MARTIN ESSLIN

The Theatre of the Absurd

THIRD EDITION

PENGUIN BOOKS

in association with Eyre & Spottiswoode

PENGUIN BOOKS

Published by the Penguin Group
Penguin Books Ltd, 27 Wrights Lane, London W8 5TZ, England
Penguin Putnam Inc., 375 Hudson Street, New York, New York 10014, USA
Penguin Books Australia Ltd, Ringwood, Victoria, Australia
Penguin Books Canada Ltd, 10 Alcorn Avenue, Toronto, Ontario, Canada M4V 3B2
Penguin Books (NZ) Ltd, Private Bag 102902, NSMC, Auckland, New Zealand

Penguin Books Ltd, Registered Offices: Harmondsworth, Middlesex, England

First published in the United States of America by
Anchor Books 1961
First published in Great Britain by
Eyre & Spottiswoode Ltd 1962
Second Edition first published in Great Britain in
Pelican Books 1968
Second Edition first published in the United States of America by
Anchor Books 1969
Third Edition first published in Great Britain in
Pelican Books 1980
Third Edition first published in the United States of America in
Pelican Books by arrangement with Doubleday & Company, Inc., 1983
Reprinted in Peregrine Books 1987
Reprinted in Penguin Books 1991
7 9 10 8

Printed in England by Clays Ltd, St Ives plc
Set in Monotype Bembo

CONTENTS

PREFACE TO THE THIRD PELICAN EDITION   9

PREFACE TO THE PELICAN EDITION (1968)   11

PREFACE   15

ACKNOWLEDGEMENTS   18

INTRODUCTION: *The absurdity of the Absurd*   19

1   SAMUEL BECKETT: *The search for the self*   29

2   ARTHUR ADAMOV: *The curable and the incurable*   92

3   EUGÈNE IONESCO: *Theatre and anti-theatre*   128

4   JEAN GENET: *A hall of mirrors*   200

5   HAROLD PINTER: *Certainties and uncertainties*   234

6   PARALLELS AND PROSELYTES   265
*Jean Tardieu (265), Boris Vian (274),
Dino Buzzati (277), Ezio d'Errico (279),
Manuel de Pedrolo (281), Fernando Arrabal (285),
Max Frisch (292), Wolfgang Hildesheimer (295),
Günter Grass (297), Robert Pinget (299),
Norman Frederick Simpson (302), Edward Albee (311),
Jack Gelber (315), Arthur L. Kopit (315),
The Theatre of the Absurd in Eastern Europe (316),
Slawomir Mrozek (318), Tadeusz Rózewicz (321),
Vaclav Havel (324)*

7   THE TRADITION OF THE ABSURD   327

8   THE SIGNIFICANCE OF THE ABSURD   399

9   BEYOND THE ABSURD   430

BIBLIOGRAPHY
1   The dramatists of the Absurd   437
2   Background and history of the Theatre of the
    Absurd   461

INDEX   471

PREFACE TO THE THIRD PELICAN EDITION

Habent sua fata leibelli . . . When I embarked, twenty years ago, on writing this book, it was mainly intended as a polemical contribution to the then current debate on what seemed to many an aberrant and debased form of drama. As it continued to be reprinted, read, and used as a text in colleges and universities it gradually changed its nature. For what had been a hotly controversial intervention in the give and take of argument increasingly turned into a book which was used as the definition of a new approach (often mistakenly thought to be a school, a movement or even a new *genre*), into a history or a reference handbook. Needless to say that I was, and still am, gratified by this development. But if the book is to continue to serve this newly developed function, it must be kept up to date. And that is why a revised edition has again, ten years after the first expansion and revision of the text, become necessary.

The chapters on the major dramatists of the Absurd have accordingly been brought up to date so that their newer works do not remain wholly ignored. The treatment of the plays of Harold Pinter (who had barely emerged when the first edition of the book appeared in 1961, and whose subsequent output had swelled the section devoted to him in the chapter on Parallels and Proselytes in the second edition) has now been moved forward and given the status of a full chapter, as, indeed, befits his position as one of the major playwrights of our time. Not *all* the subsequent work of *all* the other authors discussed, and even less so the vast amount of drama by authors writing in this vein who have since come to the fore, could be dealt with without greatly exceeding the scope and bulk of this volume. But the Bibliography has been considerably expanded, again

9

mainly with regard to the major authors. And the final chapter which deals with the impact of the Absurdist theatre on the subsequent development of drama now takes note of the state of affairs at the end of the 1970's.

I hope that all this will maintain the usefulness of the work to the readers and students who come to the book with a desire to derive understanding and information from it.

Winchelsea, Sussex, October 1978   MARTIN ESSLIN

PREFACE TO THE PELICAN EDITION
(1968)

ON 30 December 1964 *Waiting for Godot* was revived at the Royal Court Theatre in London with Nicol Williamson as Vladimir. The production was extremely favourably received by the critics. As to the play – the general verdict seemed to be that it was a modern classic now but had one great fault: its meaning and symbolism were a little too obvious. . . . When the same play made its first appearance in London in August 1955 it had met with a wide measure of incomprehension. Indeed, the verdict of most critics was that it was completely obscure, a farrago of pointless chit-chat.

The speed with which the incomprehensible avant-garde work turns into the all too easily understood modern classic in our epoch is astonishing and is only equalled by everyone's readiness to forget his own first reactions when confronted with works of art that break new ground.

The impulse which prompted the writing of this book largely sprang from its author's feeling that works in a new convention, which mirrored a new attitude to the world in our time, *could* be made comprehensible. If most critics have by now caught up with some of the more outstanding and more frequently produced plays in the new genre, this does not mean that there are not still, and will not always be, many other members of theatre audiences and readers of plays to whom an introduction of this kind might still be helpful. The continued success of the book in Britain, the United States and elsewhere seems to bear out this contention.

Indeed, in some respects the book's success – or at least its *title's* success, and there seem to be large numbers of people who talk and write about it having *only* read its title – has given the author some cause for misgivings. 'The Theatre of the Absurd' has become a catch-phrase in its own right which is often thoughtlessly used; and, what is worse, a number of other catch-phrases, built on the same principle, have been formed in imitation. We have had Theatres of Revolt, Cruelty, Paradox, Fact, etc. Authors have been asked in interviews whether they adhered to the doctrines of the Theatre of the Absurd. In fact the term, coined to describe certain features of certain plays in order to bring out certain underlying similarities, has been treated as though it corresponded to an organized movement, like a political party or a hockey team, which made its members carry badges and banners. One might as well have asked a palaeolithic potter whether he agreed that he practised the Magdalenian style. The artists of an epoch have certain traits in common, but they are not necessarily conscious of them. Nor does the fact that they have these traits in common preclude them from being widely different in other respects. Both a mouse and an elephant can be classified as mammals, but that does not mean that they are identical in size or habits of life. All it does mean is that they resemble each other in certain basic structural respects.

A term like Theatre of the Absurd is a working hypothesis, a device to make certain fundamental traits which seem to be present in the works of a number of dramatists accessible to discussion by tracing the features they have in common. That and no more. How could that have led to the assumption that Beckett and Ionesco should behave towards each other as members of the same club or party? Or that Pinter subscribed to the same views on politics or law as Genet? Only by a profound misunderstanding. And even less justified is the view that the development of the theatre proceeds by a series of such movements, each of which comes to power as the previous one abdicates or is overthrown.

The new edition of *The Theatre of the Absurd* has been brought up to date by the inclusion of material on important plays published or produced since its first appearance, by additions to the bibliography, and by a short new final chapter which attempts to set the dramatists discussed in the book in perspective against the development of drama as a whole in our time. To have included accounts of *all* new plays which in one way or other might have been relevant, or to have discussed all the many new dramatists whose work bears the mark of the influence of the major playwrights dealt with in the book, would clearly have been impracticable; it would have increased the bulk of the volume beyond all reason. However, a brief account of the emergence of an approach closely related to the Theatre of the Absurd in Poland and Czechoslovakia has been added. A few mistakes have been corrected and a certain amount of less important matter omitted.

MARTIN ESSLIN

London, April 1967

PREFACE

THIS is a book on a development in the contemporary theatre: the type of drama associated with the names of Samuel Beckett, Eugène Ionesco, Arthur Adamov, Jean Genet, and a number of other avant-garde writers in France, Britain, Italy, Spain, Germany, the United States, and elsewhere.

Books on theatre subjects have a tendency to be ephemeral; in most bookshops the shelves with the autobiographies of star actors and collections of last year's hits have a tired look. I should never have written this book had I not been convinced that its subject had an importance transcending the somewhat confined world of theatre literature. For the theatre, in spite of its apparent eclipse through the rise of the mass media, remains of immense and growing significance – precisely because of the spread of the cinema and television. These mass media are too ponderous and costly to indulge in much experiment and innovation. So, however restricted the theatre and its audience may be, it is on the living stage that the actors and playwrights of the mass media are trained and gain their experience, and the material of the mass media is tested. The avant-garde of the theatre today is, more likely than not, the main influence on the mass media of tomorrow. And the mass media, in turn, shape a great deal of the thought and feeling of people throughout the Western world.

Thus the type of theatre discussed in this book is by no means of concern only to a narrow circle of intellectuals. It may provide a new language, new ideas, new approaches, and a new, vitalized philosophy to transform the modes of thought and feeling of the public at large in a not too distant future.

Moreover, an understanding of this kind of theatre, which is still misunderstood by some of the critics, should, I believe, also cast light on current tendencies of thought in other fields, or at least show how a new convention of this sort reflects the changes in science, psychology, and philosophy that have been taking place in the last half-century. The theatre, an art more broadly based than poetry or abstract painting, without being, like the mass media, the collective product of corporations, is the point of intersection where the deeper trends of changing thought first reach a larger public.

There has been some comment on the fact that the Theatre of the Absurd represents trends that have been apparent in the more esoteric kinds of literature since the 1920's (Joyce, Surrealism, Kafka) or in painting since the first decade of this century (Cubism, abstract painting). This is certainly true. But the theatre could not put these innovations before its wider public until these trends had had time to filter into a wider consciousness. And, as this book hopes to show, the theatre can make its own very original contribution to this new type of art.

This book is an attempt to define the convention that has come to be called the Theatre of the Absurd; to present the work of some of its major exponents and provide an analysis and elucidation of the meaning and intention of some of their most important plays; to introduce a number of lesser-known writers working in the same or similar conventions; to show that this trend, sometimes decried as a search for novelty at all costs, combines a number of very ancient and highly respectable modes of literature and theatre; and, finally, to explain its significance as an expression – and one of the most representative ones – of the present situation of Western man.

It has been rightly said that what a critic wants to understand he must, at one time, have deeply loved, even if only for a fleeting moment. This book is written from the point of view of a critic who has derived some memorable experiences from watching and reading the work of the dramatists of the Absurd; who is convinced that as a trend the Theatre of the Absurd is important and significant, and has produced some of the finest dramatic achievements of our time. On the other hand, if the concentration here on this one type of theatre gives the impression that its author is a partisan exclusively of its particular convention and cannot derive pleasure from any other type of theatre, this is due simply to his deliberate limitation of the book to one subject. The rise of this new, original, and valuable dramatic convention certainly does not, in the opinion of this critic, wipe out all that has gone before, or invalidate the work of important dramatists, past, present, and to come, in other theatrical forms.

In writing this book I have been greatly helped by some of the authors discussed in it. The meetings I have had with these dramatists have been exhilarating experiences that, by themselves, have already richly rewarded me for writing it. I have been deeply touched by their kindness and am sincerely grateful to them, notably to Mr Samuel Beckett; M. Arthur Adamov; M. and Mme Eugène Ionesco; Señor Fernando Arrabal; Señor Manuel de Pedrolo; Mr N. F. Simpson; and Mr Harold Pinter.

I am also greatly indebted to Mr Eric Bentley, who combines great scholarship with an inspiring enthusiasm for the theatre, and without whose encouragement and help this book might not have been written; to Dr Herbert Blau; Mr Edward Goldberger; Mr Christopher Holme; Señor F. M. Lorda; and Mr David Tutaev for drawing my attention to writers and plays that fall within the purview of this book and for the loan of valuable books and manuscripts. My thanks are also due to Signora Connie Martellini Ricono, Mr Charles Ricono, Miss Margery Withers, Mr David Schendler, Mrs Cecilia Gillie, and Mr Robin Scott for helping me gain access to valuable material and information, and to Miss Nancy Twist and Messrs Grant and Cutler for bibliographical assistance.

My wife helped me greatly by providing constructive criticism and encouragement.

London, March 1961   MARTIN ESSLIN

ACKNOWLEDGEMENTS

My thanks for permission to make use of copyright material are due to: Faber & Faber Ltd for quotations from Beckett's *Waiting for Godot, Endgame, Krapp's Last Tape*, and *Embers*; John Calder (Publishers) Ltd for quotations from Beckett's *Molloy*, Ionesco's essay 'The world of Ionesco' in *International Theatre Annual*, no. 2 and from Ionesco's plays *Victims of Duty, Amédée, Improvisation*, and *The Killer* in Donald Watson's translation; M. Jean Genet and his translator Mr Bernard Frechtman for quotations from *Deathwatch* and *The Blacks* (published in the U.K. by Faber & Faber Ltd and in the U.S.A. by Grove Press); Methuen & Co. Ltd for quotations from Harold Pinter's plays *The Birthday Party, The Caretaker*, and *The Dwarfs*; Mrs W. B. Yeats for an extract from 'The trembling of the veil' in the volume *Autobiographies*; Mr N. F. Simpson for a quotation from *A Resounding Tinkle*; and the *Observer* for permission to quote from articles by Eugène Ionesco and Kenneth Tynan. M.E.

INTRODUCTION

The absurdity of the Absurd

ON 19 November 1957, a group of worried actors were preparing to face their audience. The actors were members of the company of the San Francisco Actors' Workshop. The audience consisted of fourteen hundred convicts at the San Quentin penitentiary. No live play had been performed at San Quentin since Sarah Bernhardt appeared there in 1913. Now, forty-four years later, the play that had been chosen, largely because no woman appeared in it, was Samuel Beckett's *Waiting for Godot*.

No wonder the actors and Herbert Blau, the director, were apprehensive. How were they to face one of the toughest audiences in the world with a highly obscure, intellectual play that had produced near riots among a good many highly sophisticated audiences in Western Europe? Herbert Blau decided to prepare the San Quentin audience for what was to come. He stepped on to the stage and addressed the packed, darkened North Dining Hall – a sea of flickering matches that the convicts tossed over their shoulders after lighting their cigarettes. Blau compared the play to a piece of jazz music 'to which one must listen for whatever one may find in it'. In the same way, he hoped, there would be some meaning, some personal significance for each member of the audience in *Waiting for Godot*.

The curtain parted. The play began. And what had bewildered the sophisticated audiences of Paris, London, and New York was immediately grasped by an audience of convicts. As the writer of 'Memos of a first-nighter' put it in the columns of the prison paper, the *San Quentin News*:

The trio of muscle-men, biceps overflowing . . . parked all 642 lbs on the aisle and waited for the girls and funny stuff. When this didn't appear they audibly fumed and audibly decided to wait until the house lights dimmed before escaping. They made one error. They listened and looked two minutes too long – and stayed. Left at the end. All shook . . .[1]

Or as the writer of the lead story of the same paper reported, under the headline, 'San Francisco Group Leaves S.Q. Audience Waiting for Godot':

From the moment Robin Wagner's thoughtful and limbo-like set was dressed with light, until the last futile and expectant handclasp was hesitantly activated between the two searching vagrants, the San Francisco company had its audience of captives in its collective hand. . . . Those that had felt a less controversial vehicle should be attempted as a first play here had their fears allayed a short five minutes after the Samuel Beckett piece began to unfold.[2]

A reporter from the San Francisco *Chronicle* who was present noted that the convicts did not find it difficult to understand the play. One prisoner told him, 'Godot is society.' Said another: 'He's the outside.'[3] A teacher at the prison was quoted as saying, 'They know what is meant by waiting . . . and they knew if Godot finally came, he would only be a disappointment.'[4] The leading article of the prison paper showed how clearly the writers had understood the meaning of the play:

It was an expression, symbolic in order to avoid all personal error, by an author who expected each member of his audience to draw his own conclusions, make his own errors. It asked nothing in point, it forced no dramatized moral on the viewer, it held out no specific hope. . . . We're still waiting for Godot, and shall continue to wait. When the scenery gets too drab and the action too slow, we'll call each other names and swear to part forever – but then, there's no place to go![5]

1. *San Quentin News*, San Quentin, Calif., 28 November 1957.
2. ibid.
3. *Theatre Arts*, New York, July 1958.
4. ibid.
5. *San Quentin News*, 28 November 1957.

It is said that Godot himself, as well as turns of phrase and characters from the play, has since become a permanent part of the private language, the institutional mythology of San Quentin.

Why did a play of the supposedly esoteric avant-garde make so immediate and so deep an impact on an audience of convicts? Because it confronted them with a situation in some ways analogous to their own? Perhaps. Or perhaps because they were unsophisticated enough to come to the theatre without any preconceived notions and ready-made expectations, so that they avoided the mistake that trapped so many established critics who condemned the play for its lack of plot, development, characterization, suspense, or plain common sense. Certainly the prisoners of San Quentin could not be suspected of the sin of intellectual snobbery, for which a sizeable proportion of the audiences of *Waiting for Godot* have often been reproached; of pretending to like a play they did not even begin to understand, just to appear in the know.

The reception of *Waiting for Godot* at San Quentin, and the wide acclaim given to plays by Ionesco, Adamov, Pinter, and others, testify that these plays, which are so often superciliously dismissed as nonsense or mystification, *have* something to say and *can* be understood. Most of the incomprehension with which plays of this type are still being received by critics and theatrical reviewers, most of the bewilderment they have caused and to which they still give rise, come from the fact that they are part of a new and still developing stage convention that has not yet been generally understood and has hardly ever been defined. Inevitably, plays written in this new convention will, when judged by the standards and criteria of another, be regarded as impertinent and outrageous impostures. If a good play must have a cleverly constructed story, these have no story or plot to speak of; if a good play is judged by subtlety of characterization and motivation, these are often without recognizable characters and present the audience with almost mechanical puppets; if a good play has to have a fully explained theme, which is neatly exposed and finally solved, these often have neither a beginning nor an end; if a good play is to hold the mirror up to nature and portray the manners and mannerisms of the age in finely observed sketches, these seem often to be reflections of dreams and nightmares; if a good play relies on witty repartee and pointed dialogue, these often consist of incoherent babblings.

But the plays we are concerned with here pursue ends quite different from those of the conventional play and therefore use quite different methods. They can be judged only by the standards of the Theatre of the Absurd, which it is the purpose of this book to define and clarify.

It must be stressed, however, that the dramatists whose work is here discussed do not form part of any self-proclaimed or self-conscious school or movement. On the contrary, each of the writers in question is an individual who regards himself as a lone outsider, cut off and isolated in his private world. Each has his own personal approach to both subject-matter and form; his own roots, sources, and background. If they also, very clearly and in spite of themselves, have a good deal in common, it is because their work most sensitively mirrors and reflects the preoccupations and anxieties, the emotions and thinking of many of their contemporaries in the Western world.

This is not to say that their works are representative of mass attitudes. It is an oversimplification to assume that any age presents a homogeneous pattern. Ours being, more than most others, an age of transition, it displays a bewilderingly stratified picture: medieval beliefs still held and overlaid by eighteenth-century rationalism and mid-nineteenth-century Marxism, rocked by sudden volcanic eruptions of prehistoric fanaticisms and primitive tribal cults. Each of these components of the cultural pattern of the age finds its own artistic expression. The Theatre of the Absurd, however, can be seen as the reflection of what seems to be the attitude most genuinely representative of our own time.

The hallmark of this attitude is its sense that the certitudes and unshakable basic assumptions of former ages have been swept away, that they have been tested and found wanting, that they have been discredited as cheap and somewhat childish illusions. The decline of religious faith was masked until the end of the Second World War by the substitute religions of faith in progress, nationalism, and various totalitarian fallacies. All this was shattered by the war. By 1942, Albert Camus was calmly putting the question why, since life had lost all meaning, man should not seek escape in suicide. In one of the great, seminal heart-searchings of our time, *The Myth of Sisyphus*, Camus tried to diagnose the human situation in a world of shattered beliefs:

A world that can be explained by reasoning, however faulty, is a familiar world. But in a universe that is suddenly deprived of illusions and of light, man feels a stranger. His is an irremediable exile, because he is deprived of memories of a lost homeland as much as he lacks the hope of a promised land to come. This divorce between man and his life, the actor and his setting, truly constitutes the feeling of Absurdity.[1]

'Absurd' originally means 'out of harmony', in a musical context. Hence its dictionary definition: 'out of harmony with reason or propriety; incongruous, unreasonable, illogical'. In common usage, 'absurd' may simply mean 'ridiculous', but this is not the sense in which Camus uses the word, and in which it is used when we speak of the Theatre of the Absurd. In an essay on Kafka, Ionesco defined his understanding of the term as follows: 'Absurd is that which is devoid of purpose. . . . Cut off from his religious, metaphysical, and transcendental roots, man is lost; all his actions become senseless, absurd, useless.'[2]

This sense of metaphysical anguish at the absurdity of the

1. Albert Camus, *Le Mythe de Sisyphe* (Paris: Gallimard, 1942), p. 18.
2. Eugène Ionesco, '*Dans les armes de la ville*', *Cahiers de la Compagnie Madeleine Renaud–Jean–Louis Barrault*, Paris, no. 20, October 1957.

human condition is, broadly speaking, the theme of the plays of Beckett, Adamov, Ionesco, Genet, and the other writers discussed in this book. But it is not merely the subject-matter that defines what is here called the Theatre of the Absurd. A similar sense of the senselessness of life, of the inevitable devaluation of ideals, purity, and purpose, is also the theme of much of the work of dramatists like Giraudoux, Anouilh, Salacrou, Sartre, and Camus himself. Yet these writers differ from the dramatists of the Absurd in an important respect: they present their sense of the irrationality of the human condition in the form of highly lucid and logically constructed reasoning, while the Theatre of the Absurd strives to express its sense of the senselessness of the human condition and the inadequacy of the rational approach by the open abandonment of rational devices and discursive thought. While Sartre or Camus express the new content in the old convention, the Theatre of the Absurd goes a step further in trying to achieve a unity between its basic assumptions and the form in which these are expressed. In some senses, the *theatre* of Sartre and Camus is less adequate as an expression of the *philosophy* of Sartre and Camus – in artistic, as distinct from philosophic, terms – than the Theatre of the Absurd.

If Camus argued that in our disillusioned age the world has ceased to make sense, he did so in the elegantly rationalistic and discursive style of an eighteenth-century moralist, in well-constructed and polished plays. If Sartre argues that existence comes before essence and that human personality can be reduced to pure potentiality and the freedom to choose itself anew at any moment, he presents his ideas in plays based on brilliantly drawn characters who remain wholly consistent and thus reflect the old convention that each human being has a core of immutable, unchanging essence – in fact, an immortal soul. And the beautiful phrasing and argumentative brilliance of both Sartre and Camus in their relentless probing still, by implication, proclaim a tacit conviction that logical discourse can offer valid solutions, that the analysis of language will lead to the uncovering of basic concepts – Platonic ideas.

This is an inner contradiction that the dramatists of the Absurd are trying, by instinct and intuition rather than by conscious effort, to overcome and resolve. The Theatre of the Absurd has renounced arguing *about* the absurdity of the human condition; it merely *presents* it in being – that is, in terms of concrete stage images. This is the difference between the approach of the philosopher and that of the poet; the difference, to take an example from another sphere, between the *idea* of God in the works of Thomas Aquinas or Spinoza and the *intuition* of God in those of St John of the Cross or Meister Eckhart – the difference between theory and experience.

It is this striving for an integration between the subject-matter and the form in which it is expressed that separates the Theatre of the Absurd from the Existentialist theatre.

It must also be distinguished from another important, and parallel, trend in the contemporary French theatre, which is equally preoccupied with the absurdity and uncertainty of the human condition: the 'poetic avant-garde' theatre of dramatists like Michel de Ghelderode, Jacques Audiberti, Georges Neveux, and, in the younger generation, Georges Schehadé, Henri Pichette, and Jean Vauthier, to name only some of its most important exponents. This is an even more difficult dividing line to draw, for the two approaches overlap a good deal. The 'poetic avant-garde' relies on fantasy and dream reality as much as the Theatre of the Absurd does; it also disregards such traditional axioms as that of the basic unity and consistency of each character or the need for a plot. Yet basically the 'poetic avant-garde' represents a different mood; it is more lyrical, and far less violent and grotesque. Even more important is its different attitude toward language: the 'poetic avant-garde' relies to a far greater extent on consciously 'poetic' speech; it aspires to plays that are in effect poems, images composed of a rich web of verbal associations.

ie Theatre of the Absurd, on the other hand, tends toward a
al devaluation of language, toward a poetry that is to
emerge from the concrete and objectified images of the stage
itself. The element of language still plays an important part in
this conception, but what *happens* on the stage transcends, and
often contradicts, the *words* spoken by the characters. In
Ionesco's *The Chairs*, for example, the poetic content of a
powerfully poetic play does not lie in the banal words that are
uttered but in the fact that they are spoken to an ever-growing
number of empty chairs.

The Theatre of the Absurd is thus part of the 'anti-literary'
movement of our time, which has found its expression in
abstract painting, with its rejection of 'literary' elements in
pictures; or in the 'new novel' in France, with its reliance on the
description of objects and its rejection of empathy and anthro-
pomorphism. It is no coincidence that, like all these movements
and so many of the efforts to create new forms of expression in
all the arts, the Theatre of the Absurd should be centred in Paris.

This does not mean that the Theatre of the Absurd is
essentially French. It is broadly based on ancient strands of the
Western tradition and has its exponents in Britain, Spain,
Italy, Germany, Switzerland, Eastern Europe and the United
States as well as in France. Moreover, its leading practitioners
who live in Paris and write in French are not themselves
Frenchmen.

As a powerhouse of the modern movement, Paris is an
international rather than a merely French centre: it acts as a
magnet attracting artists of all nationalities who are in search of
freedom to work and to live nonconformist lives unhampered
by the need to look over their shoulder to see whether their
neighbours are shocked. That is the secret of Paris as the capital
of the world's individualists: here, in a world of cafés and small
hotels, it is possible to live easily and unmolested.

That is why a cosmopolitan of uncertain origin like Apollinaire; Spaniards like Picasso or Juan Gris; Russians like

Kandinsky and Chagall; Rumanians like Tzara and Brancusi; Americans like Gertrude Stein, Hemingway, and E. E. Cummings; an Irishman like Joyce; and many others from the four corners of the world could come together in Paris and shape the modern movement in the arts and literature. The Theatre of the Absurd springs from the same tradition and is nourished from the same roots. An Irishman, Samuel Beckett; a Rumanian, Eugène Ionesco; a Russian of Armenian origin, Arthur Adamov, not only found in Paris the atmosphere that allowed them to experiment in freedom, they also found there the opportunities to get their work produced.

The standards of staging and production in the smaller theatres of Paris are often criticized as slapdash and perfunctory. That may indeed sometimes be the case; yet the fact remains that there is no other place in the world where so many first-rate men of the theatre can be found who are adventurous and intelligent enough to champion the experimental work of new playwrights and to help them acquire a mastery of stage technique – from Lugné-Poë, Copeau, and Dullin to Jean-Louis Barrault, Jean Vilar, Roger Blin, Nicolas Bataille, Jacques Mauclair, Sylvain Dhomme, Jean-Marie Serreau, and a host of others whose names are indissolubly linked with the rise of much that is best in the contemporary theatre.

Equally important, Paris also has a highly intelligent theatre-going public, which is receptive, thoughtful, and as able as it is eager to absorb new ideas. This does not mean that the first productions of some of the more startling manifestations of the Theatre of the Absurd did not provoke hostile demonstrations or, at first, play to empty houses. What matters is that these scandals were the expression of passionate concern and interest, and that even the emptiest houses contained enthusiasts articulate enough to proclaim loudly and effectively the merits of the original experiments they had witnessed.

Yet in spite of these favourable circumstances, inherent in the fertile cultural climate of Paris, the success of the Theatre of the

Absurd, achieved within a short span of time, remains one of the most astonishing aspects of this astonishing phenomenon. That plays so strange and puzzling, so clearly devoid of the traditional attractions of the well-made drama, should within less than a decade have reached the stages of the world from Finland to Japan, from Norway to the Argentine, and that they should have stimulated a large body of work in a similar convention, are in themselves powerful and entirely empirical tests of the importance of the Theatre of the Absurd.

The study of this phenomenon as literature, as stage technique, and as a manifestation of the thinking of its age must proceed from the examination of the works themselves. Only then can they be seen as part of an old tradition that may at times have been submerged but that can be traced back to antiquity. Only after the movement of today has been placed within its historical context can an attempt be made to assess its significance and to establish its importance and the part it has to play within the pattern of contemporary thought.

A public conditioned to an accepted convention tends to receive the impact of artistic experiences through a filter of critical standards, of predetermined expectations and terms of reference, which is the natural result of the schooling of its taste and faculty of perception. This framework of values, admirably efficient in itself, produces only bewildering results when it is faced with a completely new and revolutionary convention – a tug of war ensues between impressions that have undoubtedly been received and critical preconceptions that clearly exclude the possibility that any such impressions could have been felt. Hence the storms of frustration and indignation always caused by works in a new convention.

It is the purpose of this book to provide a framework of reference that will show the works of the Theatre of the Absurd within their own convention so that their relevance and force can emerge as clearly to the reader as *Waiting for Godot* did to the convicts of San Quentin.

SAMUEL BECKETT

The search for the self

IN his last will and testament, Murphy, the hero of Samuel Beckett's early novel of that name, enjoins his heirs and executors to place his ashes in a paper bag and take them to 'the Abbey Theatre, Lr Abbey Street, Dublin ... into what the great and good Lord Chesterfield calls the necessary house, where their happiest hours have been spent, on the right as one goes down into the pit ... and that the chain be there pulled upon them, if possible during the performance of a piece.'[1] This is a symbolic act in the true irreverent spirit of the anti-theatre, but one that also reveals where the author of *Waiting for Godot* received his first impressions of the type of drama against which he reacted in his rejection of what he has called 'the grotesque fallacy of realistic art – "that miserable statement of line and surface" and the penny-a-line vulgarity of a literature of notations'.[2]

Samuel Beckett was born in Dublin in 1906, the son of a quantity surveyor. Like Shaw, Wilde, and Yeats, he came from the Protestant Irish middle class and was, though he later lost his faith, brought up 'almost a Quaker', as he himself once put it.[3] It has been suggested that Beckett's preoccupation with the problem of being and the identity of the self might have sprung from the Anglo-Irishman's inevitable and perpetual concern with finding his own answer to the question 'Who am I?', but

1. Samuel Beckett, *Murphy* (New York: Grove Press, no date), p. 269.
2. Beckett, *Proust* (New York: Grove Press, no date), p. 57.
3. Beckett, quoted by Harold Hobson, 'Samuel Beckett, dramatist of the year', *International Theatre Annual*, no. 1 (London: John Calder, 1956).

while there may well be a grain of truth in this, it is surely far from providing a complete explanation for the deep existential anguish that is the keynote of Beckett's work and that clearly originates in levels of his personality far deeper than its social surface.

At the age of fourteen, Beckett was sent to one of the Anglo-Irishman's traditional boarding schools, Portora Royal School, at Enniskillen, County Fermanagh, founded by King James I, where Oscar Wilde had also been a pupil. It is characteristic of Beckett that he, whose writing reveals him as one of the most tormented and sensitive of human beings, not only became a popular and brilliant scholar but also excelled at games, batting left-handed and bowling right at cricket, and playing scrum-half at rugger.

In 1923, Beckett left Portora and entered Trinity College, Dublin, where he read French and Italian, receiving his Bachelor of Arts degree in 1927. Such was his academic distinction that he was nominated by his university as its representative in a traditional exchange of lecturers with the famous Ecole Normale Supérieure, in Paris. Accordingly, after a brief spell of teaching in Belfast, he went to Paris for a two-year stint as a *lecteur d'anglais* at the Ecole Normale in the autumn of 1928.

Thus began his lifelong association with Paris. In Paris he met James Joyce and soon became a member of his circle, contributing, at the age of twenty-three, the brilliant opening essay of that strange book entitled *Our Exagmination round his Factification for Incamination of Work in Progress*, a collection of twelve articles by twelve apostles, as a defence and exegesis of their master's as yet unnamed *magnum opus*. Beckett's contribution, headed 'Dante . . . Bruno. Vico . . . Joyce', culminates in a spirited assertion of the artist's duty to express the totality and complexity of his experience regardless of the public's lazy demand for easy comprehensibility:

Here is direct expression – pages and pages of it. And if you don't understand it, Ladies and Gentlemen, it is because you are too decadent to receive it. You are not satisfied unless form is so strictly divorced from content that you can comprehend the one almost without bothering to read the other. This rapid skimming and absorption of the scant cream of sense is made possible by what I may call a continuous process of copious intellectual salivation. The form that is an arbitrary and independent phenomenon can fulfil no higher function than that of stimulus for a tertiary or quartary conditioned reflex of dribbling comprehension.[1]

These are the articles of his faith that Beckett has put into practice in his own life's work as a writer, with an uncompromising consistency almost terrifying in its purity.

In a letter to Harriet Shaw Weaver dated 28 May 1929,[2] Joyce speaks of his intention of having Beckett's essay published in an Italian review. In the same letter he mentions a country picnic planned by Adrienne Monnier to celebrate the twenty-fifth anniversary of Bloomsday. This was the '*Déjeuner Ulysse*' held on 27 June 1929, at the Hôtel Léopold at Les Vaux-de-Cernay, near Versailles. From Richard Ellman's biography of Joyce, we learn that Beckett was one of the guests, who included Paul Valéry, Jules Romains, Léon-Paul Fargue, Philippe Soupault, and many other distinguished names, and that on the return journey Beckett aroused the wrath of Paul Valéry and Adrienne Monnier by repeatedly prevailing upon Joyce to have the bus stopped so that they might have yet another drink at some wayside café.

During his first stay in Paris, Beckett also made his mark as a poet by winning a literary prize – ten pounds, for the best poem on the subject of time – in a competition inspired by Nancy Cunard and judged by her and Richard Aldington. Beckett's poem, provocatively entitled 'Whoroscope', presents the

1. Beckett, 'Dante . . . Bruno. Vico . . . Joyce', in *Our Exagmination round his Factification for Incamination of Work in Progress* (Paris: Shakespeare & Co., 1929), p. 13.

2. *Letters of James Joyce*, ed. Stuart Gilbert (London: Faber & Faber, 1957), pp. 280–81.

31

philosopher Descartes meditating on time, hens' eggs, and evanescence. The little booklet, published in Paris by the Hours Press in an edition of a hundred signed copies at five shillings, and two hundred unsigned ones at a shilling, has become a collector's piece, with the little slip pasted on it that informs the reader of the award of the prize and that this is 'Mr Samuel Beckett's first separately published work'.

For his newly found friend James Joyce, Beckett also embarked on a daring attempt at rendering the 'Anna Livia Plurabelle' passage from *Work in Progress* into French. But this undertaking, in which he was assisted by Alfred Péron, had to be abandoned (and was carried to completion by Joyce, Soupault, and a number of others) in the course of 1930, when Beckett returned to Dublin to take the post of assistant to the professor of Romance languages at Trinity College.

Thus, at the age of twenty-four, Beckett seemed to be launched on a safe and brilliant academic and literary career. He obtained his Master of Arts degree. His study of Proust, commissioned by a London publisher and written while he was still in Paris, appeared in 1931. It is a penetrating interpretation of Proust's work as an exploration of time, but it also foreshadows many of Beckett's themes in the works he was still to write – the impossibility of possession in love, and the illusion of friendship: '. . . if love . . . is a function of man's sadness, friendship is a function of his cowardice; and if neither can be realized because of the impenetrability (isolation) of all that is not "*cosa mentale*", at least the failure to possess may have the nobility of that which is tragic, whereas the attempt to communicate where no communication is possible is merely a simian vulgarity, or horribly comic, like the madness that holds a conversation with the furniture.'[1] For an artist therefore, 'the only possible spiritual development is in the sense of depth. The artistic tendency is not expansive, but a contraction. And art is the apotheosis of solitude. There is no communication

1. *Proust*, p. 46.

because there are no vehicles of communication.'[1] Although these ideas are expositions of Proust's thought, and although today he stresses that he wrote the little book on order, not out of any deep affinity with Proust, Beckett clearly put many of his personal feelings and views into it.

To one who felt that habit and routine was the cancer of time, social intercourse a mere illusion, and the artist's life of necessity a life of solitude, the daily grind of a university lecturer's work must have appeared unbearable. After only four terms at Trinity College, he had had enough. He threw up his career and cut himself loose from all routine and social duties. Like Belacqua, the hero of his volume of short stories *More Pricks than Kicks*, who, though indolent by nature, 'enlivened the last phase of his solipsism . . . with the belief that the best thing he had to do was to move constantly from place to place',[2] Beckett embarked on a period of *Wanderjahre*. Writing poems and stories, doing odd jobs, he moved from Dublin to London to Paris, travelled through France and Germany. It is surely no coincidence that so many of Beckett's later characters are tramps and wanderers, and that all are lonely.

More Pricks than Kicks is set in Dublin; the next volume, a slim collection of poems, *Echo's Bones and Other Precipitates* (1935), widens its references to landmarks from Dublin (Guinness's barges by O'Connell Bridge) to Paris (the American Bar in the Rue Mouffetard) and London (the 'grand old British Museum', Ken Wood, and Tower Bridge). Beckett's stay in London also left its mark on his first novel, *Murphy* (1938): the 'World's End' on the fringes of Chelsea; the area around the Caledonian market and Pentonville; Gower Street.

Whenever he passed through Paris, Beckett went to see Joyce. In Richard Ellmann's words,

Beckett was addicted to silences, and so was Joyce; they engaged

1. ibid., p. 47.
2. Beckett, *More Pricks than Kicks* (London: Chatto & Windus, 1934), p. 43.

in conversations which consisted often in silences directed towards each other, both suffused with sadness, Beckett mostly for the world, Joyce mostly for himself. Joyce sat in his habitual posture, legs crossed, toe of the upper leg under the instep of the lower; Beckett, also tall and slender, fell into the same gesture. Joyce suddenly asked some such question as 'How could the idealist Hume write a history?' Beckett replied, 'A history of representations.'[1]

Beckett read Joyce passages from the works of Fritz Mauthner, whose *Critique of Language* was one of the first works to point to the fallibility of language as a medium for the discovery and communication of metaphysical truths. But 'though he liked having Beckett with him, Joyce at the same time kept him at a distance. Once he said directly: "I don't love anyone except my family" in a tone which suggested, "I don't like anyone except my family either."'[2] Once or twice Joyce, whose sight had long been failing, dictated passages from *Finnegans Wake* to Beckett. This may be the origin of the oft-repeated assertion that Beckett was at one time Joyce's private secretary. He never held such a position. If anyone ever acted as Joyce's secretary it was Paul Léon.

Richard Ellmann also tells the story of the infatuation of Joyce's unhappy daughter, Lucia, for Beckett. Beckett some-times took Lucia, already high-strung and neurotic, to restau-rants and theatres. 'As her self-control began to leave her, she made less effort to conceal the passion she felt for him, and at last her feelings became so overt that Beckett told her bluntly he came to the Joyce flat primarily to see her father. He felt he had been cruel and later told Peggy Guggenheim that he was dead and had no feelings that were human; hence he had not been able to fall in love with Lucia.'[3]

Peggy Guggenheim, patron of the arts and a famous collector

1. Richard Ellmann, *James Joyce* (New York and London: Oxford University Press, 1959), p. 661.
2. ibid.
3. ibid., p. 662.

of modern paintings, was herself, as she reports in her memoirs, 'terribly in love' with Beckett a few years later. She describes him as a fascinating young man, but afflicted with an apathy that sometimes kept him in bed till mid-afternoon; with whom it was difficult to converse, as 'he was never very animated and it took hours and lots of drink to warm him up before he finally unravelled himself.'[1] Like Belacqua, who sometimes wanted 'to be back in the caul on my back in the dark forever',[2] Beckett, according to Peggy Guggenheim, 'had retained a terrible memory of life in his mother's womb. He was constantly suffering from this and had awful crises, when he felt he was suffocating. He always said our life would be all right one day, but if I ever pressed him to make a decision it was fatal and he took back everything he had previously said.'[3]

Murphy, published in 1938 with the help and support of Herbert Read, is to some extent concerned with an analogous situation between the hero and his girl-friend Celia, who vainly tries to make him take up regular employment so they can get married, but has to see him elude her again and again.

Beckett's first play, *Eleutheria* (written in French shortly after the war, but so far unpublished and unperformed), is also concerned with a young man's efforts to cut himself loose from his family and social obligations. *Eleutheria* is in three acts. The stage is divided in the middle. On the right the hero lies in his bed, apathetic and passive. On the left his family and friends discuss his case without ever directly addressing him. Gradually, the action shifts from left to right, and eventually the hero summons up the energy to free himself from his shackles and cut himself loose from society.

Murphy and *Eleutheria* mirror Beckett's search for freedom and the right to live his own life. In fact he found himself a

1. Peggy Guggenheim, *Confessions of an Art Addict* (London: André Deutsch, 1960), p. 50.
2. *More Pricks than Kicks*, p. 32.
3. Peggy Guggenheim, op. cit., p. 50.

permanent home: in Paris. In 1937 he acquired his apartment on the top floor of a block of flats in outer Montparnasse, which was to become his base throughout the war and post-war years.

About this time an episode occurred that might have come straight out of Beckett's own writings: he was stabbed in a Paris street by an underworld character who had accosted him for money, and had to be taken to a hospital with a perforated lung. Later, when his wound had healed, Beckett went to see his assailant in prison. He asked the *apache* why he had stabbed him, and received the answer, '*Je ne sais pas, Monsieur.*' It might well be the voice of this man that we hear in *Waiting for Godot* and *Molloy*.

When war came, in September 1939, Beckett was in Ireland, visiting his widowed mother. He immediately returned to Paris. He had long been a decided opponent of the National Socialist regime in Germany, appalled by its brutality and anti-Semitism. Now that war had broken out, he argued with Joyce, who regarded the war as useless and futile. Beckett firmly maintained that its objectives were indeed justified. Being a citizen of Eire, and thus a neutral, he was able to stay in Paris even after the city had been occupied by the Germans. He joined a Resistance group, and led the dangerous and precarious life of a member of the underground movement.

One day in August 1942, he returned to his apartment and found a message informing him that some of the members of his Resistance group had been arrested. He left his home immediately and made his way into the unoccupied zone, where he found shelter and work as an agricultural labourer in a peasant's house in the Vaucluse, near Avignon. (The Vaucluse is mentioned in the French version of *Waiting for Godot*, when Vladimir argues that Estragon must know the Vaucluse country, while Estragon hotly denies ever having been anywhere except where he is at that moment, in the Merdecluse. In the English version, the Vaucluse has become 'the Mâcon country', the Merdecluse the 'Cackon country'.)

To keep his hand in as a writer while working on the farm in the Vaucluse, Beckett began to write a novel, *Watt*. It deals with a lonely and eccentric individual who finds refuge as a servant in a house in the country ruled by a mysterious, capricious, and unapproachable master, Mr Knott, who has some of the attributes later ascribed to the equally mysterious Mr Godot.

After the liberation of Paris, in 1945, Beckett returned there briefly before making his way to Ireland, where he volunteered for a Red Cross unit. He came back to France in the autumn of 1945 and spent some time as an interpreter and storekeeper in a field hospital at Saint-Lô. Later that winter, he finally returned to Paris, to his old apartment, which he found intact and waiting for him.

This homecoming marked the beginning of the most productive period in Beckett's life. Seized by a powerful and sustained creative impulse, he wrote in the five years that followed a succession of important works: the plays *Eleutheria*, *Waiting for Godot*, and *Endgame*; the novels *Molloy*, *Malone Dies*, *The Unnamable*, and *Mercier et Camier*, as well as the short stories and fragments of prose published under the title *Nouvelles et Textes pour Rien*. All these works, some of which have become the foundation of Beckett's reputation as one of the major literary forces and influences of his time, were written in French.

This is a curious phenomenon. There have been many writers who have risen to fame with works written in a language other than their own, but usually they are compelled by circumstances to write in a foreign language: the necessities of exile; a desire to break the connection with their country of origin for political or ideological reasons; or the wish to reach a world audience, which might induce the citizen of a small language community, a Rumanian or a Dutchman, to write in French or English. But Beckett was certainly not an exile in that sense, and his mother tongue is the accepted lingua franca of the twentieth century. He chose to write his masterpieces in French because he felt that he needed the discipline that the use of an acquired language would impose upon him. As he told a student writing a thesis on his work who asked him why he used French, 'Parce qu'en français c'est plus facile d'écrire sans style.'[1] In other words, while in his own language a writer may be tempted to indulge in virtuosity of style for its own sake, the use of another language may force him to divert the ingenuity that might be expended on mere embellishments of style in his own idiom to the utmost clarity and economy of expression.

When the American director Herbert Blau suggested to Beckett that by writing in French he might be evading some part of himself, 'he said yes, there were some things about himself he didn't like, that French had the right "weakening" effect. It was a weakness he had chosen, as Melville's Bartleby "preferred not to" live . . .'[2] Possibly, too, Beckett wanted to avoid the tendency of English toward allusion and evocation. Yet the fact that in his own translations the English language perfectly renders his meaning and intention shows that it is not just a surface quality that he prefers in French, but the challenge and discipline it presents to his powers of expression.

Works like Beckett's, which spring from the deepest strata of the mind and probe the darkest wells of anxiety, would be destroyed by the slightest suggestion of glibness or facility; they must be the outcome of a painful struggle with the medium of their expression. As Claude Mauriac has pointed out in his essay on Beckett, anyone 'who speaks is carried along by the logic of language and its articulations. Thus the writer who pits himself against the unsayable must use all his cunning so as not to say what the words make him say against his will, but to express instead what by their very nature they are

1. Niklaus Gessner, *Die Unzulänglichkeit der Sprache* (Zürich: Juris Verlag, 1957), p. 32.
2. Letter from Herbert Blau to members of San Francisco Actors' Workshop, dated London, 28 October 1959.

designed to cover up: the uncertain, the contradictory, the unthinkable.'[1] The danger of being carried along by the logic of language is clearly greater in one's mother tongue, with its unconsciously accepted meanings and associations. By writing in a foreign language, Beckett ensures that his writing remains a constant struggle, a painful wrestling with the spirit of language itself. That is why he considers the radio plays and occasional pieces he has since written in English as a relaxation, a rest from this hard struggle with meaning and language. But accordingly he also attaches less importance to these works. They came too easily.

The French translation of *Murphy*, which appeared in 1947, attracted little attention, but when *Molloy* was published in 1951, it created a stir. Beckett's real triumph, however, came when *Waiting for Godot*, which had appeared in book form in 1952, was first produced on 5 January 1953, at the little Théâtre de Babylone (now defunct), on the Boulevard Raspail. Roger Blin, always at the forefront of the avant-garde in the French theatre, directed, and himself played the part of Pozzo. And against all expectations, the strange tragic farce, in which nothing happens and which had been scorned as undramatic by a number of managements, became one of the greatest successes of the post-war theatre. It ran for four hundred performances at the Théâtre de Babylone and was later transferred to another Parisian theatre. It has been translated into more than twenty languages and been performed in Sweden, Switzerland, Finland, Italy, Norway, Denmark, Holland, Spain, Belgium, Turkey, Yugoslavia, Brazil, Mexico, the Argentine, Israel, Czechoslovakia, Poland, Japan, Western Germany, Great Britain, the United States, and even in Dublin, being seen in the first five years after its original production in Paris by more than a million spectators – a truly astonishing reception for a play so enigmatic, so exasperating, so complex,

1. Claude Mauriac, *La Littérature Contemporaine* (Paris: Albin Michel, 1958), p. 83.

and so uncompromising in its refusal to conform to any of the accepted ideas of dramatic construction.

This is not the place to trace in detail the strange history of *Waiting for Godot*. Suffice it to say that the play found the approval of accepted dramatists as diverse as Jean Anouilh (who described the production at the Théâtre de Babylone as equal in importance to the first performance of a Pirandello play in Paris by Pitoeff, in 1923), Thornton Wilder, Tennessee Williams, and William Saroyan (who said, 'It will make it easier for me and everyone else to write freely in the theatre'); that it reached London in August 1955, in a production that met with Beckett's disapproval but was so successful that it was transferred from the Arts Theatre Club to the West End and ran for a long time; that it reached the shores of the United States at the Miami Playhouse on 3 January 1956, where, with Bert Lahr and Tom Ewell in the parts of the tramps, it was billed as 'the laugh hit of two continents' and bitterly disappointed its audience's expectations, but that it finally reached Broadway with Bert Lahr but without Tom Ewell, and was acclaimed by the critics.

Beckett's second play, *Endgame*, originally in two acts but later reduced to one, was to have had its world première in French under the direction of Roger Blin in Paris, but when it met with some hesitation by the management and lost its Paris venue, the Royal Court Theatre, in London, hospitably offered its stage, so that London witnessed the rare occasion of a world première in French (3 April 1957). It later found another theatre in Paris and ran for a considerable time at the Studio des Champs Elysées. Productions in English in London (again at the Royal Court), in New York (at the Cherry Lane Theatre, off Broadway), and in San Francisco (by the Actors' Workshop) have also been notably successful.

In its original production in French, *Endgame* was coupled with the mimeplay *Act Without Words I*, performed by Deryk Mendel and with music by Beckett's cousin, John Beckett. At the performance in English (28 October 1958), *Endgame* shared the bill with the short play *Krapp's Last Tape*, which was written by Beckett in English and has since been performed in Paris, in Beckett's own translation, and in New York.

Krapp's Last Tape was directed by Donald McWhinnie, the distinguished radio producer who was instrumental in getting Beckett to write two plays especially for the B.B.C.'s Third Programme: *All That Fall* (first broadcast on 13 January 1957) and *Embers* (28 October 1959). And so tenuous is the dividing line between Beckett's dramatic works and his later novels, which are all cast in the form of dramatic monologues, that extracts from these have also been performed on the B.B.C.'s Third Programme: *Molloy* (10 December 1957); the fragment *From an Abandoned Work* (14 December 1957); *Malone Dies* (18 June 1958); and *The Unnamable* (19 January 1959).

In the novel *Comment C'Est* (1961) Beckett reached a new level of austerity – a mythical universe peopled by lonely creatures crawling through the mud on their bellies, occasionally encountering another, similar individual for a brief interval of grotesque attempts at communication, then crawling on, endlessly. The play *Happy Days* (first performed under Alan Schneider's direction at the Cherry Lane Theatre, New York, on 17 September 1961 with Ruth White in the leading role; then at the Royal Court, London, directed by George Devine, on 1 November 1962; and by the company of the Odéon with Madeleine Renaud as Winnie at the Venice Festival in October 1963, before starting a highly successful run at the Odéon itself) comes from a similarly bleak world, and so does *Play* (first performed in a German translation at Ulm on 14 June 1963, followed by performances in the original English in New York, 4 January 1964, and at the National Theatre in London on 7 April 1964).

The miniature playlet *Come and Go* (first performed in a German version on 14 January 1966 at the Studio of the Schiller Theatre, West Berlin) represents a further step on the road to conciseness, amounting almost to miniaturization.

Beckett, who had always been fascinated by the technical problems of the new mass media, continued to write for radio, putting special emphasis on the fusion of text and music. *Words and Music*, with an important contribution by the composer John Beckett, was first broadcast by the B.B.C. Third Programme on 13 November 1962. *Cascando* (written in French), with music by the Rumanian composer Marcel Mihalovici, had its first performance on the French radio on 13 October 1963, followed by a broadcast in German from Stuttgart on 16 October 1963 and in English on the B.B.C. Third Programme on 28 October 1964.

Beckett made his first foray into the medium of the cinema when Grove Press of New York started a project for a film to consist of three short contributions written by Beckett, Ionesco, and Pinter. Only Beckett's of the three short films has materialized up to now. It was directed by Alan Schneider in 1965 and first shown at the Venice Biennale in August of that year. Buster Keaton, the great comedian of the silent film, whom Beckett had long admired, played the lead. It was his last major role before he died.

The television play *Eh Joe*, written in 1965 and since performed in Germany as well as on the B.B.C. (with Jack McGowran, one of Beckett's favourite actors, in the lead), showed that here was another medium of which Beckett could exploit the possibilities to the full while remaining extremely simple.

As he entered the seventh decade of his life Beckett's tendency towards extreme conciseness, the concentration on a single but complex and multi-faceted image, became ever more pronounced in the dramatic works he wrote for the stage as well as for television. As he took an ever more active part in the actual production process, sometimes even openly being billed as the director, he became able to control the visual side of his work more directly so that, in effect, he could be regarded as the creator of moving, three-dimensional images rather than merely a dramatic poet.

The image in *Not I* (a short stage play first performed at the Lincoln Center, New York, in September 1972) is that of a mouth suspended in mid-stage, surrounded by total darkness, from which the voice of an old woman emerges in a rapid stream of jumbled words, while a mysterious figure in a long Arab cloak, the Auditor, listens at the side of the stage and occasionally makes a silent, deprecatory gesture. In *Footfalls* (first performed at the Royal Court Theatre, London, in May 1976) the eyes of the audience are concentrated upon a strip of light on the floor, over which the feet of an elderly woman are seen passing to and fro, while her voice and that of her mother (who remains invisible) are heard. And in *That Time* (also first performed at the Royal Court in May 1976) the audience sees the head of an old man with white beard and hair suspended in darkness; he is listening to his own voice which emerges from three points – left, right, and centre – above the stage, reciting three episodes from his past life.

For a poet who has become a painter in moving images, television offers the additional advantage that the image can be fixed, once and for all, on videotape. Here the words, even more than in his stage plays, become, as he once put it, merely 'what pharmacists call the excipient', the relatively less important matter that surrounds the effective element, the image. *Ghost Trio* (B.B.C. TV, 17 April 1977) and '...*but the clouds...*' (also B.B.C. TV, 17 April 1977) are powerful images of loss, guilt and regret in a life irretrievably past.

In the years of his world fame – he was awarded the Nobel Prize for Literature in 1969 – Samuel Beckett remained as elusive, as intent on preserving his privacy as ever. He has always refused to appear on radio or television or give newspaper interviews and declines to comment on his work. Married to Suzanne Dumesnil, with whom he shared work in the French underground movement and the years in hiding during the war, he divides his time between his apartment in Montparnasse and a small country cottage at Ussy-sur-Marne near Paris. He likes directing his own plays in Germany, above all in Berlin, where he has established special relations with the Schiller Theater for whom he directed *Endgame* (1967), *Krapp's Last Tape* (1969), *Waiting for Godot* (1975), and *Play* (1978) in what must be regarded as the definitive performances of those plays.

When Alan Schneider, who was to direct the first American production of *Waiting for Godot*, asked Beckett who or what was meant by Godot, he received the answer, 'If I knew, I would have said so in the play.'[1]

This is a salutary warning to anyone who approaches Beckett's plays with the intention of discovering *the* key to their understanding, of demonstrating in exact and definite terms *what they mean*. Such an undertaking might perhaps be justified in tackling the works of an author who had started from a clear-cut philosophical or moral conception, and had then proceeded to translate it into concrete terms of plot and character. But even in such a case the chances are that the final product, if it turned out a genuine work of the creative imagination, would transcend the author's original intentions and present itself as far richer, more complex, and open to a multitude of additional interpretations. For, as Beckett himself has pointed out in his essay on Joyce's *Work in Progress*, the form, structure, and mood of an artistic statement cannot be separated from its meaning, its conceptual content; simply because the work of art as a whole *is* its meaning, *what* is said in it is indissolubly linked with the *manner* in which it is said, and cannot be said in any other way. Libraries have been filled with attempts to reduce the meaning of a play like *Hamlet* to a few short and simple lines, yet the play itself remains the clearest

1. Alan Schneider, 'Waiting for Beckett', *Chelsea Review*, New York, Autumn 1958.

and most concise statement of its meaning and message, pre-cisely because its uncertainties and irreducible ambiguities are an essential element of its total impact.

These considerations apply, in varying degrees, to all works of creative literature, but they apply with particular force to works that are essentially concerned with conveying their author's sense of mystery, bewilderment, and anxiety when confronted with the human condition, and his despair at being unable to find a meaning in existence. In *Waiting for Godot*, the feeling of uncertainty it produces, the ebb and flow of this uncertainty – from the hope of discovering the identity of Godot to its repeated disappointment – are themselves the essence of the play. Any endeavour to arrive at a clear and certain interpretation by establishing the identity of Godot through critical analysis would be as foolish as trying to dis-cover the clear outlines hidden behind the chiaroscuro of a painting by Rembrandt by scraping away the paint.

Yet it is only natural that plays written in so unusual and baffling a convention should be felt to be in special need of an explanation that, as it were, would uncover their hidden mean-ing and translate it into everyday language. The source of this fallacy lies in the misconception that somehow these plays must be reducible to the conventions of the 'normal' theatre, with plots that can be summarized in the form of a narrative. If only one could discover some hidden clue, it is felt, these difficult plays could be forced to yield their secret and reveal the plot of the conventional play that is hidden within them. Such at-tempts are doomed to failure. Beckett's plays lack plot even more completely than other works of the Theatre of the Absurd. Instead of a linear development, they present their author's intuition of the human condition by a method that is essentially polyphonic; they confront their audience with an organized structure of statements and images that inter-penetrate each other and that must be apprehended in their totality, rather like the different themes in a symphony, which gain meaning by their simultaneous interaction.

But if we have to be cautious in our approach to Beckett's plays, to avoid the pitfall of trying to provide an oversimplified explanation of their meaning, this does not imply that we cannot subject them to careful scrutiny by isolating sets of images and themes and by attempting to discern their structural groundwork. The results of such an examination should make it easier to follow the author's intention and to see, if not the *answers* to his questions, at least what the *questions* are that he is asking.

Waiting for Godot does not tell a story; it explores a static situation. 'Nothing happens, nobody comes, nobody goes, it's awful.'[1] On a country road, by a tree, two old tramps, Vladimir and Estragon, are waiting. That is the opening situation at the beginning of act I. At the end of act I they are informed that Mr Godot, with whom they believe they have an appointment, cannot come, but that he will surely come tomorrow. Act II repeats precisely the same pattern. The same boy arrives and delivers the same message. Act I ends:

ESTRAGON: Well, shall we go?
VLADIMIR: Yes, let's go.
[*They do not move.*]

Act II ends with the same lines of dialogue, but spoken by the same characters in reversed order.

The sequence of events and the dialogue in each act are different. Each time the two tramps encounter another pair of characters, Pozzo and Lucky, master and slave, under differing circumstances; in each act Vladimir and Estragon attempt suicide and fail, for differing reasons; but these variations merely serve to emphasize the essential sameness of the situation – *plus ça change, plus c'est la même chose.*

Vladimir and Estragon – who call each other Didi and Gogo,

1. Beckett, *Waiting for Godot* (London: Faber & Faber, 1959), p. 41.

although Vladimir is addressed by the boy messenger as Mr
Albert, and Estragon, when asked his name, replies without
hesitation, Catullus – are clearly derived from the pairs of
cross-talk comedians of music halls. Their dialogue has the
peculiar repetitive quality of the cross-talk comedians' patter.

ESTRAGON: So long as one knows.
VLADIMIR: One can bide one's time.
ESTRAGON: One knows what to expect.
VLADIMIR: No further need to worry.[1]

And the parallel to the music hall and the circus is even explicitly
stated:

VLADIMIR: Charming evening we're having.
ESTRAGON: Unforgettable.
VLADIMIR: And it's not over.
ESTRAGON: Apparently not.
VLADIMIR: It's only the beginning.
ESTRAGON: It's awful.
VLADIMIR: It's worse than being at the theatre.
ESTRAGON: The circus.
VLADIMIR: The music hall.
ESTRAGON: The circus.[2]

In accordance with the traditions of the music hall or the
circus, there is an element of crudely physical humour:
Estragon loses his trousers, there is a protracted gag involving
three hats that are put on and off and handed on in a sequence
of seemingly unending confusion, and there is an abundance
of pratfalls – the writer of a penetrating thesis on Beckett,
Niklaus Gessner, lists no fewer than forty-five stage directions
indicating that one of the characters leaves the upright position,
which symbolizes the dignity of man.[3]

As the members of a cross-talk act, Vladimir and Estragon
have complementary personalities. Vladimir is the more prac-

1. Beckett, *Waiting for Godot*, p. 37.
2. ibid., p. 34.   3. Gessner, op. cit., p. 37.

tical of the two, and Estragon claims to have been a poet. In eating his carrot, Estragon finds that the more he eats of it the less he likes it, while Vladimir reacts the opposite way – he likes things as he gets used to them. Estragon is volatile, Vladimir persistent. Estragon dreams, Vladimir cannot stand hearing about dreams. Vladimir has stinking breath, Estragon has stinking feet. Vladimir remembers past events, Estragon tends to forget them as soon as they have happened. Estragon likes telling funny stories, Vladimir is upset by them. It is mainly Vladimir who voices the hope that Godot will come and that his coming will change their situation, while Estragon remains sceptical throughout and at times even forgets the name of Godot. It is Vladimir who conducts the conversation with the boy who is Godot's messenger and to whom the boy's messages are addressed. Estragon is the weaker of the two; he is beaten up by mysterious strangers every night. Vladimir at times acts as his protector, sings him to sleep with a lullaby, and covers him with his coat. The opposition of their temperaments is the cause of endless bickering between them and often leads to the suggestion that they should part. Yet, being complementary natures, they also are dependent on each other and have to stay together.

Pozzo and Lucky are equally complementary in their natures, but their relationship is on a more primitive level: Pozzo is the sadistic master, Lucky the submissive slave. In the first act, Pozzo is rich, powerful, and certain of himself; he represents worldly man in all his facile and shortsighted optimism and illusory feeling of power and permanence. Lucky not only carries his heavy luggage, and even the whip with which Pozzo beats him, he also dances and thinks for him, or did so in his prime. In fact, Lucky taught Pozzo all the higher values of life: 'beauty, grace, truth of the first water'.[1] Pozzo and Lucky represent the relationship between body and mind, the material and the spiritual sides of man, with the intellect

1. *Waiting for Godot*, p. 33.

subordinate to the appetites of the body. Now that Lucky's powers are failing, Pozzo complains that they cause him untold suffering. He wants to get rid of Lucky and sell him at the fair. But in the second act, when they appear again, they are still tied together. Pozzo has gone blind, Lucky has become dumb. While Pozzo drives Lucky on a journey without an apparent goal, Vladimir has prevailed upon Estragon to wait for Godot.

A good deal of ingenuity has been expended in trying to establish at least an etymology for Godot's name, which would point to Beckett's conscious or subconscious intention in making him the objective of Vladimir's and Estragon's quest. It has been suggested that Godot is a weakened form of the word 'God', a diminutive formed on the analogy of Pierre-Pierrot, Charles-Charlot, with the added association of the Charlie Chaplin character of the little man, who is called Charlot in France, and whose bowler hat is worn by all four main characters in the play. It has also been noted that the title *En Attendant Godot* seems to contain an allusion to Simone Weil's book *Attente de Dieu*, which would furnish a further indication that Godot stands for God. Yet the name Godot may also be an even more recondite literary allusion. As Eric Bentley has pointed out, there is a character in a play by Balzac, a character much talked about but never seen, and called Godeau.[1] The play in question is Balzac's comedy *Le Faiseur*, better known as *Mercadet*. Mercadet is a Stock Exchange speculator who is in the habit of attributing his financial difficulties to his former partner Godeau, who, years before, absconded with their joint capital: '*Je porte le poids du crime de Godeau!*' On the other hand, the hope of Godeau's eventual return and the repayment of the embezzled funds is constantly dangled by Mercadet before the eyes of his numerous creditors. '*Tout le monde a son Godeau, un faux Christophe Colomb! Après tout Godeau ... je crois qu'il m'a déjà rapporté plus d'argent qu'il ne m'en a pris!*' The plot of

1. Eric Bentley, *What is Theatre?* (Boston: Beacon Press, 1956), p. 158.

Mercadet turns on a last, desperate speculation based on the appearance of a spurious Godeau. But the fraud is discovered. Mercadet seems ruined. At this moment the real Godeau is announced; he has returned from India with a huge fortune. The play ends with Mercadet exclaiming, '*J'ai montré tant de fois Godeau que j'ai bien le droit de le voir. Allons voir Godeau!*'[1]

The parallels are too striking to make it probable that this is a mere coincidence. In Beckett's play, as in Balzac's, the arrival of Godot is the eagerly awaited event that will miraculously save the situation; and Beckett is as fond as Joyce of subtle and recondite literary allusions.

Yet whether Godot is meant to suggest the intervention of a supernatural agency, or whether he stands for a mythical human being whose arrival is expected to change the situation, or both of these possibilities combined, his exact nature is of secondary importance. The subject of the play is not Godot but waiting, the act of waiting as an essential and characteristic aspect of the human condition. Throughout our lives we always wait for something, and Godot simply represents the objective of our waiting – an event, a thing, a person, death. Moreover, it is in the act of waiting that we experience the flow of *time* in its purest, most evident form. If we are active, we tend to forget the passage of time, we *pass* the time, but if we are merely passively waiting, we are confronted with the action of time itself. As Beckett points out in his analysis of Proust, 'There is no escape from the hours and the days. Neither from tomorrow nor from yesterday because yesterday has deformed us, or been deformed by us. ... Yesterday is not a milestone that has been passed, but a daystone on the beaten track of the years, and irremediably part of us, within us, heavy and dangerous. We are not merely more weary because of yesterday, we are other, no longer what we were before the calamity of yesterday.'[2] The flow of time confronts us with the basic problem of being – the

1. Honoré de Balzac, *Œuvres Complètes* (Paris, 1866), XIX.
2. *Proust*, pp. 2–3.

problem of the nature of the self, which, being subject to constant change in time, is in constant flux and therefore ever outside our grasp – 'personality, whose permanent reality can only be apprehended as a retrospective hypothesis. The individual is the seat of a constant process of decantation, sluggish, pale and monochrome, to the vessel containing the fluid of past time, agitated and multicoloured by the phenomena of its hours.'[1]

Being subject to this process of time flowing through us and changing us in doing so, we are, at no single moment in our lives, identical with ourselves. Hence 'we are disappointed at the nullity of what we are pleased to call attainment. But what is attainment? The identification of the subject with the object of his desire. The subject has died – and perhaps many times on the way.'[2] If Godot is the object of Vladimir's and Estragon's desire, he seems naturally ever beyond their reach. It is significant that the boy who acts as go-between fails to recognize the pair from day to day. The French version explicitly states that the boy who appears in the second act is the same boy as the one in the first act, yet the boy denies that he has ever seen the two tramps before and insists that this is the first time he has acted as Godot's messenger. As the boy leaves, Vladimir tries to impress it upon him: 'You're sure you saw me, eh, you won't come and tell me tomorrow that you never saw me before?' The boy does not reply, and we know that he will again fail to recognize them. Can we ever be sure that the human beings we meet are the same today as they were yesterday? When Pozzo and Lucky first appear, neither Vladimir nor Estragon seems to recognize them; Estragon even takes Pozzo for Godot. But after they have gone, Vladimir comments that they have changed since their last appearance. Estragon insists that he didn't know them.

VLADIMIR: Yes you do know them.
ESTRAGON: No I don't know them.

1. *Proust*, pp. 4–5.   2. ibid., p. 13.

VLADIMIR: We know them, I tell you. You forget everything. [*Pause. To himself*] Unless they're not the same. . . .

ESTRAGON: Why didn't they recognize us, then?

VLADIMIR: That means nothing. I too pretended not to recognize them. And then nobody ever recognizes us.[1]

In the second act, when Pozzo and Lucky reappear, cruelly deformed by the action of time, Vladimir and Estragon again have their doubts whether they are the same people they met on the previous day. Nor does Pozzo remember them: 'I don't remember having met anyone yesterday. But tomorrow I won't remember having met anyone today.'[2]

Waiting is to experience the action of time, which is constant change. And yet, as nothing real ever happens, that change is in itself an illusion. The ceaseless activity of time is self-defeating, purposeless, and therefore null and void. The more things change, the more they are the same. That is the terrible stability of the world. 'The tears of the world are a constant quantity. For each one who begins to weep, somewhere else another stops.'[3] One day is like another, and when we die, we might never have existed. As Pozzo exclaims in his great final outburst:

'Have you not done tormenting me with your accursed time? . . . One day, is that not enough for you, one day like any other day he went dumb, one day I went blind, one day we'll go deaf, one day we were born, one day we'll die, the same day, the same second. . . . They give birth astride of a grave, the light gleams an instant, then it's night once more.'[4]

And Vladimir, shortly afterwards, agrees: 'Astride of a grave and a difficult birth. Down in the hole, lingeringly, the gravedigger puts on the forceps.'[5]

Still Vladimir and Estragon live in hope: they wait for

1. *Waiting for Godot*, p. 48.   2. ibid., p. 88.
3. ibid., p. 32.   4. ibid., p. 89   5. ibid., p. 91.

Godot, whose coming will bring the flow of time to a stop. 'Tonight perhaps we shall sleep in his place, in the warmth, dry, our bellies full, on the straw. It is worth waiting for that, is it not?'[1] This passage, omitted in the English version, clearly suggests the peace, the rest from waiting, the sense of having arrived in a haven, that Godot represents to the two tramps. They are hoping to be saved from the evanescence and instability of the illusion of time, and to find peace and permanence outside it. Then they will no longer be tramps, homeless wanderers, but will have arrived home.

Vladimir and Estragon wait for Godot although their appointment with him is by no means certain. Estragon does not remember it at all. Vladimir is not quite sure what they asked Godot to do for them. It was 'nothing very definite . . . a kind of prayer . . . a vague supplication'. And what had Godot promised them? 'That he'd see . . . that he would think it over . . .'[2]

When Beckett is asked about the theme of *Waiting for Godot*, he sometimes refers to a passage in the writing of St Augustine: 'There is a wonderful sentence in Augustine. I wish I could remember the Latin. It is even finer in Latin than in English. "Do not despair: one of the thieves was saved. Do not presume: one of the thieves was damned."' And Beckett sometimes adds, 'I am interested in the shape of ideas even if I do not believe in them. . . . That sentence has a wonderful shape. It is the shape that matters.'[3]

The theme of the two thieves on the cross, the theme of the uncertainty of the hope of salvation and the fortuitousness of the bestowal of grace, does indeed pervade the whole play. Vladimir states it right at the beginning: 'One of the thieves

1. Beckett, *En Attendant Godot* (Paris: Les Editions de Minuit, 1952), p. 30.
2. *Waiting for Godot*, p. 18.
3. Beckett, quoted by Harold Hobson, op. cit., and by Alan Schneider, op. cit.

was saved. . . . It's a reasonable percentage.'[1] Later he enlarges
on the subject: 'Two thieves. . . . One is supposed to have been
saved and the other . . . damned. . . . And yet how is it that of
the four evangelists only one speaks of a thief being saved? The
four of them were there or thereabouts, and only one speaks of a
thief being saved. . . . Of the other three two don't mention
any thieves at all and the third says that both of them abused
him.'[2] There is a fifty-fifty chance, but as only one out of four
witnesses reports it, the odds are considerably reduced. But, as
Vladimir points out, it is a curious fact that everybody seems
to believe that one witness: 'It is the only version they know.'
Estragon, whose attitude has been one of scepticism throughout,
merely comments, 'People are bloody ignorant apes.'[3]

It is the shape of the idea that fascinated Beckett. Out of all
the malefactors, out of all the millions and millions of criminals
that have been executed in the course of history, two, only two,
had the chance of receiving absolution in the hour of their death
in so uniquely effective a manner. One happened to make a
hostile remark; he was damned. One happened to contradict
that hostile remark; he was saved. How easily could the roles
have been reversed. These, after all, were not well-considered
judgements, but chance exclamations uttered at a moment of
supreme suffering and stress. As Pozzo says about Lucky,
'Remark that I might easily have been in his shoes and he in
mine. If chance had not willed it otherwise. To each one his
due.'[4] And then our shoes might fit us one day and not the
next: Estragon's boots torment him in the first act; in act II
they fit him miraculously.

Godot himself is unpredictable in bestowing kindness and
punishment. The boy who is his messenger minds the goats, and
Godot treats him well. But the boy's brother, who minds the
sheep, is beaten by Godot. 'And why doesn't he beat you?' asks
Vladimir. 'I don't know, sir' – *Je ne sais pas, Monsieur* – the

1. *Waiting for Godot*, p. 11.   2. ibid., pp. 12–13.
3. ibid.   4. ibid., p. 31.

boy replies, using the words of the *apache* who had stabbed Beckett. The parallel to Cain and Abel is evident: there too the Lord's grace fell on one rather than on the other without any rational explanation – only that Godot beats the minder of the sheep and cherishes the minder of the goats. Here Godot also acts contrary to the Son of Man at the Last Judgement: 'And he shall set the sheep on his right hand, but the goats on the left.' But if Godot's kindness is bestowed fortuitously, his coming is not a source of pure joy; it can also mean damnation. When Estragon, in the second act, believes Godot to be approaching, his first thought is, 'I'm accursed.' And as Vladimir triumphantly exclaims, 'It's Godot! At last! Let's go and meet him,' Estragon runs away, shouting, 'I'm in hell!'[1]

The fortuitous bestowal of grace, which passes human understanding, divides mankind into those that will be saved and those that will be damned. When, in act II, Pozzo and Lucky return, and the two tramps try to identify them, Estragon calls out, 'Abel! Abel!' Pozzo immediately responds. But when Estragon calls out, 'Cain! Cain!' Pozzo responds again. 'He's all mankind,' concludes Estragon.[2]

There is even a suggestion that Pozzo's activity is concerned with his frantic attempt to draw that fifty-fifty chance of salvation upon himself. In the first act, Pozzo is on his way to sell Lucky 'at the fair'. The French version, however, specifies that it is the '*marché de Saint-Sauveur*' – the Market of the Holy Saviour – to which he is taking Lucky. Is Pozzo trying to sell Lucky to redeem himself? Is he trying to divert the fifty-fifty chance of redemption from Lucky (in whose shoes he might easily have been himself) to Pozzo? He certainly complains that Lucky is causing him great pain, that he is killing him with his mere presence – perhaps because his mere presence reminds Pozzo that it might be Lucky who will be redeemed. When Lucky gives his famous demonstration of his thinking, what is the thin thread of sense that seems to underlie the opening

1. ibid., pp. 73–4.   2. ibid., pp. 83–4.

passage of his wild, schizophrenic 'word salad'? Again, it seems to be concerned with the fortuitousness of salvation: 'Given the existence ... of a personal God ... outside time without extension who from the heights of divine apathia divine athambia divine aphasia loves us dearly with some exceptions for reasons unknown ... and suffers ... with those who for reasons unknown are plunged in torment. . . .'[1] Here again we have the personal God, with his divine apathy, his speechlessness (aphasia), and his lack of the capacity for terror or amazement (athambia), who loves us dearly – with some exceptions, who will be plunged into the torments of hell. In other words, God, who does not communicate with us, cannot feel for us, and condemns us for reasons unknown.

When Pozzo and Lucky reappear the next day, Pozzo blind and Lucky dumb, no more is heard of the fair. Pozzo has failed to sell Lucky; his blindness in thinking that he could thus influence the action of grace has been made evident in concrete physical form.

That *Waiting for Godot* is concerned with the hope of salvation through the workings of grace seems clearly established both from Beckett's own evidence and from the text itself. Does this, however, mean that it is a Christian, or even that it is a religious, play? There have been a number of very ingenious interpretations in this sense. Vladimir's and Estragon's waiting is explained as signifying their steadfast faith and hope, while Vladimir's kindness to his friend, and the two tramps' mutual interdependence, are seen as symbols of Christian charity. But these religious interpretations seem to overlook a number of essential features of the play – its constant stress on the uncertainty of the appointment with Godot, Godot's unreliability and irrationality, and the repeated demonstration of the futility of the hopes pinned on him. The act of waiting for Godot is shown as essentially *absurd*. Admittedly it might be a case of '*Credere quia absurdum est*', yet it might even more

1. ibid., p. 42.

56

forcibly be taken as a demonstration of the proposition '*Absurdum est credere.*'

There is one feature in the play that leads one to assume there is a better solution to the tramps' predicament, which they themselves both consider preferable to waiting for Godot – that is, suicide. 'We should have thought of it when the world was young, in the nineties. . . . Hand in hand from the top of the Eiffel Tower, among the first. We were respectable in those days. Now it's too late. They wouldn't even let us up.'[1] Suicide remains their favourite solution, unattainable owing to their own incompetence and their lack of the practical tools to achieve it. It is precisely their disappointment at their failure to succeed in their attempts at suicide that Vladimir and Estragon rationalize by waiting, or pretending to wait, for Godot. 'I'm curious to hear what he has to offer. Then we'll take it or leave it.'[2] Estragon, far less convinced of Godot's promises than Vladimir, is anxious to reassure himself that they are not tied to Godot.

ESTRAGON: I'm asking you if we are tied.
VLADIMIR: Tied?
ESTRAGON: Ti–ed.
VLADIMIR: How do you mean tied?
ESTRAGON: Down.
VLADIMIR: But to whom? By whom?
ESTRAGON: To your man.
VLADIMIR: To Godot? Tied to Godot? What an idea! No question of it. [*Pause.*] For the moment.[3]

When, later, Vladimir falls into some sort of complacency about their waiting – 'We have kept our appointment . . . we are not saints – but we have kept our appointment. How many people can boast as much?' – Estragon immediately punctures it by retorting, 'Billions.' And Vladimir is quite ready to admit that they are waiting only from irrational habit. 'What's

1. *Waiting for Godot*, p. 10.   2. ibid., p. 18.
3. ibid., p. 20.

certain is that the hours are long . . . and constrain us to beguile them with proceedings . . . which may at first sight seem reasonable until they become a habit. You may say it is to prevent our reason from foundering. No doubt. But has it not long been straying in the night without end of the abyssal depths?'[1]

In support of the Christian interpretation, it might be argued that Vladimir and Estragon, who are waiting for Godot, are shown as clearly superior to Pozzo and Lucky, who have no appointment, no objective, and are wholly egocentric, wholly wrapped up in their sadomasochistic relationship. Is it not their faith that puts the two tramps on to a higher plane?

It is evident that, in fact, Pozzo is naïvely over-confident and self-centred. 'Do I look like a man that can be made to suffer?'[2] he boasts. Even when he gives a soulful and melancholy description of the sunset and the sudden falling of the night, we know he does not believe the night will ever fall on him – he is merely giving a performance; he is not concerned with the meaning of what he recites, but only with its effect on the audience. Hence he is taken completely unawares when night does fall on him and he goes blind. Likewise Lucky, in accepting Pozzo as his master and in teaching him his ideas, seems to have been naïvely convinced of the power of reason, beauty, and truth. Estragon and Vladimir *are* clearly superior to both Pozzo and Lucky – not because they pin their faith on Godot but because they are less naïve. They do not believe in action, wealth, or reason. They are aware that all we do in this life is as nothing when seen against the senseless action of time, which is in itself an illusion. They are aware that suicide would be the best solution. They are thus superior to Pozzo and Lucky because they are less self-centred and have fewer illusions. In fact, as a Jungian psychologist, Eva Metman, has pointed out in a remarkable study of Beckett's plays, 'Godot's function seems

1. ibid., p. 80.
2. ibid., p. 34.

to be to keep his dependents unconscious.'[1] In this view, the hope, the habit of hoping, that Godot might come after all is the last illusion that keeps Vladimir and Estragon from facing the human condition and themselves in the harsh light of fully conscious awareness. As Dr Metman observes, it is at the very moment, toward the end of the play, when Vladimir is about to realize he has been dreaming, and must wake up and face the world as it is, that Godot's messenger arrives, rekindles his hopes, and plunges him back into the passivity of illusion.

For a brief moment, Vladimir is aware of the full horror of the human condition: 'The air is full of our cries. . . . But habit is a great deadener.' He looks at Estragon, who is asleep, and reflects, 'At me too someone is looking, of me too someone is saying, he is sleeping, he knows nothing, let him sleep on. . . . I can't go on!'[2] The routine of waiting for Godot stands for habit, which prevents us from reaching the painful but fruitful awareness of the full reality of being.

Again we find Beckett's own commentary on this aspect of *Waiting for Godot* in his essay on Proust: 'Habit is the ballast that chains the dog to his vomit. Breathing is habit. Life is habit. Or rather life is a succession of habits, since the individual is a succession of individuals. . . . Habit then is the generic term for the countless treaties concluded between the countless subjects that constitute the individual and their countless correlative objects. The periods of transition that separate consecutive adaptations . . . represent the perilous zones in the life of the individual, dangerous, precarious, painful, mysterious, and fertile, when for a moment the *boredom of living* is replaced by the *suffering of being*.'[3] 'The suffering of being: that is the free play of every faculty. Because the pernicious devotion of habit paralyses our attention, drugs those handmaidens of per-

1. Eva Metman, 'Reflections on Samuel Beckett's plays', *Journal of Analytical Psychology*, London, January 1960, p. 51.
2. *Waiting for Godot*, p. 91.
3. *Proust*, p. 8 [my italics – M.E.].

ception whose cooperation is not absolutely essential.'[1]

Vladimir's and Estragon's pastimes are, as they repeatedly indicate, designed to stop them from thinking. 'We're in no danger of thinking any more.... Thinking is not the worst.... What is terrible is to have thought.'[2]

Vladimir and Estragon talk incessantly. Why? They hint at it in what is probably the most lyrical, the most perfectly phrased passage of the play:

VLADIMIR: You are right, we're inexhaustible.
ESTRAGON: It's so we won't think.
VLADIMIR: We have that excuse.
ESTRAGON: It's so we won't hear.
VLADIMIR: We have our reasons.
ESTRAGON: All the dead voices.
VLADIMIR: They make a noise like wings.
ESTRAGON: Like leaves.
VLADIMIR: Like sand.
ESTRAGON: Like leaves.
  [Silence.]
VLADIMIR: They all speak together.
ESTRAGON: Each one to itself.
  [Silence.]
VLADIMIR: Rather they whisper.
ESTRAGON: They rustle.
VLADIMIR: They murmur.
ESTRAGON: They rustle.
  [Silence.]
VLADIMIR: What do they say?
ESTRAGON: They talk about their lives.
VLADIMIR: To have lived is not enough for them.
ESTRAGON: They have to talk about it.
VLADIMIR: To be dead is not enough for them.
ESTRAGON: It is not sufficient.
  [Silence.]
VLADIMIR: They make a noise like feathers.

1. ibid., p. 9.
2. *Waiting for Godot*, p. 64.

ESTRAGON: Like leaves.
VLADIMIR: Like ashes.
ESTRAGON: Like leaves.
 [*Long silence.*][1]

This passage, in which the cross-talk of Irish music-hall comedians is miraculously transmuted into poetry, contains the key to much of Beckett's work. Surely these rustling, murmuring voices of the past are the voices we hear in the three novels of his trilogy; they are the voices that explore the mysteries of being and the self to the limits of anguish and suffering. Vladimir and Estragon are trying to escape hearing them. The long silence that follows their evocation is broken by Vladimir, '*in anguish*', with the cry 'Say anything at all!' after which the two relapse into their wait for Godot.

The hope of salvation may be merely an evasion of the suffering and anguish that spring from facing the reality of the human condition. There is here a truly astonishing parallel between the Existentialist philosophy of Jean-Paul Sartre and the creative intuition of Beckett, who has never consciously expressed Existentialist views. If, for Beckett as for Sartre, man has the duty of facing the human condition as a recognition that at the root of our being there is nothingness, liberty, and the need of constantly creating ourselves in a succession of choices, then Godot might well become an image of what Sartre calls 'bad faith' – 'The first act of bad faith consists in evading what one cannot evade, in evading what one *is*.'[2]

While these parallels may be illuminating, we must not go too far in trying to identify Beckett's vision with any school of philosophy. It is the peculiar richness of a play like *Waiting for Godot* that it opens vistas on so many different perspectives. It is open to philosophical, religious, and psychological interpretations, yet above all it is a poem on time, evanescence, and the mysteriousness of existence, the paradox of change and stabili-

1. ibid., pp. 62–3.
2. Jean-Paul Sartre, *L'Être et le Néant* (Paris: Gallimard, 1943), p. 111.

ty, necessity and absurdity. It expresses what Watt felt about the household of Mr Knott: '. . . nothing changed in Mr Knott's establishment, because nothing remained, and nothing came or went, because all was a coming and a going.'[1] In watching *Waiting for Godot*, we feel like Watt contemplating the organization of Mr Knott's world: 'But he had hardly felt the absurdity of those things, on the one hand, and the necessity of those others, on the other (for it is rare that the feeling of absurdity is not followed by the feeling of necessity), when he felt the absurdity of those things of which he had just felt the necessity (for it is rare that the feeling of necessity is not followed by the feeling of absurdity).'[2]

If *Waiting for Godot* shows its two heroes whiling away the time in a succession of desultory, and never-ending, games, Beckett's second play deals with an 'endgame', the final game in the hour of death.

Waiting for Godot takes place on a terrifying empty open road, *Endgame* in a claustrophobic interior. *Waiting for Godot* consists of two symmetrical movements that balance each other; *Endgame* has only one act that shows the running down of a mechanism until it comes to a stop. Yet *Endgame*, like *Waiting for Godot*, groups its characters in symmetrical pairs.

In a bare room with two small windows, a blind old man, Hamm, sits in a wheelchair. Hamm is paralysed, and can no longer stand. His servant, Clov, is unable to sit down. In two ash-cans that stand by the wall are Hamm's legless parents, Nagg and Nell. The world outside is dead. Some great catastrophe, of which the four characters in the play are, or believe themselves to be, the sole survivors, has killed all living beings.

Hamm and Clov (ham actor and clown? Hammer and Nail – French '*clou*'?) in some ways resemble Pozzo and Lucky. Hamm is the master, Clov the servant. Hamm is selfish, sensuous, domineering. Clov hates Hamm and wants to leave

1. Beckett, *Watt* (Paris: Olympia Press, 1958), pp. 144–5.
2. ibid., p. 146.

him, but he must obey his orders. 'Do this, do that, and I do it. I never refuse. Why?'[1] Will Clov have the force to leave Hamm? That is the source of the dramatic tension of the play. If he leaves, Hamm must die, as Clov is the only one left who can feed him. But Clov also must die, as there is no one else left in the world, and Hamm's store is the last remaining source of food. If Clov can muster the will power to leave, he will not only kill Hamm but commit suicide. He will thus succeed where Estragon and Vladimir have failed so often.

Hamm fancies himself as a writer – or, rather, as the spinner of a tale of which he composes a brief passage every day. It is a story about a catastrophe that caused the death of large numbers of people. On this particular day, the tale has reached an episode in which the father of a starving child asks Hamm for bread for his child. Finally the father begs Hamm to take in his child, should it still be alive when he gets back to his home. It appears that Clov might well be that very child. He was brought to Hamm when he was too small to remember. Hamm was a father to him, or, as he himself puts it, 'But for me . . . no father. But for Hamm . . . no home.'[2] The situation in *Endgame* is the reverse of that in Joyce's *Ulysses*, where a father finds a substitute for a lost son. Here a foster son is trying to leave his foster father.

Clov has been trying to leave Hamm ever since he was born, or as he says, 'Ever since I was whelped.'[3] Hamm is burdened with a great load of guilt. He might have saved large numbers of people who begged him for help. 'The place was crawling with them!'[4] One of the neighbours, old Mother Pegg, who was 'bonny once, like a flower of the field' and perhaps Hamm's lover, was killed through his cruelty: 'When old Mother Pegg asked you for oil for her lamp and you told her to get out to hell . . . you know what she died of, Mother Pegg?

1. Beckett, *Endgame* (New York: Grove Press, 1958), p. 43.
2. ibid., p. 38.   3. ibid., p. 14.
4. ibid., p. 68.

Of darkness.'[1] Now the supplies in Hamm's own household are running out: the sweets, the flour for the parents' pap, even Hamm's painkiller. The world is running down. 'Something is taking its course.'[2]

Hamm is childish; he plays with a three-legged toy dog, and he is full of self-pity. Clov serves him as his eyes. At regular intervals he is asked to survey the outside world from the two tiny windows high up in the wall. The right-hand window looks out on land, the left-hand on to the sea. But even the tides have stopped.

Hamm is untidy. Clov is a fanatic of order.

Hamm's parents, in their dustbins, are grotesquely senti-mental imbeciles. They lost their legs in an accident while cycling through the Ardennes on their tandem, on the road to Sedan. They remember the day they went rowing on Lake Como – the day after they became engaged – one April afternoon (cf. the love scene in a boat on a lake in *Krapp's Last Tape*), and Nagg, in the tones of an Edwardian raconteur, retells the funny story that made his bride laugh then and that he has since repeated *ad nauseam*.

Hamm hates his parents. Nell secretly urges Clov to desert Hamm. Nagg, having been awakened to listen to Hamm's tale, scolds him: 'Whom did you call when you were a tiny boy, and were frightened in the dark? Your mother? No. Me.' But he immediately reveals how selfishly he ignored these calls. 'We let you cry. Then we moved out of earshot, so that we might sleep in peace. . . . I hope the day will come when you'll really need to have me listen to you. . . . Yes, I hope I'll live till then, to hear you calling me like when you were a tiny little boy, and were frightened, in the dark, and I was your only hope.'[3]

As the end approaches, Hamm imagines what will happen when Clov leaves him. He confirms Nagg's forecast: 'There I'll be in the old shelter, alone against the silence and . . . the

1. ibid., p. 75.   2. ibid., p. 13.   3. ibid., p. 56.

stillness. . . . I'll have called my father and I'll have called my . . . son,'[1] which indicates that he does indeed regard Clov as his son.

For a last time, Clov looks out of the windows with his telescope. He sees something unusual. 'A small . . . boy!' But it is not entirely clear whether he has really seen this strange sign of continuing life, 'a potential procreator'.[2] In some way, this is the turning point. Hamm says, 'It's the end, Clov, we've come to the end. I don't need you any more.'[3] Perhaps he does not believe that Clov will really be able to leave him. But Clov has finally decided that he will go: 'I open the door of the cell and go. I am so bowed I only see my feet, if I open my eyes, and between my legs a little trail of black dust. I say to myself that the earth is extinguished, though I never saw it lit. . . . It's easy going. . . . When I fall I'll weep for happiness.'[4] And as blind Hamm indulges in a last monologue of reminiscence and self-pity, Clov appears, dressed for departure in a Panama hat, tweed coat, raincoat over his arm, and listens to Hamm's speech, motionless. When the curtain falls, he is still there. It remains open whether he will really leave.

The final tableau of *Endgame* bears a curious resemblance to the ending of a little-known but highly significant play by the brilliant Russian dramatist and man of the theatre Nikolai Evreinov, which appeared in an English translation as early as 1915 – *The Theatre of the Soul*.[5] This one-act play is a mono-drama that takes place *inside a human being* and shows the con-stituent parts of his ego, his emotional self and his rational self, in conflict with each other. The man, Ivanov, is sitting in a café, debating with himself whether to run away with a night-club singer or go back to his wife. His emotional self urges him to leave, his rational self tries to persuade him of the advantages,

1. ibid., p. 69.   2. ibid., p. 78.
3. ibid., p. 79.   4. ibid., p. 81.
5. Nikolai Evreinov, *The Theatre of the Soul, Monodrama*, trans. M. Potapenko and C. St John (London, 1915).

moral and material, of staying with his wife. As they come to blows, a bullet pierces the heart that has been beating in the background. Ivanov has shot himself. The rational and emotional selves fall down dead. A third figure, who has been sleeping in the background, gets up. He is dressed in travelling clothes and carries a suitcase. It is the immortal part of Ivanov that now has to move on.

While it is unlikely that Beckett knew this old and long-forgotten Russian play, the parallels are very striking. Evreinov's monodrama is a purely rational construction designed to present to a cabaret audience what was then the newest psychological trend. Beckett's play springs from genuine depths. Yet the suggestion that *Endgame* may also be a monodrama has much to be said for it. The enclosed space with the two tiny windows through which Clov observes the outside world; the dustbins that hold the suppressed and despised parents, and whose lids Clov is ordered to press down when they become obnoxious; Hamm, blind and emotional; Clov, performing the function of the senses for him – all these might well represent different aspects of a single personality, repressed memories in the subconscious mind, the emotional and the intellectual selves. Is Clov then the intellect, bound to serve the emotions, instincts, and appetites, and trying to free himself from such disorderly and tyrannical masters, yet doomed to die when its connection with the animal side of the personality is severed? Is the death of the outside world the gradual receding of the links to reality that takes place in the process of ageing and dying? Is *Endgame* a monodrama depicting the dissolution of a personality in the hour of death?

It would be wrong to assume that these questions can be definitely answered. *Endgame* certainly was not planned as a sustained allegory of this type. But there are indications that there is an element of monodrama in the play. Hamm describes a memory that is strangely reminiscent of the situation in *Endgame*: 'I once knew a madman who thought the end of the world had come. He was a painter – an engraver. . . . I used to go and see him in the asylum. I'd take him by the hand and drag him to the window. Look! There! All that rising corn! And there! Look! The sails of the herring fleet! All that loveliness! . . . He'd snatch away his hand and go back into his corner. Appalled. All he had seen was ashes. . . . He alone had been spared. Forgotten. . . . It appears the case is . . . was not so . . . so unusual.'[1] Hamm's own world resembles the delusions of the mad painter. Moreover, what is the significance of the picture mentioned in the stage directions? 'Hanging near door, its face to wall, a picture'.[2] Is that picture a memory? Is the story a lucid moment in the consciousness of that very painter whose dying hours we witness from behind the scenes of his mind?

Beckett's plays can be interpreted on many levels. *Endgame* may well be a monodrama on one level and a morality play about the death of a rich man on another. But the peculiar psychological reality of Beckett's characters has often been noticed. Pozzo and Lucky have been interpreted as body and mind; Vladimir and Estragon have been seen as so complementary that they might be the two halves of a single personality, the conscious and the subconscious mind. Each of these three pairs – Pozzo–Lucky; Vladimir–Estragon; Hamm–Clov – is linked by a relationship of mutual interdependence, wanting to leave each other, at war with each other, and yet dependent on each other. '*Nec tecum, nec sine te*'. This is a frequent situation among people – married couples, for example – but it is also an image of the interrelatedness of the elements within a single personality, particularly if the personality is in conflict with itself.

In Beckett's first play, *Eleutheria*, the basic situation was, superficially, analogous to the relationship between Clov and Hamm. The young hero of that play wanted to leave his family; in the end he succeeded in getting away. In *Endgame*, however, that situation has been deepened into truly universal

1. *Endgame*, p. 44.   2. ibid., p. 1.

significance; it has been concentrated and immeasurably enriched precisely by having been freed from all elements of a naturalistic social setting and external plot. The process of contraction, which Beckett described as the essence of the artistic tendency in his essay on Proust, has here been carried out triumphantly. Instead of merely exploring a surface, a play like *Endgame* has become a shaft driven deep down into the core of being; that is why it exists on a multitude of levels, revealing new ones as it is more closely studied. What at first might have appeared as obscurity or lack of definition is later recognized as the very hallmark of the density of texture, the tremendous concentration of a work that springs from a truly creative imagination, as distinct from a merely imitative one.

The force of these considerations is brought out with particular clarity when we are confronted by an attempt to interpret a play like *Endgame* as a mere exercise in conscious or subconscious autobiography. In an extremely ingenious essay[1] Lionel Abel has worked out the thesis that in the characters of Hamm and Pozzo Beckett may have portrayed his literary master, James Joyce, while Lucky and Clov stand for Beckett himself. *Endgame* then becomes an allegory of the relationship between the domineering, nearly blind Joyce and his adoring disciple, who felt himself crushed by his master's overpowering literary influence. Superficially the parallels are striking: Hamm is presented as being at work on an interminable story, Lucky is being made to perform a set piece of thinking, which, Mr Abel argues, is in fact a parody of Joyce's style. Yet on closer reflection this theory surely becomes untenable; not because there may not be a certain amount of truth in it (every writer is bound to use elements of his own experience of life in his work) but because, far from illuminating the full content of a play like *Endgame*, such an interpretation reduces it to a trivial level. If *Endgame* really were nothing but a thinly disguised account of

1. Lionel Abel, 'Joyce the father, Beckett the son', *The New Leader*, New York, 14 December 1959.

the literary, or even the human, relationship between two particular individuals, it could not possibly produce the impact it has had on audiences utterly ignorant of these particular, very private circumstances. Yet *Endgame* undoubtedly has a very deep and direct impact, which can spring only from its touching a chord in the minds of a very large number of human beings. The problems of the relationship between a literary master and his pupil would be very unlikely to elicit such a response; very few people in the audience would feel directly involved. Admittedly, a play that presented the conflict between Joyce and Beckett openly, or thinly disguised, might arouse the curiosity of audiences who are always eager for autobiographical revelations. But this is just what *Endgame* does *not* do. If it nevertheless arouses profound emotion in its audience, this can be due only to the fact that it is felt to deal with a conflict of a far more universal nature. Once that is seen, it becomes clear that while it is fascinating to argue about the aptness of such autobiographical elements, such a discussion leaves the central problem of understanding the play and exploring its many-layered meanings still to be tackled.

As a matter of fact, the parallels are by no means so close: Lucky's speech in *Waiting for Godot*, for example, is anything but a parody of Joyce's style. It is, if anything, a parody of philosophical jargon and scientific double-talk – the very opposite of what either Joyce or Beckett ever wanted to achieve in their writing. Pozzo, on the other hand, who would stand for Joyce, is utterly inartistic in his first persona, and becomes reflective in a melancholy vein only after he has gone blind. And if Pozzo is Joyce, what would be the significance of Lucky's dumbness, which comes at the same time as Pozzo's blindness? The novel that Hamm composes in *Endgame* is characterized by its attempt at scientific exactitude, and there is a clear suggestion that it is not a work of art at all but a thinly disguised vehicle for the expression of Hamm's sense of guilt about his behaviour at the time of the great mysterious calamity, when he refused to save his neighbours. Clov, on the other hand, is shown as totally uninterested in Hamm's 'Work in Progress', so that Hamm has to bribe his senile father to listen to it – surely a situation as unlike that of Joyce and Beckett as can be imagined.

The experience expressed in Beckett's plays is of a far more profound and fundamental nature than mere autobiography. They reveal his experience of temporality and evanescence; his sense of the tragic difficulty of becoming aware of one's own self in the merciless process of renovation and destruction that occurs with change in time; of the difficulty of communication between human beings; of the unending quest for reality in a world in which everything is uncertain and the borderline between dream and waking is ever shifting; of the tragic nature of all love relationships and the self-deception of friendship (of which Beckett speaks in the essay on Proust), and so on. In *Endgame* we are also certainly confronted with a very powerful expression of the sense of deadness, of leaden heaviness and hopelessness, that is experienced in states of deep depression: the world outside goes dead for the victim of such states, but inside his mind there is ceaseless argument between parts of his personality that have become autonomous entities.

This is not to say that Beckett gives a clinical description of psychopathological states. His creative intuition explores the elements of experience and shows to what extent all human beings carry the seeds of such depression and disintegration within the deeper layers of their personality. If the prisoners of San Quentin responded to *Waiting for Godot*, it was because they were confronted with *their own experience* of time, waiting, hope, and despair; because they recognized the truth about *their own human relationships* in the sadomasochistic interdependence of Pozzo and Lucky and in the bickering hate–love between Vladimir and Estragon. This is also the key to the wide success of Beckett's plays: to be confronted with concrete projections of the deepest fears and anxieties, which have been only vaguely experienced at a half-conscious level, constitutes a process of catharsis and liberation analogous to the therapeutic effect in psychoanalysis of confronting the subconscious contents of the mind. This is the moment of release from deadening habit, through facing up to the suffering of existence, that Vladimir almost attains in *Waiting for Godot*. This also, probably, is the release that could occur if Clov had the courage to break his bondage to Hamm and venture out into the world, which may not, after all, be so dead as it appeared from within the claustrophobic confines of Hamm's realm. This, in fact, seems to be hinted at by the strange episode of the little boy whom Clov observes in the last stage of *Endgame*. Is this boy a symbol of life outside the closed circuit of withdrawal from reality?

It is significant that in the original, French version, this episode is dealt with in greater detail than in the later, English one. Again Beckett seems to have felt that he had been too explicit. And from an artistic point of view he is surely right; in his type of theatre the half-light of suggestion is more powerful than the overtly symbolical. But the comparison between the two versions is illuminating nevertheless. In the English version, Clov, after expressing surprise at what he has discovered, merely says:

CLOV [*dismayed*]: Looks like a small boy!
HAMM [*sarcastic*]: A small ... boy!
CLOV: I'll go and see. [*He gets down, drops the telescope, goes towards the door, turns.*] I'll take the gaff. [*He looks for the gaff, sees it, picks it up, hastens towards the door.*]
HAMM: No!
    [*Clov halts.*]
CLOV: No? A potential procreator?
HAMM: If he exists he'll die there or he'll come here.And if he doesn't ... [*Pause.*][1]

In the original, French version, Hamm shows far greater

1. *Endgame*, p. 78.

interest in the boy, and his attitude changes from open hostility to resignation.

CLOV: There is someone there! Someone!

HAMM: Well, go and exterminate him! [*Clov gets down from the stool.*] Somebody! [*With trembling voice*] Do your duty! [*Clov rushes to the door.*] No, don't bother. [*Clov stops.*] What distance?
  [*Clov climbs back on the stool, looks through the telescope.*]

CLOV: Seventy . . . four metres.

HAMM: Approaching? Receding?

CLOV [*continues to look*]: Stationary.

HAMM: Sex?

CLOV: What does it matter? [*He opens the window, leans out. Pause. He straightens, lowers the telescope, turns to Hamm, frightened.*] Looks like a little boy.

HAMM: Occupied with?

CLOV: What?

HAMM [*violently*]: What is he doing?

CLOV [*also violently*]: I don't know what he's doing. What little boys used to do. [*He looks through the telescope. Pause. Puts it down, turns to Hamm.*] He seems to be sitting on the ground, with his back against something.

HAMM: The lifted stone. [*Pause.*] Your eyesight is getting better. [*Pause.*] No doubt he is looking at the house with the eyes of Moses dying.

CLOV: No.

HAMM: What is he looking at?

CLOV [*violently*]: I don't know what he is looking at. [*He raises the telescope. Pause. Lowers the telescope, turns to Hamm.*] His navel. Or thereabouts. [*Pause.*] Why this cross-examination?

HAMM: Perhaps he is dead.[1]

After this, the French text and the English version again coincide: Clov wants to tackle the newcomer with his gaff, Hamm stops him, and, after a brief moment of doubt as to whether Clov has told him the truth, realizes that the turning

1. Beckett, *Fin de Partie* (Paris: Les Editions de Minuit, 1957), pp. 103–5.

point has come: 'It's the end, Clov, we've come to the end. I don't need you any more.'[1]

The longer, more elaborate version of this episode clearly reveals the religious or quasi-religious symbolism of the little boy; the references to Moses and the lifted stone seem to hint that the first human being, the first sign of life discovered in the outside world since the great calamity when the earth went dead, is not, like Moses, dying within sight of the promised land, but, like Christ the moment after the resurrection, has been newly born into a new life, leaning, a babe, against the lifted stone. Moreover, like the Buddha, the little boy contemplates his navel. And his appearance convinces Hamm that the moment of parting, the final stage of the endgame, has come.

It may well be that the sighting of this little boy – undoubtedly a climactic event in the play – stands for redemption from the illusion and evanescence of time through the recognition, and acceptance, of a higher reality: the little boy contemplates his own navel; that is, he fixes his attention on the great emptiness of nirvana, nothingness, of which Democritus the Abderite has said, in one of Beckett's favourite quotations, 'Nothing is more real than nothing.'[2]

There is a moment of illumination, shortly before he himself dies, in which Murphy, having played a *game of chess*, experiences a strange sensation: '... and Murphy began to see nothing, that colourlessness which is such a rare post-natal treat, being the absence ... not of *percipere* but of *percipi*. His other senses also found themselves at peace, an unexpected pleasure. Not the numb peace of their own suspension, but the positive peace that comes when the somethings give way, or perhaps simply add up, to the Nothing, than which in the guffaw of the Abderite naught is more real. Time did not cease, that would be asking too much, but the wheels of rounds and

1. *Endgame*, p. 79.
2. Beckett, *Malone Dies*, in *Molloy/Malone Dies/The Unnamable* (London: John Calder, 1959), p. 193.

pauses did, as Murphy with his head among the armies [i.e. of the chessmen] continued to suck in, through all the posterns of his withered soul, the accidentless One-and-Only, conveniently called Nothing.'[1]

Does Hamm, who has shut himself off from the world and killed the rest of mankind by holding on to his material possessions – Hamm, blind, sensual, egocentric – then die when Clov, the rational part of the self, perceives the true reality of the illusoriness of the material world, the redemption and resurrection, the liberation from the wheels of time that lies in union with the 'accidentless One-and-Only, conveniently called Nothing'? Or is the discovery of the little boy merely a symbol of the coming of death – union with nothingness in a different, more concrete sense? Or does the reappearance of life in the outside world indicate that the period of loss of contact with the world has come to an end, that the crisis has passed and that a disintegrating personality is about to find the way back to integration, 'the solemn change towards merciless reality in Hamm and ruthless acceptance of freedom in Clov', as the Jungian analyst Dr Metman puts it?[2]

There is no need to try to pursue these alternatives any further; to decide in favour of one would only impair the stimulating coexistence of these and other possible implications. There is, however, an illuminating commentary on Beckett's views about the interrelation between material wants and a feeling of restlessness and futility in the short mime play *Act Without Words I*, which was performed with *Endgame* during its first run. The scene is a desert on to which a man is 'flung backwards'. Mysterious whistles draw his attention in various directions. A number of more or less desirable objects, notably a carafe of water, are dangled before him. He tries to get the water. It hangs too high. A number of cubes, obviously designed to make it easier for him to reach the water, descend from the flies. But however ingeniously he piles them on top

1. *Murphy*, p. 246. 2. Metman, op. cit., p. 58.

of one another, the water always slides just outside his reach. In the end he sinks into complete immobility. The whistle sounds – but he no longer heeds it. The water is dangled in front of his face – but he does not move. Even the palm tree in the shade of which he has been sitting is whisked off into the flies. He remains immobile, looking at his hands.[1]

Here again we find man flung on to the stage of life, at first obeying the call of a number of impulses, having his attention drawn to the pursuit of illusory objectives by whistles from the wings, but finding peace only when he has learned his lesson and refuses any of the material satisfactions dangled before him. The pursuit of objectives that forever recede as they are attained – inevitably so through the action of time, which changes us in the process of reaching what we crave – can find release only in the recognition of that nothingness which is the only reality. The whistle that sounds from the wings resembles the whistle with which Hamm summons Clov to minister to his material needs. And the final, immobile position of the man in *Act Without Words I* recalls the posture of the little boy in the original version of *Endgame*.

The activity of Pozzo and Lucky, the driver and the driven, always on the way from place to place; the waiting of Estragon and Vladimir, whose attention is always focused on the promise of a coming; the defensive position of Hamm, who has built himself a shelter from the world to hold on to his possessions, are all aspects of the same futile preoccupation with objectives and illusory goals. All movement is disorder. As Clov says, 'I love order. It's my dream. A world where all would be silent and still and each thing in its last place, under the last dust.'[2]

Waiting for Godot and *Endgame*, the plays Beckett wrote in French, are dramatic statements of the human situation itself.

1. Beckett, *Act Without Words I*, in *Krapp's Last Tape and Other Dramatic Pieces* (New York: Grove Press, 1960).
2. *Endgame*, p. 57.

They lack both characters and plot in the conventional sense because they tackle their subject-matter at a level where neither characters nor plot exist. Characters presuppose that human nature, the diversity of personality and individuality, is real and matters; plot can exist only on the assumption that events in time are significant. These are precisely the assumptions that the two plays put in question. Hamm and Clov, Pozzo and Lucky, Vladimir and Estragon, Nagg and Nell are not characters but the embodiments of basic human attitudes, rather like the personified virtues and vices in medieval mystery plays or Spanish *autos sacramentales*. And what passes in these plays are not *events* with a definite beginning and a definite end, but types of *situation* that will forever repeat themselves. That is why the pattern of act I of *Waiting for Godot* is repeated with variations in act II; that is why we do not see Clov actually leave Hamm at the close of *Endgame* but leave the two frozen in a position of stalemate. Both plays repeat the pattern of the old German students' song Vladimir sings at the beginning of act II of *Waiting for Godot*, about the dog that came into a kitchen and stole some bread and was killed by the cook and buried by its fellow-dogs, who put a tombstone on its grave which told the story of the dog that came into the kitchen and stole some bread – and so on *ad infinitum*. In *Endgame* and *Waiting for Godot*, Beckett is concerned with probing down to a depth in which individuality and definite events no longer appear, and only basic patterns emerge.

In the plays he has written for the stage and for radio in English, his probing does not go quite so deep, and both individual characters and individualized plots do appear, reflecting the same patterns but reflecting them in the lives of particular human beings. *Krapp's Last Tape* deals with the flow of time and the instability of the self, *All That Fall* and *Embers* with waiting, guilt, and the futility of pinning one's hopes on things or human beings.

All That Fall (the title is taken from Psalm 145: 'The Lord upholdeth all that fall and raiseth up all those that he bowed down') shows an old Irishwoman, Maddy Rooney, very fat, very ill, hardly able to move, on her way to the railway station of Boghill to fetch her blind husband, Dan Rooney, who is due to arrive on the twelve-thirty train. Her progress is slow as in a nightmare. She meets a number of people with whom she wants to establish contact but fails. 'I estrange them all.'[1] Mrs Rooney has lost a daughter, Minnie, more than forty years ago. When she reaches the railway station, the train is mysteriously delayed. When it arrives, it is said to have stopped for a long while on the open track. Dan and Maddy Rooney set out for home. As children jeer at them, Dan Rooney asks, 'Did you ever wish to kill a child? . . . Nip some young doom in the bud?'[2] and he admits that often in winter he is tempted to attack the boy who leads him home from the station. When they are almost home, the same little boy runs after them; he is returning an object Mr Rooney is believed to have left in his compartment on the train. It is a child's ball. The boy also knows why the train had to stop on the line: a child had fallen out of the train and been killed on the tracks. Did Dan Rooney push a child out of the train? Did his impulse to destroy young lives overcome him during the journey? And has his hatred of children something to do with Maddy's childlessness? Maddy Rooney stands for the forces of life and procreation, Dan for the death-wish that sees a young child only as a young doom that could be nipped in the bud. Does the Biblical quotation of the title support Dan Rooney's point of view? 'The Lord upholdeth all that fall. . . .' Was the child who was killed and redeemed from existence saved the troubles of life and old age and thus upheld by the Lord? When the text from the psalm is mentioned as the subject of next Sunday's sermon, both Maddy and Dan Rooney break out in 'wild laughter'.[3] *All That Fall* touches many of the chords that are sounded in *Waiting for*

1. Beckett, *All That Fall*, in *Krapp's Last Tape*, p. 53.
2. ibid., p. 74.   3. ibid., p. 88.

Godot and *Endgame* – but in a somewhat lighter and less searching manner.

In *Krapp's Last Tape*, a one-act play that has been performed with great success on the stage in Paris, London, and New York, Beckett makes use of the tape recorder to demonstrate the elusiveness of human personality. Krapp is a very old man who throughout his adult life has annually recorded an account of the past year's impressions and events on to magnetic tape. We see him, old, decrepit, and a failure (he is a writer, but only seventeen copies of his book have been sold in the current year, 'eleven at trade price to free circulating libraries beyond the seas'), listening to his own voice recorded thirty years earlier. But his voice has become the voice of a stranger to him. He even has to get a dictionary to look up one of the more elaborate words used by his former self. When the tape reaches the description of the great moment of insight that then seemed a miracle to be treasured 'against the day when my work will be done', he cannot be bothered to listen to it and winds the tape on. The only description that visibly arouses his attention is one of love-making in a punt on a lake. Having heard his earlier self's report on his thirty-ninth year, the sixty-nine-year-old Krapp proceeds to record the current year's balance sheet. 'Nothing to say, not a squeak.' His only moment of happiness: 'Revelled in the word spool. [*With relish*] Spoool! Happiest moment in the past half million.'[1] There are memories of love-making with an old hag. But then Krapp returns to the old tape. Again the voice of his former self is heard describing the love scene on the lake. The old tape ends with a summing up: 'Perhaps my best years are gone. When there was a chance of happiness. But I wouldn't want them back. Not with the fire in me now. No, I wouldn't want them back.'[2] The curtain falls on old Krapp staring motionless before him, with the tape running on in silence.

1. Beckett, *Krapp's Last Tape*, in op. cit., p. 25.
2. ibid., p. 28.

Through the brilliant device of the autobiographical library of annual recorded statements, Beckett has found a graphic expression for the problem of the ever-changing identity of the self, which he had already described in his essay on Proust. In *Krapp's Last Tape*, the self at one moment in time is confronted with its earlier incarnation only to find it utterly strange. What, then, is the identity between Krapp now and Krapp then? In what sense are they the same? And if this is a problem with an interval of thirty years, it is surely only a difference in degree if the interval is reduced to one year, one month, one hour. Beckett at one time planned to write a long play of three Krapps: Krapp with his wife, Krapp with his wife and child, Krapp alone – further variations on the theme of the identity of the self. But he has now abandoned this project.

The radio play *Embers* resembles *Krapp's Last Tape* in that its hero is also an old man musing on the past. Against the background of the roar of the sea, Henry remembers his youth, his father who was drowned in the sea at this very spot, his father who was a sporty man and despised his son as a washout. It seems as if Henry wanted to establish contact with his dead father, but 'he doesn't answer any more.'[1] Henry's wife, Ada, although probably dead too, does respond. They remember love-making by the sea, their daughter's riding and music lessons, but then Ada recedes, and Henry is left alone with his thoughts, which revolve around a scene he seems to have witnessed as a child between two men at night, Bolton and Holloway, Holloway being a doctor, their family doctor, whom Bolton (Henry's father?) implored for some medical help the nature of which remains unclear. With the winter night outside and the fire dying – no more flames, only the embers glowing – Henry remains alone with his thoughts of his loneliness: 'Saturday ... nothing. Sunday ... Sunday

1. Beckett, *Embers*, in *Krapp's Last Tape and other Dramatic Pieces*, p. 115.

... nothing all day. ... Nothing, all day nothing. ... not a sound.'[1]

Henry resembles the heroes of Beckett's later novels in his recall of memories in the form of 'stories' and in his compulsive need to talk. As his wife, or the memory of his wife, tells him, 'You should see a doctor about your talking, it's worse, what must it be like for Addie? ... Do you know what she said to me once, when she was quite small, she said, Mummy, why does Daddy keep on talking all the time? She heard you in the lavatory, I didn't know what to answer.' To which Henry replies, 'I told you to tell her I was praying. Roaring prayers at God and his saints.'[2]

The compulsion to talk, to tell oneself stories, which is the thread that runs through the three novels of Beckett's great trilogy, also forms the subject of his radio play *Cascando*. There are two voices here: the 'Opener' and the 'Voice' which he turns on and off. 'They say,' the Opener confesses, 'it's his own, it's his voice, it's in his head.' The 'Voice' we hear – and which must be presumed to be in the Opener's head – reports haltingly and breathlessly on its pursuit of an elusive individual, called – in the English version – Woburn. And it is suggested that once Woburn has been reached, suffering will finish: '... no more stories ... sleep. ...' The play ends inconclusively. As in *Endgame*, as in *Waiting for Godot* we are left uncertain whether the final consummation, the attainment of salvation, of the cessation of suffering through consciousness has in fact been, or can ever be, reached. In *Cascando* the droning of the voice, of verbal consciousness, which is for ever compelled to fill the void with words, i.e. compelled to tell itself stories, is accompanied by surges of non-verbal consciousness, the swell of emotion expressed in the music. Similarly, in the radio play *Words and Music* we find a tyrannical master, Croak, issuing orders to his two servants, Words and Music, to fill the time with improvisations on such subjects as Sloth,

1. ibid., p. 121.   2. ibid., p. 111.

Age, and Love. Always unsatisfied, Croak savagely clouts his servants and calls for more. The parallel between Croak and the 'Opener' of *Cascando* is thus quite clear. And so is the yearning for Peace from consciousness which emerges from Words' final improvisation:

> Then down a little way
> Through the trash
> Towards where
> All dark no begging
> No giving no words
> No sense no need
> Through the scum
> Down a little way
> To whence one glimpse
> Of that wellhead.

In the short film, laconically entitled *Film*, which Beckett wrote for Grove Press, the same flight from self-perception is put into a visual form. The manuscript of the film opens with the statement: '*Esse est percipi*. All extraneous perception suppressed, animal, human, divine, self-perception maintains in being. Search of non-being in flight from extraneous perception breaking down in inescapability of self-perception.' Beckett, as always, eager to disclaim any pretension to be a philosopher dispensing general truths, hastens to add: 'No truth value attaches to above, regarded as of merely structural and dramatic convenience.' Nevertheless, dramatically and structurally, the flight from self-perception in an attempt to reach the positive nothingness of non-being, *is* an important theme of all of Beckett's work. In *Film* it is concretized as the flight of the hero from a pursuer, who eventually is revealed to be none other than himself.

Yet the attainment of the release from consciousness, from the need to tell oneself the tale of one's own life, seems impossible. For the true release would lie in *one's knowing* that one is no longer conscious. Yet with death consciousness ceases, so we can never know that we no longer exist. Hence the last moment of a dying man's consciousness can be imagined as remaining suspended forever in the limbo of an eternal unawareness of its cessation. This is the situation dramatized by Beckett in *Play*. The heads of two women and one man are seen protruding from grey funerary urns. At the bidding of a beam of light, which turns their speech on and off (just as the Opener in *Cascando* turns on the Voice), they recite the broken fragments of what is clearly meant to be the trivial story of a French bedroom farce that has gone wrong by leading to a tragic ending – three suicides. And here are the three dead characters, the husband, the wife, and the mistress, unaware of each other's presence, only dimly aware that they are dead, endlessly repeating the contents of their last moment of consciousness. How can Eternity itself be put on to the stage within the confines of a text that runs to barely half an hour? Beckett has attempted to achieve the impossible by having the entire text of *Play* spoken twice, identically, except that the words become faster and softer. When the third time round is reached the play fades from our view, but we remain aware that it will go on, ever faster, ever more softly, forever and forever. Told by three characters in unrelated snippets, the story is not easy to take in the first time round; hence the device of repeating the entire play also provides the audience with the opportunity of getting another chance at piecing the little novelette together; thus the use of repetition brilliantly combines the solution of two different problems with which the author of so intricate a dramatic structure finds himself confronted.

In *Happy Days*, which preceded *Play*, Beckett (who is fascinated by the dramatic possibilities of a character immobilized and forced to put all his expressiveness into the words issuing from his mouth) portrays the human condition in the image of a cheerful, plump woman, Winnie, who is slowly sinking into a mound of earth. In the first act Winnie is embedded up to her waist, with her arms free; in the second act only her head is still protruding. Her husband Willie can move but is so absorbed in his newspaper that he hardly takes any notice of Winnie. Winnie's preoccupation with her few possessions, her cheerfulness and optimism create the poignant irony of the play. On the one hand it is tragic that Winnie should be so cheerful in her terrible and hopeless predicament, on the other it is funny; in one sense her cheerfulness is sheer folly and the author seems to make a deeply pessimistic comment on human life; in another sense, however, Winnie's cheerfulness in the face of death and nothingness is an expression of man's courage and nobility, and thus the play provides a kind of catharsis. Winnie's life does consist of happy days, because she refuses to be dismayed.

The miniature playlet *Come and Go* also deals with the theme of our reluctance to face our own predicament, while we are only too eager to gossip about that of our fellow men. We are confronted with three female characters, called Flo, Vi, and Ru. Each of these leaves in turn, allowing the two remaining characters to inform each other of some impending disaster (her death?) which is about to descend on the absent lady. After all possible permutations of this situation are completed, the three ladies again face the audience together in silence.

The same economy and terseness characterize Beckett's first television play, *Eh Joe*. Here we are introduced to a lonely, elderly man, sitting on his bed in a bare room. He never speaks, but listens with increasing terror to a woman's voice reproaching him with his hardness of heart towards her which drove her to suicide. As the voice drones on, the camera relentlessly jerks nearer and nearer to Joe's face, until in the end only his eyes are visible in a huge close-up. Then all is darkness. This is a theme Beckett has often dealt with before – regret about love not given, love refused in the past. What is astonishing is his mastery of the new medium. This is a television play which could not exist in any other medium. The concentration on a single close-up growing larger and larger would be intolerable on the huge cinema screen; on the television screen it always remains within a human scale. And the combination of a visible silent, and an invisible speaking, character also brilliantly exploits television's dual nature: its ability to project an image of the outside world, combined with radio's unique capacity of evoking an inner universe, a psychological inscape.

In *Eh Joe* the voice Joe hears has the timbre of a woman's voice, yet that voice too, in another sense, being inside his head, is his own, is the droning on of his own consciousness, of his compulsion to tell himself his own story. For to be alive is to be aware of oneself, to be aware of oneself is to hear one's thoughts, that endless, relentless stream of words. As a human being suffering from this compulsion Beckett rejects language; as a poet, endlessly compelled to work with language, he loves it. This is the source of the ambivalence of his attitude to language: sometimes it appears to him as a divine instrument, sometimes as mere senseless buzzing.

In the radio plays, *Embers* and *All That Fall*, this compulsive talking blends into a background of natural sound – the sound of the sea in *Embers*, the sounds of the road in *All That Fall*. And articulate sound, language, is somehow equated with the inarticulate sounds of nature. In a world that has lost its meaning, language also becomes a meaningless buzzing. As Molloy says at one point,

. . . the words I heard, and heard distinctly, having quite a sensitive ear, were heard a first time, then a second, and often even a third, as pure sounds, free of all meaning, and this is probably one of the reasons why conversation was unspeakably painful to me. And the words I uttered myself, and which must nearly always have gone with an effort of the intelligence, were often to me as the buzzing of an insect. And this is perhaps one of the reasons I was so untalkative, I mean this trouble I had in understanding not only what others said to me but also what I said to them. It is true that in the end, by dint of patience, we made ourselves understood, but understood with regard to what, I ask of you, and to what purpose? And to the noises of nature too, and of the works of men, I reacted I think in my own way and without desire of enlightenment.[1]

When we hear Beckett's characters (and hence Beckett himself) using language, we often feel like Celia when she was talking to Murphy: '. . . spattered with words that went dead as soon as they sounded; each word obliterated, before it had time to make sense, by the word that came next; so that in the end she did not know what had been said. It was like difficult music heard for the first time.'[2] And in fact the dialogue in Beckett's plays is often built on the principle that each line obliterates what was said in the previous line. In his thesis on Beckett, *Die Unzulänglichkeit der Sprache – The Inadequacy of Language* – Niklaus Gessner has drawn up a whole list of passages from *Waiting for Godot* in which assertions made by one of the characters are gradually qualified, weakened, and hedged in with reservations until they are completely taken back. In a meaningless universe, it is always foolhardy to make a positive statement. 'Not to want to say, not to know what you want to say, not to be able to say what you think you want to say, and never to stop saying, or hardly ever, that is the thing to keep in mind, even in the heat of composition,'[3] as Molloy puts it, summing up the attitude of most of Beckett's characters.

If Beckett's plays are concerned with expressing the difficulty of finding meaning in a world subject to incessant change, his use of language probes the limitations of language both as a means of communication and as a vehicle for the expression of valid statements, an instrument of thought. When Gessner asked him about the contradiction between his writing and his obvious conviction that language could not convey meaning, Beckett replied, '*Que voulez-vous, Monsieur? C'est les mots; on n'a rien d'autre.*' But in fact his use of the dramatic medium shows that he has tried to find means of expression beyond language. On the stage – witness his two mimeplays – one can

1. Beckett, *Molloy*, in *Molloy/Malone Dies/The Unnamable*, p. 50.
    2. *Murphy*, p. 40.   3. *Molloy*, p. 28.

dispense with words altogether, or at least one can reveal the reality behind the words, as when the actions of the characters contradict their verbal expression. 'Let's go,' say the two tramps at the end of each act of *Waiting for Godot*, but the stage directions inform us that 'they don't move'. On the stage, language can be put into a contrapuntal relationship with action, the facts behind the language can be revealed. Hence the importance of mime, knockabout comedy, and silence in Beckett's plays – Krapp's eating of bananas, the pratfalls of Vladimir and Estragon, the variety turn with Lucky's hat, Clov's immobility at the close of *Endgame*, which puts his verbally expressed desire to leave in question. Beckett's use of the stage is an attempt to reduce the gap between the limitations of language and the intuition of being, the sense of the human situation he seeks to express in spite of his strong feeling that words are inadequate to formulate it. The concreteness and three-dimensional nature of the stage can be used to add new resources to language as an instrument of thought and exploration of being.

Beckett's whole work is an endeavour to name the unnamable: 'I have to speak, whatever that means. Having nothing to say, no words but the words of others, I have to speak.... I have the ocean to drink, so there is an ocean then.'[1]

Language in Beckett's plays serves to express the breakdown, the disintegration of language. Where there is no certainty, there can be no definite meanings – and the impossibility of ever attaining certainty is one of the main themes of Beckett's plays. Godot's promises are vague and uncertain. In *Endgame*, an unspecified something is taking its course, and when Hamm anxiously asks, 'We're not beginning to ... to ... mean something?' Clov merely laughs. 'Mean something! You and I mean something!'[2]

1. Beckett, *The Unnamable*, in *Molloy/Malone Dies/The Unnamable*, p. 316.
2. *Endgame*, pp. 32–3.

Niklaus Gessner has tabulated ten different modes of disintegration of language observable in *Waiting for Godot*. They range from simple misunderstandings and *double-entendres* to monologues (as signs of inability to communicate), clichés, repetitions of synonyms, inability to find the right words, and 'telegraphic style' (loss of grammatical structure, communication by shouted commands) to Lucky's farrago of chaotic nonsense and the dropping of punctuation marks, such as question marks, as an indication that language has lost its function as a means for communication, that questions have turned into statements not really requiring an answer.

But more important than any merely formal signs of the disintegration of language and meaning in Beckett's plays is the nature of the dialogue itself, which again and again breaks down because no truly dialectical exchange of thought occurs in it – either through loss of meaning of single words (Godot's boy messenger, when asked if he is unhappy, replies, 'I don't know, sir') or through the inability of characters to remember what has just been said (Estragon: 'Either I forget immediately or I never forget'[1]). In a purposeless world that has lost its ultimate objectives, dialogue, like all action, becomes a mere game to pass the time, as Hamm points out in *Endgame*: '. . . babble, babble, words, like the solitary child who turns himself into children, two, three, so as to be together and whisper together in the dark . . . moment upon moment, pattering down'.[2] It is time itself that drains language of meaning. In *Krapp's Last Tape*, the well-turned idealistic professions of faith Krapp made in his best years have become empty sounds to Krapp grown old. Instead of establishing a bridge of friendliness, Mrs Rooney's attempts to communicate with the people she meets on the road in *All That Fall* merely serve to make her more estranged from them. And in *Embers* the old man's musings are equated with the beating of the waves upon the shore.

But, if Beckett's use of language is designed to devalue

1. *Waiting for Godot*, p. 61. 2. *Endgame*, p. 70.

language as a vehicle of conceptual thought or as an instrument for the communication of ready-made answers to the problems of the human condition, his continued use of language must, paradoxically, be regarded as an attempt to communicate on his own part, to communicate the incommunicable. Such an undertaking may be a paradox, but it makes sense nevertheless: it attacks the cheap and facile complacency of those who believe that to name a problem is to solve it, that the world can be mastered by neat classification and formulations. Such complacency is the basis of a continuous process of frustration. The recognition of the illusoriness and absurdity of ready-made solutions and prefabricated meanings, far from ending in despair, is the starting point of a new kind of consciousness, which faces the mystery and terror of the human condition in the exhilaration of a new-found freedom: 'For to know nothing is nothing, not to want to know anything likewise, but to be beyond knowing anything, that is when peace enters in, to the soul of the incurious seeker.'[1]

Beckett's entire work can be seen as a search for the reality that lies behind mere reasoning in conceptual terms. He may have devalued language as an instrument for the communication of ultimate truths, but he has shown himself a great master of language as an artistic medium. *'Que voulez-vous, Monsieur? C'est les mots; on n'a rien d'autre.'* For want of better raw material, he has moulded words into a superb instrument for his purpose. In the theatre he has been able to add a new dimension to language – the counterpoint of action, concrete, many-faceted, not to be explained away, but making a direct impact on an audience. In the theatre, or at least in Beckett's theatre, it is possible to bypass the stage of conceptual thinking altogether, as an abstract painting bypasses the stage of the recognition of natural objects.

Visual images, what we actually see and what appears to us in dreams and memories and the non-verbal consciousness of

1. *Molloy*, p. 64.

pure emotion (which, to follow Schopenhauer, one of Beckett's favourite philosophers, is most perfectly expressed by the non-verbal art-form of music), are as vital constituents of our awareness of ourselves as words are – the words which run in an endless stream through our minds and which can be perceived as a sort of endless story we tell ourselves about ourselves. Hamm writing his story in *Endgame*, Krapp listening to the recordings of what he was telling himself in his past, as well as the protagonists of the great trilogy, exemplify that aspect of the mystery of the self. In the last phase of his dramatic *oeuvre* Beckett increasingly concentrates on this aspect of the search for the self. Are the words which run through our minds, or which occasionally break out of us in streams of logorrhoea (like the outbursts of Henry in *Embers*, when he had to retreat to the lavatory and his daughter had to be told that Daddy was praying), are these words, this story, our real self? In *Not I* Beckett tackled this problem. The words issue forth from the mouth that we see suspended in the darkness high up on the stage, a tiny, moving point. Where do these words, these thoughts, come from? They are not part of the material world and yet they issue forth from a very material, very flesh-bound organ, the mouth. Thus the mouth is the point of intersection between a non-material world and the world of flesh, of matter. The voice, that of a woman seventy years old, speaks of the moment when, late in life, in April, in a field, she was suddenly seized by the voice which began spluttering out of her mouth – after a life of speechlessness. Five times in the course of the short play the voice is tempted to say 'I', but each time it corrects itself: 'No, SHE!' ... The voice does not perceive itself as being identical with the Self, the I. Similarly in *Footfalls* the old woman tramping up and down, to and fro, endlessly, insisting that the footfalls must be heard – as a material evidence of her existence, an evidence beyond merely immaterial words – tells a story; it is a story of a girl who when asked about something that happened during a church service replies that she does not know what happened because *she was not there*. Here again the self, materially present, – there can be no doubt about that, – was not *really* there, because the self is a mystery, ever elusive: there and yet not there. In *That Time* the elusiveness of the self is, as in *Krapp's Last Tape*, exemplified by the impermanence of the human personality in time: at each point in time our self is a distinct and different entity: the three voices that pass through the mind of the old man – on his deathbed? – are inter-cut segments of memories of very different selves, present in his consciousness at one and the same time. And in the two late television plays memory is mingled with guilt and regret: the old man in *Ghost Trio* (originally to be entitled *Tryst*) is listening to a tape of Beethoven's Fifth Piano Trio, the ghost trio of the title, and waiting for the arrival of someone who is not coming. When someone is outside it is a little boy (reminiscent perhaps of the little boy at the end of *Endgame*) who looks at the old man for a moment and leaves, down the corridor. Is he the unborn child that might have been the fruit of some unconsummated love? Or is he the earlier, submerged and regretted self of the old man himself? In '. . . *but the clouds* . . .' a very similar old man (played in the B.B.C. production supervised by Beckett by the same actor, Ronald Pickup) traverses a circle of light, to and fro (an image, no doubt, of the daily routine of rising and going to bed, of light and darkness, day and night) and is haunted by the image of a woman's face and the phrase '*but the clouds of the sky*', taken from W. B. Yeats's 'The Tower':

> The death of friends, or death
> Of every brilliant eye
> That made a catch in the breath –
> Seem but the clouds of the sky
> When the horizon fades;
> Or a bird's sleepy cry
> Among the deepening shades.

These television plays are very short; they are clearly attempts to capture the totality of an emotion in its most concentrated form. For if the self is ever elusive, split into perceiver and perceived, the teller of the tale and the listener to the tale – and also ever changing through time, from moment to moment – then the only authentic experience that can be communicated is the experience of the single moment in the fullness of its emotional intensity, its existential totality.

And that, after all, is what all art is trying to capture. That is the aim and objective of Samuel Beckett's art.

2

ARTHUR ADAMOV
The curable and the incurable

ARTHUR ADAMOV, the author of some of the most powerful
plays in the Theatre of the Absurd, later rejected all his work
that might be classified under that heading. The development
that led him toward this type of drama, however, and the
development that led him away from it again, are of particular
interest to any inquiry into its nature. Adamov, who was not
only a remarkable dramatist but also a remarkable thinker, has
provided us with a well-documented case history of the
preoccupations and obsessions that made him write plays
depicting a senseless and brutal nightmare world, the theoretical considerations that led him to formulate an aesthetic of the
absurd, and, finally, the process by which he gradually returned
to a theatre based on reality, the representation of social conditions, and a definite social purpose. How did it happen that a
dramatist who in the late nineteen-forties so thoroughly rejected the naturalistic theatre that to use even the name of a
town that could actually be found on a map would have appeared to him as 'unspeakably vulgar' could by 1960 be
engaged in writing a full-scale historical drama firmly situated
in place and time – the Paris Commune of 1871?

Arthur Adamov, born in Kislovodsk, in the Caucasus, in
1908, the son of a wealthy oil-well proprietor of Armenian
origin, left Russia at the age of four. His parents could afford to
travel, and, like the children of many well-to-do Russian
families, Adamov was brought up in France, a fact that explains
his mastery of French literary style. The first book he ever read
was Balzac's *Eugénie Grandet*, at the age of seven. The outbreak
of the First World War found Adamov's family at Freuden-

stadt, a resort in the Black Forest. It was only through the special intervention of the King of Württemberg, who was acquainted with Adamov's father, that the family escaped internment as enemy citizens, and were given special permission to leave for Switzerland, where they settled in Geneva.

Adamov received his early education in Switzerland and later in Germany (at Mainz). In 1924, at the age of sixteen, he went to Paris and was drawn into Surrealist circles. He wrote Surrealist poetry, edited an avant-garde periodical, *Disconti-nuité*, became a friend of Paul Eluard, and led the life of the Parisian literary nonconformists.

Gradually he stopped writing, or at least stopped publishing what he had written. He himself later described the severe spiritual and psychological crisis that he went through in a small book that must be among the most terrifying and ruthless documents of self-revelation in world literature, *L'Aveu* (*The Confession*). The earliest section of this Dostoevskian master-piece, dated 'Paris, 1938', opens with a brilliant statement of the metaphysical anguish that forms the basis of Existentialist literature and of the Theatre of the Absurd:

> What is there? I know first of all that I am. But who am I? All I know of myself is that I suffer. And if I suffer it is because at the origin of myself there is mutilation, separation.
>
> I am separated. What I am separated from – I cannot name it. But I am separated.

In a footnote Adamov adds, 'Formerly it was called God. Today it no longer has any name.'[1]

A deep sense of alienation, the feeling that time weighs on him 'with its enormous liquid mass, with all its dark power',[2] a deep feeling of passivity – these are some of the symptoms of his spiritual sickness.

> Everything happens as though I were only one of the particular

1. Arthur Adamov, *L'Aveu* (Paris: Editions du Sagittaire, 1946), p. 19.
2. ibid., p. 23.

existences of some great incomprehensible and central being. ...
Sometimes this great totality of life appears to me so dramatically
beautiful that it plunges me into ecstasy. But more often it seems like a
monstrous beast that penetrates and surpasses me and which is everywhere, within me and outside me. ... And terror grips and envelops
me more powerfully from moment to moment. ... My only way
out is to write, to make others aware of it, so as not to have to feel all
of it alone, to get rid of however small a portion of it.[1]

It is in dreams and in prayer that the writer of this haunting
confession seeks escape – in dreams that are 'the great silent
movement of the soul through the night'[2]; in prayer that is the
'desperate need of man, immersed in time, to seek refuge in the
only entity that could save him, the projection outward from
himself of that in him which partakes of eternity'.[3] Yet what
is there to pray to? 'The name of God should no longer come
from the mouth of man. This word that has so long been
degraded by usage no longer means anything. ... To use the
word God is more than sloth, it is a refusal to think, a kind of
short cut, a hideous shorthand. ...'[4] Thus the crisis of faith is
also a crisis of language. 'The words in our ageing vocabularies
are like very sick people. Some may be able to survive, others
are incurable.'[5]

In the next section of *L'Aveu*, dated 'Paris, 1939' (it has been
published in English, under the title 'The endless humiliation')[6]
Adamov gives a ruthlessly frank description of his own sickness, his desire to be humiliated by the lowest of prostitutes, his
'incapacity to complete the act of carnal possession'.[7] Fully
aware of the nature of his neurosis – he was well versed in
modern psychology and even translated one of Jung's works

1. ibid., pp. 25–6.   2. ibid., p. 28.   3. ibid., p. 42.
4. ibid., p. 45.   5. ibid.
6. Adamov, 'The endless humiliation', trans. Richard Howard,
Evergreen Review, New York, II, 8, 1959, pp. 64–95.
7. *L'Aveu*, p. 69; 'The endless humiliation', loc. cit., p. 75.

ARTHUR ADAMOV: THE CURABLE AND THE INCURABLE

into French[1] – Adamov was also aware of the *value* of neurosis, which 'grants its victim a peracute lucidity, inaccessible to the so-called normal man',[2] and which may thus give him the vision that 'permits him, through the singularity of his sickness, to accede to the great general laws by which the loftiest comprehension of the world is expressed. And since the particular is always a symbolic expression of the universal, it follows that the universal is most effectively symbolized by the extreme of the particular, so that the neurosis which exaggerates a man's particularity of vision defines that much more completely his universal significance.'[3]

Having given a brutally detailed description, itself a symptom of masochism by the violence of its self-humiliation, of his neurosis, with its obsessions, rites, and automatisms, Adamov returns to a diagnosis of our epoch in a section entitled *'Le temps de l'ignominie'*. He defines ignominy as that which has no name, the *unnamable*, and the poet's task is not only to call each thing by its name but also to 'denounce . . . the degenerated concepts, the dried-up abstractions that have usurped . . . the dead remnants of the old sacred names'.[4] The degradation of language in our time becomes the expression of its deepest sickness. What has been lost is the sense of the sacred, 'the unfathomable wisdom of the myths and rites of the dead old world'.[5]

The disappearance of meaning in the world is clearly linked to the degradation of language, and both, in turn, to the loss of faith, the disappearance of sacred rites and sacred myths. But perhaps this degradation and despair are necessary steps toward a renewal: 'Perhaps the sad and empty language that today's flabby humanity pours forth, will, in all its horror, in all its

1. Carl Gustav Jung, *Le Moi et l'Inconscient*, trans. Adamov (Paris: 1938).
2. *L'Aveu*, p. 37; 'The endless humiliation', loc. cit., p. 67.
3. *L'Aveu*, p. 58; 'The endless humiliation', loc. cit., p. 67.
4. *L'Aveu*, p. 106.   5. ibid., p. 110.

boundless absurdity, re-echo in the heart of a solitary man who is awake, and then perhaps that man, suddenly realizing that he does not understand, will begin to understand.'[1] Therefore the only task left to man is to tear off all that dead skin until 'he finds himself in the hour of the great nakedness.'[2]

In this document of ruthless self-revelation, Adamov outlined a whole philosophy of the Theatre of the Absurd, long before he started to write his first play.

In the pages of *L'Aveu*, we can follow him through the war years – still in Paris in May and June 1940; in Cassis in July; in Marseille by August; then, between December 1940 and November 1941, at the internment camp of Agelès, months passed in a stupor of dejection; back in Marseille at the end of 1941; returning to Paris in the last month of 1942. The last section of *L'Aveu* and the preface are dated 1943.

In reading this astonishing book, we are witnessing a mind laying the foundations of its salvation through self-examination and a merciless recognition of its own predicament. In his contributions to the short-lived literary review *L'Heure Nouvelle*, of which he became editor shortly after the end of the war in Europe, Adamov returned to the same themes, but already in a spirit of detachment, in the posture of a thinker called upon, at a great turning point in history, to work out a programme of action for a new beginning in a new epoch.

It is a programme characterized by a complete absence of illusions and easy solutions: 'We are accused of pessimism, as though pessimism were but one among a number of possible attitudes, as if man were capable of choosing between two alternatives – optimism and pessimism.'[3] Such a programme would of necessity be destructive in its rejection of all existing dogmatisms. It insists on the artist's duty to avoid selecting just one aspect of the world – 'religious, psychological, scientific,

1. ibid., p. 114.   2. ibid., p. 115.
3. Adamov, '*Une fin et un commencement*', *L'Heure Nouvelle*, no. II (Paris: Editions du Sagittaire, 1946), p. 17.

social – but to evoke behind each of these the shadow of the whole in which they must merge.'[1] And again this search for wholeness, for the reality underlying the bewildering multiplicity of appearances, is seen as a search for the sacred: 'the crisis of our time is essentially a religious crisis. It is a matter of life or death.'[2] Yet the concept of God is dead. We are on the threshold of an era of impersonal aspects of the absolute, hence the revival of creeds like Taoism and Buddhism. This is the tragic impasse in which modern man finds himself: 'From whatever point he starts, whatever path he follows, modern man comes to the same conclusion: behind its visible appearances, life hides a meaning that is eternally inaccessible to penetration by the spirit that seeks for its discovery, caught in the dilemma of being aware that it is impossible to find it, and yet also impossible to renounce the hopeless quest.'[3] Adamov points out that this is not, strictly speaking, a philosophy of the absurd, because it still presupposes the conviction that the world *has* a meaning, although it is of necessity outside the reach of human consciousness. The awareness that there may be a meaning but that it will never be found is tragic. Any conviction that the world is wholly absurd would lack this tragic element.

In the social and political sphere, Adamov finds the solution in Communism. But his is a very personal form of support for the Communist cause. He finds in Communism no supernatural, sacred element. Its ideology confines itself to purely human terms, and for him it remains open to question 'whether anything that confines itself to the human sphere could ever attain anything but the subhuman.'[4] If this is the case, why support Communism?

If we turn to Communism nevertheless, it is merely because one

1. Adamov, '*Assignation*', L'Heure Nouvelle, no. I, p. 3.
2. ibid., footnote on p. 6.
3. '*Le refus*', L'Heure Nouvelle, no. II, footnote on p. 6.
4. '*Une fin et un commencement*', loc. cit., p. 16.

day, when it will seem quite close to the realization of its highest aim – the victory over all the contradictions that impede the exchange of goods among men – it will meet, inevitably, the great 'no' of the nature of things, which it thought it could ignore in its struggle. When the material obstacles are overcome, when man will no longer be able to deceive himself as to the nature of his unhappiness, then there will arise an anxiety all the more powerful, all the more fruitful for being stripped of anything that might have hindered its realization. It goes without saying that such a purely negative hope does not seem to us to entail an adherence that, to be complete, would have to manifest itself in action.[1]

This was Adamov's position in 1946. Later, largely as a consequence of the emergence of General de Gaulle after the events of May 1958, he took a more active line in support of the extreme Left. Yet when asked in 1960 whether he had changed his attitude since 1946, Adamov confirmed that he still subscribed to what he had written fourteen years earlier.

It was towards the end of the Second World War that Adamov began to write for the theatre. He was reading Strindberg at the time, and under the influence of Strindberg's plays, notably *A Dream Play*, he began to discover the stuff of drama all around him, in 'the most ordinary everyday happenings, particularly street scenes. What struck me above all were the lines of passers-by, their loneliness in the crowd, the terrifying diversity of their utterance, of which I would please myself by hearing only snatches that, linked with other snatches of conversation, seemed to grow into a composite entity the very fragmentariness of which became a guarantee of its symbolic truth.'[2] One day he witnessed a scene that confronted him, in a sudden flash, with the dramatic reality he had wanted to express. A blind beggar passed by two pretty girls singing a refrain from some popular song: 'I had closed my eyes, it was wonderful!' This gave him the idea of showing 'on the stage,

1. ibid.
2. Adamov, *Théâtre II* (Paris: Gallimard, 1955), '*Note préliminaire*', p. 8.

as crudely and as visibly as possible, the loneliness of man, the absence of communication'.[1]

La Parodie, Adamov's first play, is the fruit of this idea. In a succession of rapidly sketched scenes, it shows two men infatuated with the same empty-headed, commonplace girl, Lili. One of them, the 'employee', is brisk, businesslike, and ever optimistic, while the other, 'N', is passive, helpless, and despondent. The employee, who, in a chance meeting, has gained the wholly erroneous impression that he has a date with Lili, never loses his hope and constantly turns up at imagined rendezvous. N, on the other hand, spends his time lying in the street, waiting for Lili to pass by chance. In the end the optimistic, buoyant attitude of the employee and the abject passivity of N lead to precisely the same result – nothing. Lili cannot even tell her two rival suitors apart. The employee lands in prison, where he goes on making plans for the future and still hopes to maintain his position, although he has gone blind. N is run over by a car and swept into the garbage by the street-cleaners. Lili is flanked by relatively successful men – a journalist with whom she seems in love and who keeps her waiting when they have a date, and the editor of his paper, who treats her as his kept mistress. The editor also takes the place, as and when the action requires it, of a number of other persons in authority – the manager of a restaurant, the director of a firm for which the employee works as a salesman, the receptionist of a hotel where he fails to get a room. While N and the employee are seen, as it were, from their own point of view, the journalist and the editor are seen wholly from the outside, as 'the other people', who, inexplicably, seem to be able to master the human situation, to whom nothing calamitous ever happens. Two identical and interchangeable couples act as a kind of chorus, the faceless crowd that surrounds us; they age as the action proceeds, but remain anonymous and interchangeable throughout.

1. ibid.

Time is constantly evoked: the characters keep on asking each other the time without ever receiving an answer. A clock without hands is a recurring feature of the décor. The action of time is also illustrated by the gradual shrinkage of space. A dance hall shown in the beginning appears again in scene II – but now the set has become much narrower.

At one point, N is shown with a prostitute whom he begs to humiliate him. As Adamov himself has pointed out, *La Parodie* served to justify his own attitude: 'Even if I am like N, I shall not be punished any more than the employee.'[1] Buoyant activity is as pointless as cringing apathy and self-humiliation.

La Parodie is an attempt to come to terms with neurosis, to make psychological states visible in concrete terms. As Adamov defines it in the introduction to the first edition, the performance of a play of this type is 'the projection into the world of sensations of states of mind and images that constitute its hidden content. A stage play ought to be the point of intersection between the visible and invisible worlds, or, in other words, the display, the manifestation of the hidden, latent contents that form the shell around the seeds of drama.'[2]

In its determined rejection of individuality in favour of schematic types – in which it resembles German Expressionist drama – *La Parodie* represents a revolt against the complexities of the psychological theatre. It is a deliberate return to primitivism. Adamov does not want to represent the world, he wants to parody it. 'When I arraign the world around me, I often reproach it for being nothing more than a parody. But the sickness I admit to – is it anything more than a parody?'[3] Parody is direct, harsh, and oversimplified. *La Parodie* deliberately eschews all subtleties of plot, characterization, or language. This is a theatre of gesture – N lying in the road, the employee bustling about, the interchangeable couples going through the

1. ibid., p. 9.
2. Adamov, *La Parodie*, *L'Invasion* (Paris: Charlot, 1950), p. 22.
3. *L'Aveu*, p. 85; 'The endless humiliation', loc. cit., p. 85.

motions of human existence without being recognizable individuals.

Adamov felt that, having parodied the world in such simple terms, he had reached a dead end. In his next play, *L'Invasion*, he took the first steps toward portraying real characters in real human relationships. The isolated, lonely individuals of *La Parodie* are replaced by a family. It is still a family composed of lonely individuals, unable to communicate. But they are strongly linked together nevertheless – curiously enough, by a shared loyalty to a dead hero.

This hero is a dead writer, Jean, who has left an enormous mass of undeciphered papers to his friend and disciple, Pierre, the husband of the dead man's sister Agnes. The apartment where they live, together with Pierre's mother, is in a state of complete disorder, which expresses the disorder reigning in the minds of the characters. The task of deciphering Jean's literary remains is an impossible one. His writing is not only illegible but the characters themselves have faded. One can never know what he really wrote, and there is a constant danger that the literary executor will simply invent what he thinks the master ought to have written. And even if a scrap of paper, a single sentence, is finally deciphered, it still must be placed in the context of the vast mass of disordered papers.

There is another disciple of Jean's who tries to help, Tradel, but he is suspect precisely because he tends to read things into Jean's writing. The disorder within the room where the action takes place is matched by the disorder of the whole country: immigrants are streaming across the frontiers, the social structure is disintegrating. In the second act the disorder in the room, now cluttered up with furniture, has increased. Pierre finds it ever more difficult to understand the meaning of the manuscripts. A man who is looking for someone in the apartment next door enters and strikes up a conversation with Agnes. He is 'the first one who comes along' with whom Agnes will run away. In the third act, this man has become a fixture in the room, and Pierre wants to retire to his own private den downstairs to work in peace. Agnes duly leaves him and goes off with the 'first one who comes along'. In act IV the room has been cleaned up, the papers are neatly stacked. Order has also returned in the country. Pierre has decided to give up his work. He begins to tear up the manuscripts. Agnes appears – she wants to borrow the typewriter. Her lover is ill, she is unable to manage his business. Pierre, who has gone down to his den, is found there by Tradel; he is dead.

L'Invasion is a play about the hopeless search for meaning, the quest for a message that will make sense in a jumble of undecipherable papers; but it is concerned with order and disorder in society as well as in the family. It almost seems that Agnes stands for disorder. Has Pierre, in marrying her, not at the same time married her dead brother with his confused manuscripts? When she leaves, order returns, and disorder and business failure enter the household of the man whose mistress she has become. Yet when Pierre abandons his work on the manuscripts, he dies. He loses Agnes to the first man who comes along because he is withdrawing more and more from human contact. The disorder that Agnes brings also represents the bewildering nature of reality and of relationships with other human beings, which Pierre is unable to cope with. He withdraws from contact with others, because he finds communication more and more difficult. Language is disintegrating before his eyes: 'Why does one say, "It happens?" Who is that "it", what does it want from me? Why does one say "on the ground" rather than "at" or "over"? I have lost too much time thinking about these things. What I want is not the meaning of words, but their volume and their moving body. I shall no longer search for anything. . . . I'll wait in silence, motionless.'[1]

Pierre begs his mother, who will bring him his food in his den, never to speak to him – a sign of his complete withdrawal.

1. Adamov, *Théâtre I* (Paris: Gallimard, 1953), p. 86.

It is when he abandons his attitude of withdrawal, when he decides that he wants to lead a life like everybody else, that he learns that Agnes has left him. 'She left too late, or too soon. Had she had a little more patience, we could have started all over again,'[1] he says, and returns to his den – to die, just missing Agnes, who comes to ask 'to borrow the typewriter', yet is clearly begging to be taken back. But Pierre's mother does not, or does not want to, understand, and fails to call Pierre upstairs.

Here the tragedy turns on a misunderstanding. Had Pierre's mother not taken Agnes's demand for the typewriter literally, rather than as a symbolic request to be taken back and participate in the work of the family, Pierre might not have died rejected and unloved. Adamov has described how he thought that he had found an important new dramatic device – indirect dialogue, the characters' oblique reference to the subject under discussion, since they cannot find the courage to display their feelings openly and thereby expose themselves to tragic misunderstandings. Later he realized that he had merely reinvented a technique already used by other dramatists, notably by Chekhov.

L'Invasion is a haunting play. André Gide was deeply impressed by it; he felt that it dealt with the greatness of a dead writer and the process by which his influence and power gradually fade away – surely a curious misunderstanding on the part of the venerable old man of letters, applying the conceptions of his own generation to the works of a new age. To a contemporary reader, the most striking feature of *L'Invasion* is precisely the unreality of the dead hero, the fact that his much vaunted message is essentially meaningless – absurd.

Jean Vilar, the great French director, who had produced Adamov's adaptation of Büchner's *Danton's Death* at the Avignon Festival of 1948, saw *L'Invasion* with the eyes of a contemporary. He praised Adamov for renouncing 'the lace ornaments of dialogue and intrigue, for having given back to

1. ibid., p. 94.

the drama its stark purity'[1] of clear and simple stage symbols. He contrasted this stark modern theatre with that of Claudel, 'which borrows its effect from the alcohols of faith and the grand word'[2] and, posing the alternatives Adamov or Claudel, clearly answered – Adamov.

Gide's and Vilar's tributes to Adamov, together with comments by other distinguished literary and stage figures like René Char, Jacques Prévert, and Roger Blin, are contained in the slim volume in which Adamov, having failed to get them performed on the stage, presented his first two plays to the reading public in the spring of 1950. The response to this publication had the desired effect; on 14 November, 1950, *L'Invasion*, directed by Jean Vilar, opened at the Studio des Champs-Elysées. Three days earlier, Adamov's third play, *La Grande et la Petite Manœuvre*, had been presented at the Théâtre des Noctambules, directed by another of the outstanding pioneers of the French avant-garde, Jean-Marie Serreau, and with Roger Blin in the leading part.

Adamov himself has explained the title of *La Grande et la Petite Manœuvre* as referring to the small manoeuvre of the social disorder depicted in the play, in contrast to the large manoeuvre of the human condition itself, which envelops and dwarfs the former,[3] the word 'manoeuvre' in this context having a double military and psychological sense.

La Grande et la Petite Manœuvre combines the theme of the parallel lives of *La Parodie* with that of the social and political disorders in the background of *L'Invasion*. The active, self-sacrificing struggle of a revolutionary leader is shown to be as futile as the passivity of a tormented victim of hidden psychological forces, who is compelled to execute the shouted orders of invisible monitors who drive him to the gradual loss of all

1. *La Parodie, L'Invasion*, p. 16.
2. *La Parodie, L'Invasion*, p. 16.
3. Adamov, quoted by Carlos Lynes, Jr, 'Adamov or "*le sens littéral*" in the theatre', *Yale French Studies*, no. 14, Winter 1954–5.

his limbs. The action takes place in a country oppressed by a brutal dictatorship. The active character, *le militant*, leads the victorious struggle against the forces of the police state; in the end he collapses while making a speech admitting that the revolutionaries have been compelled to use methods of brutal terror to gain their victory. Moreover, the *militant* has caused the death of his own child, because the disorders he himself had provoked made it impossible for the doctor to reach its sickbed. Once again the activist has achieved no more than the passive character, *le mutilé*, who, a legless, armless cripple, on a pushcart, is kicked into the road by the woman he adores, to be crushed in the crowd.

The *mutilé*, who must obey the orders of the voices that compel him to put his hands into the machine that will cut them off, to walk in front of the car that will run him over, is clearly the chief character in the play, embodying the author's own attitude. His mutilations, like the deaths of N and Pierre in the earlier plays, are the direct outcome, and the expression, of his inability to make human contact, his incapacity for love. He himself says that if he could live with a woman and have a child by her, the voices of his monitors would lose their power over him[1]; the accidents in which he loses limb after limb usually follow his repeated failures to hold the affection of the woman he loves, Erna, who at times suggests that she really cares for him, while at others she appears to be merely spying on him on behalf of a secret-police agent who is her lover.

Adamov himself has interpreted the play, which is based on a particularly vivid and terrifying dream, as an attempt to justify himself for his failure to take a more active part in the political struggle of the Left. To the outside observer, this may seem an incomplete account of the complex content of *La Grande et la Petite Manœuvre*. The play not only argues (as Adamov later believed, unfairly) that the efforts of the revolutionary to eliminate political terror are vain because all power is ulti-

1. *Théâtre I*, p. 107.

mately based on the exercise of brute force; it also shows, very graphically, that there is an essential similarity between the activist fighter for justice and the passive slave of the irrational forces of his own subconscious mind. The categorical imperative that forces the *militant* to risk his life, to leave his wife in fear and trembling and ultimately to cause the death of his sick child, is shown as springing, basically, from the same inability to love as the implacable self-destructive commands of the subconscious mind that force the *mutilé* into masochistic self-destruction. The aggressive impulses of the *militant* are merely the reverse side of the *mutilé*'s aggression against himself.

The very ambivalence of possible interpretations is an indication of the power of *La Grande et la Petite Manœuvre* as a dramatic projection of an intense and tormented experience of fundamental human dilemmas. This play also shows Adamov in full command of the technical resources he needed to put his ideas into practice. The action not only moves forward in a succession of effectively contrasted scenes that follow each other with the flow of cinematic montage, it is also a perfect realization of Adamov's conception that the theatre should be able to translate ideas and psychological realities into simple and concrete images, so that 'the manifestation of ... content should literally, concretely, *corporally* coincide with that content itself.'[1] This leads to a shift of emphasis from the language of drama toward visible action. The language of the play ceases to be the main vehicle of poetry, as it is in the theatre of Claudel, with which Vilar contrasted Adamov's work. As Adamov defines this shift, 'It is in this growth of gesture in its own right ... that I see the emergence of a dimension to which language by itself would be unable to do justice, but, in turn, when language is carried along by the rhythm of bodily action that has become autonomous, the most ordinary, everyday speech will regain a power that might still be called poetry, but that I

1. *La Parodie, L'Invasion*, p. 22.

shall be content merely to call functionally effective.'[1] In *La Grande et la Petite Manœuvre* the transmutation of content into visible, literal outward expression is completely realized.

The instrument he had perfected seemed available to Adamov to be used at will. Its only drawback was the narrowness of its field of application; there are relatively few basic human situations that can be expressed in such simple and general terms. Yet while his next play, *Le Sens de la Marche* (*The Direction of the March*), contains many of the elements and themes of its predecessors, Adamov again succeeded in finding a new expression for his basic preoccupation, while introducing an important new element indicating his progress in mastering his obsessions. In *Le Sens de la Marche*, the hero for the first time refuses to submit, and counterattacks. That action may not be directed against the real author of his troubles, but it is an action nevertheless. The hero, Henri, the son of a tyrannical father, goes through a number of episodes in which he confronts that father figure in a whole series of incarnations: in the commanding officer of the barracks where he goes for his military service, in the leader of a religious sect whose daughter is his fiancée for a time, in the headmaster of a school where he becomes a teacher. He submits to all these, but when he returns to his old home and finds his dead father's sinister *masseur* installed as the domestic tyrant and lover of his sister, he strangles him. As Adamov has pointed out, the idea from which he started was that 'in this life of which the basic circumstances themselves are terrifying, where the same situations fatally recur, all we can do is destroy, and too late at that, what we consider, mistakenly, to be the real obstacle, but what in fact is merely the last item in a maleficent series.'[2] This is a very original idea, and it is most imaginatively realized. Some of the themes of earlier plays recur, such as the revolutionaries, who are again unsuccessful; the hero's inability to love; and the sister figure.

1. ibid., p. 23.   2. *Théâtre II*, p. 11.

Adamov was dissatisfied with *Le Sens de la Marche* and had put it aside for a while when another dream presented him not only with an idea for a play but with an entire, almost ready-made play itself. And this play, *Le Professeur Taranne*, became a turning point in Adamov's development.

The professor of the title is accused of indecent exposure on a beach. He denies the allegation by indignantly pointing out that he is a distinguished scholar who has even been invited to lecture abroad, in Belgium. But the more he protests his innocence, the more deeply he becomes involved in contradictions that make his guilt more probable. A lady who comes into the police station seems to recognize him, she addresses him as Professor – but she has taken him for another professor, Menard, whom Taranne superficially resembles. The scene changes to the hotel where he is staying. Again Taranne is accused of an offence, that of having left litter in a bathing cabin at the seaside. He protests that he did not undress in a cabin at all – and thus confirms the earlier allegation. The policemen produce a notebook that has been found. Taranne eagerly recognizes it as his, but is unable to read the handwriting. What is more, the notebook consists mostly of empty pages, although Taranne insists that he had used it up entirely. A roll of paper is delivered to the professor – it is the seating plan of the dining-room of an ocean liner, with his place marked at the table of honour. Jeanne, a woman relative or secretary, brings a letter that has arrived for the professor. It is from Belgium, from the rector of the University. This will confirm Taranne's claims! But in fact it is an angry refusal to invite him again. His lectures have been found to have been plagiarisms of those of the famous professor Menard. Taranne remains alone. He hangs the seating plan of the liner's dining-room on a hook on the wall – it is a perfectly blank piece of paper. Slowly the professor begins to undress, performing the very act of indecent exposure of which he was accused at the beginning. Having been exposed as a fraud, he exposes himself. It is the nightmare of man trying to hold on to his identity, unable to establish conclusive proof of it.

In his dream, which the play transcribes as it was dreamed, without any attempt to 'give it a general meaning, to prove anything',[1] everything that happens to Taranne happened to Adamov himself, the only difference being that instead of shouting, 'I am Professor Taranne,' he exclaimed, 'I am the author of *La Parodie*!'[2]

Adamov considered *Le Professeur Taranne* of particular importance in his progress as a playwright. In transcribing an actual dream he was, as it were, forced to cross a decisive threshold. For the first time in one of his plays, he named an actual place, a place existing in the real world. Taranne claims that he has lectured abroad, *in Belgium*, and he receives a letter that is recognized as coming from that country by its stamp, which bears the Belgian Lion. 'This looks like a trifle, but it was, nevertheless, the first time that I emerged from the no man's land of poetry and dared to call things by their name.'[3]

And indeed for the tormented author of *L'Aveu*, suffering from the sense of loneliness and separation described in that book, it was a tremendous step forward to have established a link, however tenuous, with reality, the reality of the world outside his own nightmares, even if at first it appears only in the form of the name of a real country heard within a nightmare. Of course, in *L'Aveu* itself Adamov had described real scenes from his own life. But there is a vast difference between the deliberate humiliating *exposure* of his own suffering (reminiscent of Taranne's indecent exposure) and the ability to deal with the real world in the process of creative imaginative writing, which implies the ability to confront and master a reality outside oneself.

As Maurice Regnaut has pointed out in a penetrating essay on

1. ibid., p. 12.
2. ibid., p. 12.
3. ibid., p. 13.

Adamov,[1] *Le Professeur Taranne* also marks another important stage in Adamov's development. In previous plays, to express his sense of the futility and absurdity of life, Adamov had projected the two basically contradictory attitudes that in the end amount to the same thing – namely, nothing – in pairs of characters: the employee and N, Pierre and his complacent mother, the *militant* and the *mutilé*, Henri and the revolutionaries. The dream on which *Le Professeur Taranne* is based showed him, for the first time, the way in which affirmative and self-destructive attitudes can be fused in a single character simultaneously – in the very act of asserting his worth as a citizen, his achievements as a scholar, Taranne reveals these claims to be fraudulent. And it is by no means clear whether the play is meant to show a fraud unmasked, or an innocent man confronted by a monstrous conspiracy of circumstances engineered to destroy his claims. In fact, as Adamov identifies himself with Taranne, the latter is the more tenable view; after all, in his dream Adamov cried out, 'I am the author of *La Parodie*,' which he undoubtedly was, and yet his claim was disproved by a succession of nightmare confrontations. Of course, if all activity is futile and absurd, then the claim to have written a play or to have lectured in Belgium is, in the final reckoning, a claim to nothing; death and oblivion will blot out all achievements. Thus, in *Le Professeur Taranne*, the hero is both an active scholar and a fraud, a respectable citizen and an exhibitionist, an optimistic hard-working paragon and a self-destructive, slothful pessimist. This opened a way for Adamov toward the creation of ambivalent, three-dimensional characters to take the place of schematic expressions of clearly defined psychological forces.

Adamov wrote *Le Professeur Taranne* in two days in 1951. It had taken him several years to complete his first two plays – a

1. Maurice Regnaut, '*Arthur Adamov et le sens du fétichisme*', *Cahiers de la Compagnie Madeleine Renaud – Jean-Louis Barrault*, Paris, nos. 22–3, May 1958.

clear indication of how far he had succeeded in mastering his neurosis by harnessing it to a creative effort.

After completing *Le Sens de la Marche*, the writing of which he had interrupted to note down his nightmare of *Le Professeur Taranne*, Adamov returned to a subject that had preoccupied him before: the disorder of the times, social upheaval, and persecution. In *Tous Contre Tous*, we are again in a country that has been flooded by refugees from abroad; they are easily identifiable because they all limp. The hero, Jean Rist, loses his wife to one of the refugees and becomes a demagogue ranting against them. For a brief moment he is in power but when the wheel of political fortune turns and the persecutors become the persecuted, he escapes arrest by assuming a limp himself and pretending to be a refugee. He lives in obscurity, upheld by the love of a refugee girl. When there is another upheaval and the refugees are again persecuted, he might perhaps escape death by declaring his true identity. But in confirming that he is the well-known hater of refugees, he would lose the love of the girl. He refuses to do so, and goes to his death.

In Jean Rist, the persecutor and the victim of persecution, Adamov again fused two opposite tendencies in one character, not simultaneously, as in *Le Professeur Taranne*, but consecutively, in the ups and downs of the passage of time, and thus less successfully. The ending, with its self-sacrifice for the sake of love, has been criticized as a lapse into the sentimental heroics of a quite different, romantic convention of drama. This may be unjust: Jean Rist's refusal to save himself might also be interpreted as an act of resignation; of suicide in the face of an absurd, circular destiny. What the play does suffer from (in Adamov's own view) is its failure to come to grips with the reality of the problem it deals with. It is fairly obvious that this is the Jewish problem, or at least the problem of racial persecution. Yet by not situating his characters within a clearly defined social framework at one particular moment in history, at one particular point on the map, the author has deprived himself of the opportunity to do justice to the subject; he is unable to provide the background that would explain the rights and wrongs at issue: Why have the refugees taken away the jobs of the inhabitants of the country in question? Are those inhabitants justified in trying to exclude them again? Adamov himself recognized these flaws. On the one hand, he said, he wanted to show that all sides are equally reprehensible in such a conflict, yet he acknowledged that he made a larger number of the victims 'good' characters, simply because they are made to suffer innocently. But, he added, 'I suffered from the limitation imposed on me by the vagueness of the place, the schematization of the characters, the symbolism of the situations, but I did not feel that I had the power to tackle a social conflict, and to see it as such, detached from the world of archetypes.'[1]

In *Le Professeur Taranne* he had found the courage to let in a glimpse of the real world, if only in a dream. So he decided to return to a world of dreams in two plays with very similar themes: *Comme Nous Avons Été* (*As We Were*, published in the *Nouvelle Revue Française* in March 1953) and *Les Retrouvailles* (undated, but written *c.* 1952). Both plays deal with a grown man's regression to childhood, just when he is on the threshold of marriage. In *Comme Nous Avons Été*, the character A is having a nap in his room just before setting out to get married. Two women, mother and aunt, enter in search of a little boy who, they believe, must have wandered into the house. A does not know them, but as the play proceeds he himself gradually turns into the little boy the two women have been looking for. In *Les Retrouvailles*, Edgar is about to leave Montpellier, where he is reading law, to return to his home near the Belgian frontier, when he encounters two ladies, one elderly, the other young, and is persuaded to stay in the house of the elderly woman while becoming engaged to the younger. He neglects his new fiancée, and she is killed in a train accident. Having finally returned home, he hears that his former fiancée, who

1. *Théâtre II*, p. 14.

had been waiting for him there, has also been killed in a train accident. His mother forces him into a perambulator and pushes him offstage.

These are dream plays with very obvious psychological implications; they are both attacks against the mother figure, who is trying to keep the son from establishing an adult relationship with another woman. Adamov completely repudiated *Comme Nous Avons Eté*, to the point of not having given it a place in the edition of his collected plays (although he allowed it to be published in an English translation in 1957).[1] *Les Retrouvailles*, technically most intriguing in the way it establishes the dream atmosphere by gradual scene changes and by the reduplication of the two pairs of mother–fiancée characters, has been published in Adamov's collected plays. But in his preface, Adamov rejects the play as a dream that he did not have but merely constructed. Yet he declares, '*Les Retrouvailles* has been most important for me; for, having finished the play, having reread it and examined it well, I understood that the time had come to put an end to the exploitation of the half-dream and the old family conflict. Or, to put it in more general terms, I think that thanks to *Les Retrouvailles* I have liquidated all that which, after having made it possible for me to write, now had become a hindrance to my writing.'[2]

In other words, Adamov had reached a stage where he felt capable of writing a play that, though still an expression of his vision of the human condition, could people the stage not with mere emanations of his own psyche but with characters existing in their own right as objective human beings observed from the outside. This play is *Le Ping-Pong*, one of the masterpieces of the Theatre of the Absurd.

Le Ping-Pong presents the life story of two men – Victor, a medical student when the play starts, and Arthur, an art

1. Adamov, *As We Were*, trans. Richard Howard, *Evergreen Review*, I, 4, 1957.
2. *Théâtre II*, p. 15.

student. They meet at Mme Duranty's café and play the pinball machine installed there. The machine fascinates them as a business proposition, for they observe the employee of the company coming to collect the coins that have been dropped into it; as a technical problem, for it has flaws that could surely be eliminated; and even as a challenge to their poetic instinct – the machine has a poetry of its own, flashing lights, and is in some ways a work of art. Victor and Arthur suggest an improvement in the machine. They penetrate to the headquarters of the consortium that controls it, and gradually the machine becomes the dominating influence in their lives, controlling their dreams and their emotions. If they fall in love, it is with the girl who works at the headquarters of the consortium. If they have quarrels between themselves, they are about that girl and the machine. If they fear anyone, it is the boss of the consortium. Their interest in the society around them is dictated by the relevance of political and social developments to the rise or fall of pinball machines.

And so they grow old. In the last scene we see them as two old men, playing ping-pong, a contest as childish and as futile as their lifelong preoccupation with a plaything. Victor collapses and dies. Arthur remains alone.

Le Ping-Pong, like Adamov's first play, La Parodie, is concerned with the futility of human endeavour. But while La Parodie merely asserted that whatever you do, in the end you die, Le Ping-Pong provides a powerful and closely integrated argument to back that proposition – it also shows how so much of human endeavour becomes futile, and why. It is in losing themselves to a thing, a machine that promises them power, money, influence over the woman they desire, that Victor and Arthur waste their lives in the futile pursuit of shadows. By making a machine, a means to an end, an end in itself, they pervert all those values of their lives that are genuine ends in themselves – their creative instinct, their capacity to love, their sense of being part of a community. Le Ping-Pong is a powerful image of the alienation of man through the worship of a false objective, the deification of a machine, an ambition, or an ideology.

The pinball machine in *Le Ping-Pong* is more than just a machine; it is the centre-piece of an organization and of a body of thought. The moment the objective – the improvement of pinball machines – becomes an ideal, it embodies itself in an organization with its own struggles for power, its own intrigues and politics, its own tactics and strategies. As such it becomes a matter of life and death for all who serve the ideal. A number of the characters in the play are destroyed in the service of the organization, or in its internal struggle for power. All this is conducted with the utmost fervour, seriousness, and intensity. And what is it all about? A childish game, a pinball machine – nothing. But are most of the objectives men devote their lives to in the real world – the world of business, politics, the arts, or scholarship – essentially different from Arthur's and Victor's dominating obsession? It is the power and beauty of *Le Ping-Pong* that it very graphically raises this very question. Adamov achieves the difficult feat of elevating the pinball machine to a convincing image of the objectives of *all* human endeavour. He does so by the poetic intensity with which he invests his characters when they talk about the most absurd aspects of that absurd apparatus with a conviction and obsessive concentration that sound utterly true.

The play contains the elements of reality and fantasy in exactly the right dosage; time and place are sufficiently real to carry conviction, yet the world in which the action takes place is hermetically sealed off from anything outside the characters' field of preoccupation. This is not because of a lack of realism on the part of the playwright; it springs directly from the obsession of the characters, which effectively confines them in so narrow a segment of the real world that we see the world through their confined field of vision.

The characters in *Le Ping-Pong* are fully realized individuals.

No longer merely compelled by forces outside their control, or moving through the action like somnambulists, they have an element of freedom in determining their lives – we actually watch Arthur and Victor making the decision to devote themselves to pinball machines. And although Victor is the more practical of the two, and Arthur a poet, they are no longer merely personifications of complementary characteristics.

What is perhaps the most original feature of *Le Ping-Pong* is the way in which an inner contradiction, a dialectical relationship, is established between the action and the dialogue. This is a play that may well appear completely meaningless if it is merely read. The speeches about improvements in the construction of pinball machines may seem trivial nonsense: the meaning of the play emerges precisely at the moment when the actor delivers these nonsensical lines with a depth of conviction worthy of the loftiest flights of poetry. It is a play that has to be acted *against* the text rather than with it. This is a technique analogous to the indirect dialogue Adamov thought he had invented for *L'Invasion* and later discovered in Chekhov, but it is here raised to quite a different level. Chekhov used indirect dialogue in situations where the characters are too shy to express their real thoughts and hide their emotions behind trivial subjects. Here the characters believe in absurd propositions, with such intensity that they put forward their nonsensical ideas with the fervour of prophetic vision. In Chekhov, real feelings are suppressed behind meaningless politeness; in *Le Ping-Pong* absurd ideas are proclaimed as if they were eternal truths.

Adamov has given an interesting account of the genesis of *Le Ping-Pong*. He started with the final scene of the two old men playing ping-pong before he had even decided what the subject of the rest of the play would be. All he knew was that he wanted once more to show how, in the end, all human endeavour comes down to the same futility – senile whiling away of the remaining time before death reduces everything to final absurdity. But, Adamov said, 'this peculiar method of work, paradoxically enough, saved me. Once I was sure that, as usual, I should be able to show the identity of all human destiny . . . I found myself free to make the characters act, to create situations. . . .'[1] Once he had decided to put a pinball machine into the centre of the action, moreover, he was compelled to specify the time (the present) and the place (a city very much like Paris) of the action.

Nevertheless *Le Ping-Pong* belongs in the category of the Theatre of the Absurd; it shows man engaged in purposeless exertions, in a futile frenzy of activity that is bound to end in senility and death. The pinball machine has all the fascinating ambiguity of a symbol. It may stand for capitalism and big business, but it may equally well stand for any religious or political ideology that secretes its own organization and apparatus of power, that demands devotion and loyalty from its adherents.

Yet while he was working on the play, Adamov was moving away from the idea of a theatre dealing with such general human questions. He has criticized *Le Ping-Pong* on two counts – the last scene, which, having been written before the rest of the play, as it were, prejudged the issue and cramped his style; and, second, the schematic nature of the consortium, which remains

incompletely detached from allegory. In fact, the social developments that, in the course of years, modify the internal organization of the consortium are not really indicated, so that one does not sufficiently feel the state of society on the one hand, the flow of time on the other. If I had gone so far as to tackle the 'coin-operated machine', I had to examine the wheels of the great social machine with the same thoroughness that I examined the bumpers and flippers of the pinball machine. This is the examination I am trying to carry out in a new play, even more clearly situated in a specific time and milieu than *Le Ping-Pong*.[2]

1. ibid.   2. ibid., p. 17.

This play on which Adamov was working at the beginning of 1955, when he wrote his introduction to the second volume of his collected plays, was *Paolo Paoli*, completed the next year and performed by Roger Planchon's brilliant young company at Lyon on 17 May 1957. It marks Adamov's abandonment of the Theatre of the Absurd and his adherence to another, equally significant movement of the modern stage – the Brechtian 'epic theatre'. He came to regard Brecht as the greatest of contemporary playwrights and put him next to Shakespeare, Chekhov, and Büchner among the dramatists of world literature he admired most. Having freed himself from compulsions and obsessions, he felt at liberty to follow models outside his own experience. (He had previously translated and adapted works by Büchner and Chekhov.)

Paolo Paoli is an epic drama depicting the social and political causes of the outbreak of the First World War and examining the relationship between a society based on profit and the forces of destruction to which it gives rise. The play spans the period from 1900 to 1914. Each of the twelve scenes is preceded by a survey of the social background of its period – quotations from the newspapers of the time are projected on to a screen, accompanied by current popular tunes.

The characters are most ingeniously chosen to represent a whole microcosm of the political, religious, national, and social forces involved in the origins of the First World War. Adamov's brilliance as a dramatist is shown by the astonishing ingenuity with which he has condensed all this – and extremely convincingly – into a cast of only seven characters.

Paolo Paoli is a dealer in rare butterflies; Florent Hulot-Vasseur, a collector of rare butterflies and Paolo's customer, is an importer and manufacturer of ostrich feathers. He also becomes the lover of Paolo's German-born wife, Stella. An abbé and a captain's wife represent clericalism and chauvinist nationalism. A worker and trade unionist, Robert Marpeaux, and his young wife, Rose, complete the cast.

The role played by pinball machines in *Le Ping-Pong* is in *Paolo Paoli* taken by commodities no less absurd – butterflies and ostrich feathers. Yet these objects of trade and manufacture have far greater reality. As one of the newspaper projections before the first scene points out, ostrich feathers and products manufactured from them formed France's fourth largest export in 1900. Adamov brilliantly shows the far-reaching social and political ramifications and implications of the trade in these absurd articles: Paolo's business is founded on the fact that his father, a small Corsican civil servant, served in the public-works department on Devil's Island. This enabled the young man to organize the convicts there as part-time and ill-paid butterfly hunters. Marpeaux, the young workman who was serving a sentence for a petty theft, has escaped to the mainland and the swamps of Venezuela; he is wholly at Paolo's mercy, depending on the butterflies he catches for his livelihood. When troubles break out in China, butterfly hunting becomes more difficult there and the price of rare Chinese specimens goes up. The abbé, whose brother is a missionary in China, is able to provide Paolo with these precious goods. And so, in a few strokes, Adamov has shown the connection between the seemingly absurd object of trade and the penal system of French society, foreign politics, and the workings of the Church. The same is true of Hulot-Vasseur's ostrich feathers in relation to the Boer War, and, as the plot develops, the labour and trade-union troubles of his factory and his fight against German competition are very convincingly made explicit within the narrow circle of the play.

As in *Le Ping-Pong*, the characters are obsessed with their pursuit of money and power, represented by the absurd commodities they deal in. Paolo grows rich, for a time at least, by becoming a manufacturer of knick-knacks made from butterflies' wings – ashtrays, tea trays, even religious pictures, which flourish in a period of clericalism and slump when clericalism fades and German competition raises its ugly head. He loses his wife when he sets her up as a milliner, which makes her dependent for her supplies of ostrich feathers on Hulot-Vasseur, whose mistress she becomes. Stella, the German-born woman, also embodies the absurdities of European nationalism; she leaves France at the height of the anti-German feeling over Morocco, because people hate her as a German, and returns on the eve of the First World War, when her German neighbours persecute her as the wife of a Frenchman.

The only characters free of these obsessions are Marpeaux and his wife, Rose (though she for a time becomes Paolo's mistress). When Marpeaux returns, illegally, from Venezuela, Paolo suggests that he should spend the time till his pardon is granted by going to Morocco to hunt butterflies. (The crisis over Morocco has driven the prices up.) Of course, Morocco has become very dangerous; the French are fighting the natives. And here lies the moral of the play – the commodity that seems the object of trade is absurd, mere butterflies, but the commodity that is *really* traded is man, who has to sell his health and safety in the pursuit of butterflies. The ultimate object of trade is man, who himself becomes a commodity. (This is also the point of Adamov's very effective dramatization of Gogol's novel *Dead Souls*.) Moreover, the commodities are being bought and sold in deadly earnest; trade leads to war.

Marpeaux, the victim of the social system, realizes what is at stake. After he has received his pardon (at a time when war between France and Germany seemed imminent over Morocco, and volunteers could gain amnesty), he returns to France and joins the Socialists. Working in Hulot-Vasseur's factory, he opposes the 'yellow' Catholic unions managed by the abbé and also distributes pacifist pamphlets to the soldiers in their barracks. To get rid of him, the abbé denounces him for subverting the fighting forces. As the first troops march off to war, Rose tells Paolo that Marpeaux has been arrested, and this leads to a somewhat unconvincing change of heart in Paolo, who, in the closing speech of the play, vows that henceforth he will use his money to help the hungry and needy, rather than let it circulate in the endless, iniquitous cycle of exchange, the buying and selling of useless commodities.

Paolo Paoli is a political play, brilliantly constructed and executed as a drama, not very original as a political argument. (Paolo's last speech certainly makes little sense even in terms of Marxist economics: money spent on food for the victims of Right Wing persecution is by no means effectively withdrawn from the cycle of capitalist exchange.) Nevertheless, as a *tour de force* the play shows Adamov as the sovereign master of his material, handling it with remarkable powers of invention, construction, and compression.

The question arises – does this piece of powerfully constructed didactic special pleading equal the haunting, dream-like poetry of far less cleverly structured plays like *La Parodie*, *La Grande et la Petite Manœuvre*, or *Le Professeur Taranne*? Is the highly explicit social framework of *Paolo Paoli*, for all the virtuosity with which it is handled, equal in depth, or even in its power to convince, to the vaguer, more general, but therefore all-embracing images of *Le Ping-Pong*?

There can be no doubt that for Adamov the development from *La Parodie* to *Paolo Paoli* represented a gradual liberation, through the artist's creative power, from the incubus of neurosis and deep personal suffering. In the whole history of literature it will be difficult to find a more triumphant example of the healing power of the creative processes of sublimation. It is fascinating to watch the gradual breaking down of the barriers that keep the writer of this series of plays from dealing with the realities of everyday life; to watch him gain the confidence that he needs to turn the nightmares that mastered him into mere material that *he* can mould and master. His early plays are, as it were, emanations of his subconscious mind, projected on to the stage as faithful transcripts of terrifying fantasies. *Paolo Paoli* is consciously planned and rationally controlled. Yet it might be argued that this gain in rationality and conscious control represents a loss of the fine frenzy, the haunting power of neurosis that gave the earlier plays their magnetic, poetical impact. What is more, by concentrating his attack on the political and social front, Adamov narrowed his field of vision.

If in *La Grande et la Petite Manœuvre* it was the revolutionaries' futile struggle that represented the small manoeuvre, and the all-enveloping absurdity of the human condition dwarfing the social struggle that stood for the big manoeuvre, then in *Paolo Paoli* the small manoeuvre looms large and the large manoeuvre has receded into a barely perceptible background. 'We all know,' says the revolutionary leader in the earlier play, 'that death surrounds us. But if we do not have the courage to detach ourselves from that idea, we shall retreat from the demands of the future, and all our sacrifices will have been in vain.'[1] This is the argument that Paolo Paoli represents. In the earlier play Adamov had supplied his own bitterly ironical comment on it: at the very moment when the revolutionary leader speaks these defiant words, his voice becomes slower, the pace of his delivery slackens, and he collapses.

Adamov was far too acute a thinker to be unaware of the implications of his later position. Having in his earlier phase concentrated on the absurdity of the human condition, he later maintained that 'the theatre must show, simultaneously but well-differentiated, both the curable and the incurable aspect of things. The incurable aspect, we all know, is that of the inevitability of death. The curable aspect is the social one.'[2]

It is precisely because it does succeed in maintaining the extremely delicate balance between the incurable and the curable aspects of the human condition that *Le Ping-Pong* must be regarded as Adamov's finest achievement. The pinball

1. *Théâtre I*, p. 136.
2. '*Qui êtes-vous Arthur Adamov?*', *Cité Panorama* (programme bulletin of Planchon's Théâtre de la Cité), Villeurbanne, no. 9, 1960.

machine stands for all illusory objectives, material and ideological, the pursuit of which secretes ambition, self-seeking,
and the urge to dominate other human beings. There is no
necessity to fall victim to such illusory aims, so there *is* a social
lesson in the play. And yet the absurdity of all human endeavour
in the face of death is never quite forgotten, and is finally put
before our eyes by a telling and compelling image. *Paolo Paoli*,
on the other hand, is marred not only by the intrusion of
oversimplified economic and social theories, but, above all, by
the introduction of a wholly positive and therefore less than
human character, Marpeaux, and by the even less credible conversion of a hitherto negative character, Paolo, to provide a
climax and a solution. This noble character and this noble
action are clearly the consequence of the author's special pleading for the curable aspect of things, which leads to an under-
playing of the incurable side of the human situation. Marpeaux's
efforts, in the last resort, are as futile as those of the employee
in *La Parodie* – he is arrested and the war breaks out in spite of
him. Yet the author has to make this into a noble failure, due
to the special wickedness of individual enemies, or of social
conditions, at a given period of history. And that is the point
at which the pathetic fallacy enters a politically biased theatre.
Brecht, who was well aware of this danger, avoided similar
pitfalls by forgoing all positive characters in some of his more
successful plays (*Mother Courage, Galileo*), so that the positive
message might emerge by inference rather than by concrete
demonstration – but with the result that the effect on the
audience tends to be one of a negative theatre that concentrates
on the incurable aspect of things.

In some respects, *Paolo Paoli* contains an important promise –
it shows the way in which some of the elements of the Theatre
of the Absurd can be combined with those of the conventional
well-made play to produce a very fruitful fusion of two different traditions. In the simplicity of its construction, the boldness of its characterization, the use of butterflies and ostrich

feathers as symbols that are at the same time perfectly valid in the world of economic realities, *Paolo Paoli* contained some useful lessons for the future development of a theatre combining elements of both the didactic epic style and the Theatre of the Absurd.

Nor was Adamov's rejection of a nonrealistic style as complete as it might appear. It is surely significant that in the autumn of 1958, when he felt himself called upon to take an active part in the campaign against the new Gaullist constitution, Adamov found it easier to resort to allegorical techniques than to make his point in the form of realistic didactic drama. Of the three short pieces he contributed to the volume *Théâtre de Société*,[1] two are allegorical and only one is realistic – and an acknowledged failure.

The most ambitious of these three sketches, *Intimité*, uses personified collective concepts rather like those we find in medieval mystery plays – de Gaulle is caricatured as The Cause Incarnate, the Socialists as Cause's servile and stupid lackey, the young bloods among the Algerian *colons* as a bullying ruffian labelled The Elite. The Cause Incarnate is protected by a bodyguard of brutal strong-arm men; they are called The Effects of the Cause. In the short monologue *La Complainte du Ridicule*, the personification of ridicule laments the sad fact that it seems to have lost the power to kill it possessed in former, happier times in France. Both these playlets, although clearly ephemeral *pièces d'occasion*, are successful as robust topical satire. The third, *Je ne Suis pas Français*, fails even on this level; it shows the way French parachutists in Algiers were reported to have coerced the Moslem population into demonstrating for France in May 1958, but remains unconvincing in spite, or because, of its documentary technique. The political purpose is so obvious that the more realistically the subject is presented, the more it seems to lose the effect of reality.

1. *Théâtre de Société. Scènes d'Actualité* (Paris: Les Editeurs Français Réunis, 1958).

Realism and fantasy are also combined in the radio play *En Fiacre* (1959), by the device of presenting a real, historically authenticated event involving characters who are demented – three old ladies who, having lost the house they lived in, spend the night in horse-drawn cabs they hire to drive around and around the streets of old-time Paris. The incident, presented as based on the casebook of a psychiatrist, and as having actually happened in February 1902, might well have sprung from the dream world of one of Adamov's early plays. One of the three sisters is killed when she falls out of the moving cab. Has she been pushed out by the other two? And why have these three old women become homeless wanderers in the night? It appears that they learned only after their father died that the house they lived in had been the headquarters of a chain of brothels. There is also a suggestion that the dead sister, the youngest of the three, might have been in on the secret, that she might have been involved in what went on in those brothels, that she had a lover, that she was in the habit of occasionally paying the cabdrivers for those nightly journeys in currency other than mere money. But then all this may be the outcome of the fantasies of insane old women. *En Fiacre* is strictly documentary, but, in the nature of a scientific case-book, it does not seek to explain too much; it merely sets down what has been reported, leaving the motives of the action as unexplained as the solution. And while the treatment is naturalistic, the theme is madness, fantasies, dreams, irrational fears, and jealousies. The streets of Paris at night, pitiful victims of neurosis exposed to the insults of cabdrivers – this is a world not too far removed from that of *L'Aveu*.

In *Le Printemps '71* (*Spring '71*, 1961), a vast canvas of the Paris Commune in twenty-six scenes, nine interludes, and an epilogue, Adamov finally broke through to the large-scale portrayal of historical reality. The tragic suppression of the revolutionary city government of Paris is shown in an intricate mosaic of minutely observed scenes involving dozens of characters. But even here Adamov could not do without the grotesquely allegorical element; the nine interludes, which he himself calls *guignols* (puppet shows), point the moral of the action through the grotesque cavortings of historical and allegorical personages: Bismarck, Thiers, the Commune itself, the Bank of France sitting inside her vaults, the National Assembly, a sleepy old woman knitting socks, and so on. These are the cartoons of Daumier come to life, and while the realistic action, impressive as it is, appears somewhat diffuse, these allegorical cartoon scenes are concise, witty, and make their point with astonishing force.

Adamov's next major play, *Sainte Europe* (1966), was an immense political cartoon in which Charles de Gaulle merges into the Emperor Charlemagne. It is an attempt to marry political realism with the dream world of political nightmare. I personally, however, doubt very much whether it succeeds as drama.

In the last years of his life Adamov was greatly hampered by persistent serious illness not unconnected with bouts of alcoholism. His last plays show a distinct falling-off of his powers. They mingle elements of his old neuroses with his political and propagandist preoccupations. *La Politique des Restes* (written 1961–2; first performed 1967) deals with racial oppression in the United States; *M. le Modéré* (1967) shows the futility of a moderate attitude in politics. *Off Limits* (1968) is a further bitter attack against the American style of life, while *Si l'Été Revenait* (1969) is situated in an affluent bourgeois Sweden and explores guilt in a middle-class family.

On 15 March 1970 Arthur Adamov died from an overdose of barbiturates, probably suicide.

Adamov's development from a tormented, deeply neurotic individual who haunted the streets where prostitutes congregate in order to provoke them into insulting and beating him, to a highly respected militant of the left, is one of the most fascinating and best-documented case histories in European literature. (He added a second part to *L'Aveu* and republished it as *Je ... Ils ...* in 1969; another autobiographical volume, *L'Homme et l'Enfant*, appeared in 1968.) His early absurdist plays exorcized his neurosis, so that he gradually became able to deal with the real world. In *Le Ping-Pong* and *Paolo Paoli* he found the ideal synthesis between his poetic and his political commitment. In the later, highly tendentious plays, the needs of political commitment and partisanship again, ironically, removed him from the real world; now he merely dramatized the clichés and myths of the totalitarian left, and the political fanaticism which drove him could be seen as merely another – and a less productive – aspect of his neurosis. The difference lies precisely in the fact that while the plays which reflect his personal neurosis spring from a soul in torment and thus communicate powerful insights into the human condition, the fanaticism of his political drama merely reflects the ready-made truisms of a political machine. In the output of his last years, when he was in constant pain and in deep psychological anguish, the personal neurosis occasionally came to the surface, but by this time his creative powers had been eroded.

Adamov was a fascinating human being: slight, dark, with enormous piercing, probing eyes in a saturnine, unshaven face, always most raggedly dressed, he was the archetypal Paris Bohemian and *poète maudit*. He was a man of immense erudition, widely read in psychology and psychopathology, translator of Jung, Rilke, Dostoevski (*Crime and Punishment*), Strindberg (*The Father*), Gogol, Büchner, Gorki, and Chekhov, author of an excellent monograph on Strindberg, compiler of an anthology of the Paris Commune. He was the friend of Artaud and played an important part in liberating him from the asylum; a man of immense charm, passion and commitment. His work for the theatre is uneven, but his best plays will surely endure.

3

EUGÈNE IONESCO

Theatre and anti-theatre

THE development of Arthur Adamov clearly poses the alternative between the theatre as an instrument for the expression of the individual's obsessions, nightmares, and anxiety, and the theatre as an instrument of political ideology and collective social action. Adamov has given his own emphatic answer to the question. Eugène Ionesco, who started from the same premises as Adamov and initially developed along parallel lines, has equally emphatically reached the opposite conclusions.

And Ionesco, however obscure and enigmatic he might appear in his plays, has shown that he can be highly lucid and brilliantly persuasive in expounding his ideas when he is provoked to defend himself by attacks, such as the one Kenneth Tynan, the dramatic critic of the London *Observer*, launched against him in the summer of 1958. In reviewing a revival of *The Chairs* and *The Lesson* at the Royal Court, Tynan warned his readers of the danger that Ionesco might become the messiah of the enemies of realism in the theatre. 'Here at last was a self-proclaimed advocate of *anti-théâtre*: explicitly anti-realist and by implication anti-reality as well. Here was a writer ready to declare that words were meaningless and that all communication between human beings was impossible.' Tynan conceded that Ionesco presented a valid personal vision, but 'the peril arises when it is held up for general emulation as the gateway to the theatre of the future, that bleak new world from which the humanist heresies of faith in logic and belief in man will forever be banished.' Ionesco was moving away from realism, with 'characters and events [that] have traceable roots in life' – from plays such as those of Gorki, Chekhov, Arthur

Miller, Tennessee Williams, Brecht, O'Casey, Osborne, and Sartre.[1]

Tynan's attack opened one of the most interesting discussions on this subject ever conducted in public. Ionesco replied that he certainly did not see himself as a messiah,

because I do not like messiahs and I certainly do not consider the vocation of the artist or the playwright to lie in that direction. I have a distinct impression that it is Mr Tynan who is in search of messiahs. But to deliver a message to the world, to wish to direct its course, to save it, is the business of the founders of religions, of the moralists or the politicians. . . . A playwright simply writes plays, in which he can offer only a testimony, not a didactic message. . . . Any work of art which was ideological and nothing else would be pointless . . . inferior to the doctrine it claimed to illustrate, which would already have been expressed in its proper language, that of discursive demonstration. An ideological play can be no more than the vulgarization of an ideology . . .[2]

Ionesco protested against the imputation that he was a deliberate anti-realist, that he maintained the impossibility of communication by language. 'The very fact of writing and presenting plays is surely incompatible with such a view. I simply hold that it is difficult to make oneself understood, not absolutely impossible.'[3] After a dig at Sartre (as the author of political melodramas), Osborne, Miller, Brecht, et al., as 'auteurs du boulevard – representatives of a Left Wing conformism which is just as lamentable as the Right Wing sort', Ionesco stated his conviction that society itself formed one of the barriers between human beings, that the authentic community of man is wider than society. 'No society has been able to abolish human sadness, no political system can deliver us from the pain of living, from our fear of death, our thirst for the absolute; it is the human condition that directs the social con-

1. Kenneth Tynan, 'Ionesco, man of destiny?', Observer, London, 22 June 1958.
2. Ionesco, 'The playwright's role', Observer, 29 June 1958.
3. ibid.

dition, not vice versa.' Hence the need to break down the language of society, which 'is nothing but clichés, empty formulas and slogans'. That is why the ideologies with their fossilized language must be continually re-examined and 'their congealed language . . . relentlessly split apart in order to find the living sap beneath'.

To discover the fundamental problem common to all mankind, I must ask myself what *my* fundamental problem is, what *my* most ineradicable fear is. I am certain then to find the problems and fears of literally everyone. That is the true road into my own darkness, our darkness, which I try to bring to the light of day. . . . A work of art is the expression of an incommunicable reality that one tries to communicate – and which sometimes can be communicated. That is its paradox and its truth.[1]

Ionesco's article provoked a wide and varied response – a clear indication that both he and Tynan had touched on a vital issue. There were those who congratulated Ionesco on having written 'one of the most brilliant refutations of the current theory of "social realism"', but added, 'If only M. Ionesco were able to put some of its clarity and wisdom into his own plays, he might yet become a great playwright!' (H. F. Garten, the critic and expert on modern German drama), as well as those who agreed with Kenneth Tynan that a repudiation of politics in itself amounted to a political ideology (John Berger, the Marxist art critic). George Devine, the artistic director of the Royal Court Theatre, supported Ionesco, but insisted that Arthur Miller, John Osborne, and Brecht were by no means exclusively concerned with social purposes: 'The framework of these plays is consciously social but the core of them is human', while Philip Toynbee pointed out that he considered Ionesco frivolous and thought Arthur Miller a greater dramatist anyway.

In the same issue of the *Observer*, Tynan himself took up Ionesco's challenge. His argument hinged on Ionesco's contention that artistic expression could be independent of, and in

1. ibid.

some ways superior to, ideologies and the needs of the 'real world'. 'Art and ideology often interact on each other, but the plain fact is that both spring from a common source. Both draw on human experience to explain mankind to itself. . . . They are brothers, not child and parent.' Ionesco's emphasis on introspection, the exploration of his private anxieties, Tynan argued, opened the door to subjectivism, which would make objective value judgement, and thus criticism of such plays, impossible. 'Whether M. Ionesco admits it or not, every play worth serious consideration is a statement. It is a statement addressed in the first person singular to the first person plural, and the latter must retain the right to dissent. . . . If a man tells me something I believe to be an untruth, am I forbidden to do more than congratulate him on the brilliance of his lying?'[1]

The controversy raged on in the pages of the next issue of the *Observer* – with distinguished contributions from Orson Welles (mainly on the role of the critic and critical standards), Lindsay Anderson, the young dramatist Keith Johnstone, and others. Ionesco's own second riposte, however, was not published in the paper. It has since appeared in *Cahiers des Saisons*[2] and in a volume of Ionesco's collected essays. In it, Ionesco tackles the real issue behind the controversy – the problem of form and content.

'Mr Tynan reproaches me with letting myself be seduced by the means of expressing "objective reality" (Yet what is objective reality? That is another question) to such an extent that I forget the objective reality for the sake of the means of expression. . . . In other words, I think that I am accused of formalism.' But, Ionesco maintains, the history of art, of literature, is essentially the history of modes of expression. 'To approach the problem of literature through the study of its ways of expression (which is what the critic ought to do, in my

1. Tynan, 'Ionesco and the phantom', *Observer*, 6 July 1958.
2. Ionesco, '*Le cœur n'est pas sur la main*', *Cahiers des Saisons*, Paris, no. 15, Winter 1959.

opinion) amounts to approaching its basis, to fathom its essence.' Thus Ionesco's own attack against fossilized forms of language, which is itself an attempt at revitalizing dead forms, appears to him to be as deeply concerned with objective reality as any social realism. 'To renew the language is to renew the conception, the vision of the world. Revolution consists in bringing about a change in mental attitudes.' As all really creative artistic expression is an attempt at saying new things in a new way, it cannot, by definition, merely serve for the restatement of existing ideologies. Form and structure, which must obey their own internal laws of consistency and cohesion, are as important as conceptual content. 'I do not believe that there is a contradiction between creative and cognitive activity, for the structures of the mind probably reflect universal structures.'

A temple or a cathedral, although not representational, reveals the fundamental laws of structure, and its value as a work of art lies in this, rather than in its utilitarian purpose. Formal experiment in art thus becomes an exploration of reality more valid and more useful (because it serves to enlarge man's understanding of the real world) than shallow works that are immediately comprehensible to the masses. Since the beginning of our century there has been a great upsurge of such creative exploration, which has transformed our understanding of the world, particularly in music and painting. 'In literature, and above all in the theatre, this movement seems to have come to a stop since, perhaps, 1925. I should like to be able to hope to be considered one of the modest craftsmen who have taken it up again. I have, for example, tried to exteriorize the anxiety . . . of my characters through objects; to make the stage settings speak; to translate the action into visual terms; to project visible images of fear, regret, remorse, alienation; to play with words. . . . I have thus tried to extend the language of the theatre. . . . Is this to be condemned?'

Formal experiment, Ionesco argues, is more closely concerned with reality than social realism as it was displayed at an exhibition of Soviet painting Ionesco visited. The dull representational pictures of the Soviet artists were liked by the local capitalist Philistines and, what is more, 'the social-realist painters were formalist and academic precisely because they had paid insufficient attention to the formal means of expression and had thus been unable to achieve any depth.' In the paintings of an artist like Masson, on the other hand, there was both truth and life:

Because Masson, the craftsman, had left human reality alone, because he had not tried to capture it, thinking only of the act of painting, human reality and its tragic elements had revealed themselves, for that very reason, rightly, freely. Thus what Mr Tynan calls anti-reality had become real, something incommunicable had communicated itself, and there too, behind the apparent repudiation of all human, concrete, and moral reality, its living heart had been hidden all the time, while on the other side, that of the antiformalists, there had been only dried-up forms – empty, dead. The heart is not worn on the sleeve.[1]

The Ionesco–Tynan controversy, brilliantly conducted on both sides, shows that Eugène Ionesco is by no means merely the author of hilarious nonsense plays, as he is so often represented in the press, but a serious artist dedicated to the arduous exploration of the realities of the human situation, fully aware of the task that he has undertaken, and equipped with formidable intellectual powers.

Ionesco was born in Slatina, Rumania, on 26 November 1912. His mother, whose maiden name was Thérèse Icard, was French, and shortly after he was born, his parents went to live in Paris. French is his first language – he had to acquire most of his Rumanian after his return to Rumania at the age of thirteen. His first impressions and memories are of Paris:

When I was a child I lived near the Square de Vaugirard. I remember – it was so long ago! – the badly lit street on an autumn or winter evening. My mother held me by the hand; I was afraid, as children are afraid; we were out shopping for the evening meal. On

1. ibid.

the sidewalks sombre silhouettes in agitated movement, people in a hurry – phantomlike, hallucinatory shadows. When that image of that street comes to life again in my memory, when I think that almost all those people are now dead, everything seems a shadow, evanescence. I am seized by a vertigo of anxiety . . .[1]

Evanescence, anxiety – and the theatre:

. . . my mother could not tear me away from the Punch and Judy show at the Luxembourg Gardens. I stayed there, I could stay there, enrapt, for whole days. The spectacle of the Punch and Judy show held me there, as if stupefied, through the sight of these puppets that talked, moved, clubbed each other. It was the spectacle of the world itself, which, unusual, improbable, but truer than truth, presented itself to me in an infinitely simplified and caricatured form, as if to underline its grotesque and brutal truth . . .[2]

After a few years at school, the local *école communale* in Paris, the boy developed anaemia and was sent to the country. He has described how he arrived, before he had reached the age of nine, together with his sister, who was a year younger, at the village of La Chapelle-Anthenaise, where they were to board with farmers. 'The failing light; my tiredness; the mysterious light of the countryside; the imaginary vision of the long dark corridors of "the castle" [which he took the steeple of the local church to be]; and then the thought that I was about to leave my mother, I could no longer resist. . . . I flung myself, crying, against my mother's skirts.'[3]

When he revisited the village of La Chapelle-Anthenaise on the eve of war, in 1939, Ionesco recalled fragments of memories of playing 'theatre' there with other children, of his experiences in the village school and with fellow-boarders at the farm, of nightmares and strange apparitions 'like figures out of

1. Ionesco, '*Lorsque j'écris* . . .', *Cahiers des Saisons*, no. 15.

2. Ionesco, '*Expérience du théâtre*', *Nouvelle Revue Française*, Paris, 1 February 1958, p. 253.

3. Ionesco, '*Printemps 1939. Les débris du souvenir. Pages de journal*', *Cahiers de la Compagnie Madeleine Renaud – Jean-Louis Barrault*, Paris, no. 29, February 1960, p. 104.

Brueghel or Bosch – large noses, distorted bodies, horrible smiles, clubfooted. Later, back in Rumania, I was still childish enough to have such nightmares. But now the phantoms of my anxiety had a different appearance – they were two-dimensional, sad rather than hideous, with enormous eyes. One is led to believe that there are both Gothic and Byzantine hallucinations.'[1]

He has recalled how at that time he dreamed of becoming a saint but, reading the religious books available in the village, he learned that it is wrong to seek after glory. So he abandoned the idea of sainthood. Shortly afterwards he read the lives of Turenne and Condé and decided to become a great warrior. At the age of thirteen, back in Paris, he wrote his first play, a patriotic drama.

The family returned to Rumania; Ionesco encountered a rawer, more brutal world: 'Shortly after my arrival in my second homeland, I saw a man, still young, big and strong, attack an old man with his fists and kick him with his boots. . . . I have no other images of the world except those of evanescence and brutality, vanity and rage, nothingness or hideous, useless hatred. Everything I have since experienced has merely confirmed what I had seen and understood in my childhood: vain and sordid fury, cries suddenly stifled by silence, shadows engulfed forever in the night. . . .'[2]

In Rumania, Ionesco went through school and became a student of French at the University of Bucharest. He wrote his first poems, elegies influenced by Maeterlinck and Francis Jammes. He also ventured into the realm of literary criticism, publishing a withering attack on three then fashionable and leading Rumanian writers – the poets Tudor Arghezi and Ion Barbu and the novelist Camil Petresco – accusing them of narrow provincialism and lack of originality. But a few days later he published a second pamphlet, praising the same authors

1. ibid.
2. 'Lorsque j'écris . . .', loc. cit.

to the skies as great and universally valid figures of Rumanian national literature. Finally he presented the two essays side by side, under the title *No!*, to prove the possibility of holding opposite views on the same subject, and the identity of contraries.

Having finished his studies, Ionesco became a teacher of French at a Bucharest *lycée*. In 1936, he married Rodica Burileano, a petite woman with an exotic cast of features not uncommon in Eastern Europe, whose Oriental beauty has given rise to the wholly unwarranted rumour that Ionesco's wife is Chinese. In 1938, Ionesco obtained a government grant to enable him to go to France to undertake research for a thesis he planned on 'the themes of sin and death in French poetry since Baudelaire'. He went back to France but is reputed never to have written a single line of this great work.

In the spring of 1939, he revisited La Chapelle-Anthenaise, searching for his childhood, putting down his memories in his diary. 'I am writing, writing, writing. All my life I have been writing; I have never been able to do anything else.[1] . . . To whom can all this be of interest? Is my sadness, my despair communicable? It cannot have significance for anyone. No one knows me. I am nobody. If I were a writer, a public figure, it might assume some interest perhaps. And yet I am like all the others. Anyone can recognize himself in me.'[2]

At the outbreak of war Ionesco was at Marseille. Later he returned to Paris, and worked in the production department of a publishing house. His daughter Marie-France was born in 1944. When the war ended, Ionesco was almost thirty-three. There was nothing to indicate that he was soon to become a famous dramatist. In fact, he disliked the theatre intensely: 'I read fiction, essays, I went to the cinema with pleasure. I listened to music from time to time, I visited art galleries, but I hardly ever went to the theatre.'[3]

Why did he dislike the theatre? He had loved it as a boy, but

1. '*Printemps 1939*', loc. cit., p. 98.   2. ibid., p. 103.
3. '*Expérience du théâtre*', loc. cit., p. 247.

he had begun to dislike it ever since, 'having acquired a critical sense, I became aware of the strings, the crude strings of the theatre.' The acting of the cast embarrassed him, he felt embarrassed for the actors. 'Going to the theatre to me meant going to see people, apparently serious people, making a spectacle of themselves.' And yet Ionesco liked fiction, he was even convinced that the truth of fiction is superior to that of reality. Nor did he dislike acting in the cinema. But in the theatre

it was the presence on the stage of flesh-and-blood people that embarrassed me. Their material presence destroyed the fiction. I was confronted, as it were, by two planes of reality – the concrete, material, impoverished, empty, limited reality of these living, everyday human beings, moving about and talking on the stage, and the reality of the imagination, the two face to face and not coinciding, unable to be brought into relation with each other; two antagonistic worlds incapable of being unified, of merging.[1]

In spite of his dislike of the theatre, Ionesco wrote a play, almost against his will. This is how it happened. In 1948, he decided that he ought to learn English, and so he acquired an English course. Learned research, published in the august pages of the *Cahiers du Collège de Pataphysique*, has since, by close textual analysis, established that the text in question was *L'Anglais sans Peine*, of the *Assimil* method.[2] Ionesco himself has described what happened next:

I set to work. Conscientiously I copied whole sentences from my primer with the purpose of memorizing them. Rereading them attentively, I learned not English but some astonishing truths – that, for example, there are seven days in the week, something I already knew; that the floor is down, the ceiling up, things I already knew as well, perhaps, but that I had never seriously thought about or had forgotten, and that seemed to me, suddenly, as stupefying as they were indisputably true.[3]

1. ibid., p. 253.
2. Lutembi, '*Contribution à une étude des sources de* La Cantatrice Chauve', *Cahiers du Collège de Pataphysique*, nos. 8–9, 1953.
3. Ionesco, '*La tragédie du langage*', *Spectacles*, Paris, no. 2, July 1958.

As the lessons became more complex, two characters were introduced, Mr and Mrs Smith:

To my astonishment, Mrs Smith informed her husband that they had several children, that they lived in the vicinity of London, that their name was Smith, that Mr Smith was a clerk, that they had a servant, Mary – English, like themselves. . . . I should like to point out the irrefutable, perfectly axiomatic character of Mrs Smith's assertions, as well as the entirely Cartesian manner of the author of my English primer; for what was truly remarkable about it was its eminently methodical procedure in its quest for truth. In the fifth lesson, the Smiths' friends the Martins arrive; the four of them begin to chat and, starting from basic axioms, they build more complex truths: 'The country is quieter than the big city . . .'[1]

Here was a comic situation, already in dialogue form: two married couples solemnly informing each other of things that must have been obvious to all of them all along. But then 'a strange phenomenon took place. I don't know how – the text began imperceptibly to change before my eyes, and in spite of me. The very simple, luminously clear statements I had copied diligently into my . . . notebook, left to themselves, fermented after a while, lost their original identity, expanded and overflowed.' The clichés and truisms of the conversation primer, which had once made sense although they had now become empty and fossilized, gave way to pseudo-clichés and pseudo-truisms; these disintegrated into wild caricature and parody, and in the end language itself disintegrated into disjointed fragments of words.

While writing the play (for it had become a kind of play or anti-play; that is, a parody of a play, a comedy of comedy) I felt sick, dizzy, nauseated. I had to interrupt my work from time to time and, wondering all the while what demon was prodding me on, lie down on my couch for fear of seeing my work sink into nothingness, and me with it.[2]

That is how Ionesco's first play came into being. At first he

1. ibid.   2. ibid.

wanted to call it *L'Anglais sans Peine*, later *L'Heure Anglaise*, but in the end it was called *La Cantatrice Chauve* (*The Bald Prima Donna*).

Ionesco read his play to a group of friends. They found it funny, although *he* believed himself to have written a very serious piece, 'the tragedy of language'. One of these friends, Monique Saint-Côme, who had translated novels from the Rumanian and was at that time, at the end of 1949, working with a group of avant-garde actors under the direction of Nicolas Bataille, asked Ionesco to lend her the manuscript.

Nicolas Bataille, then twenty-three years old, liked the play and wanted to meet its author. Ionesco came to see him at the little Théâtre de Poche. Nicolas Bataille has described that meeting:

... tradition demands that I should tell what was the first impression I had of him. Well, to follow that usage, I shall say that he seemed to me to resemble Mr Pickwick. I told him that we wanted to stage his play. He replied, '*Pas possible!*' He had already submitted it, without success, to, among others, Jean-Louis Barrault and ... the Comédie Française![1]

At first the director tried to stage the play in a wildly parodistic style. But that did not work. Finally, all concerned realized that, to have its full effect, the text would have to be acted in deadly seriousness, like a play by Ibsen or Sardou. In fact, when asking Jacques Noël to design the set, Bataille did not give him the play to read. He merely told him to design the drawing room for *Hedda Gabler*. Another model the production followed was the conception of the English character conveyed by the novels of Jules Verne, whose English people have a peculiar decorum and *sang-froid*, which has been brilliantly captured by the original illustrators in the stiff, bewhiskered figures of the Editions Hetzel.

The title of the play was found during rehearsals; in the long

1. Nicolas Bataille, '*La bataille de* La Cantatrice', *Cahiers des Saisons*, no. 15.

and pointless anecdote entitled 'The Headcold', which the fire chief tells, there is a reference to an *institutrice blonde*, a blonde schoolteacher. During one run-through, Henri-Jacques Huet, who played the fire chief, made a mistake and said *'cantatrice chauve'* instead. Ionesco, who was present, immediately realized that this was a far better title than *L'Heure Anglaise* or even *Big Ben Follies* (which he had considered at one time). And so the play became *The Bald Prima Donna*. A brief reference to the *'cantatrice chauve'* was introduced at the end of Scene 10, when the fire chief, as he is about to leave, creates general embarrassment by asking about the bald soprano, and after a painful silence receives the answer that she still wears her hair the same way.

Another important change that occurred during rehearsals concerned the end of the play. Originally Ionesco had intended that after the final quarrel between the two couples the stage should be left empty for a moment, then some extras in the audience were to start booing and protesting; this would lead to the appearance of the manager of the theatre on the stage, followed by the police. The police would 'machine-gun' the audience, while the manager and the police sergeant would congratulate each other by shaking hands. But this would have necessitated a number of additional actors and thereby have increased the costs. So, as an alternative, Ionesco had planned to let the maid, at the height of the quarrel, announce, 'The Author!', after which the author would appear, the actors would respectfully step aside and applaud him while the author would approach the footlights with sprightly steps, but suddenly raise his fists and shout at the audience, 'You bunch of crooks! I'll get you!' But, Ionesco reports, this ending was considered 'too polemical' and so eventually, as no other ending could be found, it was decided that there would be no end at all and that instead the play would start all over again from the beginning.

La Cantatrice Chauve, billed as an 'anti-play', was first

performed at the Théâtre des Noctambules on 11 May 1950. It was coldly received. Only Jacques Lemarchand, at that time the critic of *Combat*, and the playwright Armand Salacrou gave it favourable notices. There was little money for publicity, so the actors turned themselves into sandwich men and paraded the streets with their boards for about an hour before the performance. But the theatre remained almost empty. More than once, when there were fewer than three people in the theatre, they were given their money back and the actors went home. After about six weeks they gave up.

For Ionesco, this first encounter with the living theatre became a turning point; not only was he amazed to hear the audience laugh at what he considered a tragic spectacle of human life reduced to passionless automatism through bourgeois convention and the fossilization of language, he was also deeply moved by seeing the creatures of his imagination come to life:

One cannot resist the desire of making appear, on a stage, characters that are at the same time real and invented. One cannot resist the need to make them speak, to make them live before our eyes. To incarnate phantasms, to give them life, is a prodigious, irreplaceable, adventure to such an extent that I myself was overcome when, during the rehearsals of my first play, I suddenly saw characters move on the stage who had come out of myself. I was frightened. By what right had I been able to do this? Was this allowed? . . . It was almost diabolical.[1]

Suddenly Ionesco realized that it was his destiny to write for the theatre. He who had been embarrassed when he saw actors trying to identify themselves with the characters they portrayed to the point of finding such attempts indecent (as Brecht had before him), but who had been equally repelled by Brechtian acting, which 'made the actor a mere pawn in a chess game' and dehumanized him, now realized what it had been that made him uneasy:

1. '*Expérience du théâtre*', loc. cit., p. 258.

... if the theatre had embarrassed me by enlarging and thereby coarsening nuances, that was merely because it had enlarged them insufficiently. What seemed too crude was not crude enough; what seemed to be not subtle enough was in fact too subtle. For if the essence of the theatre lay in the enlargement of effects, it was necessary to enlarge them even more, to underline them, to emphasize them as much as possible. To push the theatre beyond that intermediary zone that is neither theatre nor literature was to put it back into its proper framework, to its natural limits. What was needed was not to disguise the strings that moved the puppets but to make them even more visible, deliberately apparent, to go right down to the very basis of the grotesque, the realms of caricature, to transcend the pale irony of witty drawing-room comedies ... to push everything to paroxysm, to the point where the sources of the tragic lie. To create a theatre of violence – violently comic, violently dramatic.[1]

To reach this point, Ionesco has since argued, the theatre must work with veritable shock tactics; reality itself, the consciousness of the spectator, his habitual apparatus of thought – language – must be overthrown, dislocated, turned inside out, so that he suddenly comes face to face with a new perception of reality. Thus Ionesco, the persistent critic of Brecht, is in fact postulating a far more radical, a far more fundamental alienation effect. What made him uneasy in the Brechtian style of acting was precisely that 'it appeared as an unacceptable mixture of the true and the false'; that, in effect, it did not carry alienation, the abandonment of a simulation of reality, far enough.

La Cantatrice Chauve (known as *The Bald Prima Donna* in Britain and as *The Bald Soprano* in the United States) has been so widely performed and published that it is unnecessary to outline its contents in detail. Some of its features have already become proverbial: the clock that, in a spirit of contradiction, always indicates the opposite of the correct time, or the classic recognition scene between a married couple, who, after a feat of logical deduction, to their great surprise reach the conclusion

1. *'Expérience du théâtre'*, loc. cit., pp. 258–9.

that as they seem to be living in the same street, the same house, the same floor, the same room, the same bed, they must necessarily be man and wife. (This scene is said to be based on an episode when Ionesco and his wife found themselves entering the same Métro carriage by different doors and went through an elaborate pantomime of recognition.)[1]

Nor is there any doubt left of the meaning and intention of the play. Ionesco himself, who has said that he never has ideas before writing a play, but has a good many ideas about its meaning after he has completed it,[2] has explained it most convincingly. It is in fact a tragicomic picture of life in an age when

we can no longer avoid asking ourselves what we are doing here on earth and how, having no deep sense of our destiny, we can endure the crushing weight of the material world. ... When there is no more incentive to be wicked, and everyone is good, what shall we do with our goodness, or our non-wickedness, our non-greed, our ultimate neutrality? The people in *The Bald Prima Donna* have no hunger, no conscious desires; they are bored stiff. They feel it vaguely, hence the final explosion – which is quite useless, as the characters and situations are both static and interchangeable, and everything ends where it started.[3]

The play is an attack against what Ionesco has called the 'universal petty-bourgeoisie... the personification of accepted ideas and slogans, the ubiquitous conformist'. What he deplores is the levelling of individuality, the acceptance of slogans by the masses, of ready-made ideas, which increasingly turn our mass societies into collections of centrally directed automata. 'The Smiths, the Martins can no longer talk because they can no longer think; they can no longer think *because they can no longer be moved, can no longer feel passions*. They can no longer be; they

1. *Observer*, 14 July 1958.
2. 'Expérience du théâtre', loc. cit., p. 268.
3. Ionesco, 'The world of Ionesco', *International Theatre Annual*, London, no. 2, 1957.

can "become" anybody, anything, for, having lost their identity, they assume the identity of others ... they are interchangeable.'[1]

We live in a world that has lost its metaphysical dimension, and therefore all mystery. But to restore the sense of mystery we must learn to see the most commonplace in its full horror: 'To feel the absurdity of the commonplace, and of language – its falseness – is already to have gone beyond it. To go beyond it we must first of all bury ourselves in it. What is comical is the unusual in its pure state; nothing seems more surprising to me than that which is banal; the surreal is here, within grasp of our hands, in our everyday conversation.'[2]

Having rediscovered his childhood passion for the theatre, Ionesco even adventured into becoming an actor. He accepted an offer from the director of *La Cantatrice Chauve*, Nicolas Bataille, and the well-known theatrical scholar and director, Akakia Viala, to play the part of Stepan Trofimovich, in an adaptation of Dostoevski's *The Possessed* by Bataille and Akakia Viala. He who had always regarded the effort an actor must make as unbearable, bordering on the absurd or a kind of sainthood, now learned what it means 'to take on another human being, when one finds it hard enough already to bear with oneself; to understand him with the help of the director, when one does not understand oneself.'[3]

Ionesco did not like the character he had undertaken to act, 'because he was another, and in allowing myself to be inhabited by him, I really had the impression of being "possessed" or "dispossessed", of losing myself, of renouncing my personality, which I don't like particularly but to which I have at last

1. Ionesco, 'The tragedy of language', *Tulane Drama Review*, Spring 1960.

2. Ionesco, '*Le point du départ*', *Cahiers des Quatre Saisons*, Paris, no. 1, August 1955.

3. Ionesco, Preface to *Les Possédés*, adapted from Dostoevski by Akakia Viala and Nicolas Bataille (Paris: Editions Emile-Paul, 1959).

become accustomed.'¹ And yet, after many attempts to desert, having been held back merely by the sense of his moral obligation, suddenly the moment came when he discovered that precisely because he had lost himself in the character of Stepan Trofimovich, he was finding his own self in a new sense. 'I had learned that each of us is all the others, that my solitude had not been real and that the actor can, better than anyone else, understand human beings by understanding himself. In learning to act, I have also, in a certain sense, learned to admit that the others are oneself, that you yourself are the others, and that all lonelinesses become identified.'²

The run of *The Possessed* at the Théâtre des Noctambules, which gave Ionesco these insights into the art of acting, came to an end on 18 February 1951. Two days later, his second play, written in June 1950, had its first night at the tiny Théâtre de Poche. This was *La Leçon* (*The Lesson*). As Jacques Lemarchand has pointed out, it was a disconcerting occasion for those who after *The Bald Prima Donna* – a play in which no prima donna appeared, and no bald person either – expected that in *The Lesson* there would be no question of a lesson. To their surprise, the whole play consisted of an hour's reproduction of a lesson, an unusual one, no doubt, but a lesson nevertheless: an aged professor giving private instruction to an eager but obtuse girl pupil, a lesson in geography, addition, multiplication, linguistics, and other subjects – in short, as Jacques Lemarchand put it, almost 'a faithful reproduction of a lesson given by Marshal Foch at the *école de guerre*'.³

The Lesson, like *The Bald Prima Donna*, is concerned with language, and not only in the long dissertation on the neo-Spanish language group, which includes a large number of real and imaginary languages that are superficially all the same yet are all distinguished by subtle differences, imperceptible to the

1. ibid.   2. ibid.
3. Jacques Lemarchand, Preface to Ionesco, *Théâtre I* (Paris: Gallimard, 1954).

ear but very real nevertheless. Thus the word '*grandmère*' in French is pronounced '*grand-mère*' in Spanish, in Sardanapali, or in Rumanian as well, and yet there is a world of subtle difference between these languages. That is, if one man says 'Grandmother' and another man says 'Grandmother', they *seem* to be saying the same thing, but are in fact talking about vastly different people! So, as the professor learnedly points out, if an Italian says 'my country', he means Italy, but if an Oriental says 'my country', he means the Orient, the same word signifying completely different things. This is a demonstration of the basic impossibility of communication – words cannot convey meanings because they leave out of account the personal associations they carry for each individual. This is one of the reasons why the professor seems unable to break through to his pupil. Their minds work along different lines and will never meet. The pupil can add but fails to grasp the possibility of subtraction, yet she can multiply astronomical figures in a flash, explaining to the baffled professor that she has merely learned all possible multiplication tables by heart. And yet, she says, she can count only to sixteen.

But there is more about language in *The Lesson* than a demonstration of the difficulties of communication. Here language is also shown as an *instrument of power*. As the play proceeds, the pupil who was eager, lively, and alert is gradually drained of her vitality, while the professor, who was timid and nervous at the beginning, gradually gains in assurance and domination. It is clear that the professor derives his progressive increase of power from his role as a giver, a very arbitrary prescriber of meanings. Because words must have the significance *he* decides to give them, the pupil comes under his dominance, which finds its concrete, theatrical expression in her rape and murder. The maid, who in turn dominates the professor like a malignant mother figure, is immune when he attacks her with the same knife – simply because she is not one of his pupils. It is the maid who finally sums up the situation –

'arithmetic leads to philology, and philology leads to crime...'

The discomfiture of the pupil announces itself when she is suddenly overtaken by a violent toothache, 'the final, great symptom', as the maid puts it. In some ways this toothache indicates the pupil's loss of the power to speak, her loss of the gift of language, but it also announces the victory of physical reality over that of the mind. Progressively, all the parts of her body begin to ache until, in an act of complete physical subjection, she allows the professor to plunge the knife into her, accepting the professor's final proposition – 'The knife kills.'

The sexual connotation of this climactic moment of the play is quite openly indicated. The pupil flops into a chair 'in an immodest position ... her legs spread wide and hanging over both sides of the chair. The professor remains standing in front of her, his back to the audience.' Murderer and victim shout 'Aaah!' at the same moment. In Marcel Cuvelier's production, the repeated rhythmic enunciation of the key word '*couteau*' by murderer and victim was also unambiguously orgastic.

Pierre-Aimé Touchard has argued that *The Lesson* expresses in caricatured form the spirit of domination always present in teacher–pupil relationships, and that the professor kills the girl because her toothache enables her to escape from having to listen to his instruction. This, according to Touchard's ingenious interpretation, is in turn a symbol for all forms of dictatorship. When dictators feel that their domination of their people is on the wane, they want to annihilate the rebellious ones, abolishing their own power in doing so.[1] This interpretation is somewhat rationalistic, although it is supported by the maid's handing the professor a swastika armband at the end of the play. The political implication of domination is certainly present in *The Lesson*, but it is only one, and perhaps a minor, aspect of its main proposition, which hinges on the sexual nature of all power and the relationship between language and power as the basis of all human ties. The professor dominates

1. P. A. Touchard, '*La loi du théâtre*', *Cahiers des Saisons*, no. 15.

the pupil, but he in turn is dominated by the maid, who treats him like a fond, if disapproving, mother, spoiling her naughty child by ultimately overlooking his most flagrant pranks. The point of the play surely is that the pupils *always* get a toothache, and that the professor *always* rapes and kills them. The murder we witness is his *fortieth* on that single day. And the play ends with the forty-first victim arriving for her lesson.

It is all authority, therefore, which is shown up in its sexual, sadistic nature. What Ionesco is saying is that even behind so apparently harmless an exercise of authority as the teacher–pupil relationship, all the violence and domination, all the aggressiveness and possessiveness, the cruelty and lust are present that make up any manifestation of power. The technique of non-literary theatre, which allows the author and director to treat the text of a play as expendable, enables Ionesco to bring this hidden content into the open. While the language remains on the plane of question and answer, of information asked for and imparted, the *action* can become more and more violent, sensuous, and brutal. All that remains of the elaborate body of knowledge, information (in its parodied form), and conceptual apparatus is the basic fact that the professor wants to dominate and to possess the pupil. Ionesco labelled *The Lesson* a '*drame comique*'. It certainly is very funny, but it is a stark and pessimistic drama nevertheless.

Jacques, ou La Soumission (*Jacques or Obedience* in the British translation, *Jack, or The Submission* in the American), which Ionesco completed after *The Lesson*, in the summer of 1950, has a very similar theme – the individual cowed into conformism by society and convention through the operation of the sexual instinct. Jacques at first refuses to pronounce the words that would confirm his acceptance of the standards of his family, all the members of which are called Jacques as well, thus revealing their renunciation of individuality in the same way the family of Bobby Watsons symbolized the conformity of petty-bourgeois existence in *The Bald Prima Donna*. Jacques resists the pressure of his family for a while; he refuses to accept the need to pronounce the fatal words and even cries out, 'Oh, words, what crimes are committed in your name!' but when his sister Jacqueline points out to him that he is '*chronométrable*' – i.e. (probably) subject to the working of time, subject to the law of the clock – he collapses and finally pronounces the family creed: '*J'adore les pommes de terre au lard.*' (This is translated as 'I love potatoes in their jackets' in the British edition, 'I adore hashed brown potatoes' in the American, but probably just means 'I adore potatoes fried in bits of lard' or 'potatoes with bacon', as emerges in the sequel to the play *The Future is in Eggs*, where the bits of bacon play a part and have made the English translator, Derek Prouse, adopt the term 'potatoes with bacon'.)

The acceptance of the bourgeois creed by the rebellious ex-bohemian son is, according to the French tradition, the signal for settling down and marriage. Jacques is accordingly brought together with the daughter of the Robert family, Roberte, a girl with two noses. Once more Jacques is rebellious – two noses are not enough for him; he needs three noses in his future wife, regardless of the extra expense in handkerchiefs that this implies. Although Roberte with two noses was their only daughter, the Robert family find a way out – they produce a second only daughter, Roberte II, who has three noses. But not even she at first satisfies Jacques's individualist spirit; she is not ugly enough. He cannot love her: 'I have done all I could! I am what I am. . . .' And yet, when left alone with Roberte, he finally succumbs. Roberte wins him with a speech about a dream in which little guinea pigs grow out of their mother at the bottom of a bathtub; suddenly he tells her of his secret longings to be different. The conversation shifts to images of fire (rather like the maid's fiery poem in *The Bald Prima Donna*) and back to Roberte's description of herself in terms of humidity. Jacques cries out, '*Cha-a-armant!*' and this leads on to the famous passage in which the two lovers converse in a long succession of terms containing the syllable '*chat*', with its obvious erotic implications in French – from *cha-peau* to *cha-touille* and *cha-pitre* to the point when Roberte proclaims that henceforth all concepts will be called *chat* without distinction. Jacques and Roberte embrace, the family enters and performs an obscene dance around them. Jacques and Roberte squat down on the ground, the light fades, and the stage is filled with animal noises. The stage direction insists, 'All this must produce in the audience a feeling of embarrassment, awkwardness, and shame.'

In fact, therefore, Jacques submits twice. He submits to the bourgeois conformism of his family, and, second and finally, to the irresistible, animal lure of the sexual impulse. And it is his second submission that is decisive. It is man's enslavement to the sexual instinct that forces him into the iron mould of bourgeois conformity.

This point is reinforced by the later play that takes up the story: *L'Avenir est dans Les Œufs, ou Il faut de tout pour faire un monde* (*The Future is in Eggs, or It takes all sorts to make a world*) (written in 1951), which starts with a further orgy of '*chat*' and ends with Roberte hatching unending basketfuls of eggs destined to become the emperors, policemen, Marxists, drunkards, and so on, of the future, all to be turned into sausage meat, cannon fodder, and omelettes. 'Long live production! Long live the white race!' is the despairing cry that concludes the play.

The horror of proliferation – the invasion of the stage by evergrowing masses of people or things – which appears in *The Future is in Eggs* is one of the most characteristic images we find in Ionesco's plays. It expresses the individual's horror at being confronted with the overwhelming task of coping with the world, his solitude in the face of its monstrous size and duration. This is also the theme of *The Chairs*, written at about the same time as the second part of *Jacques* (April–June 1951) and often considered one of Ionesco's greatest achievements.

In a circular tower on an island (very similar to that of Beckett's *Endgame*) live two old people, man and wife, aged 95 and 94 respectively; the man works as a concierge, although it seems difficult to imagine how he could do so in a lonely tower on an island. The couple is expecting the visit of a crowd of distinguished people who have been invited to listen to the message that, at the end of his life, the old man wants to pass on to posterity – the fruit of a long lifetime's experience. He himself is no orator, so he has engaged a professional orator to deliver the message. The guests arrive; they are neither heard nor seen, but the two old people are filling the stage with increasing numbers of chairs to accommodate them and pouring forth torrents of polite conversation. The crowd becomes more and more dense, the two old people have greater and greater difficulty in moving among them, finally the emperor himself arrives; the scene is set for the appearance of the orator. He comes – and is a real character. Satisfied that his message will be delivered, the old man, followed by his wife, jumps to his death into the sea. The orator faces the crowd of chairs and tries to speak, but he is deaf and dumb and can only make an inarticulate, gurgling sound. He writes something on a blackboard – it is a jumble of meaningless letters.

The power and poignancy of this situation are as great as its effectiveness as theatre. The simulation of a crowd of invisible characters is a *tour de force* for the actors involved, which, if it is successfully carried through, is bound to be a most impressive scenic spectacle. A play like *The Chairs* is a poetic image brought to life – complex, ambiguous, multi-dimensional. The beauty and depth of the image, as symbol and myth, transcends any search for interpretations. Of course it contains the theme of the incommunicability of a lifetime's experience; of course it dramatizes the futility and failure of human existence, made bearable only by self-delusion and the admiration of a doting, uncritical wife; of course it satirizes the emptiness of polite conversation, the mechanical exchange of platitudes that might as well be spoken into the wind. There is also a strong element of the author's own tragedy in the play – the rows of chairs resemble a theatre; the professional orator who is to deliver the message, dressed in the romantic costume of the mid-nineteenth century, is the interpretative artist who interposes his personality between that of the playwright and the audience. But the message is meaningless, the audience consists of rows of empty chairs – surely this is a powerful image of the absurdity of the artist's, the playwright's, own situation.

All these themes intertwine in *The Chairs*. But Ionesco himself has defined its basic preoccupation: 'The subject of the play', he wrote to the director of the first performance, Sylvain Dhomme,

is not the message, nor the failures of life, nor the moral disaster of the two old people, but the chairs themselves; that is to say, the absence of people, the absence of the emperor, the absence of God, the absence of matter, the unreality of the world, metaphysical emptiness. The theme of the play is *nothingness* . . . the invisible elements must be more and more clearly present, more and more real (to give unreality to reality one must give reality to the unreal), until the point is reached – inadmissible, unacceptable to the reasoning mind – when the unreal elements speak and move . . . and nothingness can be heard, is made concrete . . .[1]

The Chairs was Ionesco's third play to reach the stage, and it did not do so without the greatest difficulties. It took Sylvain Dhomme and the two actors of the old couple, Tsilla Chelton and Paul Chevalier, three months to find the style of acting suitable for the play – a mixture of extreme naturalness of detail and the utmost unusualness of the general conception. None of the established managements in Paris wanted to risk putting on *The Chairs*, so in the end the actors themselves hired an old unused hall, the Théâtre Lancry, where they opened on

1. Letter from Ionesco to Sylvain Dhomme, quoted by F. Towarnicki, '*Des* Chaises *vides* . . . *à Broadway*', *Spectacles*, Paris, no. 2, July 1958.

22 April 1952. Financially the venture proved a disaster. Only too often the empty chairs on the stage were matched by empty seats in the auditorium, and there were evenings when only five or six tickets were sold. Most of the critics slated the play, but, on the other hand, it did find some distinguished supporters. A defence of *The Chairs* published in the magazine *Arts* was signed by Jules Supervielle, Arthur Adamov, Samuel Beckett, Luc Estang, Clara Malraux, Raymond Queneau, and others. At the end of the last performance, the poet and playwright Audiberti was heard, in the almost empty auditorium, shouting 'Bravo!' at the top of his voice.

Four years later, when Jacques Mauclair revived *The Chairs* with the same actress, Tsilla Chelton, in the part of the old woman, the climate of opinion had changed; the performance at the Studio des Champs-Elysées was a great success. The leading conservative critics, like J.-J. Gautier, of *Figaro*, still held out against Ionesco, but Jean Anouilh himself came to his defence, calling the play a masterpiece, and adding, 'I believe this to be better than Strindberg, because it has its "black" humour, *à la Molière*, in a manner that is at times terribly funny, because it is horrifying and laughable, poignant and always true, and because – with the exception of a bit of rather old-fashioned avant-garde at the end that I do not like – it is classical.'[1]

Ionesco labelled *The Chairs* a 'tragic farce', *Jacques, ou La Soumission* a 'naturalistic comedy'. He called his next play, *Victimes du Devoir* (*Victims of Duty*), a 'pseudo-drama'. This play may have been less successful than some of his earlier works, but it is certainly among his most significant statements.

Victims of Duty is a playwright's play, an argument for and against the problem drama: 'All the plays that have ever been written, from Ancient Greece to the present day, have never really been anything but thrillers. Drama has always been realistic and there has always been a detective about. Every play

1. J. Anouilh, '*Du chapitre des* Chaises', *Figaro*, Paris, 23 April 1956.

is an investigation brought to a successful conclusion. There is a riddle and it is solved in the final scene.'[1] Even the classical French tragedy, says Choubert, the hero of *Victims of Duty*, ultimately can be reduced to refined detective drama.

Choubert is a petty-bourgeois spending the evening quietly with his wife, who is darning socks. His views on the theatre are immediately put to the test. A detective arrives. He is merely looking for the neighbours, but they are out. He wants to find out whether the previous tenant of Choubert's apartment spelled his name 'Mallot' with a 't', or 'Mallod' with a 'd'. The Chouberts ask the detective in; he looks such a nice young man. But before he knows where he is, Choubert is the victim of third-degree methods. He has never known Mallot, or Mallod, but he is ordered to delve into his (Choubert's) subconscious; the answer to the problem simply *must* be there. The detective is thus turned into a psychoanalyst, the identity between the detective play and the psychological drama is demonstrated.

As Choubert dives deeper and deeper into the bottomless well of his subconscious, his wife, Madeleine, changes too – into a seductress at first, then an old woman, and finally the detective's mistress. So deep down has Choubert gone that he pierces the sound and sight barriers and actually disappears from sight. When he comes to the surface again, he has become a child and Madeleine is now his mother. The detective has become his father. Again the situation changes: Choubert holds the stage, acting out the drama of his search, while Madeleine and the detective are his audience. But all he sees is a gaping hole. Attempts are made to bring him back to the surface – he has delved too deep – and is presently going up and up, higher than Mont Blanc, and in danger of becoming airborne. New characters wander in – a lady who sits silently in the corner, but to whom the others occasionally turn with a polite '*N'est-ce pas,*

1. Ionesco, *Victims of Duty*, trans. Donald Watson, in *Plays*, vol. II (London: Calder; New York: Grove Press, 1958), p. 119.

Madame?' and a bearded man, Nicolas d'Eu (not to be confounded with Nicolas Deux, the late Czar of Russia), who brings the conversation back to the theatre, while Choubert continues his hapless quest for Mallot.

Nicolas is for a new kind of theatre, up to date, 'in harmony with the general drift of the other manifestations of the modern spirit . . . We'll get rid of the principle of identity and unity of character. . . . As for plot and motivation, let's not mention them . . . no more drama, no more tragedy: the tragic's turning comic, the comic is tragic, and life's getting more cheerful. . . .'[1] These, of course, are the well-known points of view of Ionesco himself, only slightly parodied, and Nicolas confesses that he does not want to write – after all, 'We've got Ionesco and that's enough.'[2]

In the meantime, the detective is feeding Choubert enormous quantities of bread to stop the gaping hole of his memory. Nicolas d'Eu suddenly turns against the detective, who cringes in fear and pleads for his life but is pitilessly knifed by Nicolas. He dies with the cry, 'Long live the white race!' Madeleine, who has been bringing cups of coffee throughout the proceedings, so that the entire stage is filled with cups, reminds them that they have not yet found Mallot. So Nicolas takes over the role of the detective and begins to feed the protesting Choubert with bread; he, like the detective, is merely doing his duty – he is a victim of duty as much as Choubert, as much as Madeleine. They are all victims of duty. What duty? In all likelihood that of finding a solution to the riddle posed at the beginning of the play. Being characters in a play, they have to find a solution at all costs; they *must* find the answer to the question whether Mallot spelled his name with a 't' or a 'd'. For we are here in the realm of 'pseudo-drama'.

Victims of Duty is one of Ionesco's favourite plays. It deals with the subject nearest to his heart, the problem of the essential tasks and limitations of the theatre. The policeman-psycho-

1. ibid., pp. 158–9.   2. ibid., p. 162.

analyst stands for the proposition that the mysteries of existence can be solved. 'As for me,' he says, 'I remain Aristotelically logical, true to myself, faithful to my duty, and full of respect for my bosses. . . . I don't believe in the absurd; everything hangs together, everything can be comprehended in time . . . thanks to the achievements of human thought and science.'[1] But Choubert, however deeply he descends into his subconscious, can find no solution there, only a gaping hole of nothingness. Far from containing the hidden solution to the riddle of existence, the subconscious mind opens into a bottomless pit, the absolute void.

As Serge Doubrovsky has pointed out, Freudian psychoanalysis is here confronted with Sartre's Existentialist ontology and psychology. Whether intentionally or not – more probably the latter – Ionesco here illustrates Sartre's proposition that man is a 'hole in Being', that he is 'the being through which nothingness enters the world'[2] and that 'consciousness is a being which in its being is conscious of the nothingness of its being.'[3] Man *is* nothing because he has the liberty of choice and therefore is always that which he is in the process of choosing himself to be, a permanent potentiality rather than actual being. No amount of bread that the detective, and later Nicolas d'Eu, stuff into Choubert can therefore, as Doubrovsky maintains, stop the gaping hole in Choubert's consciousness or 'give thought a substantial existence'.[4]

But if, to quote Doubrovsky again, 'consciousness is nothingness, then personality, character, disappear for good.'[5] If man can choose himself anew at each instant of his life, the conception of character as the final, irreducible essence – the Platonic idea – of each individual person disappears. As Nicolas d'Eu

1. ibid., p. 159.
2. Sartre, *L'Etre et le Néant* (Paris: Gallimard, 1943), p. 60.
3. ibid., p. 85.
4. S. Doubrovsky, '*Le rire d'Eugène Ionesco*', *Nouvelle Revue Française*, February 1960.
5. ibid.

puts it in *Victims of Duty*, 'We are not ourselves. Personality doesn't exist. Within us are only forces that are either contradictory or not contradictory. . . . The characters lose their form in the formlessness of becoming. Each character is not so much himself as another.' The brilliantly managed sequence of Choubert's descent into the depths and subsequent flight into the empyrean is a demonstration of this proposition. As he reaches the different levels of depth and height, Choubert turns into a bewildering variety of different, and not necessarily consistent, selves. At the same time the character of his wife also undergoes a series of changes, both in so far as *he* sees a different Madeleine at different levels of *his* self, and also as *she* becomes a different personality in responding to the changes in *his* character – for example, when he becomes a child, she becomes his mother, and so on.

Doubrovsky's essay is based on the assumption that Ionesco illustrates this Sartrean psychology, and parodies Freudian psychoanalysis. Yet it is possible that Ionesco might just as well be parodying both Sartre and Freud. After all, when Nicolas d'Eu, the propounder of the fluidity of character, has killed the Freudian detective, he himself resumes the search for Mallot and continues to stuff bread down Choubert's throat. In other words, the two views are interchangeable, and Choubert, the little man, suffers as much under the tyranny of the one as of the other. It is always dangerous to take Ionesco too seriously. On the other hand much of his practice seems to follow the principles of an anti-psychological drama, renouncing ready-made solutions to the problems it purports to pose, and abandoning the sacred concept of character as the essence of personality, i.e. the view enunciated by Nicolas d'Eu. But for Ionesco, the author of *No!*, that early essay on the identity of opposites, it would not be difficult to hold a belief and to parody it at the same time.

Victims of Duty, however, is not merely a play about Ionesco's theory of the theatre (the first of a number of such essays in the tradition of Molière's *Impromptu de Versailles*). It is not merely a psychological and philosophical inquiry, or a parody of such an inquiry; it is, above all, a haunting nightmare, a deeply felt and tormented expression of its author's experience of the absurdity and cruelty of existence. Ionesco, like Kafka and Beckett, is primarily concerned with trying to communicate his own sense of being, to tell the world what it feels like, what it means for him when he says, 'I am' or 'I am alive.' This is 'the point of departure' of all his work:

Two fundamental states of consciousness are at the root of all my plays. ... These two basic feelings are those of evanescence on the one hand, and heaviness on the other; of emptiness and of an over-abundance of presence; of the unreal transparency of the world, and of its opaqueness. ... The sensation of evanescence results in a feeling of anguish, a sort of dizziness. But all of this can just as well become euphoric; anguish is suddenly transformed into liberty. ... This state of consciousness is very rare, to be sure. ... I am most often under the dominion of the opposite feeling: lightness changes to heaviness, transparence to thickness; the world weighs heavily; the universe crushes me. A curtain, an insuperable wall, comes between me and the world, between me and myself. Matter fills everything, takes up all space, annihilates all liberty under its weight. ... Speech crumbles ...[1]

The proliferation of matter – chairs, eggs, furniture (in *The New Tenant*), or, in this case, Madeleine's coffee-cups – is one of the manifestations of the heavy, leaden, hopeless, depressive state of consciousness. The proliferation of matter expresses 'the concretization of solitude, of the victory of anti-spiritual forces'.[2] And humour is the only liberation from this anguish.

Victims of Duty clearly belongs to a depressive period in Ionesco's development. The play was first performed in February 1953, by Jacques Mauclair, the young director who later brought Ionesco his first major success with the revival of *The Chairs*. The seven short pieces which Jacques Poliéri presented

1. '*Le point du départ*'.   2. ibid.

in September of that year at the tiny Théâtre de la Huchette, on the other hand, were largely light, humorous, and euphoric. Only three of these (*Le Salon de l'Automobile*, *La Jeune Fille à Marier*, and *Le Maître*) have appeared in print. The four others (*Le Connaissez-Vous?*, *Le Rhume Onirique*, *La Nièce-Epouse*, and *Les Grandes Chaleurs* – an adaptation from the Rumanian of Caragiale) appear to be lost, the manuscripts having gone astray.

These are slight plays, actually cabaret sketches, but nevertheless very characteristic and revealing of Ionesco's comic techniques. *Le Salon de l'Automobile*[1] is based on a confusion between motor-cars and human beings. The buyer rides away in a newly acquired vehicle that is a female and that he decides to marry. The exhibition hall is filled with the farmyard noises of the exhibited vehicles. In *La Jeune Fille à Marier* the comic element is largely surprise; a lady discusses her young and innocent daughter, who has just completed her studies; an expectation of young innocence is built up. Finally the daughter appears: 'She is a man, about thirty years old, robust and virile, with a bushy black moustache, wearing a grey suit.'[2] The same comic principle is used again in *Le Maître*. A radio announcer and two young couples express mounting expectation to see in person a *great man* (the English translation reads, '*the leader*', but it is not quite clear whether the personality concerned might not just as well be a literary figure, more usually addressed as *Maître* in France). In tones of mounting adoration, his actions offstage are ecstatically described – he kisses babies, eats his soup, signs autographs, has his trousers ironed, and so on. When he finally appears, he is a headless body.[3]

1. Ionesco, *Théâtre I* (Paris: Arcanes 1953). Trans. Sasha Moorsom, *The Motor Show*, in *3 Arts Quarterly*, London, no. 2, Summer 1960.

2. Ionesco, *La Jeune Fille à Marier*, in *Théâtre II* (Paris: Gallimard, 1958). Trans. Donald Watson, in *Plays*, vol. III (London: Calder; New York: Grove Press, 1960), p. 158.

3. Ionesco, *Le Maître*, in *Théâtre II*. Trans. Derek Prouse, *The Leader*, in *Plays*, vol. IV (London: Calder; New York: Grove Press, 1960).

In the earlier phase of his career Ionesco liked to express himself in short plays, or at least in one-act plays that can develop without interruption. He found a division into three acts 'rather artificial. The play ends, then restarts, it ends again, restarts again. . . . I don't think one should try to put too much into a play. In a three-act play there are necessarily superfluous things. The theatre needs a very simple idea: a single obsession, a simple, very clear, self-evident development.'[1] His first effort to write a three-act play, *Amédée, ou Comment s'en débarrasser* (*Amédée, or How to get rid of it*), a comedy in three acts, may bear out his misgivings about the longer form, but it contains some of his most haunting images. The play springs from his darkest, most depressive mood, and presents what is probably his most powerful symbol of the proliferation of matter and its stifling of the spirit.

The hero of the play, Amédée Buccinioni, is, like Ionesco, a writer. He is, in fact, writing a play, a play about an old man and an old woman rather like the protagonists of *The Chairs*. But in fifteen years of work he has succeeded in writing only two lines of dialogue:

THE OLD WOMAN: Do you think it will do?
THE OLD MAN: It won't do by itself.[2]

Amédée and his wife, Madeleine (Madeleine again, like the wife in *Victims of Duty*), live cut off from the world. They have not left their apartment for fifteen years, and even haul their supplies through the window in a basket. Yet Madeleine is still in communication with the outside world, through her job – she works at a switchboard in the living-room, where she operates a kind of telephone exchange at certain times of the day. She connects callers even to the office of the President of the Republic, communicates new traffic regulations to inquirers, and so on. The couple are on very bad terms with each other; they quarrel constantly. Madeleine is a hard, nagging

1. Ionesco, interview in *L'Express*, 28 January 1960.
2. Ionesco, *Amédée*, trans. Donald Watson, in *Plays*, vol. II, p. 8.

creature. But the main shadow over the marriage is the presence in the next room of a corpse, the body of a young man who came to call fifteen years ago, and whom Amédée is said, but by no means with certainty, to have killed in a fit of jealousy. Perhaps the corpse is not that of the wife's lover at all. At one point, Amédée suggests that he might have left again at the time the 'crime' was committed. Or again it might be that the corpse is that of a baby a neighbour once left in their care and never called for again. But why should that baby have died?

The corpse in the next room may be dead, but it is very active. Its beard and nails are growing, its eyes glow with an eerie green light, and the dead body itself is growing larger and larger. The corpse is suffering from 'the incurable disease of the dead' – *geometrical progression*. As the play proceeds, this growth accelerates; the door of the next room bursts open, and a gigantic foot pushes into the room. As the corpse grows, mushrooms proliferate in the apartment – images of decay and corruption.

Who or what is the corpse that is growing so relentlessly? A flashback scene supplies some of the clues to the solution of this riddle. Amédée and Madeleine appear as a newly married couple. Amédée is loving, importunate, romantic; Madeleine is petulant, sullen, unwilling to accept his protestations of love, deflating his romantic notions. The imagery of the dialogue is clearly sexual; the situation is that of an ardent lover and a girl who regards all advances as acts of violation and rape: 'Your voice is so piercing! You are deafening me! Hurting me! Don't rend my darkness! S-a-dist! S-a-dist!'[1] When Amédée's younger self hears the voices of spring, children's voices, the phantom Madeleine can merely hear 'oaths and toads'. The scene comes to a climax with Amédée pleading for love: 'What is far can be near. What is withered can grow green again. What is separated can be reunited. What *is* no more, *will be* again', but as Amédée dreams of happiness in their house of

1. ibid., p. 48.

glass, Madeleine insists that their house is of brass[1] – in other words the image of lightness, happiness, and euphoria is countered by the image of heaviness, depression and opacity.

This flashback scene makes it fairly clear that the corpse in the next room is the corpse of the couple's dead love, the victim of their sexual incompatibility. It is a corpse made up of disgust, guilt, and regret. It poisons the atmosphere with the mushrooms of decay and decomposition – and it is growing from day to day, from hour to hour. Amédée quite clearly states that what is rotten in their home is the absence of love: 'Do you know, Madeleine, if we loved each other, if we really loved each other, none of this would be important?' But Madeleine has become hard, unsentimental, and matter of fact: 'Love can't help people get rid of their troubles!'[2]

Amédée must get rid of the corpse, which threatens to burst out of the apartment. With a superhuman effort, he tries to push the endless body out of the window. As Ionesco puts it in the stage direction, the body pulled near the window should give the impression that 'it is dragging the whole house with it and tugging at the entrails of the two principal characters.'[3]

The third act shows Amédée dragging the body through the streets toward the Seine. He meets various people, notably an American soldier outside a bar or brothel. Amédée explains to this foreigner, with whom he is unable to communicate, that he is writing a play in which he is taking the part of the living against the dead, a play against nihilism and for a new humanism. He, Amédée, is for commitment, and believes in progress. As the scene becomes more crowded with people, girls, soldiers, policemen, Amédée continues to assure all and sundry that he is for social realism, against disintegration and nihilism. By this time the corpse has become a kind of balloon, and Amédée is already floating in the air. Madeleine wants him to

1. In the original French the words are *verre* and *fer* (iron).
2. Ionesco, *Amédée*, trans. Donald Watson, in *Plays*, vol. II, pp. 52–3.
3. ibid., p. 62.

come back, the mushrooms are in bloom, but Amédée floats away into the sky.

In *Amédée* we see the two basic moods of Ionesco's experience of the world side by side: heaviness and the proliferation of matter in the first two acts, lightness and evanescence in the third. As Amédée gets rid of the corpse of his dead love, that stifling presence turns into lightness and lifts him into the air. The play, which is simply labelled 'Comedy in Three Acts', is a comedy of liberation, a dream of a new beginning that will abolish the past.

As in *Victims of Duty*, the polemic against the social realists runs as a secondary theme through the whole play. At one point Madeleine tells Amédée that the presence of the corpse in the next room falsifies his perception of reality, makes him see the world in a morbid light – hence his failure to write a socio-logical play. But, as the events of the third act show, the facts of the writer's personal life are more immediate than his social intentions. However much he protests his belief in progress and commitment, the corpse of his past love and personal memor-ies carries him upwards and pulls his feet off the ground.

Amédée contains some of Ionesco's most brilliant images. As a stage symbol of tremendous power and immediate impact the growing corpse is sure of its measure of immortality. The claustrophobic feelings of the couple's private world height-ened by the echoes of the offstage voices of other tenants of the house and thrown into relief when a postman comes to deliver a letter, which plunges them both into a frenzy of fear and causes them to refuse delivery – are made brilliantly concrete. The weakness of the play lies in the third act, which is intended to be rather like the final, frantic chase in the last reel of a Keystone comedy, with soldiers and policemen pursuing each other across the stage. But this intention does not allow itself to be completely realized in the theatre. And the transition from claustrophobia to openness and lightness is a very difficult one to manage on the stage.

In the short story *Oriflamme*,[1] which constitutes a preliminary sketch for the play, the events of the last act occupy barely a page, as against about twelve pages devoted to relating the action of the first two acts. The last paragraph of the story indicates the euphoria of the final floating away even more clearly than the dramatized version:

I still heard the Americans, who thought I was performing some sporting feat, greet me with a 'Hello, boy!' I dropped my clothes, my cigarettes; the policemen divided them between themselves. Then there was only the Milky Way that I traversed, an oriflamme [i.e. like the sacred gold-starred banner of France billowing in the wind] at headlong pace, at headlong pace.[2]

Amédée (the play) is dated Cerisy-la-Salle, August 1953. It was first performed at the Théâtre de Babylone on 14 April 1954, under the direction of Jean-Marie Serrau. Within a few weeks of completing *Amédée*, Ionesco wrote another play, which took him only three days to finish (14–16 September 1953) and which presents the imagery of proliferating matter with renewed force. This play is *Le Nouveau Locataire* (*The New Tenant*), and is in one act. The action consists of an empty room being filled up with the furniture of the new tenant, a mild, middle-aged gentleman who seems unencumbered with worldly goods at first and takes his time carefully placing the first few pieces, but who at the end is literally buried in the unending stream of furniture, at first brought in by two moving-men, but later pouring in by itself. We learn that all the traffic is at a standstill, all the streets of Paris are blocked by more and more furniture, and the bed of the River Seine itself is filled with it.

The New Tenant is a spectacle of terrifying simplicity. Dialogue (between the tenant and the bickering, greedy concierge; between the tenant and the moving-men) is reduced to a secondary role. Primarily, this is a play of objects on the move,

1. Ionesco, '*Oriflamme*', *Nouvelle Revue Française*, February 1954.
2. ibid.

objects overwhelming man, stifling him in a sea of inert matter. A single poetic image is built up before our eyes, first with a certain amount of surprise, later with relentless inevitability. This is a demonstration of the possibilities of *pure* theatre: the concepts of character, conflict, plot-construction have been abandoned – and yet *The New Tenant* remains drama with mounting suspense, excitement, and poetic force. What does it mean? Is the empty room filling up with furniture, slowly at first but later with increasing speed, an image of the life of man, empty at first, but gradually cluttered up with new and repetitive experiences and memories? Or is the play merely a translation into scenic terms of the claustrophobia – the feeling of being hemmed in by heavy, oppressive matter – of the depressive, leaden moods from which Ionesco suffers?

The New Tenant was first performed by a Swedish-speaking company in Finland in 1955. It was presented at the Arts Theatre in London in November 1956, and reached Paris only in September 1957. Yet in spite of setbacks, in spite of the financial disasters of the first productions of his plays, Ionesco's career was making steady progress. Towards the end of 1954, the first volume of his *Théâtre* was published by Gallimard, the leading French publisher, in whose decisions Raymond Queneau, the poet and novelist who had been deeply impressed by Ionesco's first efforts, and whose own experiments with language clearly influenced Ionesco, played an important part. Of the six plays in that first volume, only one had not yet reached the stage when it was published: *Jacques, ou La Soumission*. This omission was repaired in October of the following year, 1955, when Robert Postec presented *Jacques* and another play by Ionesco, *Le Tableau* (*The Picture*), at the Théâtre de la Huchette.

Unlike *Jacques*, which was a success, *The Picture* failed to please, and Ionesco omitted it from the second volume of his plays. But it appeared in the *Dossiers Acénonètes du Collège de Pataphysique*, that distinguished group of followers of Jarry and his Dr Faustroll, among whom Ionesco holds the high rank of a Transcendant Satrap (as do René Clair, Raymond Queneau, Jacques Prévert, and many other famous pataphysicians). It has also been broadcast, in a translation by Donald Watson, on the B.B.C.'s Third Programme (11 and 15 March 1957) and has now been published in volume IV of Ionesco's *Théâtre*.

The Picture is a curious play. It opens with a fat, wealthy gentleman who wants to buy a picture from a painter. They are haggling about the price; the painter wants the buyer to have a look at the picture before he names his price, but the fat gentleman wants to settle that detail first. The painter asks five hundred thousand francs at first, but is relentlessly driven down until, in the end, he is ready to settle for a mere four hundred francs. Only then does the shrewd businessman cast a glance at the picture, which represents a queen, and promptly criticizes it so savagely that the painter finally begs him to keep the picture without any payment. In fact the painter consents to pay the fat gentleman a fee for storing his picture.

The fat gentleman's old and ugly sister enters into the proceedings and is rudely treated by her brother. But the moment the painter has gone, the situation changes abruptly. Alice, the sister, becomes the tyrant and the fat gentleman is reduced to the role of a cowed schoolboy. Left to himself, the fat gentleman, who is starved of beauty and affection, works himself up into a state of frenzy about the picture. As Ionesco says in a footnote,[1] 'The actor playing this part must get as erotic as the censorship permits or the spectators will tolerate.' When his sister reappears, he has again become his old dominating self. He menaces his sister with a gun and finally shoots her. But instead of dying she is transformed, becoming as beautiful as the picture. An ugly woman neighbour wants to be transformed the same way. She too is shot and turned into a beautiful

1. Ionesco, *Le Tableau*, in *Dossiers Acénonètes du Collège de Pataphysique*, no. 1, 1958, p. 44.

princess. The painter returns, admires his patron's ability to create beauty by violence, is shot himself, and becomes a Prince Charming. Shots fired into the air transform the room into a fairy palace. The fat gentleman, who alone remains as fat and ugly as he was, invites the audience to shoot at him.

Ionesco calls *The Picture* a '*guignolade*' – a Punch and Judy play. He attributes its failure at its 1955 performance to the fact that the first part, the haggling over the price with the painter, was acted realistically, as a critique of a capitalist's exploitation of an artist. 'In fact, this Punch and Judy play must be acted by circus clowns in the most childish, exaggerated, idiotic manner possible. . . . The reversals of situations must happen brusquely, violently, crudely, without preparation. . . . It is only by extreme simplification . . . that the meaning of this farce can be brought out and become acceptable through its very unacceptability and idiocy.'[1] The subject of the play, according to the same note, is 'metamorphosis, treated . . . parodistically, to disguise, out of bashfulness, its serious significance'.[2]

It would be rash to attempt to read too much into this intentionally 'idiotic' spectacle. What it seems to be driving at is the vicious circle between the crude commercialism of the Philistine businessman with his mixture of meanness and sentimentality, on the one hand, and, on the other, the supposed transcendence of this ugly world by its antithesis, a world of 'beauty' redeemed by 'art'. But the mean are imprisoned in their own meanness: having killed the ugliness in themselves, having replaced it by what they consider its direct opposite, they merely enter a world of cheap *Kitsch*, a world of operetta with the Princesses and the Prince Charmings of the crudest erotic fantasies. If, at the end of the play, the fat gentleman begs the audience to shoot him, this is merely a variant of the situation in the rejected violent ending of *The Bald Prima Donna*, where the Philistine audience was to have been machine-gunned from the stage. Here the Philistine on the stage wants to

1. ibid., p. 5.   2. ibid.

be shot by the non-Philistines in the audience. And the play itself has demonstrated the futility of any such thing. Shooting, violence, cannot bring about a real transformation; the hope of changing the world or the sensibilities of people by violence is utterly vain and absurd; the changes are as idiotic as the original situation.

At the same time, the play is an experiment in the possibilities of the theatre. Ionesco once said:

I personally would like to bring a tortoise on to the stage, turn it into a race horse, then into a hat, a song, a dragoon, and a fountain of water. One can dare anything in the theatre, and it is the place where one dares the least. I want no other limits than the technical limits of stage machinery. People will say that my plays are music-hall turns or circus acts. So much the better – let's include the circus in the theatre! Let the playwright be accused of being arbitrary. Yes, the theatre is the place where one *can* be arbitrary. As a matter of fact, it is not arbitrary. The imagination is not arbitrary, it is revealing. . . . I have decided not to recognize any laws except those of my imagination, and since the imagination obeys its own laws, this is further proof that in the last resort it is not arbitrary.[1]

These two interpretations of *The Picture*, one in terms of a critique of Philistine sensibility, the other in terms of an experiment in a pure theatre of circus-like transformation-scenes, are in no way contradictory. All of Ionesco's theatre contains two strands side by side – complete freedom in the exercise of his imagination and a strong element of the polemical. His very first play, *The Bald Prima Donna*, was an anti-play, and as such a criticism of the existing theatre as well as of a type of dead society. The same, strongly pugnacious spirit manifests itself in Ionesco's entire *œuvre*, and it is therefore quite wrong to regard him as a mere clown and prankster. Ionesco's plays are a complex mixture of poetry, fantasy, nightmare – and cultural and social criticism. In spite of the fact that Ionesco rejects,

1. '*Eugène Ionesco ouvre le feu*', *World Theatre*, Paris, VIII, 3, Autumn 1959.

and detests, any openly didactic theatre ('I do not teach, I give testimony. I don't explain, I try to explain myself'[1]) he is convinced that any genuinely new and experimental writing is bound to contain a polemical element. 'The man of the avant-garde is in opposition to an existing system. ... An artistic creation is by its very novelty aggressive, spontaneously aggressive; it is directed against the public, against the bulk of the public; it causes indignation by its unusualness, which is itself a form of indignation.'[2]

Ionesco's most openly polemical play, his most direct attack against his critics, is *L'Impromptu de l'Alma, ou Le Caméléon du Berger* (English title: *Improvisation, or The Shepherd's Chameleon*), dated Paris, 1955, and first performed at the Studio des Champs-Elysées in February 1956. By the title alone, Ionesco proclaims his faith that the avant-garde is merely the renewer of tradition – Molière's *L'Impromptu de Versailles*, and Giraudoux's *L'Impromptu de Paris* are clearly alluded to. And, like Molière, Ionesco puts himself on the stage in the act of writing a play – that is, asleep with a ball-point pen in his hand. He is visited by three learned doctors dressed in the gowns of the pompous doctors of Molière's *Malade Imaginaire*, and all three called Bartholomeus – Bartholomeus I, Bartholomeus II, and Bartholomeus III. To the first of these, Ionesco explains that he is in the process of writing a play to be called *The Shepherd's Chameleon*, which is based on a real incident: 'Once, in a large country town, in the middle of the street, during the summer, I saw a young shepherd, about three o'clock in the afternoon, who was embracing a chameleon. ... It was such a touching scene, I decided to turn it into a tragic farce.'[3] But, of course, this is merely the pretext, the starting point of the play he is writing. In reality, Ionesco explains, it will be a play about his

1. Ionesco, '*Pages de journal*', *Nouvelle Revue Française*, February 1960.
2. '*Eugène Ionesco ouvre le feu*'.
3. Ionesco, *Improvisation*, trans. Donald Watson, in *Plays*, vol. III, pp. 112–13.

ideas on playwriting: 'You can say I am the shepherd, if you like, and the theatre is the chameleon. Because I have embraced a theatrical career, and the theatre, of course, changes, for the theatre is life.'[1]

Prevailed upon to read what he has written up to now, Ionesco proceeds to read exactly what the public has seen performed – an ingenious and very characteristic mirror effect, which is immediately reduplicated once again by the arrival of the second Bartholomeus, who repeats the same lines as the first; whereupon the third arrives, repeats the same lines as the first two, asks Ionesco to read his play, Ionesco starts off with the same opening passage. There is a new knock on the door and it seems as though a vicious circle had been established that would go on forever. But this time the person who knocked is not let in, and the discussion can begin. The three doctors are purveyors of a half-Existentialist, half-Brechtian farrago of dramatic theory, with allusions to Adamov, who discovered the Aristotelian principles before Aristotle, Sartre, and, of course, above all, Ionesco's special *bête noire*, Brecht.

Ionesco is rescued from complete stultification by the doctors through the arrival of his charwoman (who has been knocking at the door all the time); she represents common sense and demystification. Ionesco recovers his poise and launches into a confession of his faith as a dramatist. He condemns the three critics for having peddled truisms clothed in extravagant jargon, whereas

the critic should describe and not prescribe ... he should only judge a work on its own terms, according to the laws that govern artistic expression, according to each work's own mythology, by penetrating into its own world. One does not set chemistry to music, one does not judge biology by the criteria of painting or architecture. ... For my part, I believe sincerely in the poverty of the poor, I deplore it, it is real and can serve as material for the theatre; I also believe in the grave cares and anxieties that may beset the rich. But in my case

1. ibid., pp. 113–14.

it is neither from the wretchedness of the poor nor the unhappiness of the rich that I draw the substance of my drama. For me, the theatre is the projection on to the stage of the world within – it is in my dreams, my anguish, my dark desires, my inner contradictions that I reserve the right to find the stuff of my plays. As I am not alone in the world – as each one of us, in the depths of his being, is at the same time everyone else – my dreams and desires, my anguish and my obsessions do not belong to myself alone; they are part of the heritage of my ancestors, a very ancient deposit to which all mankind may lay claim.[1]

At this point, Ionesco's manner becomes more and more pontifical. He begins to quote the names of German and American authorities, and is finally asked whether he is really taking himself seriously after all. Abashed, he recognizes that he has fallen into his own trap and is in danger of himself becoming didactic. He apologizes that this, in his case, is the exception, not the rule, a dig at Brecht's play *The Exception and the Rule*.

L'Impromptu de l'Alma takes us back into the thick of the controversy about the didactic, political theatre, of which the exchange with Kenneth Tynan later became one brilliant, but by no means central, episode. The main attack against Ionesco had been launched by some of the critics who had at first hailed him as a master of the new avant-garde, in the pages of such periodicals as Sartre's *Les Temps Modernes* and the influential *Théâtre Populaire*. It is no concidence that the same number of the latter periodical (dated 1 March 1956) that contained a rather pained notice of *L'Impromptu de l'Alma* and the revival of *The Chairs* with which it shared the bill at the Studio des Champs-Elysées, also published an essay by Adamov on 'Theatre, money and politics', in which he made public confession of his error in having omitted the social theme from his plays that had been performed to date, and called for a revival of a historical, sociological theatre. No wonder that the review of *The Chairs* by Maurice Regnaut, in spite of high praise for

1. ibid., pp. 149–50.

direction and performance, culminates in the question, 'Why, then, in spite of all this, should we too feel ourselves "cheated"? It is because we have been provoked into taking an interest in what basically does not concern us at all. This piece has objective reality only to that extent to which the postulate of the lyrical confession is true. More than Ionesco himself, we need to believe that "one is all people". But the old mystification cannot long conceal the emptiness of this theatre. To transform the theatre into music is the last artistic dream of the petty-bourgeois as Gorki has defined him: man who prefers himself.'[1]

Thus the battle was joined between the historical, sociological, epic theatre and the lyrical, poetical theatre of the world within, the theatre of dream, mood, and being. We shall return to a discussion of these two basic points of view of the contemporary theatre in a later chapter. Here it must be noted that the final parting of the ways between Ionesco's conception and that of Brecht and his newly converted follower Adamov coincided with the breakthrough of Ionesco into the world of acceptance and success – a sure sign in the eyes of his opponents that the bourgeoisie had at last recognized the man who best expressed their decadent point of view.

Not only in France but in other countries as well, performances of Ionesco's plays became more frequent. There were still scandals like the one in Brussels where the audience at a performance of *The Lesson* demanded their money back, and the leading actor had to escape through a back door, but also surprising successes in countries like Yugoslavia and Poland, where *The Chairs* was performed with the old couple in workmen's overalls. Within six years of the first disastrous performance of *The Bald Prima Donna*, Ionesco had arrived.

Being an accepted author involved Ionesco in some strange adventures that might have come straight out of one of his own plays. In May 1957, some London papers reported that 'the Duke and Duchess of Windsor and ten other guests were

1. *Théâtre Populaire*, Paris, no. 17, 1 March 1956, p. 77.

present at a remarkable theatre performance given recently in the Paris home of the Argentine millionaire, M. Anchorena'[1] and that the play presented had been by Ionesco, with music specially composed by Pierre Boulez. A few days later, London papers speculated on the possibility that this play, *Impromptu pour la Duchesse de Windsor*, might be performed in England, but, as the *Daily Mail* put it, 'It's going to cause some head-aches' to the Lord Chamberlain. The *Evening News* of the same day, 31 May 1957, even spoke of the Duchess of Windsor having refused permission to have the little play performed in London. Yet, according to the *Daily Mail* again, Ionesco had commented that the Duke and Duchess 'seemed quite amused'.

In fact Ionesco's second *Impromptu* is a very slight, but witty and utterly harmless party joke: a short scene in which The Lady of the House discusses with the author and an actress what they might present to amuse the Duke and Duchess of Windsor. This leads to a discussion of Ionesco's own work and of his favourite theme of the identity of comedy and tragedy. When the lady of the house asks Ionesco not to present 'a sad play, one of those modern dramas like those by Beckett or Sophocles, which might make people cry,' he answers, 'Some-times, Madame, comedies make people cry even more than dramas . . . the comedies that I write. When I want to write a tragedy I make them laugh, when I write a comedy, I make them cry.'[2] There is also a very amusing nonsense version of English history as seen by a Frenchman, and an equally charac-teristic sequence of semantic misunderstandings about spirits: when offered a glass of whisky by the lady of the house, the author maintains that it is gin, while the actress tastes it and pronounces it Bénédictine. When the author, out of politeness, comes round to accepting it as whisky, the others, also from politeness, accept each other's interpretations, increasing the

1. Sam White, 'Paris Newsletter', *Evening Standard*, London, 24 May 1957.

2. Ionesco, *Impromptu pour la Duchesse de Windsor*, ms., pp. 6–7.

confusion. The discussion of what might amuse the royal guests finally ends in complete deadlock and the piece concludes with the apologies of the hostess. As, according to the *Evening Standard*, Mme Marcel Achard, the wife of the playwright, remarked after the performance, 'Only Ionesco could have handled such a delicate subject.' Salvador Dali, another of the privileged number of guests, merely remarked, 'It was most moving.'

The composition of such a lighthearted trifle did not distract Ionesco overmuch from more ambitious and artistically more rewarding objectives. In November 1955, the *Nouvelle Revue Française* had published a short story by him that was later to grow into one of his major plays. (Altogether five of Ionesco's plays are elaborations of drafts written in the form of stories: *Une Victime du Devoir*, published in the review *Medium*, which later became *Victims of Duty*; *Oriflamme*, in the *Nouvelle Revue Française*, February 1954, which became *Amédée*; *Rhinocéros*, in *Les Lettres Nouvelles*, September 1957; *La Photo du Colonel*, in the *Nouvelle Revue Française*, November 1955; and *Le Piéton de l'Air* in the *Nouvelle Revue Française*, February 1961.) This particular story was *La Photo du Colonel* (*The Photograph of the Colonel*),[1] which became the basis of the play Ionesco completed during a stay in London in August 1957 – *Tueur Sans Gages*, entitled in the English translation *The Killer*, which does not quite do justice to the implications of the French, which means *Killer Without Reward* (or payment); that is, a gratuitous, purposeless killer.

Tueur Sans Gages is Ionesco's second three-act work, and not only one of his most ambitious, but also probably his finest play. Bérenger, its hero, is a Chaplinesque little man, simple, awkward, but human. As the play opens, he is being shown round an ambitious new housing project by its creator, the municipal architect. This is a beautiful new quarter of the town,

1. Trans. Stanley Read, *Evergreen Review*, I, 3, 1957. Another trans., by Jean Stewart, in *The Colonel's Photograph*, London: Faber & Faber, 1967.

well-designed, with pleasant gardens and a pond. What is more, as the architect explains, permanent sunshine is built into the project; however much it may rain in other parts of the city, the moment you cross the boundary of the *cité radieuse*, the radiant city, you enter a climate of perpetual spring.

Bérenger, who never realized that such perfection of modern design or planning existed, and who strayed into this new world by pure chance, is deeply moved. But why, he asks, are the streets of this lovely quarter so deserted? He is shattered to hear that the inhabitants have either left or have locked themselves into their houses, because a mysterious killer is abroad in this happy place, who lures his victims to their death by promising to show them 'the photograph of the colonel'. The architect, who reveals that he also exercises the functions of a police commissar and those of a doctor, cannot understand Bérenger's horror at his revelation. After all, the world is full of misery: 'Children murdered, starved old men, widows in distress, orphans, people in agony, judicial errors, houses that collapse on their inhabitants . . . mountains that come down in landslides . . . massacres, floods, dogs run over by cars – that's how the journalists earn their daily bread.' Bérenger is appalled. And when news comes that among the latest victims is Mlle Dany, the architect's young secretary, whom he had just met and with whom he had fallen in love, he resolves to track down the killer.

The second act opens in Bérenger's dingy room, where a visitor, Edouard, is silently waiting for him. Outside we hear the voices of the inhabitants of the block conversing in absurd fragments of small talk; a teacher giving a nonsensical history lesson; an efficiency expert calculating the money to be saved by stopping employees from going to the lavatory five times each day and making them concentrate these natural functions into one session of four and a half hours per month instead; old men talking of old times – a whole symphony of grotesque snippets of talk that take up and expand the voices on the

landing heard offstage in *Amédée*. Bérenger returns, tells
Edouard the horrible news about the killer, and is astonished to
find that Edouard, in fact everybody, has long known about
him, that everyone is used to the idea that such a killer is abroad.
Edouard's briefcase opens and is revealed to contain the implements of the killer – the knick-knacks he pretends to be selling,
stacks of photos of a colonel, even the killer's identity card.
Edouard says he must have picked up the briefcase by mistake,
but mysteriously he has further evidence in his coat pocket – the
diary of the killer, a map on which the exact spots of past and
even future murders are marked. Bérenger wants to go to the
police. Edouard is reluctant. Finally they go, but Edouard
leaves the briefcase behind.

In the street a political meeting is in progress; a monstrous
woman, *la mère Pipe*, described as the keeper of the public geese
and resembling Bérenger's concierge, makes a speech composed of totalitarian clichés. In the world after her victory,
everything will be different, at least in name, although the
substance of things will remain the same. Tyranny will then be
called liberty, occupation will be called liberation. A drunk
interrupts the speech; he represents the opposite (Ionesco's
own) point of view – the real revolution, he argues, as Ionesco
did in his final reply to Tynan, is made not by politicians but by
artists and thinkers like Einstein, Breton, Kandinsky, Picasso,
who change mankind's way of seeing and thinking. In a Punch
and Judy fight, the drunk is knocked out. Bérenger discovers
that the briefcase has been lost. In a nightmare sequence, he tries
to wrest similar briefcases from the hands of passers-by, attempts to interest the police in finding the killer, but the police
have more important things to do. They have to control the
traffic.

Bérenger is alone. He walks through the empty streets, the
décor changing as he progresses. Suddenly he finds himself face
to face with a grinning, giggling dwarf in shabby clothes. He
knows that this is the killer. In a long speech (covering about

ten closely printed pages in the French edition), Bérenger tries to persuade the killer, who is obviously a degenerate idiot, to desist from his murderous and senseless activity. He uses every known argument for philanthropy and goodness – patriotism, self-interest, social responsibility, Christianity, reason, the vanity of all activity, even that of murder. The killer never speaks a word, he merely giggles idiotically. In the end Bérenger pulls out two old guns and tries to kill the killer, but he cannot do it. He drops the guns and silently submits to the killer's raised knife.

In a note, Ionesco underlines the intention of this last scene, which, as he says, 'is a short act in itself'. The speech should be presented in a manner designed 'to bring out the gradual breaking down of Bérenger, his falling apart and the vacuity of his own rather commonplace morality, which collapses like a leaking balloon. In fact Bérenger finds within himself, in spite of himself and against his own will, arguments in favour of the killer.'[1] The killer (who, Ionesco suggests in a stage direction, might not be seen at all, only his giggle being heard in the shadows) represents the inevitability of death, the absurdity of human existence itself. This is the murderous presence that lurks behind even the most euphoric moods of lightness and radiant happiness and turns them back into the cold, grey, rainy November of our everyday existence.

In the first act, Bérenger describes at length the experience the *cité radieuse* expresses – the warmth that in former times used to fill his soul from within, the indescribable feeling of euphoria and light that made him cry out with joy, 'I am, I am, everything is, everything is!' And then suddenly a feeling of emptiness invaded his soul as at the moment of a tragic separation, 'old women came out of their courtyards and pierced my ears with their loud, vulgar voices; dogs barked; and I felt myself abandoned among all these people, all these things.' This is the mood we are presented with in the second act in the

1. *The Killer*, trans. Donald Watson, in *Plays*, vol. III, p. 9.

symphony of gossiping voices in the courtyard, and later, in the horrible political meeting, in the traffic regulated by policemen. It is the realization, accepted by everybody else – that life is futile in the face of inevitable death – which changes euphoria into depression. Death is the photograph of the colonel, which exercises such a fatal fascination on the killer's victims. No argument of morality or expediency can prevail against the half-witted, idiotic futility of the human condition.

Once again the whole play elaborates a single poetic image, but this time its power is sustained and deepened as the action proceeds and, in contrast to the decline of tension in the third act of *Amédée*, the final scene of *Tueur Sans Gages* is so brilliant a *tour de force* that it is capable of forming a climax even after the astonishing poetic invention of the *cité radieuse* in the first scene.

It is significant that the last brilliant speech is hardly fore-shadowed in the short story that was the germ of the play. There the hero merely realizes that 'no words, friendly or authoritative, could have convinced him; all the promise of happiness, all the love in the world, could not have reached him; beauty would not have made him relent, nor irony have shamed him, nor all the wise men in the world make him com-prehend the vanity of crime as well as charity.' The translation of this brief paragraph into a breathtakingly dramatic speech shows Ionesco's immense power as a dramatist.

There is another element not present in the short story of 1955 that occupies an important place in the play of 1957 – the political meeting and the argument about the true revolution. This is a measure of Ionesco's growing preoccupation with the polemic against his left-wing critics. It might be argued that the introduction of this anti-political – but for that very reason itself political – element distracts from the main poetic image of the play. After all, the *cité radieuse* of the opening scene is a more powerful argument for the same position. It is an image of a world in which all social problems have been solved, all irritation eliminated; and yet, even there, the presence of death makes life futile and absurd. On the other hand, the crowd scenes, with their nightmare tumult and agitation, are a legitimate extension of the images of proliferation and heaviness in Bérenger's diagnosis of his depressive mood.

Tueur Sans Gages was staged with considerable success at the Théâtre Récamier in February 1959. When it reached New York in April 1960, it met with less understanding and had to close after a few performances. Brooks Atkinson found the third act 'bad theatre writing' because the last scene is static and therefore 'unbearable nervously as well as esthetically'.[1] Yet this is precisely what the scene is supposed to be – unbearable. For in spite of its being laced with a bitter, farcically tragic humour, Ionesco's is a far harsher convention of the theatre than one based on mere pleasantness. The mixture of the farcical and the tragic also confronts the public with an entirely new convention; no wonder Brooks Atkinson found the play an accumulation of 'helter-skelter gibes'. Within its own terms of reference, *Tueur Sans Gages* is a work of classical purity of style as well as language – at least in the original French.

Tueur Sans Gages, moreover, is not only based on a brilliant overall conception, it is full of the most felicitous touches of detail: the *cité radieuse*, for example, has such perfect built-in sunshine that to produce plants that need rain, special glass houses have to be provided. The architect, showing Bérenger round the new quarter, continues his office routine on a telephone he casually pulls out of his pocket. The architect's secretary, Mlle Dany, cannot stand her office routine and decides to quit. This is the reason for her murder – the killer does not attack municipal employees, and by choosing freedom she chooses death. But the architect merely shrugs his shoulders at people's mania, 'the mania of the victims always to return to the place of the crime'. Among the killer's implements in Edouard's briefcase there is a box that has another box inside it, which in turn has another inside it, and so on *ad infinitum*. In the

1. *New York Times*, 3 April 1960.

crowd at the political meeting, a little old man asks the way to the Danube, although he is aware of being in Paris and is in fact a Parisian. All this is a wealth of invention that helps to conjure up Ionesco's own peculiar world of nightmare, Chaplinesque humour, and wistful tenderness. *Tueur Sans Gages* must rank as one of the major works of the Theatre of the Absurd.

Before *Tueur Sans Gages* had its first stage performance, Ionesco revealed that he had completed another full-length play, *Rhinocéros*. On 25 November 1958, he gave a public reading of the third act at the Vieux-Colombier, after having told the audience that 'a play is made to be acted, not to be read. If I were you, I should not have come.' By the following spring the play had appeared in book form (but in a note in the *Cahiers du Collège de Pataphysique*,[1] Ionesco insisted that his publishers had got the title wrong by calling the play *Le Rhinocéros* instead of simply *Rhinocéros*). On 20 August 1959, the play, already translated into English by Derek Prouse, had its first performance – on the radio, in the B.B.C.'s Third Programme; on 6 November, it had its world première on the stage in Düsseldorf; on 25 January 1960, it opened at the Odéon in Paris, directed and acted by Jean-Louis Barrault, and on 28 April of the same year at the Royal Court in London, directed by Orson Welles, with Sir Laurence Olivier as Bérenger. The era of Ionesco's international acceptance as a major figure in the theatre undoubtedly dawned with *Rhinocéros*.

Rhinocéros again has Bérenger as its hero – inexplicably, if we assume that Bérenger was killed at the end of *Tueur Sans Gages*; an assumption, however, that is by no means a certainty, for, after all, the short story *The Photograph of the Colonel* is narrated in the first person singular, proof that its hero lived to tell the tale, and in the play the curtain falls before any fatal blow has been struck. But these pataphysical speculations are in vain if the character of Bérenger in the two plays is compared, for then a subtle difference between the two is certain to be detected.

1. *Cahiers du Collège de Pataphysique, Dossier 7, 1959.*

The Bérenger of *Rhinocéros* is less sombre, though more dissipated; more poetical, though less idealistic than the Bérenger of *Tueur Sans Gages*. While the latter lives in Paris, the former inhabits a small provincial city. In short, they are not necessarily the same person; or it may be that the Bérenger of *Rhinocéros* is a younger Bérenger, in an earlier phase of his career.

The Bérenger of *Rhinocéros* works (as Ionesco did at one time) in the production department of a firm of law publishers. He is in love with a colleague, Mlle Daisy (whose name curiously resembles that of the first Bérenger's love, Dany); he has a friend named Jean. On a Sunday morning the two are involved in an incident in which one, or perhaps two, rhinos are observed, or believed to be observed, charging down the main street of the town. Gradually more and more rhinos appear. They are the inhabitants who have been infected by a mysterious disease, rhinoceritis, which not only makes them change into rhinos but actually makes them want to turn themselves into these strong, aggressive, and insensitive pachyderms. At the end, only Bérenger and Daisy remain human in the whole town, then even Daisy cannot resist the temptation of doing what came naturally to all the others. Bérenger is left alone, the last human being, and defiantly proclaims his intention never to capitulate.

It has been said that *Rhinocéros* represents Ionesco's feelings before he left Rumania in 1938, when more and more of his acquaintances adhered to the Fascist movement of the Iron Guard. As he himself has said:

As usual, I went back to my personal obsessions. I remembered that in the course of my life I have been very much struck by what one might call the current of opinion, by its rapid evolution, its power of contagion, which is that of a real epidemic. People allow themselves suddenly to be invaded by a new religion, a doctrine, a fanaticism. . . . At such moments we witness a veritable mental mutation. I don't know if you have noticed it, but when people no longer share your opinions, when you can no longer make yourself understood by them, one has the impression of being confronted with monsters – rhinos, for example. They have that mixture of candour and ferocity. They would kill you with the best of consciences. And history has shown us during the last quarter of a century that people thus transformed not only resemble rhinos, but really become rhinoceroses.[1]

During the first performance at the Düsseldorf Schauspiel-haus, the German audience instantly recognized the arguments used by the characters who feel they must follow the trend as those they themselves had heard, or used, at a time when people in Germany could not resist the lure of Hitler. Some of the characters in the play opt for a pachydermatous existence because they admire brute force and the simplicity that springs from the suppression of over-tender humanistic feelings; others do so because one can try to win the rhinos back to humanity only by learning to understand their way of think-ing; still others, notably Daisy, simply cannot bear being differ-ent from the majority. Rhinoceritis is not only the disease of the totalitarians of the Right as well as of the Left, it is also the pull of conformism. *Rhinocéros* is a witty play. It abounds in brilliant touches, and – unlike most plays by Ionesco – it seems easily understood. The London *Times* headed its review of *Rhinocéros*, 'Ionesco Play All Easily Comprehensible'.[2]

Yet, is it really as easily comprehensible as all that? As Bernard Francueil pointed out in an ingenious article in the *Cahiers du Collège de Pataphysique*,[3] Bérenger's final confession of faith and his previous assertions of the superiority of human beings over rhinos curiously resemble the cries of 'Long live the white race!' in *L'Avenir est dans les Œufs* and in *Victimes du Devoir*. If we examine Bérenger's final reasoning with his friend Dudard, we find that he defends his desire to remain

1. Ionesco, interview with Claude Sarraute, *Le Monde*, 17 January 1960.

2. *The Times*, London, 29 April 1960.

3. *Cahiers du Collège de Pataphysique*, Dossiers *10–11*, 1960.

human with the same recourse to *instinctive* feelings that he condemns in the rhinos, and when he notices this error, he merely corrects himself by replacing instinct with intuition. Moreover, at the very end, Bérenger bitterly regrets that he seems unable to change into a rhinoceros! His final defiant profession of faith in humanity is merely the expression of the fox's contempt for the grapes he could not have. Far from being a heroic last stand, Bérenger's defiance is farcical and tragicomic, and the final meaning of the play is by no means as simple as some critics made it appear. What the play conveys is the absurdity of defiance as much as the absurdity of conformism, the tragedy of the individualist who cannot join the happy throng of less sensitive people, the artist's feelings as an outcast, which forms the theme of writers like Kafka and Thomas Mann. In a sense, Bérenger's situation at the end of *Rhinocéros* resembles that of the victim of another metamorphosis, Kafka's Gregor Samsa. Samsa was transformed into a giant bug while the rest of humanity remained normal; Bérenger, having become the last human being, is in exactly the same position as Samsa, for now that being a rhinoceros is normal, to be human is a monstrosity. In his last speech, Bérenger deplores the whiteness and flabbiness of his skin and longs for the hardness and dark-green colour of the pachyderm's armour. 'I am a monster, just a monster,' he cries, before he finally decides to make a stand for humanity.

If *Rhinocéros* is a tract against conformism and insensitivity (which it certainly is), it also mocks the individualist who merely makes a virtue of necessity in insisting on his superiority as a sensitive, artistic being. That is where the play transcends the oversimplification of propaganda and becomes a valid statement of the fatal entanglement, the basic inescapability and absurdity of the human condition. Only a performance that brings out this ambivalence in Bérenger's final stand can do justice to the play's full flavour.

Bérenger reappears in two further plays: *Le Piéton de l'Air (A*

Stroll in the Air) and *Le Roi se Meurt* (*Exit the King*). The latter play, which Ionesco completed after *Le Piéton de l'Air*, reached the stage slightly earlier. It was first performed under Jacques Mauclair's direction in Paris on 15 December 1962, while *Le Piéton de l'Air* followed at the Odéon, with Jean-Louis Barrault again as Bérenger and under his direction, on 8 February 1963.

Le Piéton de l'Air brings Bérenger, accompanied this time by wife and daughter, to an England conceived in the style of Douanier Rousseau, Chagall or Utrillo. Many of the clichés about England we know from *The Bald Prima Donna* reappear. But the climax of the play comes when Bérenger, who has acquired the ability to fly through the air and has floated out of sight, returns and recounts a veritable vision of hell. Here Bérenger is clearly the artist who alternates between elation and depression and alienates the bystanders by the deep gloom of his insights into the human condition.

Le Roi se Meurt, equally dark as a play, marks Ionesco's breakthrough to a new level of almost classical formal control. Now Bérenger is a king, but his powers are failing, his kingdom is shrinking, and he is informed that he will die within an hour and a half. The whole play thus becomes a relentless, preordained ritual of King Bérenger's decline and death. As he loses his power over his guard – the last remaining soldier – his servant and his two wives, his world disintegrates, even the furniture disappears. And in the end he is all alone in the void, sitting on his throne. Then that too dissolves into thin air.

With *La Soif et la Faim* (*Hunger and Thirst*) Ionesco achieved final acceptance as a modern classic. The play was acquired by the Comédie Française and opened there, with Robert Hirsch in the leading part, on 28 February 1966. It shows a Bérenger-like hero, now simply called Jean, leaving his wife and family, vainly waiting for a romantic lady with whom he thinks he has a rendezvous; and finally watching a strange ceremony at a mixture of monastery, barracks and prison, called La Bonne Auberge, the torture of two figures in cages, Tripp and Brechtoll, who clearly represent different conceptions of life and of drama (the allusion to Brecht – always one of Ionesco's favourite bugbears – is only too clear). While effective as theatre, *La Soif et la Faim* has little coherence and sometimes falls into a romanticism reminiscent of a far earlier period of drama. It is ironical that Ionesco should have reached official acceptance in France with a play which seems not particularly successful, nor particularly characteristic of Ionesco's own peculiar world.

In the plays which followed, Ionesco returned to a more openly parodic vein: *Jeux de Massacre* (1970) derives its title (*Here Comes a Chopper* in the English, *Killing Game* in the American translation) from the fairground booth which provides visitors with the pleasure of knocking down large numbers of doll-like figures. The play, inspired to a certain extent by Defoe's *Journal of the Plague Year*, shows a community invaded by a mysterious disease which suddenly and instantly kills large numbers of people, in all the varying situations of daily life. The politician making a speech drops dead, the lover declaring his love drops dead, everybody suddenly drops dead. At first this spectacle is disturbing, but as the number of characters who die in a loose sequence of sketch-like scenes increases the mechanical succession of deaths does become funny, so that the play can be described as a riotously hilarious Dance of Death, a powerfully grotesque and at the same time tragic image.

The mechanical recurrence of horror is again the main theme of *Macbett* (1972) which is also a parody – or perhaps a modernized and extended variation on Shakespeare's *Macbeth*. Here the future Lady Macbett is the wife of Duncan; she incites Macbett to kill her husband and so becomes Lady Macbett. She is also one of the witches who arouse Macbett's and Banco's – these are Ionesco's spellings of the names – ambitions. And at the end, as in Shakespeare's play, Macbett in turn is overthrown by Macol (Ionesco's Malcolm) who, however, ends the play with the speech, taken from Shakespeare, in which he describes the wickedness of his character and the horrors of his reign to come, not, as in the original play, to test Macduff's loyalty, but as a sincere declaration of his intentions. Thus the wheel of power turns incessantly – and inexorably all power corrupts.

Ce Formidable Bordel (1973), (*Oh What a Bloody Circus* in the English, *A Hell of a Mess* in the American translation), Ionesco's next full-length play, is based on his novel *Le Solitaire* (1973) and tells the story of a middle-aged man, merely called *le Personnage* (the person or character), who, after years of drudgery in an office job, achieves independence through an inheritance and then gradually withdraws from the world while outside revolution and civil war rage.

L'Homme aux Valises (1975) (*Man with Bags*) presents a similarly alienated character, simply called *Premier Homme*, first man, who is carrying two suitcases, having lost a third, and is seeking recognition of his identity. The action is fluid and episodic and is clearly meant to portray a dream-situation: time and place are undefined and constantly changing; Paris becomes Venice and the past the present. The characters have lost any individuality, even that of types, and have become mere emanations of the dreamer's solipsistic preoccupation with his own elusive self.

In *L'Homme aux Valises*, as in the film *La Vase* (1971; in which Ionesco himself played the lead, a man who withdraws from the world and in the end sinks into the mud and dissolves), the main theme is one of rejection of the world which is depicted as a bungled creation.

It is perhaps ironic that these sentiments were expressed by Ionesco in the period of his acceptance by the world and his recognition by the powers that be as a member of the establishment. Production of his plays by the Comédie Française was followed, in 1971, by Ionesco's reception into the most august body of French literary life, the Académie Française. With this the little Rumanian immigrant had finally arrived.

Ionesco's flowering into a dramatist of world-wide fame has been an astonishing phenomenon. He did not begin writing

The Bald Prima Donna until he was thirty-six. It is a case of a long-pent-up power of expression, which had been seeking for the right form, suddenly finding its true medium – dialogue. The ready-made dialogue of the English primer revealed to Ionesco where his true vocation lay – in the theatre that he had disliked hitherto, precisely because its prevailing convention ran counter to his own personal dramatic perceptions and intuitions. He had been *writing* all his life, as he confesses in the fragment of his diaries for 1939 that has been published,[1] but the reflections and notes he put down did not amount to more than a personal record. Yet in the same extract from Ionesco's diary we already find him jotting down the idea for a dramatic sketch – a woman talking to a man offstage, and enacting what is obviously a highly emotional scene entirely in fragments of clichés and repetitions of the same stereotyped phrases, without the reader (or spectator) ever knowing what is actually at issue. This short sketch shows that Ionesco's mind was running along the lines of his later dramatic writing ten years before his encounter with the *Assimil* method finally sparked off his latent powers as a dramatist.

Ionesco is a highly intuitive writer. He himself described his method of work in a slightly bantering and exaggerated, but nevertheless convincing, way when he said:

It is obviously difficult to write a play; it requires considerable physical effort. One has to get up, which is tiresome, one has to sit down, just when one had got used to the idea of standing up, one has to take a pen, which is heavy, one has to get some paper, which one cannot find, one has to sit at a table, which often breaks down under the weight of one's elbows. . . . It is relatively easy, on the other hand, to compose a play without writing it down. It is easy to imagine it, to dream it, stretched out on the couch between sleep and waking. One only has to let oneself go, without moving, without controlling oneself. A character emerges, one does not know whence; he calls

1. '*Printemps 1939*', loc. cit., p. 98.

others. The first character starts talking, the first retort is made, the first note has been struck, the rest follows automatically. One remains passive, one listens, one watches what is happening on the inner screen . . .[1]

Ionesco regards spontaneity as an important creative element. 'I have no ideas before I write a play. I have them when I have written the play or while I am not writing at all. I believe that artistic creation is spontaneous. It certainly is so for me.'[2] But this does not mean that he considers his writing to be meaningless or without significance. On the contrary, the workings of the spontaneous imagination are a cognitive process, an exploration. 'Fantasy is revealing; it is a method of cognition; everything that is imagined is true; nothing is true if it is not imagined.'[3] Everything that springs from the imagination expresses a psychological reality: 'Because the artist apprehends reality directly, he is a true philosopher. And it is from the range, the depth and the sharpness of his truly philosophical vision that his greatness springs.'[4]

The spontaneity of the creative vision is in itself an instrument of philosophical exploration and discovery. But spontaneity does not mean artlessness; the true artist has mastered his technical means to such an extent that he can apply them without conscious reflection, just as a good ballet dancer has so thoroughly mastered the technique of dancing that she can concentrate wholly on expressing the music and the feelings of the character she portrays. Ionesco is far from neglecting the formal aspect of playwriting – he is a master craftsman and a classicist. He believes that 'the aim of the avant-garde should be to rediscover – not invent – in their purest state the permanent forms and forgotten ideals of the theatre. We must cut through

1. Preface to *Les Possédés*.
2. '*Expérience du théâtre*', loc. cit., p. 268.
3. Ionesco, '*La démystification par l'humour noir*', *L'Avant-Scène*, Paris, 15 February 1959.
4. '*Expérience du théâtre*', loc. cit., p. 270.

the clichés and break free from a hidebound "traditionalism";
we must rediscover the one true and living tradition.'[1]

This is why Ionesco is preoccupied with isolating the 'pure'
elements of theatre, with discovering and laying bare the
mechanism of action even if it is devoid of sense. This is why,
although he does not like Labiche, he is fascinated by Feydeau
and was astonished to find some similarities to his own plays in
Feydeau's farces –

not in the subject-matter but in the rhythm. In the organization of a
play like *La Puce à l'Oreille*, for example, there is a kind of acceleration
of movement, a progression, a kind of madness. In it one might
discover the essence of theatre, or at least the essence of the comic. . . .
For, if Feydeau pleases, it is not for his ideas (he has none) nor for the
stories of his characters (they are silly); it is this madness, this seemingly regulated mechanism that, however, comes apart through its
very progression and acceleration.[2]

Ionesco compares his classicism, his attempt to rediscover
'the mechanism of the theatre in its pure state', with this principle of acceleration in Feydeau's farces: 'In *The Lesson*, for
example, there is no story, but there is a progression nevertheless. I try to bring about a progression by a kind of progressive
condensation of states of mind, of a feeling, a situation, an
anxiety. The text is merely a pretext for the acting of the cast,
starting from the comic toward a progressive heightening. The
text is merely a prop, a pretext for this intensification.'[3] From
The Bald Prima Donna to *Rhinocéros*, this condensation and intensification of the action represent the basic formal principle,
the shape of Ionesco's plays, in contrast to those of Beckett and
Adamov (until his breach with the Theatre of the Absurd),
which have a circular shape, returning to the initial situation or
to its equivalent, a zero point from which the preceding action
is seen to be futile, so that it would have made no difference if it
had never happened. It is true that *The Bald Prima Donna* and

1. 'The world of Ionesco'.
2. Interview in *L'Express*, 28 January 1960.   3. ibid.

The Lesson end as they started – with the Martins (or, in the Paris production, the Smiths) beginning to speak the same dialogue we heard at the beginning of the play, and with a new pupil arriving for a new lesson. But in the case of *The Bald Prima Donna* this ending is an afterthought; Ionesco's original intention was to top the pandemonium of the final scene by direct aggression against the audience. And in *The Lesson* we know that the forty-first pupil of that day will be murdered in the same frenzied fashion as the fortieth – that there will be another inevitable, and even more frenzied, climax. This in fact is the pattern of most of Ionesco's plays: we find the same acceleration and accumulation in the obscene final frenzy of *Jacques* as well as in the growing proliferation of furniture in *The New Tenant*, in the more and more crowded room in *The Chairs*, and in the growing number of transformations in *Rhinocéros*.

Intensification, accumulation, and progression, however, must not, Ionesco insists, be confounded with the storyteller's endeavour to build action toward a climax. In the narrative, the climax leads toward the final solution of a problem. And Ionesco detests 'the reasoning play, constructed like a syllogism, of which the last scenes constitute the logical conclusion of the introductory scenes, considered as premisses.'[1] Ionesco repudiates the well-made, storytelling play:

I do not write plays to tell a story. The theatre cannot be epic ... because it is dramatic. For me, a play does not consist in the description of the development of such a story – that would be writing a novel or a film. A play is a structure that consists of a series of states of consciousness, or situations, which become intensified, grow more and more dense, then get entangled, either to be disentangled again or to end in unbearable inextricability.[2]

To the elegant, logical construction of the well-made play, Ionesco opposes, instead, the demand for intensity, the gradual

1. Ionesco, '*Théâtre et anti-théâtre*', *Cahiers des Saisons*, no. 2, October 1955.
2. '*Pages de journal*', loc. cit., p. 231.

heightening of psychological tensions. To bring this about, the author, in Ionesco's view, is bound by no rule or restraint:

Everything is permitted in the theatre: to bring characters to life, but also to materialize states of anxiety, inner presences. It is thus not only permitted, but advisable, to make the properties join in the action, to make objects live, to animate the décor, to make symbols concrete. Just as words are continued by gesture, action, mime, which, at the moment when words become inadequate, take their place, the material elements of the stage can in turn further intensify these.[1]

Language is thus reduced to a relatively minor function. According to Ionesco, the theatre cannot hope to challenge those forms of expression in which language is entirely autonomous – the discursive speech of philosophy, the descriptive language of poetry or fiction. For this, he argues, the use of language of the theatre is too narrowly circumscribed to language as 'dialogue, words in combat, in conflict'.[2] In the theatre language is not an end in itself but merely one element among many; the author can treat it freely, he can make the action contradict the text, or can let the language of the characters disintegrate altogether. And this too is a device serving the pattern of intensification that underlies Ionesco's theatre. Language can be turned into theatrical material by 'carrying it to its paroxysm. To give the theatre its true measure, which lies in going to excess, the words themselves must be stretched to their utmost limits, the language must be made almost to explode, or to destroy itself in its inability to contain its meaning.'[3]

The pattern of Ionesco's plays is one of intensification, acceleration, accumulation, proliferation to the point of paroxysm, when psychological tension reaches the unbearable – the pattern of orgasm. It must be followed by a release that relieves the tension and substitutes a feeling of serenity. This liberation

1. 'Expérience du théâtre', loc. cit., p. 262.
2. ibid.   3. ibid.

takes the form of laughter. And that is why Ionesco's plays are comic.

'As far as I am concerned,' says Ionesco, 'I have never been able to understand the difference that is made between the comic and the tragic. As the comic is the intuition of the absurd, it seems to me more conducive to despair than the tragic. The comic offers no way out. I say "conducive to despair", but in reality it is beyond despair or hope.'[1] But this is precisely the liberating effect of laughter:

Humour makes us conscious, with a free lucidity, of the tragic or desultory condition of man. . . . It is not only the critical spirit itself . . . but . . . humour is the only possibility we possess of detaching ourselves – yet only after we have surmounted, assimilated, taken cognizance of it – from our tragicomic human condition, the malaise of being. To become conscious of what is horrifying and to laugh at it is to become master of that which is horrifying. . . . Logic reveals itself in the illogicality of the absurd of which we have become aware. Laughter alone does not respect any taboo, laughter alone inhibits the creation of new anti-taboo taboos; the comic alone is capable of giving us the strength to bear the tragedy of existence. The true nature of things, truth itself, can be revealed to us only by fantasy, which is more realistic than all the realisms.[2]

Yet if Ionesco again and again insists on the exploratory, cognitive function of his theatre, one must always keep in mind what *kind* of cognition it is he wants to communicate. Bewildered critics first confronted with an Ionesco play like *The Chairs* or *The Killer* are apt to ask what these plays seek to demonstrate; after all, we all *know* that people have difficulty in communicating their personal experience, we know that death is inevitable. Once the audience has realized what the author is driving at, the play should end. But it is not the conceptual, formulated *moral* that Ionesco tries to communicate, it is his experience, *what it feels like* to be in the situations concerned. It is precisely against the fallacy that the fruits of human experience

1. ibid., p. 260.   2. 'La démystification par l'humour noir'.

can be transmitted in the form of pre-packed, neatly formulated conceptual pills that his theatre is directed. That is why his criticism, his savage satire, tries to destroy the rationalistic fallacy that language alone, language divorced from experience, can communicate human experience from one person to another. This, if it can be done at all, can be accomplished only through the creative act of the artist, the poet who can transmit something of his own experience by making another human being capable of *feeling* what the artist, the poet had himself experienced.

No amount of clinical description can convey what it feels like, let us say, to be in love. A young person may have been told, may think he knows what it will be like, but when he really does have the experience, he will realize that any merely intellectual knowledge of it was not knowledge in any real sense. A poem, on the other hand, or a piece of music, can convey, to however limited an extent, the reality of feeling and experience. In the same way, Ionesco in a play like *The Killer* is not, as some critics thought, trying to tell us through three long acts that death is inevitable, he is trying to make us experience with him *what it feels like* to be grappling with this basic human experience; what it feels like when at the end we have to face the harsh truth that there is no argument, no rationalization that can remove that stark, final fact of life. When Bérenger, at the end, submits to the knife of the killer, he has finally fought through to the recognition that we must face death without evasion, prettification, or rationalization – and this is the equivalent of a mystical experience. It is true that the other characters in the play, the architect or Edouard, also accept the presence of the killer in their midst as inevitable. The difference is that they do so out of thoughtlessness, lack of imagination, superficial complacency; they have not grasped what it means to experience the presence of death, and, failing to face the issue of death, they are not fully alive. To wake up the audience, to deepen their awareness of the human condition, to make them experience what Bérenger experiences is the real purpose of Ionesco's play.

We do not expect to receive new information in a poem; a moving poem on time or the inevitability of death is not rejected by critics merely because it is not telling us any new truths. Ionesco's theatre is a poetic theatre, a theatre concerned with the communication of the experience of states of being, which are the most difficult matters to communicate; for language, consisting largely of prefabricated, congealed symbols, tends to obscure rather than to reveal personal experience. When A says, 'I am in love,' B will understand by it merely what *he* has experienced, or expects to experience, which may be something entirely different in kind and intensity, and so A, instead of having communicated *his* sense of being, has merely triggered off B's own mode of feeling. No real communication has taken place. Both remain imprisoned, as before, in their own experience. That is why Ionesco has spoken of his own work as an attempt to communicate the incommunicable.

If, however, language, because it is conceptual, and therefore schematic and general, and because it has hardened into impersonal and fossilized clichés, is a hindrance rather than a means toward such a genuine communication, the breakthrough into the other human being's consciousness of the poet's mode of feeling and experience has to be attempted on a more basic level, the pre- or sub-verbal level of elementary human experience. This is what the use of imagery and symbolism achieves in lyrical poetry, combined with such elements as rhythm, tonal quality, and association of words. In Ionesco's theatre the same approach is attempted through the use of basic human situations that will evoke a direct and almost physical response, such as Punch hitting the policeman in the puppet show, circus clowns falling off chairs, or the characters in a silent film throwing custard pies into each other's faces. All these evoke a direct, visceral response in audiences. And by combining such basically evocative emotional images into more and more complex structures, Ionesco gradually forges his theatre into an instrument for the transmission of more complex human situations and experiences.

In this he may not always be equally successful, but in plays like *The Lesson*, *The Chairs*, *Jacques*, the first two acts of *Amédée*, *The New Tenant*, and *Victims of Duty* he has triumphantly succeeded in putting his own experience on the stage and getting it across to the audience. It may be true that, on the whole, such basic, though multivalent and complex, states of mind lend themselves better to brief statement in the form of one-act plays or even sketches than to full-length plays. Yet a play like *The Killer* shows that it is possible to interweave a number of such basic images of experience into a more complex structure. *Rhinocéros*, which also shows Ionesco's ability to sustain a longer form, is perhaps too much of a tract, too closely approximating to a *pièce à thèse*, to serve as an argument in this context.

Of course, the traditional theatre too has always been an instrument for communicating the basic experiences of humanity. But this element has often been subordinated to other functions, such as the telling of a story or the discussion of ideas. Ionesco is attempting to isolate this one element – which he regards as the one that constitutes the theatre's supreme achievement, and in which it excels all other forms of artistic expression – and to restore a *pure*, entirely theatrical theatre.

The technical inventiveness Ionesco displays in trying to achieve his end is truly astonishing. In *The Bald Prima Donna* alone, his first and in many ways simplest play, Alain Bosquet has isolated no fewer than thirty-six 'recipes of the comic',[1] ranging from the negation of action (i.e. scenes in which nothing happens), loss of identity of characters, the misleading title, mechanical surprise, repetition, pseudo-exoticism, pseudo-logic, abolition of chronological sequence, the proliferation of

1. Alain Bosquet, '*Le théâtre d'Eugène Ionesco, ou les 36 recettes du comique*', *Combat*, Paris, 17 February 1955.

doubles (i.e. a whole family all called Bobby Watson), loss of memory, melodramatic surprise (the maid says, 'I am Sherlock Holmes'), coexistence of opposing explanations for the same thing, discontinuity of dialogue, and the raising of false expectations, to purely stylistic devices like cliché, truism, onomatopoeia, Surrealist proverbs, nonsense use of foreign languages, and complete loss of sense, the degeneration of language into pure assonance and sound patterns.

A good many other characteristic devices from Ionesco's later plays could be added to this list – above all, the animation and proliferation of objects, the loss of homogeneity of individual characters who change their natures in front of our eyes, the various mirror effects in which the play itself becomes an object of discussion within the play, the use of offstage dialogue to suggest the isolation of the individual in a sea of irrelevant small talk, the loss of distinction between animate and inanimate objects, the contradiction between the implied description and actual appearance of characters (the young girl who is in fact a mustachioed gentleman, in *Maid to Marry*; the genius who has no head, in *The Leader*), the use of onstage metamorphosis (in *The Picture* and *Rhinocéros*), and a host of others.

What, then, are the basic situations and experiences that Ionesco wants to communicate by the use of this wealth of comic – and tragicomic – invention? Ionesco's theatre has two fundamental themes, which often coexist in the same play. The lesser of these is the protest against the deadlines of present-day mechanical, bourgeois civilization, the loss of real, *felt* values, and the resulting degradation of life. Ionesco attacks a world that has lost its metaphysical dimension, in which human beings no longer feel a sense of mystery, of reverent awe in facing their own existence. Behind the violent mockery of fossilized language, there stands a plea for the restoration of a poetic concept of life:

When I wake up, on a morning of grace, from my nocturnal sleep as well as from the mental sleep of routine, and I suddenly become aware of my existence and of the universal presence, so that everything appears strange, and at the same time familiar to me, when the astonishment of being invades me – these sentiments, this institution belong to all men, of all times. We can find this state of mind expressed in almost the same words by all poets, mystics, philosophers, who feel it in exactly the same way I do . . .[1]

But if Ionesco savagely assails a mode of life that has banished mystery from existence, this does not mean that he regards a full awareness of the implications of human existence as a state of euphoria. On the contrary, the intuition of being that he tries to communicate is one of despair. The main themes that recur in his plays are those of the loneliness and isolation of the individual, his difficulty in communicating with others, his subjection to degrading outside pressures, to the mechanical conformity of society as well as to the equally degrading internal pressures of his own personality – sexuality and the ensuing feelings of guilt, the anxieties arising from the uncertainty of one's own identity and the certainty of death.

If the basic pattern in Beckett's plays is pairs of interdependent, complementary personalities, and in Adamov's theatre pairs of contrasting extrovert–introvert men, Ionesco's most frequently recurring basic pattern is the married couple, the family – Mr and Mrs Smith, Amédée and Madeleine, Choubert and his Madeleine, the old man and his wife in *The Chairs*, the Jacques family in *Jacques* and *The Future is in Eggs*, the professor and his maid (who is both wife and mother to him) in *The Lesson*, the rich man and his sister in *The Picture*. In this basic pattern, the woman usually plays the part of an admiring, but nagging, supporter of the husband. In Ionesco's later plays, Bérenger is a lonely and isolated individual, but he is also, in each case, in love with the ideal of an understanding young working-woman, Dany–Daisy, who combines grace, beauty, and *savoir-faire*.

1. '*Expérience du théâtre*', loc. cit., p. 264.

Ionesco's characters may be isolated and lonely in a meta-physical sense, but they are by no means the tramps and out-casts of Beckett and Adamov, and this, in some sense, increases the despair and absurdity of their isolation – they are lonely in spite of being members of what ought to be an organic com-munity. Yet, as we see above all in *Jacques*, the family is the agent of society's pressures toward conformity, which not even the sweet and loving Daisy can resist in *Rhinocéros*.

Nevertheless, the presence of companionship and family re-lationships lightens the despair of Ionesco's world. It would be wrong to regard his attitude as wholly pessimistic. He wants to make existence authentic, fully lived, by putting man face to face with the harsh realities of the human condition. But this is also the way to liberation. 'To attack the absurdity (of the human condition) is', Ionesco once said, 'a way of stating the possibility of non-absurdity. . . . For where else would there be a point of reference? . . . In Zen Buddhism there was no direct teaching, only the constant search for an opening, a revelation. Nothing makes me more pessimistic than the obligation not to be pessimistic. I feel that every message of despair is the state-ment of a situation from which everybody must freely try to find a way out.'[1]

The very statement of the desperate situation, the ability it gives the spectator to face it with open eyes, constitutes a catharsis, a liberation. Are not Oedipus and Lear confronted with the full despair and absurdity of their human condition? Yet their tragedies are liberating experiences.

Ionesco himself has always opposed the idea that, as an avant-garde author, he stands outside the mainstream of tradition. He insists that the avant-garde is a mere rediscovery of submerged parts of the main tradition. And so, while he admits that Corneille bores him, that he finds Schiller unbearable, Mari-vaux futile, Musset thin, Vigny unactable, Victor Hugo ridiculous, Labiche unfunny, Dumas *fils* laughably sentimental,

1. Ionesco, quoted by Towarnicki, '*Des* Chaises *vides à Broadway*'.

Oscar Wilde facile, Ibsen heavy, Strindberg clumsy, Pirandello outmoded, Giraudoux and Cocteau superficial, he does see himself as part of a tradition including Sophocles and Aeschylus, Shakespeare, Kleist, and Büchner, precisely because these authors are concerned with the human condition in all its brutal absurdity.

Only time can show to what extent Ionesco will become part of the mainstream of the great tradition. What is certain, however, is that his work constitutes a truly heroic attempt to break through the barriers of human communication.

4

JEAN GENET

A hall of mirrors

IN the most personal of his books, the autobiographical *Journal du Voleur* (*The Thief's Journal*), Jean Genet describes how he once came across Stilitano, the tall, handsome, one-handed Serbian pimp, thief, and drug peddler who was one of the heroes of his youth, lost in a hall of mirrors on a fairground. It was one of those labyrinths constructed partly of mirrors, partly of panes of transparent glass that are arranged in such a way that the crowd outside can watch the antics of those who are trying to find their way out of the maze. And so Genet could observe Stilitano caught like a trapped animal, could see, but not hear, him uttering enraged curses while the large throng of bystanders outside were splitting their sides with laughter:

Stilitano was alone. Everyone had found the way out except he. Strangely the universe veiled itself for me. The shadow that suddenly fell over things and people was the shadow of my solitude confronted with this despair, for, no longer able to shout, to butt himself against the walls of glass, resigned at being a mockery for the gaping crowd, Stilitano had crouched down on the floor, refusing to go on. . . .[1]

This image expresses the essence of Genet's theatre, the image of man caught in a maze of mirrors, trapped by his own distorted reflections, trying to find the way to make contact with the others he can see around him but being rudely stopped by barriers of glass. (Genet himself used mirrors in his ballet scenario *Adam Miroir*.) His plays are concerned with expressing his own feeling of helplessness and solitude when confronted with the despair and loneliness of man caught in the hall of mirrors of the human condition, inexorably trapped by an endless pro-

1. Jean Genet, *Journal du Voleur* (Paris: Gallimard, 1949), p. 282.

gression of images that are merely his own distorted reflection – lies covering lies, fantasies battening upon fantasies, nightmares nourished by nightmares within nightmares.

In the whole long line of *poètes maudits* that runs through French literature, like a red thread, from Villon to Sade to Verlaine, Rimbaud, and Lautréamont, Jean Genet is surely among the most extraordinary. 'On the planet Uranus', he writes, 'it seems the atmosphere is so heavy ... that the animals drag themselves about crushed by the weight of the gases. It is with these humiliated creatures always crawling on their bellies that I want to mingle. If in the transmigration of souls I am granted a new dwelling place, I shall choose that cursed planet to inhabit it with the convicts of my race.'[1]

Jean Genet was born in Paris on 19 December 1910. He was abandoned by his mother and brought up by peasant foster parents in the Morvan, in the north of the Massif Central. When he reached the age of twenty-one he was given his birth certificate. From it he learned that his mother had been called Gabrielle Genet and that he had been born at 22 Rue d'Assas, behind the Luxembourg Gardens. When he went to find the house, he discovered it was a maternity hospital.

In his monumental study of Genet, surely one of the most astonishing books of our age, Jean-Paul Sartre has described how, at the age of ten, the little boy, who had till then been considered pious and docile, was accused of stealing, and how, being described as a thief, he resolved to *be* a thief. For Sartre this was the great act of existential choice. Genet himself puts the matter in a slightly less philosophical way: 'It was not at any particular period of my life that I decided to be a thief. My laziness and my daydreaming having led me to the *maison correctionelle* at Mettray, where I was to stay till I was twenty-one, I escaped, and to gain the signing-up bonus, joined up for five years. After a few days [in the Foreign Legion] I deserted, taking with me the suitcases of some Negro officers. For a time

1. ibid., p. 47.

I loved stealing, but prostitution appealed more to my easygoing ways. I was twenty. . . .'[1]

But in the essential point of existential choice, Genet's account agrees with Sartre's. 'Abandoned by my family, I found it natural to aggravate this fact by the love of males, and that love by stealing, and stealing by crime, or complicity with crime. Thus I decisively repudiated a world that had repudiated me.'[2]

Between 1930 and 1940, Genet led the life of an itinerant delinquent. After a stay in the Barrio Chino of Barcelona, among beggars and pimps, he went back to France, made his first acquaintance with French prisons, and then went to Italy. Via Rome, Naples, and Brindisi, he reached Albania. Refused a permit to land at Corfu, he passed into Yugoslavia, Austria, Czechoslovakia. In Poland he tried to pass forged banknotes, was arrested, and eventually expelled. In Hitler's Germany he felt out of place: 'Even on Unter den Linden I had a feeling of being in a camp organized by bandits. . . . This is a nation of thieves, I felt. If I steal here, I accomplish no special act that could help me to realize myself. I merely obey the habitual order of things. I do not destroy it.'[3] And so he hastened on into a country that still obeyed the conventional moral code and therefore enabled an outlaw to feel himself outside an established order. He went to Antwerp, where he remained for some time before returning to France.

While France was occupied by the Germans, Genet was in and out of prison. It was prison that made him into a poet. Once, still on remand, he told Sartre, he was, by mistake, given prison clothes and pushed into a cell in which all the other prisoners, also not yet convicted, still had their ordinary clothes. He was thus exposed to ridicule and contempt. Among these prisoners there was one 'who made poems to his sister, idiotic and self-pitying poems that were much admired. In the end . . . I declared that I was able to make poems just as good. They dared

1. ibid., p. 48.   2. ibid., p. 92.   3. ibid., p. 131.

me and I wrote the *Condamné à Mort*[1] – a long and solemn elegy dedicated to the memory of Maurice Pilorge, executed for the murder of his friend at the prison of Saint-Brieuc on 17 March 1939.

This poetry has a strange ritualistic, incantatory quality. It has the dark splendour of a religious act, as if the verses were a magic formula by which the dead man could be brought back to life. The same quality is present in the four long prose poems (for they are prose poems rather than novels, as they are most often called) that Genet wrote between 1940 and 1948: *Notre-Dame-des-Fleurs* (dated from Fresnes prison, 1942), *Miracle de la Rose* (dated from La Santé and Tourelles prisons, 1943), *Pompes Funèbres*, and *Querelle de Brest*. All these books are in the form of stories set in a world of homosexual outlaws. Yet they are not novels, because, as Genet himself told Sartre, 'none of my characters ever makes a decision by himself'[2]; in other words, the characters are mere emanations of the whim of their creator. These books are in fact the erotic fantasies of a prisoner, the day-dreams of a solitary outcast of society, who is resolved to live up to the pattern he feels society has imposed upon him. No wonder that in these books there is a curious mixture of lyrical beauty and the most sordid subject-matter.

'I am reproached', Genet writes in *Journal du Voleur*,

with using properties like fairground shacks, prisons, flowers, the loot of sacrilege, railroad stations, frontiers, opium, sailors, ports, public lavatories, funerals, rooms in slums, in order to obtain medi-ocre melodramatic effects and with mistaking poetry for a facile picturesqueness. What am I to reply? I have already said how much I love the outlaws who have no other beauty except that of their bodies. The properties that have been named are impregnated with the violence of men, with their brutality . . .[3]

Genet's narrative prose, erotic, scabrous, scatological, is at the

1. Sartre, *Saint Genet, Comédien et Martyr* (Paris: Gallimard, 1952), p. 397.

2. ibid., p. 421.   3. *Journal du Voleur*, p. 283.

same time highly poetic, with a solemn inverted religious atmosphere – a world turned upside down, in which the dedicated pursuit of the abject is carried out with the devotion of sainthood. In his essay entitled, for that very reason, *Saint Genet*, Sartre has gone so far as to draw a comparison between St Teresa of Avila and Genet, and has reached the conclusion that if sainthood consists of carrying humility to the total acceptance of the sinfulness of the human condition, the annihilation of all pride before the absolute, Genet's claim to sainthood is the better.

Be that as it may, in writing down his erotic fantasies, in transmuting daydreams into written sentences with their own rhythm, colour, and inherent demand for objective craftsmanship, Genet learned to master his dream world. As Sartre says:

By infecting us with his evil, Genet delivers himself from it. Each of his books is a cathartic crisis of possession, a psychodrama; it seems as though each book merely reproduced the preceding one, just as his new love-affairs merely repeat his former ones. But with each book this possessed man becomes a little more the master of the demon that possesses him. Ten years of literature are equivalent to a psychoanalytic cure.[1]

It is significant that in this process of gradual mastery of his obsessions, Genet progressed from poetry to narrative prose and, finally, to the dramatic form.

This amounts to a progression from the most subjective to the more objective forms of writing. By the time he was completing his *Journal du Voleur* (about 1937), Genet was able to say, 'I have been writing books for the last five years. I can say that I have done so with pleasure, but I have finished with it. By writing, I have obtained what I had been looking for. . . .'[2] Since then Genet has written no more prose narratives. But he continued to write plays. And it is only in his plays that he has been able to free himself from purely autobiographical subject-matter, the world of prisons and homosexual outlaws.

1. *Saint Genet*, p. 501.   2. *Journal du Voleur*, p. 47.

Genet's first play, *Haute Surveillance* (*Deathwatch*), is still anchored in that world. It is a long one-act play set in a prison cell. Its theme is the one that pervades Genet's narrative prose – the hierarchy of crime. In Genet's daydreams, the prison is the equivalent of a royal palace: 'To the prisoner, the prison offers the same sense of security that a royal palace offers to the guest of a king. ... The rigour of the rules, their narrowness, their precision are of the same essential quality as the etiquette of a royal court, the exquisite but tyrannical politeness of which a guest at court is the object.'[1]

For Genet there is also a rigid order in the precedence of the prisoners. In *Deathwatch* the occupant of the highest rung of the ladder is out of sight. He is Boule-de-Neige (Snowball), a convicted murderer, a Negro. The occupants of the cell where the action takes place bathe in the reflected glory of this idol. There are three of them: Yeux-Verts (Green Eyes) is also a murderer, but of lesser rank than Snowball, who murdered for gain, while Green Eyes merely killed a prostitute in a moment when he had lost self-control. Lefranc is a thief, and Maurice, only seventeen years old, a juvenile delinquent. (In the French edition of the play, Green Eyes is described as 'very beautiful', Maurice as 'small, handsome', and Lefranc as 'tall, beautiful'. These indications, highly characteristic of Genet, are coyly omitted in the American edition.)

The plot of *Deathwatch* turns on the relationship among the three prisoners. Maurice adores Green Eyes, who knows that he will be convicted of murder and is likely to be executed. Lefranc, who has been writing letters to Green Eyes' wife because Green Eyes himself is illiterate, is jealous of Maurice. He has been using the letters he wrote to Green Eyes' wife to try to seduce her away from her husband, not so much to get her himself as to break her relationship with Green Eyes. When Green Eyes finds out about this, he suggests that either Maurice or Lefranc should kill her after their release, which is due within

1. ibid., p. 93.

a matter of days. Which of the two will have the guts to become a murderer for the sake of their idol and risk the guillotine, as he does? But then Green Eyes breaks down. He tells the story of the murder he committed – he killed a prostitute in a sadistic fury he could not help. When the guard brings him a gift of cigarettes from the authentic murderer, Snowball, he bequeaths his wife to the guard. The young hero-worshipper Maurice is deeply disappointed at the disintegration of his hero. To show that he, too, is a really tough, hardened criminal, Lefranc, whom Maurice has taunted with the fact that he will never be one of them ('You are not our kind. You'll never be. Even if you killed a man'),[1] strangles the boy in cold blood. Green Eyes still refuses to regard Lefranc as an authentic killer. 'I didn't want [my crime],' he says. 'It chose me.' Lefranc, on the other hand, insists, 'My misfortune comes from something deeper. It comes from myself.' Green Eyes wants nothing to do with him. The play ends with Lefranc's realization, 'I really am all alone!'

Thus Genet's first play is largely a dramatized form of the type of story he tells in his lyrical narratives about the lives of criminals and convicts. On the surface the play looks like a somewhat heightened and stylized prison epic; it could be the scenario of one of Hollywood's prison movies, except that it is frankly amoral. Yet the author's intention is far from straight-forward naturalism. The stage directions at the beginning read: 'The entire play unfolds as in a dream. . . . The movements of the actors should be either heavy or else extremely and incomprehensibly rapid, like flashes of lightning.'[2] In other words, Genet wants to make it clear that the play is not intended to represent real events, but is a daydream, a prisoner's fantasy come to life, the product of a feverish imagination.

And in its strange, inverted, upside-down way, the subject of

1. Genet, *Deathwatch*, in *The Maids/Deathwatch*, trans. Bernard Frechtman (New York: Grove Press, 1954), p. 128.
2. ibid., pp. 103–4.

Genet's daydream resembles that of so many of Thomas Mann's and Kafka's stories. Lefranc is the outcast who tries to emulate the authentic, instinctive beauty and intuitive belonging together of uncomplicated human beings who simply are themselves, who do not have to will themselves into being. But even when he forces himself to overcome his weakness and accomplishes the act that is to make him their equal, they reject him. Nothing he can do can make him be accepted. Green Eyes is illiterate – his misfortune chose him. Lefranc can read and write – he chooses his misfortune. But it is this consciousness that puts him beyond the pale. It is through being aware of himself that he is caught, as the man lost in the hall of mirrors is lost among the reflections of his own image.

Genet's second play, *Les Bonnes* (*The Maids*), his first to be performed, takes us much deeper into this hall of mirrors. This is the first work in which Genet freed himself, at least outwardly, from the narrow confines of a world of prisoners.

The Maids opens in a Louis XV bedroom in which an elegant lady is being dressed by her maid, whom she calls Claire. The lady is haughty, the maid servile. But the two visibly taunt each other. In the end the maid slaps the lady. Suddenly an alarm clock rings; in a flash the whole scene collapses. The lady is seen to be no lady at all, but one of two maids who have been playing at lady and maid in the absence of the real lady. And in fact the maid who has been called Claire is not Claire at all but Solange, and it was Claire who acted the part of the lady, and treated her sister as the lady treats Claire.

Whenever their lady is out, the two maids enact the fantasy game of servility and final revolt against her, each playing the lady in turn. For they are bound to their lady, who is younger and more beautiful than they, by a mixture of affection, erotic love, and deep hatred. They have just caused the arrest of Monsieur, the lady's lover, by writing anonymous letters to the police. The telephone rings; Monsieur is out on bail. The maids are terrified. Now their denunciation will be found out. They decide to kill the lady when she returns. They will pour poison into her tea. The lady arrives. They keep the news of Monsieur's release from her, but just as she is about to drink the poisoned tea, she notices that the receiver of the telephone is off, and one of the maids lets the news of Monsieur's release slip out. The lady will no longer drink her tea; she hurries off to meet her lover. The maids are left alone. They resume the game of lady and maid. Claire again plays the lady and demands that she be served the poisoned cup of tea. Solange has once before failed to kill the lady. Now Claire is going to show her courage. She drinks the poison and dies in the role of the lady.

The two maids are linked by the love-hatred of being each other's mirror images. As Claire says, 'I'm sick of seeing my image thrown back at me by a mirror, like a bad smell.'[1] At the same time, in the role of the lady, Claire sees the whole race of servants as the distorting mirror of the upper class: 'Your frightened, guilty faces, your puckered elbows, your outmoded clothes, your wasted bodies, only fit for cast-offs! You're our distorting mirrors, our loathsome vent, our shame, our dregs!'[2] Thus what they hate seeing reflected in each other is the distorted reflection of the world of the secure masters, which they adore, ape, and loathe.

But Genet's hall of mirrors is even more tortuous. When Louis Jouvet undertook to produce *The Maids* in 1947, Genet at first insisted that the three women who make up the cast be played by men. As he had put it in his very first narrative, *Notre-Dame-des-Fleurs*, 'If I ever had to stage a play with women's parts in it, I should insist that these parts should be played by young men, and I would inform the public of it by a poster that would stay attached at the right or left of the set throughout the performance.'[3] And so, in fact, the maids and their lady are young men.

1. *The Maids*, p. 61.   2. ibid., p. 86.
3. Genet, *Notre-Dame-des-Fleurs* in *Œuvres Complètes*, vol. II (Paris: Gallimard, 1951), p. 119.

As Sartre has pointed out in his brilliant analysis of *The Maids*, the play reproduces almost exactly the situation we find in *Deathwatch*. Monsieur, the absent master criminal, corresponds to Snowball, the absent murderer hero. Madame, whose beauty and wealth are a reflection of Monsieur's glory, stands for Green Eyes, and the two maids represent the two lesser figures, Maurice and Lefranc, who both love and hate to see their own inadequacy reflected in the greater glory of their hero. Just as Lefranc murders Maurice to prove himself the equal of Green Eyes, Claire braves death by forcing Solange to serve her the poisoned cup of tea. We are back in the daydream of the prisoner, the fantasy of the outcast who makes futile efforts to reach the world of acceptance and belonging.

But the lady and her lover, the masters of the maids, do not stand merely for a higher order in the hierarchy of convicts, as Snowball and Green Eyes do in *Deathwatch*. They are also an image of respectable society itself, the closed world of *les justes*, from which the orphaned foundling Genet had felt himself excluded and rejected as a monstrosity. The revolt of the maids against their masters is not a social gesture, a revolutionary action; it is tinged with nostalgia and longing, like the revolt of the fallen angel Satan against the world of light from which he is forever banished. That is why this revolt finds its expression not in protest but in ritual. Each of the maids in turn acts the part of the lady, expressing her longing to *be* the lady, and each in turn takes it upon herself to act the other maid, progressing from adoration and servility to abuse and violence – the discharge of all the hatred and envy of the outcast who sees himself as a rejected lover. This ritual, as Sartre points out, is a kind of Black Mass – the wish to murder the loved and envied object congealed and forever repeated as a ceremonial, stereotyped action. Such a ritual is frustration become flesh – an action that will never be performed in the real world is repeated over and over as a mere game. And not even this ritual ever reaches its natural climax. The lady always returns before that. As Sartre sees it, this failure is, as it were, subconsciously built into the ritual. The game is played in such a way that the time wasted on the preliminaries is always too long for the climax ever to be reached.

The ritual of wish-fulfilment is an act that is wholly absurd – it is futility mirroring itself; the wish to accomplish something which can never bridge the gulf that separates the dream from reality; the sympathetic magic of the primitive who is unable to face the cold, implacable hardness of the real world. Such ritual belongs in the world of neurosis and compulsive obsessions. It is the expression of a withdrawal from life.

The concept of the ritual act, the magical repetition of an action deprived of reality, is the key to any understanding of Genet's theatre. He himself has described his ideal of the union of the ritual with the dramatic in the letter to the publisher Pauvert that serves as preface to one of the editions of *The Maids*.

On a stage almost like ours, on a platform, it was a matter of reconstructing the end of a meal. From that starting point, which one can hardly discover in it any more, the highest modern drama has found expression through two thousand years and every day in the sacrifice of the Mass. The starting point disappears under the profusion of ornaments and symbols. . . . A performance that would not act on my soul would be in vain. . . . No doubt it is one of the functions of art to replace religious faith by the effective ingredient of beauty. At least this beauty must have the power of a poem, that is to say of a crime. But let that pass.[1]

Genet rejects the theatre as mere entertainment. He does not believe that in our Western world the theatre could ever have the effect of a real communion, a real link between human beings. He recalls that Sartre once told him that he had experienced that kind of effect in a theatrical performance only once – during a Christmas play in a prisoner-of-war camp,

1. Genet, letter to Pauvert, in Genet, *Les Bonnes–L'Atelier d'Alberto Giacometti* (Décines: L'Arbalète, 1958), pp. 145–6.

when the nostalgia of a French play on the stage suddenly recreated France herself, the homeland and its mystical unity, not on the stage but in the auditorium. But, says Genet,

I don't know what the theatre will be like in a Socialist world. I can understand better what it would be like among the Mau Mau, but in the Western world, more and more touched by death and turned toward it, it can only refine itself in the 'reflection' of a comedy of a comedy, the reflection of reflection which a ceremonious rendering could make exquisite and close to invisibility. If one has chosen to contemplate oneself dying deliciously, one must rigorously pursue and arrange the funeral symbols. Or choose to live and discover the Enemy. For me there will never be an Enemy anywhere, there will never be a homeland, not even an abstract and interior one. If I am moved, it will be by the nostalgia of what my homeland once was. Only a theatre of shadows can still touch me.[1]

Genet's theatre, in a very real sense, is a Dance of Death. If in Ionesco's theatre death is always present, in the sense that the fear of extinction pervades its sense of being, in Genet's theatre the world of being exists only as a nostalgic memory of life in a world of dream and fantasy. Sartre observes on the very first page of his monumental study of Genet: 'Genet is a dead man; if he still seems to live, he does so only in that larval existence that certain people ascribe to the dead in their tombs. All his heroes have died at least once in their life.'[2]

Genet's game of mirrors – in which each apparent reality is revealed as an appearance, an illusion, which in turn is revealed as again part of a dream or an illusion, and so on, *ad infinitum* – is a device to uncover the fundamental absurdity of being, its nothingness. The fixed point from which we feel we can safely watch the world, made up of deceptive appearances perhaps, but always reducible to an ultimate reality, is itself shown to be a mere reflection in a mirror, and the whole structure collapses. The first *coup de théâtre* in *The Maids* is a case in point. We have seen a great lady being dressed by her maid, Claire; accustomed

1. ibid., p. 147.   2. *Saint Genet*, p. 9.

as we are to follow the exposition of a play we are memorizing these relationships. But suddenly, on the ringing of an alarm clock, the fixed point of reference vanishes – what had appeared to be the lady is Claire, the maid; what had appeared to be Claire now turns out to be Solange; what appeared to be the opening scene of a conventional play is revealed to be a piece of ritual play-acting within a play.

'This moment', as Sartre put it in the technical language of his Existentialist philosophy,

in which the lights flicker, when the volatile unity of the being of non-being and the non-being of being is achieved in semi-darkness – this perfect and perverse instant makes us realize from within, the mental attitude of Genet when he dreams: it is the moment of evil. For in order to be sure of never making *good use* of appearance, Genet wants his fancies, at two or three removes from reality, to reveal themselves in their nothingness. In this pyramid of fantasies, the ultimate appearance destroys the reality of all others.[1]

Or, as Genet himself says in describing what he was trying to do in *The Maids*,

I tried to establish a *distantiation* which, in allowing a declamatory tone, would carry the theatre into the theatre. I thus hoped also to obtain the abolition of characters . . . and to replace them by symbols as far removed as possible, at first, from what they are to signify, and yet still attached to it in order to link by this sole means author and audience; in short, to make the characters on the stage merely the metaphors of what they were to represent. . . .[2]

Thus the characters themselves are only characters in appearance – they are mere symbols, reflections in a mirror, dreams within a dream.

When *The Maids* had its first performance at the Athénée in Paris on 17 April 1947, under the direction of France's foremost actor, Louis Jouvet, it seemed that Genet had finally established

1. Sartre, Introduction to *The Maids/Deathwatch*, p. 30.
2. Genet, letter to Pauvert, loc. cit., p. 144.

himself in the world of respectability. His narrative prose was already circulating in privately printed editions. In fact it was Jouvet who had suggested to Genet that he should write the play. 'Commissioned by an actor famous in his time, my play was written out of vanity, but in boredom.'[1] Brilliantly produced in a set of breathtaking beauty designed by Christian Bérard, *The Maids* achieved considerable success. But Genet had not yet redeemed himself completely. In 1948 he was faced with the prospect of a sentence of life imprisonment. It was only a petition signed by a number of great literary figures, Sartre and Cocteau among them, that, in the end, persuaded the President of the Republic to grant him a pardon.

It must be supposed that it was at this period that Genet's first film was made. *Un Chant d'Amour*, a silent picture running about half an hour, clearly restates some of the main themes from Genet's narrative prose. It is so drastically erotic that it cannot hope to get much of a public showing. Indeed, when shown in San Francisco in 1966, it had to be withdrawn. *Un Chant d'Amour* opens with a shot of the façade of a prison, with long rows of barred windows. From two of these adjoining windows two hands stretch forth, trying to grasp each other. A warder who has watched this scene goes upstairs to investigate. Through the peepholes of a number of cells he observes various prisoners in various stages of auto-erotic practices. Having traced the two culprits, an older man and a boy (whose attempts to make contact and voluptuous fantasies about each other we are made to witness), the warder rushes into one of the cells and brutally beats the inmate, the older man; but, ironically, the pain merely heightens the victim's pleasure in his erotic fantasies. Back in the prison yard the defeated warder observes how the two hands again stretch forth from the adjoining windows. Now one of them holds a garland of flowers and this finally enables contact to be established between the two lovers. There is a great deal of highly character-

1. ibid.

istically sentimental homosexual imagery in the film; genitals turn into bunches of roses, garlands of flowers bind the separated pair. Nevertheless this is a remarkable film, well made, and a terrifying document on the sexual misery of prisoners.

Genet's fortunes had taken an upward turn. One of France's leading publishers began to publish a monumental edition of his works; the first volume appeared in 1951, Sartre's great introductory study in 1952, a further volume in 1953. But Genet seemed to have stopped writing for the theatre. In fact he was reported to have forsworn the theatre after his experience with *The Maids* and *Deathwatch* (first produced at the Théâtre des Mathurins in February 1949). In his letter to Pauvert about *The Maids*, he speaks of his dislike of the theatre and its world: 'The poet who [would venture into it] would find ranged against him the haughty stupidity of the actors and theatre people. One cannot expect anything from a profession that is exercised with so little seriousness and reverence. Its starting point, its *raison d'être*, is exhibitionism.'[1] But by 1956 Genet had written another play, *Le Balcon* (*The Balcony*).

The events that surrounded the first production of this play show that in the intervening years Genet had by no means acquired a more charitable opinion of actors and stage people. *The Balcony* had its world première on 22 April 1957, in London at the Arts Theatre Club, open to members only and therefore not subject to the Lord Chamberlain's censorship. The same issues of the London papers that reviewed the play also contained the story of how the author had been banned from the theatre after he had violently objected to the way it was being produced. Peter Zadek, the young English director who had directed a French performance of *The Maids* in London as early as 1952, and had later staged its first performance in English, was accused by Genet of having vulgarized *The Balcony*.

'My play was set in a brothel of noble dimensions,' he was quoted as having said. 'Peter Zadek has put on the stage a

1. Genet, letter to Pauvert, loc. cit., p. 142.

brothel of petty dimensions.'[1] And Bernard Frechtman, Genet's excellent American translator, was cited as having commented, '[the scenes in the brothel] should be presented with the solemnity of a Mass in a most beautiful cathedral. Mr Zadek has transformed it into just an ordinary brothel.'[2] A few days later, Peter Zadek gave his own account of the controversy in a finely argued and magnanimous article, in which he paid tribute to Genet as an artist: 'It is this complete inability to compromise with his vision that makes of Genet one of the great poet-dramatists of our century.'[3] Zadek explained Genet's outburst as a manifestation of his preoccupation with the borderline between fantasy and reality:

Genet's whole life seems to repeat the pattern of the visionary who tries to make 'his fantasy penetrate into the reality of the world'. But the world has always crucified visionaries, and 'St Genet' is no exception. ... For him his own perfect dream of *The Balcony* was reality, and in an effort to make this concrete, our reality, the production of the play on a stage, with actors, had to be sacrificed.[4]

The conflict over the London production of *The Balcony* (which admittedly was a brave attempt in a small theatre and with modest means) was more than merely a picturesque incident in the life of a colourful and eccentric playwright. It illuminates the essence of Genet's whole approach – the deep inner tension arising from his search for something absolute, beautiful, a sacramental element in an inverted system of values in which evil is the greatest good, and the beautiful blooms in a soil of excrement and sordid crime. That is why it was not at all paradoxical for Genet to demand that his fantasies of sex and power should be staged with the solemnity and the outward splendour of the liturgy in one of the world's great cathedrals, while at the same time insisting to the director that the production should

1. *News Chronicle*, London, 23 April 1957.
2. *News Chronicle*, London, 24 April 1957.
3. *New Statesman*, London, 4 May 1957.
4. ibid.

be 'vulgar, violent, and in bad taste'[1] and assuring him that 'if anybody tells you that you have produced this play in good taste, you will have failed. My tarts must look like the worst prostitutes in the world.'[2] To live up to such demands is clearly very difficult, if not impossible.

As a matter of fact, the London production of *The Balcony*, although it contained many mistakes, weaknesses, and cuts of important passages, in some ways managed to put the play as a whole across the footlights in a more complete manner than Peter Brook's infinitely more polished, splendidly designed, and magnificently cast first French production, at the Théâtre du Gymnase in May 1960. The slower pace resulting from the more faithful execution of the author's intention made the performance drag to such an extent that after the first night the very essential and central scene among the revolutionaries, although rehearsed and included in the première, was omitted (as it was in the New York production of March 1960), thus depriving the final climax of the play of a point essential to its understanding. But then, at the time of the first night in Paris, Genet had become wary enough to have gone to Greece to nurse his rheumatism.

The Balcony carries the organic development of Genet's approach forward by an important step. Again, at the beginning, we have the ground pulled out from under our feet. The play opens with a magnificently robed bishop discoursing in high-flown theological language. But hardly have we adjusted ourselves to the idea that we are watching a bishop when it becomes brutally clear that we are not in a bishop's palace but in a brothel, and that the man concerned is not a bishop but a gas-man who has paid the madam for the satisfaction of indulging himself in his fantasies of sex and power. Madame Irma's brothel, the Grand Balcony, is a palace of illusions – a hall of mirrors. Here men can indulge their most secret daydreams: they can see themselves as a judge meting out punishment to a

1. ibid.   2. *Picture Post*, London, 11 May 1957.

girl thief; as a general feeling himself loved by his favourite
steed, who is also a beautiful girl; as a leper being miraculously
cured by the Madonna in person; as a dying Foreign Legionary
being succoured by a beautiful Arab maiden. The props for all
the ever recurring fantasies of grandeur are available at Madame
Irma's establishment, which is thus not only a hall of mirrors, in
the metaphorical as well as the actual sense (there are mirrors
everywhere that multiply the images of self-heroization), but
also a kind of theatre, with Madame Irma as its producer and
impresario.

The plot of the play arises from the fact that the country in
which the Grand Balcony is situated is in the throes of revolution. Machine-gun fire is heard throughout the first scenes. The
revolutionaries want to destroy the established structure of
power, represented as it is by the image of the country's queen,
chaste and remote, her bishops, her judges, and her generals.
One of the inmates of Madame Irma's establishment, a girl
called Chantal, has fallen in love with the leader of the revolutionaries, a plumber whom she met while he was doing some
repairs at the Grand Balcony; she herself has become a kind of
symbol of the revolution, its Joan of Arc. The fight against the
revolution is led by the Chief of Police, who is the real power in
the land, representing the modern apparatus of dictatorship, the
wielder of totalitarian and terroristic power. The Chief of
Police knows, however, that power is not a matter of torture
and physical force, but ultimately a question of domination
over people's minds. Such ascendancy expresses itself best in the
secret fantasies of human beings; only when there will be a
demand in Madame Irma's brothel for the trappings of the
totalitarian Police Chief will he feel secure. Anxiously he keeps
inquiring whether anyone has yet asked for this particular
setting in the brothel. Everything is prepared for that day, but
nobody has yet wanted to dream of this brand of grandeur.

We meet the revolutionaries in a scene that sets the counterpoint to the world of the Grand Balcony, but there, too, power

is based on sex fantasies. Some of the rebels want to build up Chantal into a kind of trademark of the revolution, the beautiful girl leading the attack, singing rousing tunes to fire the men to greater exertions. Roger, the leader, resists these demands but has to yield in the end, protesting, 'I didn't carry you off, I didn't steal you for you to become a unicorn or a two-headed eagle.' But Chantal goes nevertheless.

The royal palace is blown up, the queen and her court swept away. An envoy from the palace appears at the Grand Balcony. Only if the people can be made to believe that the age-old symbols of power are intact can the day still be saved. Will Madame Irma assume the part of the Queen, and her customers – the men who dressed up as bishop, general, and judge – assume these roles in earnest? Madame Irma and her customers consent. Solemnly they appear on the balcony and bow to the crowd. Chantal rushes up to the balcony and is killed by a shot from below. A stray bullet? Or a shot fired by the revolutionaries themselves to turn her into a myth? Or was it the bishop, who wanted to turn her into one of his saints?

The revolution has been defeated. But 'bishop', 'general', and 'judge', having to exercise their power in the real world, are weary and nostalgic for their fantasies. When they try to assert the reality of their functions, the Chief of Police rudely reminds them that it is he who holds the real power. Yet he, too, still longs for the day when his function will be invested with the dignity of being the centre of erotic dreams. He is having an immense mausoleum constructed for himself, in the hope that this will bring him nearer to his goal. He is trying to evolve a symbol for his dignity that will stir men's imagination. He has rejected the executioner's red coat and axe. His newest idea is that he should be represented by a gigantic phallus.

The first customer who wants to dress up as a Chief of Police arrives. It is Roger, the leader of the defeated revolutionaries. Anxiously Irma (now the Queen) and her dignitaries watch the scene through the intricate apparatus of mirrors and periscopes that enable the madam of the brothel to see what goes on in all the private rooms. Roger enacts his own fantasy of power and torture, but finally, exclaiming, 'Since I'm playing the Chief of Police . . . I've a right to lead the character I have chosen to the very limit of his destiny – no, of mine – of merging his destiny with mine,' he pulls out a knife and castrates himself. The Chief of Police, satisfied that his image has become enshrined in the fantasies of the people, has himself immured in his tomb – or its representation in the brothel. Bursts of machine-gun fire are heard. A new revolution is in progress. Madame Irma dismisses her customers, divests herself of her royal dignity, and prepares to return to her old role of the keeper of a house of illusions.

In the stage directions for *Deathwatch*, Genet had to insist that it should be acted as a dream. In *The Balcony* there is no need for such specific instructions. It is quite clear that the play represents a world of fantasy about a world of fantasy; Genet's dream about the essential nature of power and sex, which, to him, have the same roots; his wish-fantasy about the true nature of judges, policemen, officers, and bishops. The outcast child, repudiated by society and not recognizing any of its codes, unable to understand the motives of the organs of the state's coercive apparatus, weaves its own fantasy about the motives of the men who have acted as the instruments of the state. The outcast comes to the conclusion that these men are expressing their sadistic drive for domination, and that they are using the awful symbolism with which they are surrounded, the ritual and ceremonial of courtroom, army, and church, to buttress and secure their domination. Thus sex, which to Genet is essentially a matter of domination and submission; the power of the state, which manifests itself in the domination of the prisoner by the court and its policemen; and the romantic ceremonial, the manifestation of myth in sex as well as in power, are basically one.

A feeling of helplessness when confronted with the vast intricacy of the modern world, and the individual's impotence in making his own influence felt on that intricate and mysterious machinery, pervades the consciousness of Western man today. A world that functions mysteriously outside our conscious control, must appear absurd. It no longer has a religious or historical purpose; it has ceased to make sense. The convict who is being physically separated from the outside world has literally been deprived of any means to make his presence felt, to make an impact on reality; in that sense the convict experiences the human condition in our time more intensely and more directly than any of us. He, or at least a convict of Genet's sensibility and power of expression, can therefore become the spokesman for the unspoken thoughts, the subconscious malaise of Western man.

Genet's vision in *The Balcony* may be vindictive, and distorted by the outcast's violent rage at society, but it has its validity nevertheless. It would be wrong to criticize the play on the ground that the analysis of the workings of society it presents is manifestly false, that the church, the law, and the defence forces have other functions than merely those of giving expression to the lust for power of those holding responsible positions in their hierarchies (although these motives no doubt play a powerful part in the psychology of lawyers, bishops, and generals). Genet is not concerned with giving such an analysis. He is projecting the feeling of impotence of the individual caught up in the meshes of society, he is dramatizing the often suppressed and subconscious rage of the 'I', alone and terrified by the anonymous weight of the nebulous 'they'. It is this helplessness, this impotence, that seeks an outlet in the substitute explanation of myth and daydreams. They try to bring back meaning and purpose into the universe, yet they are bound to collapse again and again. Reality is an unattainable goal. Nothing the individual can do can have meaning in a world on the brink of annihilation for reasons and by means that the individual is unable to grasp and over which he appears to have no control.

The revolutionaries in *The Balcony* try to abolish a system of power based on mythical images. But in the very act of trying to break out of the iron ring of myth into the world of reality beyond it, they are compelled to construct their own myth. For it is by the fantasies of the masses that society is kept going. Chantal, who escaped from Madame Irma's brothel because she could not bear prostituting herself for the fantasies of impotent little men trying to partake of the feeling of power and sexual potency, is inevitably turned into an object of myth, a sexual image designed to lure the cannon-fodder of the revolution to its death. And after her own self-sacrifice in that heroic part, Chantal, the mythical Joan of Arc, is without difficulty appropriated by the fake bishop as part of his own liturgy. (It is noteworthy that Brecht, whose work Genet is unlikely to have known, uses exactly the same image. His saintly revolutionary girl in *St Joan of the Stockyards* is canonized by the capitalists immediately after her death.)

In the end, the leader of the revolutionaries himself faces the truth about his own motivation. The reality he wanted to break into was the reality of power, the power represented by the secret-information service and terroristic methods of the modern totalitarian state. That is why he wants to satisfy his frustrated craving by coming to the brothel to seek satisfaction in impersonating the Chief of Police. But, at the same time, he feels guilty about this realization, and is filled with a furious desire for revenge. His act of self-castration while impersonating the Police Chief is an ambivalent one; he wants to punish himself for his desire for power, and at the same time punish the Police Chief vicariously by an act of sympathetic magic. Power and virility being equated in Roger's mind as well as in Genet's, the Police Chief himself having chosen a gigantic phallus as his heraldic symbol, such an act of sympathetic magic is bound to be an act of emasculation.

Roger, although he makes only two relatively brief appearances in a long play, is the real hero of *The Balcony*. His role is analogous to that of Lefranc in *Deathwatch* and of Claire in *The Maids*. Lefranc tries to escape from his isolation and rejection by committing a murder. He fails and falls back into even more complete loneliness. Claire, having failed to murder her lady, kills herself while pretending to be the lady, in exactly the same way that Roger castrates the Chief of Police by proxy. As Claire, who really wants to become the lady whom she both loves and hates, both fulfils her craving by impersonating the loved character and punishes herself for that craving by killing herself, so Roger acknowledges his desire to *be* the Police Chief while punishing the Police Chief in his own person. But neither Claire nor Roger can break out into reality. Claire can neither become like her lady in reality nor kill her in reality. Roger can neither attain power through revolution nor really punish the Police Chief by sympathetic magic. On the contrary, his action completes the ritual acceptance of the figure of the Chief of Police in the pantheon of mankind's fantasies of sex and power. Instead of smashing a mirror to reach the outside world, Roger has merely added one further cabinet of mirrors to the many others that serve to reflect the fake images of little men dreaming of real power.

This analysis of myth and dream is itself quite clearly a dream and a myth. Even more than in *Deathwatch* and *The Maids*, the audience is left in no doubt that they are not meant to take any of the events they see as real. There are no characters in the conventional sense in *The Balcony*, merely the images of basic urges and impulses. Nor is there, strictly speaking, a plot. Essentially the play is a series of rituals, followed by their equally ritual debunking – the customers of the brothel performing their rites, the ritual presentation of the new hierarchy of power, the ritual castration of the frustrated revolutionary. The plot structure needed to link these ceremonial acts together is the weakest part of the play. That is why all critics agree that the final part is too long and less impressive than the opening of the play. It is here that the figures of fantasy are briefly supposed to be shown exercising real power, but in fact they do nothing concrete beyond discussing the relative merits of their myths and posing for press photographers – i.e. exhibiting themselves to the populace. Here Genet himself clearly fails to achieve the breakthrough into reality. On the other hand, the ceremonial or mock-ceremonial parts of the play are superb both as theatre (witness the triumphant use of the cothurnus to make the dream images of little men appear as gigantic figures) and in the splendour of their language.

This unevenness springs from Genet's basic dilemma. He strives for a theatre of ritual, but ritual is the regular repetition of mythical events and, as such, closely akin to sympathetic magic. It endeavours to influence the real world either by re-enacting the key happenings that have shaped that world or (as in fertility rites) by performing in an exemplary manner what is hoped will be happening in abundance. A theatre of ritual and ceremonial like the theatre of ancient Greece presupposes a valid and vital body of beliefs and myths. And this is precisely what our own civilization lacks. Hence in *The Balcony* Genet is faced with the need to provide a plot structure that will furnish the rationale for his mock-liturgy and mock-ceremonial. And he has not quite succeeded in integrating plot and ritual.

In *Les Nègres* (*The Blacks*) he has found an extremely ingenious solution to this problem. Here he presents a play, labelled a *clownerie* (a clown show), which is entirely ritual and therefore needs no plot devices at all. A group of Negroes performs the ritual re-enactment of their resentments and feelings of revenge before a white audience. As Genet insists, in a prefatory note to the play, it would lose its *raison d'être* if there were not at least one white person in the audience. 'But what if no white person accepted? Then let white masks be distributed to the black spectators as they enter the theatre. And if the blacks refuse the mask, then let a dummy be used.'[1] In other words, the

1. Genet, *The Blacks*, trans. Bernard Frechtman (New York: Grove Press, 1960), p. 11.

presence – even the merely symbolic presence – of at least one white spectator is indispensable to this particular ritual.

The Negro actors performing this ritual are divided into two groups: those who appear as Negroes and will enact the Negroes' fantasy, and those who appear, grotesquely and visibly masked, to represent white men. The white audience in the theatre is confronted by a grotesque mirror image of itself on the stage. The Negro actors stand between two audiences of whites. The stage audience consists, however, of the Negroes' fantasy image of the white man, embodied in the hierarchy of power in a colonial society – the queen, haughty and remote; her governor; her judge; her missionary; and her valet, who plays the part of the artist or intellectual who lends his services to the hierarchy of power while not strictly belonging to it. It is significant that queen, judge, bishop, and general (the governor is a military man) are identical with the figures of the hierarchy of power in *The Balcony*.

In front of this projected image of alien rule, the group of Negroes enacts its fantasies of resentment. The central part of the ritual is a fantasy of the ritual murder of a white woman, elaborately and lovingly imagined in lurid detail. It is this white woman who is supposed to be inside the coffin that stands in the centre of the stage. For, as one of the Negroes puts it, 'we must deserve their [i.e. the whites'] reprobation and get them to deliver the judgement that will condemn us.'[1] At first the Negro named Village, who is supposed to have committed the murder, describes the victim as an old crone they found drunk and helpless by the docks and then strangled. Later, when the actual murder is lovingly reconstructed, the victim becomes a buxom white woman who has been so seduced by her black visitor's superior sexual attractions that she had invited him into her bedroom, where she was both violated and strangled. As an additional touch of irony, the Negro who has to enact the raped white woman is supposed in private life to be a black priest,

1. ibid., p. 39.

Diouf. After his ritual murder, he takes his place among the other 'whites' on the platform backstage.

After the Negroes have acted out their hatred and resentment, but also their feelings of guilt, the next phase follows – the fantasy of final liberation. The queen and her court descend, as though engaged on a punitive expedition to the colony. They are trapped and ignominiously put to death by the blacks, the missionary bishop is castrated. Thanking the Negro actors who have impersonated the whites, Archibald, who acts as the stage manager throughout the play, sums up the significance of the ritual: 'The time has not yet come for presenting dramas about noble matters. But perhaps they suspect what lies behind this architecture of emptiness and words. We are what they want us to be. We shall therefore be it to the very end, absurdly.'[1]

The spectacle of this ritual representation of the Negroes' feelings about the whites has been made grotesquely clownish to render it bearable to an audience of whites. In opening the proceedings, Archibald informs the spectators, 'In order that you may remain comfortably settled in your seats in the presence of the drama that is already unfolding here – in order that you be assured that there is no danger of such a drama's worming its way into your precious lives – we shall even have the decency – a decency learned from you – to make communication impossible. We shall increase the distance that separates us – a distance that is basic – by our pomp, our manners, our insolence. For we are also actors.'[2] Hence the play takes the form of a ritual ceremony rather than being a direct discussion of the colour problem or colonialism. In ritual, meaning is expressed by the repetition of symbolic actions. The participants have a sense of awe, of mysterious participation rather than of conceptual communication. The difference is merely that here the audience sees a grotesque parody of a ritual, in which the bitterness that is to be communicated emerges from clowning and derision.

1. ibid., p. 127.   2. ibid., p. 22.

Yet this is only the initial deception in this complex hall of mirrors. As the action proceeds, the audience is made aware that something else, something more real than the ritual concerned, is happening offstage. One of the characters, Ville de Saint-Nazaire (or Newport News, in the translation), who was sent off with a revolver in the opening scene, returns toward the end and reports that a Negro traitor has been tried and executed. So the whole elaborate performance given on the stage is revealed as a blind, an illusion enacted as a diversion to distract attention from the real action behind the scenes. We have seen a ritual of the murder of a white woman, but the reality was the trial and execution of a Negro – a Negro traitor.

It is on the entrance of Ville de Sainte-Nazaire with the news of the traitor's execution that the actors who have been impersonating the white court remove their masks and reveal themselves as Negroes. It is only after they have heard the news that a new revolutionary delegate has been sent to Africa, to resume the work of the executed traitor, that they put on their masks again and enact the execution and torture of the white oppressors.

So the whole ritual of revenge was a grotesque diversion. Or was it? For we know that Ville de Saint-Nazaire is also an actor, and that nothing real has been going on behind the scenes – that in fact the theatrical performance is more real than the pretended reality of execution and revolution. Whether intended by Genet or not, the pretence at political action behind the smokescreen of a grotesque performance is merely another reflection in a chain of mirages.

Moreover, we know full well that the Negroes on the stage stand for more than simply Negroes. Just as the servant girls in *The Maids*, even if acted by women, are really meant to be boys playing women, but representing a world of men, the Negroes in *The Blacks*, acted by Negroes, are not really Negroes. As Genet himself puts it in a cryptic prefatory note to the play, 'One evening an actor asked me to write a play for an all-black

cast. But what exactly is a black? First of all, what is his colour?'[1]
The Negroes in the play are an image of all outcasts of society;
they stand, above all, for Genet himself, who, when called a
thief at the age of ten, decided 'to be what they want us to be'.
Or as Archibald puts it, 'On this stage we are like guilty
prisoners who play at being guilty.'[2] The blacks are again the
convicts, the prisoners who, deprived of the chance to partake
of the real world, dream their dreams of guilt and revenge –
including the trial and execution of traitors.

'We – you and I,' says Village, 'were moving along the edges
of the world, out of bounds. We were the shadow, or the dark
interior, of luminous creatures. . . .' When he speaks these lines,
Village is talking about his love for Virtue, the black prostitute.
For a moment when that love was kindled, he was at the
threshold of reality:

When I beheld you, suddenly – for perhaps a second – I had the
strength to reject everything that wasn't you and to laugh at the
illusion. But my shoulders are very frail. I was unable to bear the
weight of the world's condemnation. And I began to hate you when
everything about you would have kindled my love and when love
would have made men's contempt unbearable, and their contempt
would have made my love unbearable. The fact is, I hate you.[3]

Being denied the dignity of man, the outcasts, the blacks, are
denied the emotions of the real world. Yet at the end of the
play, when the grotesque ritual has dissolved, Village and Virtue remain alone on the stage. And Village tries to learn the
gestures of love, hard though they may be to learn. This is the
first gleam of hope in Genet's dark theatre – two of his characters who have found the courage to break out of the vicious
circle of daydreaming and establish genuine human contact
through love. Or is this too optimistic an interpretation? Is this
happy end only itself a fantasy of wish-fulfilment, and false as
such? It does not seem so. The final tableau of *The Blacks* shows

1. ibid., p. 10.   2. ibid., p. 47.   3. ibid., p. 44.

the whole cast standing at the back of the stage, with only Virtue and Village turning their backs to the audience and walking toward their fellow-actors to the strains of the minuet from *Don Giovanni*. So the lovers *have* turned their backs on the world of illusion.

The Blacks was written in 1957 and first performed by a troupe of Negro actors, Les Griots, under the direction of Roger Blin, at the Théâtre de Lutèce on 28 October 1959. Brilliantly acted, the play achieved considerable success and had a run of several months, although it bewildered a large part of the audience and a good many of the critics.

In spite of his often professed contempt for the theatre as a place to work in, and for actors as artists, Genet continued to be active as a dramatist. His next play, *Les Paravents* (*The Screens*, 1961), presents his acid comment on the Algerian war. At first sight it might appear as though Genet was following the development of Adamov in abandoning the Theatre of the Absurd and turning into a political realist. But this is not really the case, although *Les Paravents* certainly shows where Genet's sympathy in the conflict lay. In fact, *Les Paravents* resumes and restates the subject of *Les Nègres*, and, on the whole, less successfully. The play, which manipulates a very large number of characters, again sees the poorest of the poor, the Algerian peasants, as outcasts of society fighting a desperate battle against the powers that be – the authorities, *les justes*. But whereas *Les Nègres* concentrated the action in a powerful poetic image, *Les Paravents* scatters it over a vast open-air stage (Genet insists that the play must be performed in the open air) rising in four tiers. The action is to take place, often on several tiers at the same time, in front of a wide variety of screens that are to be rolled onstage on silent rubber wheels. The indication of the background for each scene is to appear painted on these screens, and will in certain cases be drawn on them by the actors themselves. The cast list comprises almost a hundred characters, but Genet specifies that each actor should play five or six parts.

The focal point of this wide canvas is occupied by Saïd, the poorest of all Arabs, so poor in fact that he can afford to marry only the ugliest girl, Leila. Saïd's mother dominates Saïd as well as the action of the play; she is, as mother figures usually are in Genet's work, a highly ambivalent character. Saïd and his mother are involved in the rebellion; the mother is killed and appears on the uppermost tier of the stage, together with a whole row of other dead, who look down on the action like the masked figures of the whites in *Les Nègres*. The life of an Arab village – with its cadi, its brothel, its market, its *colons*, its police-men – is vividly evoked. Grotesque caricatures of French soldiers perform cruel and scurrilous antics. But the anti-colonial tendency of the play is largely overlaid by a profusion of images of an anal eroticism that had not hitherto appeared so openly in Genet's dramatic works, although it has always been present in his prose fiction. On this score, and on that of its diffuseness, *Les Paravents* appears to be less successful than Genet's earlier plays. It clearly could not be performed in France while the Algerian conflict remained unsettled. It had its world première, in a much cut version, in West Berlin in May 1961.

Peter Brook, who had started his Theatre of Cruelty season early in 1964 with the express purpose of training a company of actors for a production of *Les Paravents*, only got as far as an ex-perimental – and private – production of the first twelve scenes, barely more than half of the play. It was a memorable evening in the theatre. The scene in which the Algerians' burning of the colonists' orchards is indicated by flames being painted on the screens, reached a peak of frenzy of unforgettable intensity. It was action painting transformed into drama. But censorship difficulties and the small likelihood of a success with a large public led to the abandonment of the project. The company Brook had trained triumphed in the summer of 1964 in *Marat/*

Sade.[1] History is full of exquisite ironies: after the end of the Algerian war and in the heyday of de Gaulle's rule, *Les Paravents* finally received its first French performance at the Odéon on 21 April 1966, under Roger Blin's direction and with Madeleine Renaud and Jean-Louis Barrault in leading parts. There were some demonstrations, but the performance was received with enthusiasm by the bulk of the audience.

Les Paravents was said to form part of a cycle of seven plays on which Genet was believed to be working, but none of these had seen the light of day by the late 1970's.

The film *Mademoiselle* (1966), directed by Tony Richardson with Jeanne Moreau in the lead, is highly characteristic of Genet's approach to reality. A prim little village schoolteacher has observed a gorgeously built foreign labourer (in the original script he is a Pole, in the finished film he has become an Italian) perform feats of daring in rescue work on the occasion of some village disaster. She commits a series of criminal acts (setting fire to a barn, poisoning a well, breaching a dam) merely to obtain further gratification of her suppressed desires, for each time the splendid foreigner intervenes courageously to help. Unable to explain this succession of disasters, the xenophobic villagers become convinced that the foreigner himself must be the culprit. After a wild night of real gratification with the man, the prim young woman looks on coldly and unmoved as the crowd lynches her lover. She packs her bags and primly departs to a new post. Genet's script is brilliantly written. Alas, somewhat clumsily transferred to the screen, it becomes faintly ridiculous, almost a self-parody.

Since then Genet has, at least as far as published work for the theatre is concerned, fallen silent. In the late sixties he took an

1. Peter Weiss, *The Persecution and Assassination of Marat as performed by the Inmates of the Asylum of Charenton under the Direction of the Marquis de Sade* (*Die Verfolgung und Ermordung Jean Paul Marats dargestellt durch die Schauspieltruppe des Hospizes zu Charenton unter Anleitung des Herrn de Sade*, first performed Berlin, 1964).

energetic stand in favour of the Black Panther party in the United States and made a number of public appearances on their behalf.

He leads an elusive, solitary and nomadic existence, moving, practically without luggage or possessions, from one hotel to another, appearing briefly in one continent and reappearing in another, a wanderer between the worlds.[1]

In writing for the theatre and cinema, Genet has achieved what all his characters (with the possible exception of Village and Virtue) have failed to achieve – he has broken through the vicious spiral of daydream and illusion, and by putting his fantasies on to the stage – concrete, brutal, and disturbing – he has succeeded in making his impact on the real world, if only by leaving an audience of *les justes* deeply stirred and disgusted. As Sartre puts it in summing up Genet's astonishing career, 'In willing himself to be a thief to the utmost limit, Genet plunges into dream; in willing his dream to the point of madness, he makes himself a poet; in willing poetry to the final triumph of the word, he becomes a man; and the man has become the truth of the poet, just as the poet had been the truth of the thief.'[2]

If the young outcast's anti-social acts were attempts to revenge himself on society, to destroy the whole of its fabric in symbolic acts of sympathetic magic, his activity as a writer is a direct continuation of this protest by other and more efficacious means. 'If', as Sartre points out,

Genet, confined as he is in a world of fantasy by the pitiless order of things [i.e. an outcast who can have no impact on the real world], renounced his attempt to scandalize by the action of a thief? . . . If he made . . . the imaginary sphere a permanent source of scandal? If he could bring it about that his dreams of impotence tapped, in their very impotence, an infinite power and, in defiance of all the police

1. For a portrait of Genet's mode of life see *Jean Genet in Tangiers* by Mohamed Choukri, Ecco Press, New York, 1974.
2. *Saint Genet*, p. 535.

forces of the world, put society as a whole in question? Would he not, in that case, have found a point of junction for the imaginary and the real, the ineffective and the effective, the false and the true, the right to act and the action?[1]

It is clear that in confronting society itself in the theatre, rather than as solitary readers of his narrative prose, Genet comes far closer to his objective. Here a group of living people constituting a collective unity – the audience – is confronted with the secret world of the dreams and fantasies of the outcast. What is more, the audience, by experiencing the impact of what they see, even if that impact takes the form of horror and disgust, is forced to recognize its own psychological predicament, monstrously heightened and magnified though it be, there in front of it on the stage. The fact that a large part of the audience may have been drawn into the theatre by rumours that the spectacle will be scandalous or pornographic only increases this effect of shock. For here the prurient among *les justes* will find that their own fantasies are not so dissimilar from those of the self-confessed outcast.

Genet's theatre may lack plot, character, construction, coherence, or social truth. It undoubtedly has psychological truth. His plays are not intellectual exercises (cleverly though they are constructed) but the projections of a world of private myth, conceived as such in the pre-logical modes of thought that are the hallmark of the sphere of myth and dream; hence the prevalence of magical modes of action in Genet's plays – the identification of subject and object, symbol and reality, word and concept, as well as, in some instances, the divorce of the name from the thing it signifies: the objectification of the word (Genet once told Sartre that he hated roses, but loved the word 'rose'). In the world of pre-logical thought, dream, and myth, language becomes incantation instead of communication; the word does not signify a concept but magically conjures up a thing – it becomes a magical formula. Desire and love express

1. ibid., p. 388.

themselves in the wish for possession through identification and incorporation of the beloved object. Incantation, magical substitution, and identification are the essential elements of ritual. It is the use of language as incantatory magic – the objectification of words – that makes Genet's theatre, in spite of its harshness and scabrous content, into a truly poetical theatre, a translation, as it were, of Baudelaire's *Fleurs du Mal* into dramatic imagery.

Genet's theatre is, profoundly, a theatre of social protest. Yet, like that of Ionesco, and of Adamov before his conversion to epic realism, it resolutely rejects political commitment, political argument, didacticism, or propaganda. In dealing with the dream world of the outcast of society, it explores the human condition, the alienation of man, his solitude, his futile search for meaning and reality.

Although Genet's theatre differs in many aspects of method and approach from that of the other dramatists discussed in this book, it bears many of the essential hallmarks that they have in common – the abandonment of the concepts of character and motivation; the concentration on states of mind and basic human situations, rather than on the development of a narrative plot from exposition to solution; the devaluation of language as a means of communication and understanding; the rejection of didactic purpose; and the confrontation of the spectator with the harsh facts of a cruel world and his own isolation. As such *The Balcony* and *The Blacks* can with certainty, *The Maids* with a good deal of probability, be regarded as examples of the Theatre of the Absurd.

5

HAROLD PINTER

Certainties and uncertainties

AMONG the younger generation of playwrights who followed in the footsteps of the pioneers of the Theatre of the Absurd, Harold Pinter, twenty-four years younger than Beckett, has achieved the status of a major force in the contemporary theatre. His background is very different from that of the exiles from Armenia, Rumania, Ireland, and the French criminal underworld who made the major contributions to the new approach to drama, but he too, in his own way, repeats the pattern, as he also comes from a family of relatively recent immigrants from Eastern Europe.

Harold Pinter (born in 1930), the son of a Jewish tailor in Hackney, in East London, started writing poetry for little magazines in his teens, studied acting at the Royal Academy of Dramatic Art and the Central School of Speech and Drama, and, under the stage name David Baron, embarked on an acting career, which led him around Ireland in a Shakespearean company and to years of strenuous work in provincial repertory. After starting on a novel, *The Dwarfs*, which he did not publish, he began to write plays in 1957. He himself has told the story of how he mentioned an idea for a play to a friend of his who was working in the drama department of Bristol University. The friend liked the idea so much that he wrote to Pinter asking for the play, adding that if the university was to perform it, he would have to send the manuscript within a week. 'So I wrote back and told him to forget the whole thing. And then I sat down and wrote it in four days. I don't know how it happened, but it did.'[1]

1. Harold Pinter, interview with Kenneth Tynan, B.B.C. Home Service, 28 October 1960.

This rapidly and spontaneously written one-act play, *The Room* (first performed at Bristol University in May 1957), already contains a good many of the basic themes and a great deal of the very personal style and idiom of Pinter's later and more successful work – the uncannily cruel accuracy of his reproduction of the inflections and rambling irrelevancy of everyday speech; the commonplace situation that is gradually invested with menace, dread, and mystery; the deliberate omission of an explanation or a motivation for the action. The room, which is the centre and chief poetic image of the play, is one of the recurring motifs of Pinter's work. As he himself once put it, 'Two people in a room – I am dealing a great deal of the time with this image of two people in a room. The curtain goes up on the stage, and I see it as a very potent question: What is going to happen to these two people in the room? Is someone going to open the door and come in?'[1] The starting point of Pinter's theatre is thus a return to some of the basic elements of drama – the suspense created by the elementary ingredients of pure, preliterary theatre: a stage, two people, a door; a poetic image of an undefined fear and expectation. When asked by a critic what his two people in his room are afraid of, Pinter replied, 'Obviously they are scared of what is outside the room. Outside the room there is a world bearing upon them which is frightening. I am sure it is frightening to you and me as well.'[2]

In this case, the room is inhabited by Rose, a simple-minded old woman whose husband, Bert, never speaks to her although he is pampered and fed with overwhelming motherliness. The room is in a vast house; outside it is winter and night. Rose sees the room as her only refuge, her only security in a hostile world. This room, she tells herself, is just right for her. She would not like to live downstairs in the basement, where it is cold and damp. The room becomes an image of the small area of light

1. Pinter, interview with Hallam Tennyson, B.B.C. General Overseas Service, 7 August 1960.
2. Pinter interview with Tynan.

and warmth that our consciousness, the fact that we exist, opens up in the vast ocean of nothingness from which we gradually emerge after birth and into which we sink again when we die. The room, this small speck of warmth and light in the darkness, is a precarious foothold; Rose is afraid that she may be driven from it. She is not sure of the place of her room in the scheme of things, how it fits into the house. When she asks Mr Kidd, whom she takes for the landlord but who may be merely a caretaker, how many floors there are in the house, even he is vague about the matter: 'Well, to tell you the truth, I don't count them now.'[1] Mr Kidd is an old, doddering man, vague about his own origins: 'I think my mum was a Jewess. Yes, I wouldn't be surprised to learn that she was a Jewess.'[2]

Rose's husband and Mr Kidd leave. Rose remains alone. The door assumes all the menace of an opening into the vague unknown of the house, with its uncertain number of floors, the night and the winter outside. And when Rose finally opens the door to take the refuse out, two people are seen standing outside it. A moment of genuine terror has been produced with the utmost economy of means. And even though the strangers are merely a young couple looking for the landlord, the atmosphere of terror is kept up. They are looking for a room, they have heard there is a good room to let in that very house. Wandering through the empty house, they heard a voice in the dark basement, confirming that there was a room to let. As a matter of fact it was no. 7 – Rose's room.

The strangers leave. Mr Kidd returns. There is a man downstairs who wants to see Rose. He has been there for days, waiting for Rose's husband to leave, just lying there in the basement. Mr Kidd goes out. Rose is left alone. Again the door becomes the focal point of a nameless menace. It opens. A blind Negro enters. His name is Riley. He has a message for Rose: 'Your

1. Pinter, *The Room*, in *The Birthday Party and Other Plays* (London: Methuen, 1960), p. 102.

2. ibid., p. 103.

father wants you to come. Come home, Sal.'[1] We know the woman is called Rose. But she does not deny being called Sal. She merely insists. 'Don't call me that.' Bert, Rose's husband, returns. He, who has not spoken throughout the entire first scene, now speaks: 'I got back all right.' Again, a real *coup de théâtre* is brought about by the simplest of devices. Bert speaks about the menace of the dark and how his beloved van got him back. Then he notices the Negro. He upsets the chair on which he is sitting and beats him savagely until he remains motionless. Rose clutches her eyes. She has gone blind.

The Room shows not only the main characteristics of Pinter's style fully formed; the weaknesses it displays also allow us to judge how he gradually learned to avoid the temptations into which he fell in his first bout of spontaneous enthusiasm. The weakness of *The Room* is clearly its lapse from horror, built up from elements of the commonplace, into crude symbolism, cheap mystery, and violence. The blind Negro with the message from the father calling his daughter home, the killing of this near-parody of a death symbol by the jealous husband, and Rose's own blinding – all these are melodramatic devices that are out of keeping with the subtly built-up terrors of the opening scenes. Here mystery becomes threadbare mystification.

Pinter's second one-act play still contains this element of mystification, but already it is far more subtly and wittily used. In *The Dumb Waiter* (written in 1957, first performed at the Hampstead Theatre Club in London, on 21 January 1960), we again have a room with two people in it – and the door that opens on the unknown. The two men in this dingy basement room are two hired killers employed by a mysterious organization to go around the country and assassinate their employers' victims. They are given an address and a key and told to wait for instructions. Sooner or later their victim arrives, they kill him or her, and drive off. They don't know what happens then: 'Who clears up after we have gone? I am curious about that.

1. ibid., p. 118.

Who does the clearing up? Maybe they don't clear up. Maybe they just leave them there, eh? What do you think?'[1]

Ben and Gus, the two gunmen, are very nervous. They want to make tea but are frustrated. They have no matches. An envelope with matches is mysteriously pushed under the door. But even then they don't have the shilling to put into the gas meter. At the back of the basement room there is a serving hatch, a 'dumb waiter' – this must have been the kitchen of a restaurant at one time. Suddenly this contraption begins to move; an order on a piece of paper comes down: 'Two braised steak and chips. Two sago puddings. Two teas without sugar.' The two gunmen, anxious not to be discovered, are pathetically eager to fill this mysterious order from above. They search their pockets for bits of food and send up a packet of tea, a bottle of milk, a bar of chocolate, an Eccles cake, a packet of potato crisps. But the dumb waiter comes back for more. It demands more and more complicated dishes. Greek and Chinese specialties. The two men discover a speaking-tube next to the dumb waiter, and Ben establishes contact with the powers above. He hears that 'the Eccles cake was stale, the chocolate was melted, the biscuits were mouldy.'[2] When Gus goes out to get a glass of water, the speaking-tube comes to life again. Ben gets his final instructions from above. They are to kill the next man who enters. It is Gus. He is stripped of jacket, waistcoat, tie, holster, and revolver. It is Gus who is the next victim.

The Dumb Waiter brilliantly fulfils Ionesco's postulate in completely fusing tragedy with the most hilarious farce. It also succeeds in turning the mysterious supernatural ingredient, which was merely sentimental in *The Room*, into an additional element of comedy: the spectacle of the heavenly powers bombarding two solemn gunmen with demands for '*macaroni pastitsio, ormitha macarounada*, and *char siu* and bean sprouts' is

1. Pinter, *The Dumb Waiter*, in *The Birthday Party and Other Plays*, p. 150.
2. ibid.

wildly funny. Yet the main element of comedy is provided by the brilliant small talk behind which the two men hide their growing anxiety. These discussions of which football team is playing away on that particular Saturday, whether it is correct to say 'light the kettle' or 'light the gas', the desultory discussions of trivial news in the evening paper are utterly true, wildly comic, and terrifying in their absurdity.

Pinter's first full-length play, *The Birthday Party*, combines some of the characters and situations of *The Room* and *The Dumb Waiter* while, for the first time, omitting the melodramatic, supernatural element – without any loss of mystery or horror. The safe and warm haven of *The Room* has here become a dingy seaside boarding house kept by a slovenly but motherly old woman, Meg, who has many of the features of Rose in the earlier play. Meg's husband, Petey, is almost as silent as Rose's husband Bert. But he lacks Bert's brutality. He is a kindly old man, employed as a deck-chair attendant on the promenade. Ben and Gus, the two gunmen of *The Dumb Waiter*, reappear as a sinister pair of strangers – an Irishman, brutal and silent, and a Jew, full of false *bonhomie* and spurious worldly wisdom. But there is a new central character – Stanley, a man in his late thirties, indolent and apathetic, who has somehow found refuge in Meg's boarding-house, which has not had any other visitor for years. Meg treats him with a motherliness so stifling as to be almost incestuous. Little is known about his past, except for a clearly apocryphal story that he once gave a piano recital at Lower Edmonton. It was a great success. But then, at his next concert,

they carved me up. Carved me up. It was all arranged, it was all worked out. My next concert. Somewhere else it was. In winter. I went down there to play. Then, when I got there, the hall was closed, the place was shuttered up, not even a caretaker. They'd locked it up. . . . A fast one. They pulled a fast one. I'd like to know who was responsible for that. . . . All right, Jack, I can take a tip.[1]

1. Pinter, *The Birthday Party and Other Plays*, p. 23.

Though Stanley is dreaming of a world tour, it is clear that he is taking shelter from a hostile world in Meg's sordid seaside haven.

Then, as in the two earlier plays, the door opens. Two sinister visitors, Goldberg and McCann, want a room in Meg's boarding house. It soon becomes clear that they are after Stanley. Are they the emissaries of some secret organization he has betrayed? Or male nurses sent out to fetch him back to an asylum he has escaped from? Or emissaries from another world, like the blind Negro in *The Room*? This question is never answered. We see them merely organizing a birthday party for Stanley who insists that it is not his birthday, and brainwashing him in a terrifying but nonsensical cross-examination:

GOLDBERG: You verminate the sheet of your birth.
MC CANN: What about the Albigensenist heresy?
GOLDBERG: Who watered the wicket in Melbourne?
MC CANN: What about the blessed Oliver Plunkett?
GOLDBERG: Speak up, Webber. Why did the chicken cross the road?
STANLEY: He wanted to – he wanted to – he wanted to –
MC CANN: He doesn't know!
GOLDBERG: Why did the chicken cross the road?
STANLEY: He wanted . . .
MC CANN: He doesn't know. He doesn't know which came first!
GOLDBERG: Which came first?
MC CANN: Chicken? Egg? Which came first?
GOLDBERG and MC CANN: Which came first? Which came first? Which came first?[1]

The birthday party proceeds – with Meg, oblivious of what is going on, grotesquely playing the belle of the ball; with Goldberg, who seems to have a large number of different names, seducing the dumb blonde from next door – until eventually it culminates in a game of blind man's buff. Stanley, whose glasses have been snatched by McCann, becomes more and more hysterical, tries to strangle Meg, and is finally driven upstairs by the two sinister strangers.

1. ibid., pp. 54–5.

In the third act, Goldberg and McCann take Stanley away in a big black car. He is now dressed in a black jacket and striped trousers, has a clean collar, wears a bowler hat, carries his broken glasses in his hand, and has become speechless and blank, like a puppet. When Meg comes down, she is still dreaming of the wonderful party and does not realize what has happened.

The Birthday Party has been interpreted as an allegory of the pressures of conformity, with Stanley, the pianist, as the artist who is forced into respectability and pin-stripe trousers by the emissaries of the bourgeois world. Yet the play can equally well be seen as an allegory of death – man snatched away from the home he has built himself, from the warmth of love embodied by Meg's mixture of motherliness and sexuality, by the dark angels of nothingness, who pose to him the question of which came first, the chicken or the egg. But, as in the case of *Waiting for Godot*, all such interpretations would miss the point; a play like this simply explores a situation which, in itself, is a valid poetic image that is immediately seen as relevant and true. It speaks plainly of the individual's pathetic search for security; of secret dreads and anxieties; of the terrorism of our world, so often embodied in false *bonhomie* and bigoted brutality; of the tragedy that arises from lack of understanding between people on different levels of awareness. Meg's warmth and love can never reach Stanley, who despises her stupidity and slatternliness, while, on the other hand, Meg's husband Petey is tongue-tied almost to the point of imbecility, so that his evident warmth and affection remain unexpressed and bottled up.

The possibility of an overall allegorical interpretation of a play like *The Birthday Party* would presuppose that the play had been written to express a preconceived idea. Pinter emphatically denies that he works in this manner: 'I think it is impossible – and certainly for me – to start writing a play from any kind of abstract idea. . . . I start writing a play from an image of a situation and a couple of characters involved, and these people always remain for me quite real; if they were not, the play could not be written.'[1]

For Pinter, there is no contradiction between the desire for realism and the basic absurdity of the situations that inspire him. Like Ionesco he regards life in its absurdity as basically funny – up to a point. 'Everything is funny; the greatest earnestness is funny; even tragedy is funny. And I think what I try to do in my plays is to get to this recognizable reality of the absurdity of what we do and how we behave and how we speak.'[2]

Everything is funny until the horror of the human situation rises to the surface: 'The point about tragedy is that it is *no longer funny*. It is funny, and then it becomes no longer funny.'[3] Life is funny because it is arbitrary, based on illusions and self-deceptions, like Stanley's dream that he is going on a world tour as a pianist, because it is built out of pretence and the grotesque overestimation each individual makes of himself. But in our present-day world, everything is uncertain and relative. There is no fixed point; we are surrounded by the unknown. And 'the fact that it is verging on the unknown leads us to the next step, which seems to occur in my plays. There is a kind of horror about and I think that this horror and absurdity go together.'[4]

The area of the unknown that surrounds us includes the motivation and background of the characters. What Pinter, in his search for a higher degree of realism in the theatre, rejects in the 'well-made play' is precisely that it provides too much information about the background and motivation of each character. In real life, we deal with people all the time whose early history, family relationships, or psychological motivations we totally ignore. We are interested if we see them involved in some dramatic situation. We stop and look in fascination at a quarrel in the street even if we do not know what is at

1. Pinter interview with Tynan.
2. Pinter interview with Tennyson. 3. ibid. 4. ibid.

issue. But there is more to this rejection of an over-defined motivation of characters in drama than the desire for realism. There is the problem of the *possibility* of ever knowing the real motivation behind the actions of human beings who are complex and whose psychological make-up is contradictory and unverifiable. One of Pinter's major concerns as a dramatist is precisely that of the difficulty of verification. In a note inserted in the programme of the performance of his two one-act plays at the Royal Court Theatre in London in March 1960, Pinter stated this problem as follows:

The desire for verification is understandable but cannot always be satisfied. There are no hard distinctions between what is real and what is unreal, nor between what is true and what is false. The thing is not necessarily either true or false; it can be both true and false. The assumption that to verify what has happened and what is happening presents few problems I take to be inaccurate. A character on the stage who can present no convincing argument or information as to his past experience, his present behaviour or his aspirations, nor give a comprehensive analysis of his motives, is as legitimate and as worthy of attention as one who, alarmingly, can do all these things. The more acute the experience the less articulate its expression.[1]

The problem of verification in Pinter's theatre is closely linked with his use of language. Pinter's clinically accurate ear for the absurdity of ordinary speech enables him to transcribe everyday conversation in all its repetitiveness, incoherence, and lack of logic or grammar. The dialogue of Pinter's plays is a casebook of the whole gamut of *non sequiturs* in small talk; he registers the delayed-action effect resulting from differences in the speed of thinking between people – the slower-witted character is constantly replying to the penultimate question while the faster one is already two jumps ahead. There are also the misunderstandings arising from inability to listen; incomprehension of polysyllabic words used for show by the more

1. Programme note for performance of *The Room* and *The Dumb Waiter*, Royal Court Theatre, London, March 1960.

articulate characters; mishearings; and false anticipations. Instead of proceeding logically, Pinter's dialogue follows a line of associative thinking in which sound regularly prevails over sense. Yet Pinter denies that he is trying to present a case for man's inability to communicate with his fellows. 'I feel,' he once said, 'that instead of any inability to communicate there is a deliberate evasion of communication. Communication itself between people is so frightening that rather than do that there is continual cross-talk, a continual talking about other things, rather than what is at the root of their relationship.'[1]

The Birthday Party was Pinter's first play to get a professional performance in London. (It opened at the Arts Theatre in Cambridge on 28 April 1958, and was transferred to the Lyric, Hammersmith, in May.) The play failed at first, but could not be kept down. Pinter himself directed it in Birmingham in January 1959. It achieved a brilliant success in an excellent performance by the Tavistock Players at the Tower Theatre, in Canonbury, London, in the spring of the same year, and was seen by millions of British viewers in an exciting television performance early in 1960.

The impact of so strange and demanding a play on the mass audience of television was fascinating. While viewers were clearly exasperated by the lack of the cheap and obvious motivation to which they were used in their daily fare, they were also visibly intrigued. For days one could hear people in buses and canteens eagerly discussing the play as a maddening but deeply disturbing experience. *The Birthday Party* reached the United States in July 1960, when it was very successfully staged by the Actors' Workshop in San Francisco.

Much of Pinter's astonishingly rich output since he started writing plays in 1957 has been for radio and television. In the radio play *A Slight Ache* (first performed on the B.B.C.'s Third Programme on 29 July 1959), Pinter makes brilliant use of the limitations of the medium. Of the three characters in the play,

1. Pinter interview with Tynan.

only two speak. The third remains entirely silent and is thus invested with the terror of the unknown. An old couple, Edward and Flora, are disturbed by the mysterious presence of a matchseller at the back gate of their house. He has been standing there for weeks, holding his tray without ever selling anything. They finally call him into their house. But whatever they say to him, he remains silent. As though challenged by the stubborn absence of any reaction, Edward begins to tell the man his life story. Edward insists that he is not frightened, but he is, and goes to get some fresh air in the garden. Now it is Flora's turn to address the silent visitor with a flood of reminiscences and confessions. She even talks of sex, being clearly attracted and repelled by the old tramp. 'I'm going to keep you, you dreadful chap, and call you Barnabas.' Like Meg in *The Birthday Party*, Flora's attitude toward the old man is a mixture of sexuality and motherliness. Edward becomes violently jealous. It is his turn again to address Barnabas. As he still fails to elicit any reaction, he becomes more and more personal while visibly disintegrating. The play ends with Flora installing Barnabas in the house and sending Edward away: 'Edward! Here is your tray!'[1] The tramp and the husband have changed places.

There is a curious affinity between the silent matchseller in *A Slight Ache* and Ionesco's Killer, whose silence also leads his antagonist, Bérenger, to paroxysms of eloquence and eventual disintegration. Here, as there, the silent character acts as a catalyst for the projection of the other's deepest feelings. Edward, in projecting his thoughts, is confronted with his inner emptiness and disintegrates, while Flora projects her still vital sexuality and changes partners. Yet as the silent matchseller is never heard to utter so much as the inarticulate giggle of the Killer, he might equally well be a figment of the old people's imagination. The audience of the radio play will never be able to verify whether he was real or not. But *A Slight Ache* also

1. Pinter, *A Slight Ache*, in *Tomorrow*, Oxford, no. 4, 1960. Also in *A Slight Ache and Other Plays* (London: Methuen, 1961).

proved effective when produced on the stage (Arts Theatre, London, 18 January 1961).

The element of mystery is almost entirely absent in Pinter's second radio play, *A Night Out* (first broadcast in March 1960, on the Third Programme; television version on A.B.C. Television, April 1960), and in the television play *Night School* (first broadcast by Associated Rediffusion TV in July 1960). In both of these plays, as in a number of short revue sketches he wrote at about the same time, Pinter relies entirely on his mastery of real-life idiom to produce a feeling of the absurdity and futility of the human condition.

A Night Out tells the adventures of a repressed clerk, Albert Stokes, who is kept on his mother's apron strings and stifled by a possessiveness reminiscent of Meg's motherliness towards Stanley, or Flora's towards the enigmatic matchseller. Albert has been invited to an office party. He breaks loose from his mother and goes to the party, where his office rival causes him embarrassment by egging on the girls to draw him out. He is accused of having 'interfered' with one of the girls, returns home, is received with nagging by his mother, loses his temper, throws something at her, and leaves, thinking that he has killed her. A prostitute takes him to her room, but when she too nags him about spilling cigarette ash on her carpet, he terrifies her with an outburst of temper and runs away. Returning home in the morning, he finds his mother alive but somewhat chastened by his aggressiveness. Has he really broken free during his night out? The question is left unanswered.

A Night Out is only seemingly simple. It is, in fact, extremely subtly constructed in suggesting Albert's predicament through a series of repetitions. The prostitute, in nagging Albert, repeats not only his situation with his mother but also, in making advances to him, his embarrassed situation when confronted with the girls at the party. Thus the scene with the prostitute focuses Albert's double predicament as a mother's boy – his inability to resist his mother and his timidity towards the other sex. In going to the prostitute's room, he has run away from both his mother and the party, yet there once again he encounters all he was trying to escape from.

The television play *Night School* returns to another of Pinter's main preoccupations – a room of one's own as a symbol for one's place in the world. Walter, on his return from prison for forging entries in post-office savings books, finds that his two old aunts have let his room. He is horrified to learn that it is now occupied by a girl, Sally, who describes herself as a schoolteacher and who goes out at night a good deal – allegedly to study foreign languages at night school. While fetching some things from his room, Walter discovers that the girl is in fact a night-club hostess. Although there is a good chance that he might make friends with Sally and thus regain his bed by having an affair with her or even marrying her, Walter asks a shady businessman friend of his aunts' to trace the night club in which she is working. Solto, the businessman, finds the girl, hopes to have an affair of his own with her, and inadvertently reveals that Walter sent him to spy her out. When Solto reports back to Walter, he conceals the fact that he has found the girl. But Sally, who now knows that Walter wanted to expose her, leaves. In wanting too badly to regain his room, Walter has lost the chance of winning the girl who might have given him a real place in the world. *Night School* also touches on the problem of verification and identity – to impress Sally, Walter makes himself out to be a romantic gunman; Sally herself pretends to be a teacher. These pretences prevent Walter and Sally from establishing a true relationship.

The fight for a room of one's own is also the theme of Pinter's second full-length stage play, which brought him his first great success with the public – *The Caretaker* (first performed at the Arts Theatre Club, London, on 27 April 1960). This is a play in three acts, with three characters. The room in question is in a decaying property inhabited by Aston, a kindly but somewhat slow-witted man in his thirties. As the play opens,

Aston has brought a visitor for the night – Davies, an old tramp he has rescued out of a fight at some café where he had been working. Davies has lost not only his place in the world – he is homeless – but also his identity. He soon confesses that while his real name *is* Davies, he has been using the name Jenkins for years. To prove his identity, he would have to get his papers. But he left them with a man, years ago, down in Sidcup. The trouble is he cannot get down to Sidcup because he has no suitable shoes, and because the weather is never good enough.

Davies is vain, irascible, evasive, and prejudiced. He could stay with Aston and his younger brother, Mick, who owns the place and dreams of converting it into modern flats. Davies is almost offered the job of caretaker there. But he cannot resist the temptation to play the two brothers off against each other, to try to gain the upper hand when the kindly Aston has, in a bout of confidence, revealed that he once received electric-shock treatment in a mental hospital. And so Davies is a personi-fication of human weakness. His need for a place in the world is pathetically obvious, but he is unable to subdue his own nature enough to impose upon himself the minimum of self-discipline that would help him obtain it. As Mick says to him when he finally turns him out, 'What a strange man you are. Aren't you? You're really strange. Ever since you come into this house, there's been nothing but trouble. Honest. I can take nothing you say at face value. Every word you speak is open to any number of different interpretations. Most of what you say is lies. You're nothing else but a wild animal, when you come down to it. You're a barbarian.'[1]

It is a measure of Pinter's power as a playwright that the final scene, in which Davies vainly pleads to be given another chance, is almost unbearably tragic. After Davies has been shown in all his abject unreliability, clearly undeserving of the charity offered to him by the brothers, his ejection from the dingy room that could have become his world assumes almost

1. Pinter, *The Caretaker* (London: Methuen, 1960), p. 77.

the cosmic proportions of Adam's expulsion from Paradise. Davies's lying, his assertiveness, his inability to resist any chance to impose himself as superior, are, after all, mankind's original sin – hubris, lack of humility, blindness to our own faults.

The Caretaker achieves this quality of universality and tragedy without any of the tricks of mystery and violence that Pinter used in his earlier plays to create an atmosphere of poetic terror. Even Davies's myth of the impossible journey to Sidcup remains within the bounds of strict realism. It represents simply a form of self-deception and grotesque evasion on Davies's part. Anyone can see through it, but Davies is too self-indulgent a character to notice how the rationalization of his apathy and inability to help himself deceives no one except perhaps himself.

Pinter has revealed that originally he wanted to bring in violence:

The original idea . . . was . . . to end the play with the violent death of the tramp. . . . It suddenly struck me that it was not necessary. And I think that in this play . . . I *have* developed, that I have no need to use cabaret turns and blackouts and screams in the dark to the extent that I enjoyed using them before. I feel that I can deal, without resorting to that kind of thing, with a human situation. . . . I do see this play as merely . . . a particular human situation, concerning three particular people and not, incidentally . . . symbols.[1]

Much in *The Caretaker* is very funny, and the long run of the play has been attributed in some quarters to the public's laughter over Pinter's devastatingly accurate rendering of lower-class speech. In a letter to the London *Sunday Times*, Pinter takes issue with this and clarifies his own views on the relation between tragedy and farce in the play:

An element of the absurd is, I think, one of the features of [*The Caretaker*], but at the same time I did not intend it to be merely a laughable farce. If there had not been other issues at stake, the play would not have been written. Audience reaction can't be regulated,

1. Pinter interview with Tynan.

and no one would want it to be; nor is it easy to analyse. But where the comic and the tragic (for want of a better word) are closely interwoven, certain members of an audience will always give emphasis to the comic as opposed to the other, for by so doing they rationalize the other out of existence. . . . Where this indiscriminate mirth is found, I feel it represents a cheerful patronage of the characters on the part of the merrymakers, and thus participation is avoided. . . . As far as I'm concerned *The Caretaker* is funny up to a point. Beyond that point it ceases to be funny, and it was because of that point that I wrote it.[1]

In fact, *The Caretaker* has passages of genuine poetry – Aston's great speech about the shock treatment, or Mick's description of his plans for redecorating the old house, which transmutes the jargon of contemporary brand names into a dreamlike world of wish-fulfilment:

You could have an off-white pile linen rug, a table in . . . afromosia teak veneer, sideboard, with matt black drawers, curved chairs with cushioned seats, armchairs in oatmeal tweed, beech-frame settee with woven sea-grass seat, white-topped heat-resistant coffee table, white tile surround. . . .[2]

Pinter is one of the first poets to have recognized the potentialities of laminated plastics or power-tools. Mick's brother, Aston, is that typical mid-twentieth-century species of Western man, a do-it-yourself mechanic and handyman. He is constantly fixing some electrical appliance. And he too, in his slower way, extracts poetry from technical jargon:

DAVIES: What's that then, exactly, then?

ASTON: A jig saw? Well, it comes from the same family as the fret saw. But it's an appliance, you see. You have to fix it on to a portable drill.

DAVIES: Ah, that's right. They're very handy.

ASTON: They are, yes.

DAVIES: What about a hack-saw?

1. *Sunday Times*, London, 14 August 1960.
2. *The Caretaker*, p. 63.

ASTON: Well, I've got a hack-saw, as a matter of fact.
DAVIES: They're handy.
ASTON: Yes. . . . So's a keyhole saw. . . .[1]

The laughter of the audience during the long run of *The Caretaker* was by no means merely patronizing. It was also the laughter of recognition. It is not often that the theatregoer is confronted with his own language and preoccupations, even though they are exaggerated and heightened to point up the absurdity of the primitive, magical satisfaction most of us derive from being able to name and thus to master the bewildering array of gadgets with which we are surrounding ourselves. In a world that is increasingly deprived of meaning, we seek refuge in being experts in some narrow field of irrelevant knowledge or expertise. In trying to become master of some electrical appliance, Aston is seeking to get a foothold on reality. His breakdown, which led to his receiving shock treatment, was due to a loss of contact with reality and with other people: 'They always used to listen. I thought . . . they understood what I said. I mean I used to talk to them. I talked too much. That was my mistake.'[2]

Because he suffered from hallucinations, because he felt he could see things with a strange clarity, he was subjected to the horror of the mental hospital. He tried to retain his super-lucidity, he appealed to his mother, 'but she signed their form, you see, giving them permission.' Aston is the poet whom society crushes under the weight of its machinery of legal forms and bureaucracy. His hallucinations, his clear visions, having been wiped from his brain, Aston is reduced to seeking satisfaction in the way most citizens of our affluent society obtain what poetry they can out of life, by tinkering about the house: '. . . so I decided to have a go at decorating it, so I came into this room, and I started to collect wood, for my shed, and all these bits and pieces, that I thought might come in handy for the flat, or around the house, sometime.'[3]

1. ibid., p. 25.   2. ibid., p. 57.   3. ibid., p. 60.

In the radio play *The Dwarfs* (first performed on the Third Programme on 2 December 1960), Pinter amplifies Aston's experience. Len, the hero of *The Dwarfs*, also suffers from hallucinations – he sees himself as belonging to a gang of dwarfs whom he feeds with titbits of rat meat. He fears these dwarfs, resents having to work for them, and yet, when the dream world recedes, he feels it a loss to be deprived of the warmth and the cozy litter of their squalid yard:

They've cut me off without a penny. And now they've settled down to a wide-eyed kip, cross-legged by the fire. It's unsupportable. I'm left in the lurch. Not even a stale frankfurter, a slice of bacon rind, a leaf of cabbage, not even a mouldy piece of salami, like they used to sling me in the days when we told old tales by suntime. ... Now all is bare. All is clean. All is scrubbed. There is a lawn. There is a shrub. There is a flower.[1]

Len has two friends who are invading his room, Pete and Mark, each of whom is trying to play him off against the other. Len's room, like his sense of reality, is subject to constant change: 'The rooms we live in ... open and shut ... Can't you see? They change shape at their own will. I wouldn't grumble if only they would keep to some consistency. But they don't. And I can't tell the limits, the boundaries which I've been led to believe are natural.'[2]

The Dwarfs, based on Pinter's unpublished novel, is a play without a plot; it is a set of variations on the theme of reality and fantasy. As Pete tells Len, 'The apprehension of experience must obviously be dependent upon discrimination if it's to be considered valuable. That's what you lack. You've got no idea how to preserve a distance between what you smell and what you think about it. ... How can you hope to assess and verify anything if you walk about with your nose stuck between your feet all day long?'[3] And yet Pete, who makes this plea for

1. Pinter, *The Dwarfs*, in *A Slight Ache and Other Plays* (London: Methuen, 1961), p. 116.
2. ibid., p. 97.   3. ibid., p. 99.

realism, follows it up by telling Len about a dream of his own –
people's faces peeling off them in a panic on the underground.

The Dwarfs, although outwardly simple and without any of
Pinter's earlier tricks and mystifications, is a complex and
difficult play. It is also one of his most personal statements. Len's
world of the dwarfs is that of Aston, or Stanley in *The Birthday
Party*. All three have the same experience in common – they
have been expelled from their private world, squalid but cozy,
in which they could indulge their personal vision. Stanley is
carried off by force in the midst of highly allegorical happenings; Aston and Len lose their vision in a process of healing that
is also a catastrophic loss of a dimension of their lives – the
dimension of fantasy or poetry, the ability to look behind the
scenes of the commonplace, everyday world.

In *The Collection* (originally written for television and first
broadcast by Associated Rediffusion TV on 11 May 1961,
later adapted for the stage and presented by the Royal Shakespeare Company at the Aldwych Theatre in London on 18
June 1962) Pinter returns to the problem of verification. Harry,
a wealthy homosexual textile designer, lives in a household
with Bill, a young man he has 'discovered' and made his friend.
James, also in the textile business, accuses Bill of having seduced
and spent the night with his wife Stella, when both had gone up
north, to Leeds, to look at the season's dress collections. Can
James's story be true? Or has Stella merely invented the accusa-
tion in order to make her husband jealous? Or has Bill been
trying to break out from the magic circle in which Harry, and
homosexuality, are keeping him enclosed? Pinter himself does
not, perhaps cannot, give the answer. What emerges, however,
from the verbal fencing between the three men is that James,
the husband, may well have homosexual tendencies as well. He
becomes more interested in Bill than seems normal in a man
merely trying to deal with his wife's seducer. And Harry, the
elderly protector of Bill, becomes even more jealous of Bill
than Harry the wronged husband. In the television version the

action switched from James's and Stella's flat to Harry's and Bill's house, in the stage version the two locations remain visible throughout on a split stage. Thus throughout the play we can see Stella, the wife, sitting on her sofa mostly alone and abandoned, fondling her cat. And so one point which emerges very strongly in performance – and may perhaps be overlooked in merely reading the text – is that the play highlights the tragedy of a woman in a world where the men tend to be more interested in each other than in the other sex. With *The Collection* Pinter also proved that his mastery of language extended far beyond the vernacular of the lower classes; this is a middle-class world, somewhere between the business community and the more or less 'arty' set, and Pinter brilliantly succeeds in achieving effects quite as striking as those in his earlier plays with the idiom of an entirely different section of society.

In the television play *The Lover* (first broadcast by Associated Rediffusion, London, on 28 March 1963, transferred to the stage, together with a stage version of *The Dwarfs*, at the Arts Theatre, London, on 18 September 1963) we are again in a middle-class, suburban milieu. Richard and Sarah are a suburban couple, the husband commuting to London every weekday. As he leaves in the morning he asks his wife if she is expecting her lover that afternoon. She says yes. He nods approval and leaves. When he returns in the evening he inquires casually if she had a good time with her lover, and she reports, equally casually, on his visit, while Richard equally casually admits that he regularly visits a whore. We are then introduced to Sarah's preparations on another afternoon for the coming of the lover. She changes into a tight dress. Finally the lover comes: it is her husband, also sleekly dressed. She now calls him Max. So in fact this couple act out their fantasy lives in the guise of a romantically sadistic seducer and a luscious whore. But as the play unfolds they are confronted with the impossibility of keeping the two sides of their personalities, their two selves, apart; and in the end it looks as though the fantasy figures are about to take over altogether.

In *The Lover* the theme of reality and the fantasy of wish-fulfilment is still baldly and somewhat literally stated. In his third full-length play, *The Homecoming*, Pinter brilliantly succeeds in merging the two levels into an intriguingly ambivalent whole. *The Homecoming* (first performed by the Royal Shakespeare Company at the Aldwych Theatre, London, on 3 June 1965) has greatly puzzled some members of its audience. And yet the key to its understanding is simple enough: the play presents a sequence of realistic (or at least realistically explicable) events which at the same time could be, might well be, fantasy, a wish-fulfilment dream. On either level the play makes sense. But its poetic force lies in the ambivalence between them. Max, a retired butcher, lives in North London with two of his sons: Lenny, sleek, alert, and at the opening of the play of uncertain occupation, and Joey, brawny, slow, a boxer. There is also an old uncle in the house, Sam, a cab-driver, from whose conversation it emerges that the mother of the family, Jessie, now dead, may at one time have been involved with a friend of the family called MacGregor. Into this household there suddenly comes the eldest of Max's sons, Teddy, with his wife Ruth. Teddy has long been absent from London. He has gone to America where he now teaches philosophy at a university. Ruth is English too. Teddy married her just before leaving England, but the family never had a chance to meet her. She now has three sons, who have been left behind in America. Ruth becomes erotically involved with the two sons, Lenny and Joey, and it gradually emerges that Lenny is in fact earning his living as a professional pimp. In due course Lenny coolly proposes to Ruth that she should stay in the house and he should set her up as a prostitute. She coolly accepts the proposition. Teddy, her husband, readily agrees and goes back to America and his sons. Old Sam has a heart attack as he reveals that the boys' mother once made love to MacGregor in the back of his cab. And old Max, the father, grovels in front of Ruth, begging for a scrap of her sexual favours.

Lenny's proposition to Ruth and her husband's placid acceptance of her as a whore (which closely resembles Richard's cool acceptance of his wife's affair with a romantic 'lover') are the only elements in the play which appear impossible in a realistic setting. But knowing Pinter's refusal to provide neat expositions for his plays and detailed motivations for his characters, we ought to be able to find a perfectly reasonable explanation; and indeed, it is fairly clear from what is said about Ruth in the play (she used to work as a nude model) that she may well have been a prostitute, or very nearly one, before Teddy met and married her. If she was unable to adjust herself to a life of respectability in America (being a nymphomaniac, as she is clearly shown to be) she must have caused poor Teddy a lot of embarrassment on the campus. The trip to Venice from which they are returning when calling on Teddy's family in London, may have been a last attempt to save the marriage. It clearly has failed. Hence Teddy may be genuinely relieved to find himself rid of his wife. And if Jessie, the boys' mother, also was a prostitute, or a near-prostitute, as seems indicated from Sam's hints, then Teddy as much as the rest of the family may well be used to a cool and businesslike discussion of such transactions. Hence his lack of surprise and cool acceptance of the new situation would be quite natural.

So much for the realistic level of the play. On the level of fantasy and wish-fulfilment, *The Homecoming* seems to me to represent the sons' dream of the sexual conquest of the mother and the discomfiture of the father. That Max and Teddy (the elder brother – often a father substitute) are aspects of the father figure seems clear enough. Max represents the more ridiculous aspects of senile old-age, Teddy – the philosopher – the superior intellectual claims of the father. But if this is so, then Ruth, Teddy's wife, is a duplicate of the mother. Hence the sons' desire for her, and the dreamlike ease with which the desire is fulfilled. And Max's final pleading for some scraps of Ruth's favour completes the sons' Oedipal dream: now the roles of father and son are reversed, now the sons are in proud possession of the mother's sexuality, and the father is reduced to begging for her favours.

If Richard in *The Lover* wants to treat his respectable wife as a whore, he also highlights the dichotomy between the female archetype as mother and as prostitute. Jessie, the mother in *The Homecoming*, is accused of having whored with Mac-Gregor. In other words the sons, yearning for the mother, dream of her turning into a whore whose sexual favours would be available just for the asking. If only the mother were a whore, how easily could all the taboos surrounding her be broken!

From the vantage point of *The Homecoming* a good deal of light can be seen to fall on Pinter's earlier plays. In *The Birthday Party*, Stanley can be seen as a son who has found refuge in the love of a mother figure, brutally driven from that haven by the emissaries of the father: certainly Goldberg is a father figure and he again is shown enjoying himself with a near-whore, Lulu. The correspondence between the characters in *The Caretaker* and those in *The Homecoming* is even more striking. Davies closely corresponds to the querulous and intemperate Max, the sleek pimp Lenny to Mick, and the slow giant Joey to Aston. *The Caretaker* can thus be seen as – among many other things – a dream about the sons' expulsion of the father from their home. In *The Homecoming* the mother figure also appears and so reveals what really caused the sons' contempt and hatred for the father figure in *The Caretaker*. The father figure wins along the whole line in *The Birthday Party*; he is about to be expelled at the end of *The Caretaker*. In *The Homecoming* his discomfiture is complete, his humiliation spelled out in triumphant detail.

The television play *Tea Party* (broadcast by the B.B.C. in 1965) deals with a far more conventional subject. The hero is a wealthy manufacturer of sanitary equipment who has married into an upper-class family to whom he feels socially inferior. His inferiority complex towards his wife drives him to lust after his secretary. At a tea party in his office during which the wife and her brother confront the secretary and our hero's proletarian parents, the tension becomes too great for him and he sinks into his chair, stricken, paralysed, blinded.

Another television play, *The Basement*, broadcast by the B.B.C. early in 1967, was originally planned to form part of the film project initiated by Grove Press for which Beckett wrote his *Film*. In that project it was entitled *The Compartment*. This is an intriguing script, a free association of images around Pinter's favourite concept, the room as territory to be conquered and defended. The owner of the basement room is visited by an old friend who, as soon as he is offered hospitality, brings in a girl who has waited outside in the rain and goes to bed with her. There follows a series of images all illustrating the struggle between the two men, Law and Stott, for the favours of the girl, Jane. The room itself changes character and furniture as the moods of the contest change. In the end Law has lost the room but won the girl. Now he stands with her outside in the streaming rain while Stott sits inside, snug, and warm, when the bell rings and he rises to let in his old friend . . . and the whole story seems about to start again, in reverse. . . . The television public was disconcerted by the difficulty of deciding whether the action was real or imagined. In fact, Pinter's intention seems to have been the creation of an almost abstract piece of fantasy, a permutation in the author's own mind, of all the possibilities of one archetypal situation.

Two short plays which followed, *Landscape* (1968) and *Silence* (1969), enlarged on the theme of the elusiveness of human personality; in *Landscape*, Beth and Duff, a middle-aged couple, sit in the kitchen of a large country house in which, perhaps, they have served as the butler/chauffeur and the maid. Beth has totally withdrawn from the outside world – what we hear her say is merely inside her mind; while Duff is, unsuccessfully, trying to communicate with her. The landscape of the title is in Beth's memories, a scene of love-making with an unnamed man by the seaside, tenderly and delicately recalled. Duff, on the other hand, is a coarse middle-aged ruffian, using the roughest language, and mention is made of his adultery in the past. The play raises the question of why Beth has withdrawn; is it because of Duff's adultery? Or because she was the lover of their employer, now absent or perhaps dead, Mr Sykes? Was Mr Sykes Beth's lover in her memories? Or was it Duff, who has now turned into a vulgar brute? Probably. But the charm of the play lies, precisely, in the fact that these questions remain open. *Silence* is a variation on the same theme, with a girl and two of her lovers recalling the past; and here, too, many questions remain unanswered. The form of these plays is very much more static than previous works of Pinter. The characters remain seated almost throughout the action, the drama is entirely in the language, the evocation of moods.

In Pinter's next full-length play, *Old Times* (1971), the ambiguities and the stasis of *Landscape* and *Silence* are further developed and used to splendid effect. Here a man between two women is involved in an enigmatic and subtle action which, ultimately, comes down to the problem of the nature of memory: Deeley is a middle-aged intellectual (he claims to be a film or television director) married to Kate. As the play opens this couple are discussing the impending arrival of Anna, Kate's friend of her youth twenty years earlier in the London of the 1940's, whom Kate has not seen since that time. While we witness the discussion about Anna's visit we can already see Anna, standing motionless by the window. Is she really there? Or is she merely an emanation of the fantasies of the couple? Suddenly she *is* present and enters the conversation, which gradually develops into a duel between Deeley and Anna for the possession and love of Kate. The duel is fought with contradictory memories of the old times twenty years earlier. And in the end Deeley is seen crying, between the two women. They clearly have been lesbian lovers, at least in Deeley's mind. And the play hovers between three levels of reality: it may represent no more than Deeley's fears of what might happen if Anna arrives; it may on the other hand portray the actual course of Anna's visit, in which case the mysterious presence of Anna at the opening of the action may merely be a theatrical symbol; or, indeed, Anna may *really* be present at the rise of the curtain, in which case the action might be an erotic ritual or make-believe between a *ménage à trois* on the lines of *The Lover*. The simultaneous possibility of all three options gives the play, which is also very funny, its haunting impact.

A duel of real or pretended memories is also at the centre of Pinter's next full-length play, *No Man's Land* (1974). Here the situation of *The Caretaker* has been transferred into a socially more elevated milieu. A famous writer, Hirst, has invited an old down-at-heel intellectual, Spooner, whom he has picked up on Hampstead Heath, to have a drink with him in his large and elegant house. Spooner sees an opportunity of finding a home with Hirst who at first seems to be lonely and in need of friendship. These hopes are threatened by the appearance of two lower-class young men, Briggs and Foster, who seem to be servants in the house, but also act as the master's gaolers or male nurses and at times treat him as their servant. The play ends, like *The Caretaker*, with Spooner about to be expelled from his much-desired haven. But it is made clear that this event is also a climactic moment in the life of Hirst, whose last attempt to break out of the closed circle of his strange household this must be, for in the final scene the two servants enact what almost amounts to a ceremony of entombment, a coda to his life marking his entry into the no-man's-land between life and death.

In *Betrayal* (1978) Pinter returns to the theme of the erotic triangle, again with a woman disputed by two men. It is the story of an adultery told backwards, starting with the break-up of an affair and pursuing its inception and development to its initiation ten years earlier. The question this ingeniously plotted play opens up is: whom has the wife betrayed? Is it the husband or is it the lover, who, in the last years of the affair, had not been told by her that her husband, his best friend, already knew of the relationship?

Pinter's work as a script writer for the cinema also deserves mention. Here he prefers to adapt other authors' plots and to play the role of the conscientious and highly professional craftsman. Nevertheless much of his characteristic quality remains and enriches the films, most notably the ones which have been directed by Joseph Losey, a film-maker whose sensibility is beautifully attuned to Pinter's terse, elliptic style, his silences and pauses. Losey directed *The Servant* (after a novel by Robin Maugham, 1963) and *Accident* (after a novel by Nicholas Mosley, 1967). Other films which Pinter scripted were *The Caretaker*, a faithful transfer of the play to the screen directed by Clive Donner, *The Pumpkin Eater* (after a novel by Penelope Mortimer), *The Quiller Memorandum* (based on a thriller by Donald Hall), *The Go-Between* (after the novel by L. P. Hartley, directed by Joseph Losey), and *The Last Tycoon* (after the novel by Scott Fitzgerald). A screenplay based on Aidan Higgins's novel *Langrishe, Go Down* was turned by Pinter into a television play; and his masterly adaptation of Proust's great novel *À la Recherche du Temps Perdu*, which has up till now remained unfilmed because of financial difficulties, was published as a book in 1978. It shows Pinter's astonishing ability to translate a complex narrative into a series of powerful visual images.

Yet basically Pinter is a man of the theatre. He is a poet and his theatre is essentially a poetic theatre, more so than the euphuistic verse drama of some of his contemporaries. Pinter, who acknowledges the influence of Kafka and Beckett, is, like these two writers, preoccupied with man at the limit of his being. As Len says in *The Dwarfs*,

The point is, who are you? Not why or how, not even what. . . . You are the sum of so many reflections. How many reflections? Whose reflections? Is that what you consist of? What scum does the tide leave? What happens to the scum? When does it happen? I've seen what happens. . . . The scum is broken and sucked back. I don't see where it goes, I don't see when, what do I see, what have I seen? What have I seen, the sum or the essence?[1]

It is this preoccupation with the problem of the self that separates Harold Pinter from the social realists among the young British playwrights of his generation with whom he shares the ability to put contemporary speech on to the stage. When Kenneth Tynan reproached him in a radio interview for writing plays unconcerned with ideas and showing only a very limited aspect of the life of their characters, omitting their politics, ideas, and even their sex life, Pinter replied that he was dealing with his characters 'at the extreme edge of their living, where they are living pretty much alone';[2] at a point, that is, when they are back in their rooms, confronted with the basic problem of being.

We see Pinter's characters in the process of their essential adjustment to the world, at the point when they have to solve their basic problem – whether they will be able to confront, and come to terms with, reality at all. It is only after they have made this fundamental adjustment that they will be able to become part of society and share in the games of sex or politics. Pinter repudiates the suggestion that in so presenting them he is unrealistic. After all, he maintains, his plays deal with a short, if climactic, period in the lives of his characters, a few days or, in the case of *The Caretaker*, a fortnight. 'We are only concerned with what is happening then, in this particular moment of these people's lives. There is no reason to suppose that at one time or another they did not listen at a political meeting . . . or that they haven't ever had girl friends'[3] or been concerned with ideas.

1. ibid., p. 111.
2. Pinter interview with Tynan.   3. ibid.

It is the intriguing paradox of Pinter's position that he considers himself a more uncompromising, ruthless realist than the champions of 'social realism' could ever be. For it is they who water down the reality of their picture of the world by presupposing that they have solutions for problems that have not yet been solved – and that may well be insoluble – or by implying that it is possible to *know* the complete motivation of a character, or, above all, by presenting a slice of reality that is less essential, and hence less real, less true to life, than a theatre that has selected a more fundamental aspect of existence. If life in our time is basically absurd, then any dramatic representation of it that comes up with neat solutions and produces the illusion that it all 'makes sense', after all, is bound to contain an element of oversimplification, to suppress essential factors, and reality expurgated and oversimplified becomes make-believe. For a dramatist of the Absurd, like Harold Pinter, the political, social-realist play loses its claim to realism by focusing its attention on inessentials and exaggerating their importance, as though, if only some limited objective were reached, we could live happily forever after. And by choosing the wrong slice of life altogether, it falls into the same error as the drawing-room comedy that ends when boy gets girl – at the very point when their real problems, marriage and the process of ageing, begin. After the social realist has established the need for his reform, the basic problems of existence remain – loneliness, the impenetrable mystery of the universe, death.

On the other hand, Pinter was indignant when a critic took him to task for introducing a character whose antecedents are clearly stated in the television play *Night School*, arguing that a true Pinter character should come from nowhere rather than from prison. Pinter considers *Night School* an experiment in a lighter vein and resents being told by others that a true Pinter play *must* deal exclusively in mysterious and wholly unmotivated events.

Of all the major dramatists of the Absurd, Harold Pinter

6

PARALLELS AND PROSELYTES

By its very nature, the Theatre of the Absurd is not, and never can be, a literary movement or school, for its essence lies in the free and unfettered exploration, by each of the writers concerned, of his own individual vision. Yet the wide response these, at first sight baffling and uncompromisingly difficult, plays have evoked shows not only how closely they express the preoccupations of our age, but also how great is the yearning for a new approach to the theatre. In turning their backs on the psychological or narrative theatre, and in refusing to conform to any of the old-established recipes for the 'well-made play', the dramatists of the Theatre of the Absurd are, each in his own way and independent of the others, engaged in establishing a new dramatic convention. In this enterprise of trial and error and ceaseless experimentation, the five dramatists whose work has been examined in some detail in this book by no means stand alone. A number of writers of their own generation have been experimenting on parallel lines, and a growing number of younger dramatists have been encouraged by the success of some of the work of Beckett, Ionesco, or Genet to develop their own personal idiom in a similar convention. A survey (which does not claim to be complete) of the experiments of these contemporaries and followers of the masters of the new convention may show the possible future lines of development.

JEAN TARDIEU

The writer whose work represents the most comprehensive range of experiment in this field is undoubtedly Jean Tardieu (born in 1903), who, older than Beckett, Adamov, Genet, and

Ionesco, was already well-known as a poet before the Second World War. Having tried to write plays in his early youth, Tardieu turned to an austere style of lyrical poetry based on Mallarmé, and became known as the author of the best French translations of the poems of Hölderlin. After the war, he turned to experiments with language, in the vein of Jacques Prévert and Raymond Queneau, and to exploring the limits of the possibilities of the theatre. He joined the staff of the French Radio and Television Service after the end of the war, became head of its experimental workshop, the *club d'essai*, and started to write experimental plays in 1947, at about the time Beckett, Adamov, Genet, and Ionesco also made their first steps as dramatists – a curious instance of the *Zeitgeist* at work.

Tardieu's dramatic experiments, which have been published in two volumes – *Théâtre de Chambre* (1955) and *Poèmes à Jouer* (1960) – are mostly on a very small scale. Many of them are short cabaret sketches rather than even one-act plays, but their range is wider than that of any other dramatist of the Absurd, extending from the fantastic and eerie to the purely lyrical, and beyond it into the sphere of a wholly abstract theatre in which language loses all conceptual content and merges into music.

The earliest of the sketches in *Théâtre de Chambre* anticipate Ionesco. *Qui Est Là?* (dated 1947, and earlier than *The Bald Prima Donna*) starts with exactly the same situation – a family of father, mother, and son seated around the dinner table. The father is interrogating his wife and son about their activities during the day, but as he clearly knows the answers already, he supplies them himself without waiting for any information from those he has questioned:

What did you do this morning? I went to school. And you? I went to the market. What did you get? Vegetables, more expensive than yesterday, and meat, cheaper. Just as well, one makes up for the other. And you, what did the teacher tell you? That I was making good progress. . . .[1]

1. Jean Tardieu, *Théâtre de Chambre* (Paris: Gallimard, 1955), p. 10.

A mysterious woman appears who warns the father of an approaching danger. There is someone at the door. The father opens it. A huge man stands outside. He strangles the father and carries his corpse away. The mysterious woman invites the wife to look out of the window. There are dead bodies outside as far as the eye can see. The father's body is among them. The son calls the father; he rises from the dead and returns to the room. The wife asks, 'Who killed you?' The father replies, 'It was not a human being.' 'Who are you?' asks the wife. 'I am not a human being,' replies the dead man. 'Who were you?' 'Nobody.'

The lesson of the little play seems to be the need to search for the human image that is not yet alive within any of us, but that we might find one day. In the words of the mysterious woman visitor, who concludes the play, 'The window is lighting up. Someone approaches. Let us wait!'[1] *Qui Est Là?* is an attempt to produce a poetic image of the situation at the end of the war – man faced with the fact that the routine of a bourgeois existence is as inhuman as the mass killing of the battlefields and concentration camps, and the need for finding a new, fully human way of life.

If Tardieu's first sketch of this type reproduces the opening situation and – to some extent – the message of *The Bald Prima Donna*, it is even more curious that his second short play, *La Politesse Inutile* – also dated 1947 – should open with the professor–pupil situation of *The Lesson*. Yet here the similarity is purely superficial. The professor is saying goodbye to a young man off to his exams. He impresses on him that it is not what he knows that matters but what he *is*. When the pupil has left, another visitor, a vulgar and sinister individual, enters. He receives the professor's elaborate old-world politeness with a show of extravagant rudeness and finally slaps him savagely. The professor picks himself up and addresses the audience:

I shall not explain this story to you. No doubt it happened very far

1. ibid., p. 14.

from here, at the bottom of a bad memory. It is from there that I come to warn you and to convince you. . . . Shush! There is someone asleep here who might overhear me. . . . I'll come back . . . tomorrow.[1]

The same dream, or nightmare, quality characterizes a good many of Tardieu's earlier sketches. In *Le Meuble*, an inventor is trying to sell a buyer, offstage, a fabulous piece of furniture that is designed to perform any conceivable service, including recitations of Musset's poems. But gradually the machine gets out of hand; instead of Musset it sings doggerel verse and finally it pulls out a revolver and kills the buyer. If this sketch is reminiscent of Ionesco or Adamov, *La Serrure* has overtones of Genet. In a brothel, a customer is awaiting the fulfilment of his dreams – to see his beloved girl through an outsize keyhole. In ecstasy, the client describes what he sees as the girl discards one garment after another. Yet even after she has reached a state of complete nudity she goes on undressing, discarding her cheeks, her eyes, and other parts of her body until only the bare skeleton remains. Unable to control himself any more, the customer rushes against the door and falls down dead. The madam appears: 'I think . . . the gentleman . . . is satisfied.'

A similar motif appears in *Faust et Yorick*, which also experiments with the representation of the flow of time in the manner of Thornton Wilder's *The Long Christmas Dinner*. Faust, a scientist, spends his life looking for an example of a more highly developed skull, which will represent the next stage of human evolution. We see him getting married, his child becoming a woman, Faust growing old, always neglecting his family to find that skull. He dies without having found it. Yet the skull he has been looking for all his life is his own.

In *Le Guichet*, one of the longer pieces in *Théâtre de Chambre*, we are in a world of Kafkaesque bureaucracy. A man comes to an information office to ask about the time of a train. He is subjected to a rigid cross-examination about his whole life. Finally

1. ibid., p. 23.

the official behind the counter draws up the man's horoscope and informs him that he will be killed on leaving the office. He leaves and is promptly run over.

In all these sketches, Tardieu is exploring the possibilities of reproducing a dreamlike atmosphere on the stage. In others he is more openly experimental and even didactic in trying out what can, or cannot, be done with various stage conventions, such as the use of asides (*Oswald et Zenaïde, ou Les Apartés* – what an engaged couple say to each other, and what they think) or monologues (*Il y Avait Foule au Manoir, ou Les Monologues* – a crowded stage suggested by a succession of monologues that could be spoken by a single actor), or in demonstrating the relativity of language (*Ce Que Parler Veut Dire, ou Le Patois des Familles* – each family has its private slang) or manners (*Un Geste pour un Autre* – a world traveller demonstrates how the most absurd behaviour is regarded as exquisite good manners in distant civilizations). These didactic sketches, which take the form of illustrated lectures, are Tardieu's least successful efforts – they recall the more hackneyed procedures of the little revue.

Tardieu's most interesting experiments are those in which he explores the possibilities of a wholly abstract theatre. *Eux Seuls Le Savent*, for example, presents a highly dramatic action that remains wholly unexplained. We see the characters engaged in violent quarrels referring to hidden motives and guilty secrets, without ever learning what these are or even in what relationship the four people involved stand to each other. 'Only they know it.' By presenting a wholly motiveless action that still holds the public's attention, Tardieu is in fact demonstrating the possibility of pure, plotless theatre.

But he goes further than this. Two of the short pieces in *Théâtre de Chambre* (*La Sonate et les Trois Messieurs* and *Conversation–Sinfonietta*) attempt an approximation of dialogue to music. In *La Sonate* we have three gentlemen, labelled A, B, and C, engaged in a conversation the subject of which remains undefined but which evokes a certain type of image, tempo, and rhythm to correspond to the notations of a sonata; first movement, *largo* (slow, nostalgic description of an expanse of water); second movement, *andante* (more animated discussion – what was it that they have seen?); third movement, finale (animation leading to a dying fall). *Conversation–Sinfonietta* repeats the same experiment with six voices (two basses, two contraltos, a soprano, and a tenor) under the direction of a conductor. Again there are three movements: *allegro ma non troppo*, *andante sostenuto*, and *scherzo vivace*. The text consists of the most banal fragments of small talk: '*Bonjour, Madame!*' '*Bonjour, Monsieur!*' or '*Mais oui, mais oui, mais oui, mais oui*' followed by '*Mais non, mais non, mais non, mais non!*' or lists of foods liked by the speakers, with directions as to how they are to be cooked.

Having explored the possibilities of constructing the equivalent of a symphonic poem from disjointed elements of language, Tardieu took the logical step forward. In the second volume of his collected plays, we find the results of this development.

Les Amants du Métro (*The Lovers in the Underground*), written in 1931, is described in the subtitle as 'a comic ballet without dance and without music'; that is, language in movement is to take the place of both the music and the dancing.

The first scene is a Métro station. The small talk of the waiting passengers has a thematic relationship to the main subject, the meeting of the two lovers. Two gentlemen deeply immersed in their books collide and introduce their reading matter to each other – 'St Paul!', 'Marquis de Sade!' – while a student tells his girl the story of Hero and Leander. The lovers themselves are introduced in a passage of abstract dialogue simulating a waltz rhythm: '*Un, deux, trois, amour,*' '*Un, deux, trois, Adour,*' '*Un, deux, trois, toujours,*' and so on. Later, when the lovers quarrel, they do so in strings of women's names: 'Emma! Eloa! Héloise! Diotima! Georgia! Hilda!', and so on.

In the second scene, the lovers are inside a Métro carriage, separated by a crowd of other passengers, who represent the anonymity and hostility of mass society. Another Leander, the hero has to cross this sea of puppet-like fellow-men. When he has finally managed to reach his beloved, she too has relapsed into the depersonalized anonymity of the crowd. Only when he violently slaps her face does she wake up and become an individual again.

As an experiment with the expressive possibilities of language, even when almost wholly empty of conceptual content, *Les Amants du Métro* is a fascinating *tour de force*; it shows the richness of the textural and rhythmic possibilities of language, as well as the feasibility of a purely poetic, as distinct from discursive, use of dramatic dialogue, which replaces the exchange of ideas or information between the characters by the striking up and development of poetic images and themes by a new logic of association.

This idea is carried a step further by Tardieu in *L'A.B.C. de Notre Vie* (*The A.B.C. of Our Life*), written in 1958 and first performed on 30 May 1959. Tardieu describes this as 'a poem for acting', and it is built strictly in the form of a concerto. A protagonist has the main solo part, the individual man, a day in whose life among the crowd of the great city is the subject-matter of the poem, starting with his awakening from his dreams in the morning and ending with his return to sleep at night. The choral part consists of the indistinct murmur of the crowd, against which articulated parts of sentences rise and fall. Two further characters, Monsieur Mot and Madame Parole (Mr Word and Madam Speech), illustrate the proceedings by reciting strings of words from the dictionary, which, the author states, are 'musical notes or touches of colour' rather than concepts. Other solo parts include a couple of lovers, a criminal, the voices of dreaming women. Three themes are interwoven in the movements of this concerto-in-words: the individual's illusion of his uniqueness against the indistinct murmur of the mass to which he belongs; the power of love to take man out of the flow of time and to make him into a true individual; and, finally, the recognition of man's rootedness in humanity as a whole – '*Humanité, tu es mon paysage.*' The murmuring of the mass becomes one of the sounds of nature, like the wind in the forest, like the waves of the sea.

In another 'poem for acting', *Rhythme à Trois Temps, ou Le Temple de Ségeste* (*Rhythm in Three-Time, or The Temple of Segesta*), written in 1958, Tardieu has tried to reproduce the feelings of a traveller when he first sees the Greek temple of Segesta. Six girls represent the six columns that face the traveller as he approaches, a voice offstage embodies the traveller's feelings. The girls express calm and immutability, the ecstatic traveller is rhapsodic and emotional. Both *L'A.B.C. de Notre Vie* and *Rhythme à Trois Temps* were accompanied at their first production by musical quotations from the works of Anton Webern.

In exploring the limits of the theatre, Tardieu has even tried to write a short play in which no characters at all appear: *Une Voix Sans Personne* (*A Voice Without Anyone*). The stage represents an empty room. A voice offstage recalls the memory of a room once familiar; the lighting onstage changes in accordance with the moods recalled. Only occasionally, a woman's voice is heard, like an echo from the past. This is certainly an interesting and ingenious, though by no means conclusive, experiment; it merely proves that lighting and décor have a part to play in creating poetry on the stage. But this has never been in need of proof.

In the same programme with *Une Voix Sans Personne* at the tiny Théâtre de la Huchette in 1956, Tardieu presented his nearest approximation to a straight play, *Les Temps du Verbe, ou Le Pouvoir de la Parole* (*The Tenses of the Verb, or The Power of Speech*), two acts designed to demonstrate the thesis that the tenses of the verb govern our standpoint in time. The rather melodramatic plot concerns Robert, who has lost his wife in an automobile accident. He has withdrawn from the present, lives in the past, and speaks exclusively in the past tense. When he dies, his body is found to be that of a man who died a long time ago. As the body lies on the empty stage, the moment just before the accident comes to life again. Robert hears the voices of his wife and his niece speaking in the future tense. At that moment before his wife was killed, she still had a future, but 'Past, present, future, which is true? Everything partakes of each at the same time! Everything fades away, but everything remains – and everything remains unfinished!'[1]

The volume of Tardieu's *Poèmes à Jouer* concludes with his earliest dramatic effort, the verse play *Tonnerre Sans Orage, ou Les Dieux Inutiles* (*Thunder Without Storm, or The Useless Gods*), dated 1944. This outwardly conventional poetic one-act play might almost be a programme note on the subject-matter of the Theatre of the Absurd. On the threshold of death, Asia, the mother of the titan Prometheus, reveals to her grandson Deucalion that the gods do not exist. She herself invented the myth of their existence to curb Prometheus's ambition when he was young. But far from inducing him to submit to higher powers, the supposed existence of the gods spurred Prometheus into his lifelong struggle against them. Deucalion tells Prometheus what he has learned, but Prometheus, who is about to unleash a conflagration that will destroy the gods, and the world with them, can no longer stop events from taking their course. Deucalion sails away into the unknown, 'seeking in the reflection of the two abysses an alliance with my new god – nothingness',[1] while Prometheus remains behind alone:

> I know, I know full well henceforth
> In the superb desert of the night,
> Which is the god I threaten:
> It is myself, Prometheus![2]

It is in the light of this recognition of the absurdity of the human situation in a godless world that we must see Tardieu's impressive experimental work; it is an attempt to find a means

1. Tardieu, *Théâtre II: Poèmes à Jouer* (Paris: Gallimard, 1960), p. 163.
2. ibid., pp. 240–41.

of expression adequate to represent man's efforts to situate himself in a meaningless universe. Being avowedly experimental, Tardieu's plays, though some of them contain poetry of great distinction, cannot claim to be judged as works of art in their own right. They are explorations, materials for research from which valuable experience can be gained for the creation of works of art that Tardieu himself, or others, making use of his research, might build on the foundations he has provided. This is not to deny Tardieu's very considerable achievement, but rather to emphasize his importance. Here is a playwright's playwright, a dedicated pioneer bent on enlarging the vocabulary of his art. Alone among the playwrights of the avant-garde, Tardieu can claim that his work spans the entire gamut of exploration. He straddles the poetic theatre of Schehadé as well as the sardonic anti-theatre of Ionesco and the psychological dream world of Adamov and Genet. But by its very awareness, its experimental consciousness, its playfulness in trying out new devices, Tardieu's work misses the obsessive compulsiveness, and thus the hypnotic power, the inevitability, of some of the masterpieces of the Theatre of the Absurd.

BORIS VIAN

If Tardieu's experiments pursue a course parallel to, but independent of, the development of the mainstream of the new convention, the single play by Boris Vian (1920–59) that falls within it clearly shows the signs of the direct influence of Ionesco, his fellow-satrap in the Collège de Pataphysique. This play, *Les Bâtisseurs d'Empire* (*The Empire Builders*), was first performed in Jean Vilar's experimental Théâtre Récamier on 22 December 1959, six months after the tragic death of its author. Boris Vian was one of the most remarkable figures of the post-war period in Paris. Engineer, jazz trumpeter, *chansonnier*, film actor, novelist, wit, jazz critic; one of the great characters of the Existentialist bohemia of the *caves* around

Saint Germain-des-Prés; translator of Raymond Chandler, Peter Cheney, James Cain, Nelson Algren, Strindberg, and the memoirs of General Omar N. Bradley; iconoclast and convicted pornographer; science-fiction expert, and dramatist, Boris Vian seems an epitome of his time – sardonic, practical, a working technician and inventor of gadgets, a violent enemy of cant, and at the same time a sensitive poet, an artist concerned with the ultimate reality of the human condition.

Boris Vian's first play, *L'Equarrissage pour Tous* (which might be rendered in English as *Knackery Made Easy* – written in 1946-47 and first performed in 1950), already shows him as a master of a bitter, black humour, although the play, a tragicomic farce, still fits into a traditional pattern, in spite of the fact that Jean Cocteau greeted it as an event comparable to Apollinaire's *Les Mamelles de Tirésias* and his own *Mariés de la Tour Eiffel*. Described as 'a paramilitary vaudeville in one long act', *L'Equarrissage pour Tous* takes place in a knacker's yard at Arromanches on the day of the Allied landings there, 6 June 1944. While the knacker's eccentric family go about their peaceful business of horse-slaughtering and arranging the marriage of one of their daughters to a German soldier, the place is continually invaded by military personnel of various nations, ranging from a Japanese parachutist to a Soviet Russian woman soldier, who inexplicably is one of the daughters of the house. There are also numerous Americans and members of the Free French forces. The hilarious and bawdy proceedings end when the knacker's house is blown up to make room for the glorious rebuilding schemes of the future. By this time the whole family has been killed, and the curtain falls to the strains of the 'Marseillaise'.

So soon after the war, this sardonic play provoked veritable howls of indignation from all sides, particularly for its irreverent portrayal of members of the Free French forces, although they are expressly shown as opportunists who have joined the Resistance only that very day, and spend their time looking for cars they can requisition. In fact, the play is as harmless a piece of satire as it is a brilliant example of *l'humour noir* at its blackest.

Les Bâtisseurs d'Empire also has its touches of humour, but is a play of an altogether different kind – a poetic image of mortality and the fear of death. Its three acts show a family on the run from a mysterious but terrifying noise, which they try to escape by moving on to a higher and higher floor, into an ever-smaller apartment. In act I, father, mother, daughter Zénobie, and their maid, Cruche, are shown taking possession of a two-room apartment. In act II they are one floor higher, in a one-room apartment. The maid leaves them, and their daughter, who has gone to the landing, cannot return to them when the door mysteriously closes. Only the father and mother are left. The world becomes narrower and narrower for them. In the third act the father is seen entering a tiny attic room, so terrified of the noise that he barricades the entrance before his wife can get to him. He is alone. But the noise, the terrifying noise of the approach of death, cannot be excluded. And now there is nowhere the father can escape to. He dies.

Apart from the characters named, who have speaking parts, there is a mysterious, silent character, a half-human being, called a *schmürz;* 'covered in bandages, dressed in rags, one arm in a sling, he holds a walking-stick in the other. He limps, bleeds, and is ugly to look at.'[1] This silent figure seems not to be noticed by the characters. Nevertheless they constantly rain brutal blows on him.

Simple in structure and relentless in its progression, *Les Bâtisseurs d'Empire* is a powerful and very personal statement. Proud as we are, confident that we are building our own world, our personal empire on earth, we are in fact constantly on the run; far from growing wider, our world contracts. As we approach death, we get more and more lonely, our range of vision and action becomes more and more narrow. It is increasingly

1. Boris Vian, *Les Bâtisseurs d'Empire* (Paris: L'Arche, 1959), p. 8.

difficult to communicate with the younger generation, and the subterranean noise of death grows louder and louder.

All this is clear enough. But what does the *schmürz* stand for? It is perhaps significant that Boris Vian wrote some of his contributions to the more popular magazines under the pseudonym Adolphe Schmürz. There can be little doubt that *Les Bâtisseurs d'Empire* dramatizes Vian's own feelings. He knew he was suffering from a serious heart condition, the after-effect of a fever attack. He had to give up playing his beloved jazz trumpet: 'Each note played on the trumpet shortens my life by a day,' he said. It was his own life he saw narrowing. Does the *schmürz* therefore stand for the mortal part of ourselves that we brutally flog and maltreat without noticing what we are doing? The fact that the *schmürz* collapses and dies just before the hero of the play does point in this direction. On the other hand, after the hero's death other *schmürzes* are seen invading the stage. Are they the messengers of death and is the hero's own *schmürz* his own death, silently waiting for him, thoughtlessly flogged by the hero when he is *not* aware of his own mortality? Or is *schmürz*, derived from the German word for pain – *Schmerz* – simply the silent, ever-present pain of heart disease?

Boris Vian died on 23 June 1959, while watching a private preview of a film based on one of his books. There had been a good deal of controversy about the adaptation and he had not been invited to attend, but had merely sneaked in.

DINO BUZZATI (1906–1972)

In *Les Bâtisseurs d'Empire* the flight from death takes the form of trying to escape upwards. The same image appears in the opposite direction in a remarkable play by Dino Buzzati, the eminent Italian novelist and journalist on the staff of the *Corriere della Sera* in Milan. This play, first performed by the Piccolo Teatro, Milan, in 1953, and in Paris in an adaptation by Camus in 1955, is *Un Caso Clinico*. In two parts (thirteen scenes), it shows the death of a middle-aged businessman, Giovanni Corte. Busy, overworked, tyrannized but pampered as the family's breadwinner, whose health must be preserved, he is disturbed by hallucinations of a female voice calling him from the distance and by the spectre of a woman that seems to haunt his house. He is persuaded to consult a famous specialist, and goes to see him at his ultra-modern hospital. Before he knows what has happened, he is an inmate of the hospital, about to be operated on. Everybody reassures him – this hospital is organized in the most efficient modern manner; the people who are not really ill, or merely under observation, are on the top floor, the seventh. Those who are slightly less well are on the sixth; those who are ill, but not really badly, are on the fifth; and so on downwards in a descending order to the first floor, which is the antechamber of death.

In a terrifying sequence of scenes, Buzzati shows his hero's descent. At first he is moved to the sixth floor, merely to make room for someone who needs his private ward more than he does. Further down, he still hopes that he is merely going down to be near some specialized medical facilities he needs, and before he has fully realized what has happened, he is so far down that there is no hope of escape. He is buried among the outcasts who have already been given up, the lowest class of human beings – the dying. Corte's mother comes to take him home, but it is too late.

Un Caso Clinico is a remarkable and highly original work, a modern miracle play in the tradition of *Everyman*. It dramatizes the death of a rich man – his delusion that somehow he is in a special class, exempt from the ravages of illness; his gradual loss of contact with reality; and, above all, the imperceptible manner of his descent and its sudden revelation to him. And in the hospital, with its rigid stratification, Buzzati has found a terrifying image of society itself – an impersonal organization that hustles the individual on his way to death, caring for him, providing services, but at the same time distant, rule-ridden, incomprehensible, and cruel. While *Les Bâtisseurs d'Empire* shows man in active flight from death, *Un Caso Clinico* depicts him gradually overtaken by old age and illness, while totally unaware of what is happening. In the gradual process of dying, man loses his personality. Looking at the raincoat he wore at the height of his powers, Corte says, 'Once Corte, the engineer, wore this fine raincoat. . . . Do you remember him? A dynamic man, sure of himself . . . how sure he was of himself, do you remember . . . ?'[1]

Buzzati, the author of an outstanding Kafkaesque novel (*Il Deserto dei Tartari*) and many short stories in a similar vein, followed *Un Caso Clinico* with another play, *Un Verme al Ministero* (*A Worm at the Ministry*), which, however, belongs to a different theatrical convention. It is a political satire on a totalitarian revolution, reminiscent of Orwell's *1984* but with a curiously mystical ending – the appearance of a Christ-like figure at the moment when the turncoat bureaucrat is about to insult the Crucifix to prove his sincerity in supporting the atheist dictatorship.

EZIO D'ERRICO

Another interesting Italian contribution to the Theatre of the Absurd is that of Ezio d'Errico. A man of many parts, d'Errico had made a name as a painter, a writer of thrillers in the vein of Simenon, an art critic, film writer, and journalist, when, in 1948, he turned to writing plays. His output of well over twenty plays since then has been varied, but has gradually veered in the direction of the Theatre of the Absurd. The starting point here is a criticism of the modern world, which, in *Il Formicaio* (*The Anthill*), appears as a grotesque, dehumanized place in which the hero, Casimiro, ends up by losing not only his individuality but even the gift of articulate speech. *Tempo di Cavallette* (*Time of the Locusts*) shows post-war Italy as a

1. Dino Buzzati, *Un Caso Clinico* (Milan: Mondadori, 1953), p. 182.

ruined village inhabited by selfish opportunists. When Joe, the Italo-American, arrives to share his wealth with the people of his homeland, he is murdered by a pair of juvenile delinquents. He reappears as a Christ-like figure, but the inhabitants are destroyed in a holocaust – of locusts or of atom bombs? – which incinerates the ruins of the village. Only a little boy survives, the hope of the new world. *Tempo di Cavallette* had its first performance at Darmstadt in the spring of 1958, in German.

D'Errico's experimental plays seem to have daunted the theatres of his native Italy, for his most important play to date in the convention of the Theatre of the Absurd, *La Foresta* (*The Forest*), also had its first stage appearance in German – on 19 September 1959, in Kassel.

The forest of the title consists of the grotesque relics of a mechanical civilization: broken telegraph poles, a derelict petrol pump, pylons and gallows growing out of a soil of concrete. In the spring, 'the concrete burgeons like a mould, a filthy mould that rises, stratifies, and invades everything.'[1] The people inhabiting this forest, from which there is no way out, are lost souls. Like the tramps in *Waiting for Godot*, they are hoping for a miracle, a liberation that will never happen. From time to time a train is heard passing in the distance and a ticket collector appears – he is an image of death. Those whose tickets have run out must die.

Among the derelicts are an old professor; a man of the world, and his ex-prostitute mistress; a vintner who in some ways represents Christianity and who struggles to hold on to his faith; a general whose family was killed in an air raid while he was directing operations at the front, and who lost his military unconcern with death when he saw the ruins under which they were buried; and a young poet who lost contact with reality when he was forced to take a humdrum job to support his family – he conducts animated and agonizing conversations

1. Ezio d'Errico, *La Foresta*, in *Il Dramma*, Turin, no. 278, November 1959, p. 9.

with unseen characters whose replies take the form of improvisations on the saxophone and the violin.

The main action of the play turns round the efforts of Margot, the ex-prostitute (who was forced into prostitution when captured by enemy troops during the war), to redeem the young poet. But when she offers him her love and invites him to flee, he cannot bear to return to reality, and kills himself. Margot reproaches herself for having offered romantic notions of love to the boy, rather than winning him back to reality with her body, and she goes mad. The vintner reaffirms his faith that man is not abandoned by the deity, but the play ends with the radio idiotically bawling out the morning gymnastics, and Max, Margot's lover, mechanically performing the grotesque exercises it prescribes.

The forest of concrete is an apt poetic image of an industrial civilization, and the characters who inhabit it are all sufferers from its scourges – war, intellectual pride, the suppression of the poetic impulse by commercial pressures, religious doubt, and all the horrors of the concentration camp. (Max was forced under torture to betray his best friend, the friend left him his vast fortune, and he is now roaming the world to escape from his memories. Margot was tortured into her wartime prostitution.) The play is the passionate outcry of a romantic against the deadening of sensibilities, the loss of contact with organic nature, that the spread of a civilization of concrete and iron has brought about.

MANUEL DE PEDROLO

D'Errico's dream world, absurd and harsh though it may be, has a wistful poetic symbolism, a softness that sometimes verges on sentimentality. In the work of another Latin writer, Manuel de Pedrolo (born in 1918), we are in the presence of an intelligence of almost geometrical austerity. De Pedrolo would by now be better known outside his native country but for the fact that he writes in a language – Catalan – that is little understood even by those in the English-speaking world who would normally have access to French, Spanish, or German. He is a prolific novelist and short-story writer, and also the author of a number of plays, some of which fall into the convention of the Theatre of the Absurd. After fighting in the Spanish Civil War, on the losing side, he has worked as an elementary schoolteacher, insurance agent, salesman, translator, and publisher's reader. He has gained an impressive number of literary prizes.

De Pedrolo's one-act play *Cruma* (first performed in Barcelona on 5 July 1957) is a study in human isolation. 'Cruma' is the name of an Etruscan measure or measuring instrument,[1] and the play shows an attempt to measure the human situation by standards that have become inoperative and meaningless. In an empty and bare-walled corridor that seems part of a larger apartment, a man who is at home there – and is therefore called 'the resident' – is about to measure the dimensions of the walls. He is joined by a visitor who helps him in this work – which is in vain, because they discover that the measuring tapes they are using are blank, without markings or figures.

The situation of the resident in the corridor of his apartment is as mysterious as that of the two tramps on their road in *Waiting for Godot*. The resident is unaware of an outside world. He does not know how the objects he uses have reached him. The visitor notices that he is using an ashtray, and asks him where he got it. 'I don't know,' the resident replies. 'Someone brought it and now it is here.' The visitor warns him, 'If you are not careful, objects will invade your life.'[2] The visitor, too, is oblivious of the outside world, although, as the resident reminds him, he must have come from outside.

It is in the same dreamlike atmosphere that the two are

1. See Pallottino, *The Etruscans* (Penguin Books, 1953), p. 246.
2. Manuel de Pedrolo, *Cruma*, in *Premi Joan Santamaria 1957* (Barcelona: Editorial Nereida, 1958), p. 14.

brought into contact with other characters. Voices are heard outside calling a woman's name, Nagaio. A girl passes through the corridor but is barely noticed by the resident and the visitor. When the visitor, who wants to wash his hands, opens the door to the bathroom, a stranger emerges, whom the resident takes for the visitor, a misunderstanding that makes communication almost impossible. Nagaio, the woman whom the voices have been heard calling, is seen when the window is opened in an apartment on the other side of the courtyard. Again the resident and the visitor find it difficult to communicate with her, but the stranger immediately makes friends with her and arranges a date. The stranger also has no difficulty in establishing contact with the girl, who again traverses the corridor. He decides to go out with this girl, instead of Nagaio. When the girl disappears behind a curtain leading into one of the rooms, he wants to follow her, but the curtain has turned into a solid door. The resident is able to open the door and let him reach the girl. Resident and visitor are left alone. They try to understand what has happened, and come to the conclusion that the strange beings who have disturbed them do not exist. But then they themselves cannot claim that they exist in reality. This being settled, they can return to their work. There is a knock at the door. As the resident goes to open it, the curtain falls.

This strange short play poses the problem of the reality of the 'others' and the possibility of establishing contact with them. Each character represents a different level of being. The resident occupies one end of the scale – he is an authentic being exploring his own world, hence unable to relate himself to others, unable even to distinguish his friend from a stranger. On the other end of the scale is the young girl – she exists only insofar as others want her. The other three characters represent intermediary steps on this scale. The greater the *inner* reality or authenticity of a human being, the less able he is to establish contact with the outside world, in its crudity and deceptiveness. And yet this interior solitude is bound to be disturbed; at the end of the play, the whole cycle of invasions from the inauthentic, everyday world is about to begin anew.

De Pedrolo's second, and more ambitious, play in this convention, *Homes i No* (*Humans and No*, first performed in Barcelona on 19 December 1958), is described by the author as 'an investigation in two acts'. The stage is divided into three parts by two screens of iron bars; in the compartment in the middle, the prison guard, a strange inhuman being called No, watches over the inmates of the cells to the left and right. No has fallen asleep, and the two couples, Fabi and Selena in one cage, Bret and Eliana in the other, try to overpower their jailer. But he awakes in time. The attempt of the two human couples to break out from behind the bars that imprison them fails. But the human beings, now that they have become conscious of the possibility of escape, have high hopes that in time they will succeed – and if not they themselves, their children.

In the second act, the two couples are joined by a son, Feda, in one cage, and in the other by a daughter, Sorne. Feda and Sorne are in love and resolve to do all they can to break out from the cages that prevent them from being united. They undertake a thorough examination of their prison and find that on the far side the cells end in an unbridgeable abyss. Their parents had been so fascinated by No that they had never even taken the trouble to explore the other side of their prison. Yet there seems no escape that way. Hence the young people concentrate on the back wall, and discover that this is by no means as solid as it seemed but has, rather, the appearance of a kind of curtain. Shall they tear that curtain down? No, the inhuman jailer is deeply perturbed, and begs them not to do so. If they do, it will be the end of them. Death? No, much worse. As the tension grows, Feda finally decides to take the risk and they tear the curtain down. Behind it there is another row of bars, which not only close their respective cells but reveal that No himself is merely a prisoner in a third cell. Behind this new row of bars sit three new jailers clad in black, silent and motionless. No has been a prisoner himself, but as Feda exclaims, 'even more so, because he knew it.'[1]

Homes i No is indeed an investigation – an investigation into the problem of liberty. Man is imprisoned in an infinitely receding series of enclosures. Whenever he thinks that he has broken through one of these barriers (the barrier of superstition, the barrier of myth or tyranny, or the inability to master nature), he finds himself face to face with a new barrier (the metaphysical anguish of the human condition, death, the relativity of all knowledge, and so on). But the struggle to overcome the new row of iron bars continues; it must go on, even if we know in advance that it will reveal only a further barrier beyond.

In the simplicity of its conception, and in the complete merging of the philosophical idea with its concrete representation in terms of a stage picture, *Homes i No* must occupy a high place among the most successful examples of the Theatre of the Absurd.

FERNANDO ARRABAL

Another Spaniard who may well be able to claim such a place is Fernando Arrabal, who was born in Melilla (formerly Spanish Morocco) in 1932. He completed his law studies at Madrid, but has been living in France since 1954, and writing his plays in French. Arrabal's world derives its absurdity not, like that of de Pedrolo, from the despair of the philosopher trying to probe the secrets of being but from the fact that his characters see the human situation with uncomprehending eyes of childlike simplicity. Like children, they are often cruel because they have failed to understand, or even to notice, the existence of a moral

1. De Pedrolo, *Homes i No*, in *Quaderns de Teatre A.D.B.*, Barcelona, no. 2, 1960, p. 24.

law; and, like children, they suffer the cruelty of the world as a meaningless affliction.

Arrabal's first play, *Pique-nique en Campagne* (the title is a cruel pun – it might be taken to mean 'picnic in the country', but actually stands for 'picnic on the battlefield'), already clearly shows this approach. He wrote the play at the age of twenty, under the influence of the news from the Korean War. This short one-act play shows a soldier, Zapo, isolated in the front line of the fighting. His father and mother, who are too simple to grasp the ferocity of modern war, arrive to visit him, so that they can have a Sunday picnic together. When an enemy soldier, Zepo, turns up, Zapo takes him prisoner, but later invites him to join the picnic. As the party gaily proceeds, a burst of machine-gun fire wipes out all the participants.

This is Chaplinesque comedy without the redeeming happy end; it already contains the highly disturbing mixture of innocence and cruelty so characteristic of Arrabal. This is also the atmosphere of *Oraison*, a *drame mystique* in one act, which opens the first volume of Arrabal's *Théâtre*, published in 1958. A man and a woman, Fidio and Lilbé (notice the baby talk of the names), sit by a child's coffin discussing ways and means of being good – from today. Lilbé cannot grasp what it means to be good:

LILBÉ: Shall we not be able to go and have fun, as before, in the cemetery?
FIDIO: Why not?
LILBÉ: And tear the eyes out of the corpses, as before?
FIDIO: No, not that.
LILBÉ: And kill people?
FIDIO: No.
LILBÉ: So we'll let them live?
FIDIO: Obviously.
LILBÉ: So much the worse for them.[1]

As this discussion on the nature of goodness proceeds, it is

1. Fernando Arrabal, *Théâtre* (Paris: Julliard, 1958), pp. 13–14.

gradually revealed that Fidio and Lilbé are sitting by the coffin of their own child, whom they have killed. Naïvely they discuss the example of Jesus, and come to the conclusion that they will have a try at being good, although Lilbé foresees the likelihood that they will get tired of it.

In *Les Deux Bourreaux* (*The Two Executioners*), we are faced with an analogous situation, but here conventional morality is more directly attacked as self-contradictory. A woman, Françoise, comes with her two sons, Benoît and Maurice, to denounce her husband to the two executioners of the title. He is guilty of some unspecified crime. Françoise, who hates him, wants to witness his being tortured in the next room. She rejoices in his sufferings, and even rushes into the torture chamber to put salt and vinegar on his wounds. Benoît, who is a dutiful son of his mother, accepts her behaviour, but Maurice protests. Maurice is thus a bad son, who disobeys his mother and hurts her. When the father finally dies of his tortures, Maurice persists in accusing his mother of having caused his death, yet finally he is persuaded into the path of duty. He asks to be forgiven for his insubordination, and as the curtain falls the mother and her sons embrace.

In *Fando et Lis*, a play in five scenes, Fando is pushing his beloved, Lis, who is paralysed, in a wheelchair. They are on the road to Tar. Fando loves Lis dearly, and yet, at the same time, he resents her as a burden. Nevertheless he tries to amuse her by playing her the only thing he knows on his drum, the Song of the Feather. They meet three gentlemen with umbrellas, who are also on the way to Tar, a place that they, like Fando and Lis, find it almost impossible to reach. Instead of getting to Tar, they always arrive back in the same place. Fando proudly displays Lis's beauty to the three gentlemen, raising her skirt to show off her thighs, and inviting them to kiss her. Fando loves Lis, but he cannot resist the temptation to be cruel to her. In scene 4, we learn that, to show her off to the gentlemen, he left her lying naked in the open all night. Now she is even more ill than before. Fando has her in chains, and puts handcuffs on her, just to see whether she can drag herself along with them. He beats her. Falling down, she breaks his little drum. He is so furious that he beats her unconscious. When the three gentlemen arrive, she is dead. The last scene shows the three gentlemen with umbrellas confusedly discussing what has happened. Fando appears with a flower and a dog – he promised Lis that when she died he would visit her grave with a flower and a dog. The three gentlemen decide to accompany him to the cemetery. After that the four of them can try to make their way to Tar.

In its strange mixture of *commedia dell'arte* and *grand guignol*, *Fando et Lis* is a poetic evocation of the ambivalence of love, the love a child might have for a dog, which is cuddled and tormented in turn. By projecting the emotions of childhood into an adult world, Arrabal achieves an effect that is both tragicomic and profound, because it reveals the truth hidden behind a good deal of adult emotion as well.

Le Cimetière des Voitures (*The Automobile Graveyard*), a play in two acts, attempts no less than a reconstruction of the passion of Christ seen through Arrabal's childlike eyes and placed in a grotesque landscape of squalor. The scene is a derelict graveyard of old motor-cars, which is, however, run on the lines of a luxury hotel. A valet, Milos, provides the service – breakfast in bed and a kiss from Dila, the prostitute, for every gentleman before he falls asleep. The hero, Emanou (i.e. Emanuel), a trumpet player, is the leader of a group of three musicians: his companions are Topé, the clarinettist, and Fodère, the saxophone player, a mute modelled on Harpo Marx. Emanou, like Fidio in *Oraison*, wants to be good. This desire expresses itself in his providing music for dancing to the inmates of the automobile graveyard every night, although the playing of musical instruments is strictly forbidden by the police. Throughout the play, two indefatigable athletes, a man, Tiossido, and an elderly woman, Lasca, cross the scene in a grotesque show of sportsmanship. In the second act, these two are revealed as police agents who are after Emanou. They pay Topé to betray his master for money – he will identify him by a kiss. When this happens, the mute Fodère denies him by vigorously shaking his head as he is asked whether he knows Emanou. Emanou is savagely beaten and taken away, dying, his arms tied to the handle-bars of a bicycle. The grotesque high life of the automobile graveyard continues.

Emanou's desire to be good is shown as a vague wish rather than a rational conviction. He recites his creed of goodness mechanically: 'When one is good, one feels a great interior joy, born from the peace of the spirit that one knows when one sees oneself similar to the ideal image of man,' but by the end of the play he seems to have forgotten this text and gets into a complete muddle when trying to recite it. At the same time, he earnestly discusses with his disciples whether it would not be more profitable to take up another profession – such as stealing or murder – and decides against these occupations merely on the ground that they are too difficult. When Dila tells him that she too wants to be good, Emanou replies, 'But you are good already; you allow everybody to sleep with you.'[1]

Although the parallels between Emanou and Christ are made so obvious as to border on the blasphemous (he was born in a stable, his father was a carpenter, he left home at the age of thirty to play the trumpet), the play achieves an impression of innocence – the search for goodness pursued with total dedication in a universe that is both squalid and devoid of meaning. In such a world there cannot be any understandable ethical standards and the pursuit of goodness becomes an enterprise tragic in its absurdity, as absurd as the strenuous running of the police spies in the pursuit of sportsmanship.

Arrabal's preoccupation with the problem of goodness – the relationship between love and cruelty, his questioning of all accepted ethical standards from the standpoint of an innocent

1. ibid., p. 152.

who would be only too eager to accept them if only he could understand them – is reminiscent of the attitude of Beckett's tramps in *Waiting for Godot*. Arrabal, who insists that his writing is the expression of his personal dreams and emotions, acknowledges his deep admiration for Beckett. But although he has translated some of Adamov's plays into Spanish, he does not think that he has been influenced by him.

Arrabal is greatly interested in developing an abstract theatre that would eliminate any human content altogether. In his *Orchestration Théâtrale* (first performed under the direction of Jacques Poliéri in the autumn of 1959), he tried to create a dramatic spectacle consisting entirely of the movements of abstract three-dimensional shapes, some of which were mechanical devices, while others were moved by dancers. The formal world of this strange spectacle was based on the inventions of Klee, Mondrian, Delaunay, and the mobiles of Alexander Calder. Arrabal is convinced that the incongruities of mechanical movement are a potential source of highly comic effects. The script of *Orchestration Théâtrale*, later retitled *Dieu Tenté par les Mathématiques*, which contains no dialogue whatever, resembles the notation of a gigantic game of chess (Arrabal is a passionate chess player) and is illustrated by fascinating coloured diagrams. The difficulties of putting this daring conception on the stage within the means of a struggling avant-garde company proved so formidable that the lack of public acclaim achieved by the experiment is by no means conclusive proof of the impossibility of an abstract mechanical theatre.

As he gained in fame and assurance Arrabal's fertile imagination produced a long series of plays in which an inverted ritual, a kind of black mass, recurs with considerable regularity; and this urge towards blasphemy is allied to exuberant sadomasochistic fantasies of the most extreme kind. Among this highly theatrical but mostly far too chaotically structured *œuvre*, one play stands out by the economy of its design and the brilliant simplicity of its basic concept which clearly shines through the most baroque detail. This is *L'Architecte et l'Empereur d'Assyrie* (1967), which has become Arrabal's most widely performed work and can claim the stature of a contemporary classic. The play derives its title from a passage in Artaud's writings on the theatre of cruelty, in which he speaks of the cruelty of 'Assyrian emperors' who sent each other the cutoff ears and noses of their enemies. It is also a modern variant of the theme of Shakespeare's *Tempest*. The architect, – that is, the constructive, positive, unspoilt human type, – is the Caliban of this desert island; he does not have the gift of speech because he does not need it; birds and animals and the heavens themselves obey his slightest wish, he merely has to think it. After a tremendous explosion there enters the island's Prospero, a modern man, seemingly the survivor of an air crash – or an atomic holocaust. He is power-mad and fancies himself as an Emperor, although he seems to have been no more than a lower-middle-class employee from Madrid. With the arrogance of 'civilized' man he teaches the architect his language and the airs and graces of society, with the result that the architect loses his miraculous powers. But the Emperor is also tormented by the most terrible guilt complexes and has himself tried for the murder of his mother, insisting that he be condemned to death and eaten by the architect. As the architect eats him he turns into the Emperor, who now, naked and in a state of nature, inhabits the island alone – until another explosion strands a civilized man on the island, who has the appearance of the erstwhile architect. And the cycle of history between the innocent state of nature and the corrupt, guilt-ridden world of socialized man begins anew.

The volume of Arrabal's collected plays in which *The Architect and the Emperor of Assyria* is published, carries the over-all title *Théâtre Panique*, a label which Arrabal increasingly attaches to the totality of his output. The term combines the usual sense of 'panic' (i.e. fear, anxiety, terror) with the original connotation of 'pertaining to the god Pan'; Arrabal thus stresses the elements of spontaneity and enthusiasm, the aspect of a celebration of *all* of life (Pan means 'all' in Greek), its acceptance in all its horror and glory. 'I dream of a theatre,' Arrabal proclaims, 'in which humour and poetry, panic and love would all be one. The theatrical ritual would then transform itself into an *opera mundi* like the fantasies of Don Quixote, the nightmares of Alice, the delirium of K., in fact the humanoid dreams which would haunt the nights of an IBM computer.'

This is an ambitious programme and Arrabal has given ample proof that he would be capable of putting it into practice. Yet most of his more recent output seems wildly self-indulgent and deliberately perverse. His early plays derived much of their impact from the childlike innocence of their cruel vision of the world. This is a quality which seems to be lacking, above all, in the works of his later period.

MAX FRISCH

Max Frisch (born in 1911) is an important German-Swiss dramatist and novelist; the play, *Biedermann und die Brandstifter* (*Biedermann and the Incendiaries*), first produced in the original German at the Zürich Schauspielhaus on 29 March 1958, is his first and only excursion hitherto into the realm of *humour noir* and the Theatre of the Absurd. Frisch and his compatriot, Friedrich Dürrenmatt, without doubt among the leading dramatists of the German-speaking world today, have developed a dramatic idiom of their own, a style that owes a great deal to Bernard Shaw, Thornton Wilder, and Bertolt Brecht, and one that might perhaps most aptly be described as a theatre of intellectual fantasy, airing contemporary problems in a vein of disillusioned tragicomedy. In being a sardonic commentary on a contemporary political phenomenon, *Biedermann und die Brandstifter* clearly belongs in this vein, but in the parodistic treatment of the subject and its resolute pursuit of the absurd, the play also shows the influence of the Theatre of the Absurd.

Labelled a 'didactic play without a lesson', *Biedermann und die Brandstifter* tells, in six scenes and an epilogue, the cautionary tale of a highly respectable bourgeois (Biedermann means precisely this in German), a manufacturer of hair lotion, whose house is invaded by a trio of shady characters. Biedermann knows that his home town has been the scene of a series of incendiary acts that are the work of men who have sought shelter in various houses, on the ground that they are homeless. He soon suspects that his guests are incendiaries, but even when they openly stack drums of petrol in his attic, even when they fix fuses and detonators in front of his own eyes, he believes that they will not set fire to his house, and to the whole town, if only he treats them nicely and invites them to a special dinner of goose and red cabbage. As one of the incendiaries sums up the situation, 'Jocularity is the third-best kind of camouflage; the second-best is sentimentality. . . . But the best and safest camouflage is still the pure, naked truth. Funnily enough, no one believes it. . . .'[1]

Biedermann is shown as heartless and brutal. He has driven one of his employees to suicide by dismissing him after years of faithful service, but at the same time he sees himself as an affable fellow who knows how to charm people. And this is his undoing. Two of the incendiaries, though depicted as victims of the social order, are destructive purely for the sake of destructiveness and the feeling of power they get from seeing things burn. The third is an intellectual who thinks he is serving some abstract principle. When the fuses are about to be lit, the intellectual rats on his fellow-conspirators, having discovered that they are not interested in his ideological rationalizations of destruction. But Biedermann does not believe this warning either. When the incendiaries find that they are out of matches,

1. Max Frisch, *Biedermann und die Brandstifter* (Berlin and Frankfurt: Suhrkamp, 1958), p. 78. Based on a radio play broadcast by Bayrischer Rundfunk, Munich, in March 1953; published as *Herr Biedermann und die Brandstifter* (Hamburg: Hans Bredow Institut, 6th ed., 1959).

he obligingly hands them his own, so that they can light the fuse that burns his house, his wife, himself, and the whole town.

The civilization that is being destroyed is one in which 'most people believe not in God but in the fire brigade.'[1] And the play is framed by a burlesque pseudo-Greek chorus of firemen, who are constantly affirming their readiness to intervene. In the epilogue, Biedermann and his wife are in hell, but in this un-metaphysical age the Devil himself (who is revealed as one of the incendiaries) refuses to conduct a hell for people like Biedermann. As the destroyed city has been rebuilt 'more beautiful than before' it seems that life can go on.

Biedermann und die Brandstifter is more than just a very telling piece of political satire. The political satire is certainly there: Biedermann's situation, according to Hans Bänziger, the author of an excellent study of Frisch, is based on the situation of President Beneš of Czechoslovakia, who took the Communists into his government although he knew that they were bent on destroying the country's independence.[2] It is also the situation of the German intellectuals who thought that Hitler did not mean what he said when he spoke of war and conquest, and so allowed him to start a world conflagration. And it is also, in a sense, the situation of the world in the age of the hydrogen bomb, when the attics of the world's major powers are stored with very highly inflammable and explosive material. But beyond this purely political aspect, Frisch's play describes the state of mind of the family in Ionesco's *The Bald Prima Donna* and *Jacques* – the dead world of routine and empty *bonhomie*, where the destruction of values has reached a point where the bewildered individual can no longer distinguish between the things that ought to be preserved and those that should be destroyed. The fire brigade is ready, but there is no one left

1. *Biedermann und die Brandstifter*, p. 20.
2. Hans Bänziger, *Frisch und Dürrenmatt* (Bern and Munich: Francke, 1960), p. 100.

who can recognize the incendiaries as dangerous, and so the measures taken to prevent the fire are bound to fail. What is more, in a world of dead routine, of unceasing consumption and production, the destruction of a civilization will be felt merely as a beneficial way of clearing the ground for a new building boom – so that production and consumption can continue.

WOLFGANG HILDESHEIMER

The Theatre of the Absurd has struck a responsive chord in the German-speaking world, where the collapse of a whole civilization, through the rise and fall of Hitler, has made the loss of meaning and cohesion in men's lives more evident than elsewhere. The major dramatists of the Absurd have been more successful in Germany than anywhere else to date. Yet in the vacuum left by Hitler it has taken a long time for a new generation of dramatists to arise.

Wolfgang Hildesheimer (born in 1916), one of the first German dramatists to take up the idiom of the Theatre of the Absurd, spent the war years, significantly enough, in exile abroad, and is still an Israeli citizen. Originally a painter, Hildesheimer started his career as a dramatist with a series of witty and fantastic radio plays – picaresque tales of forgers, grotesque Balkan countries, and Oriental romance. The step from this type of intellectual thriller to the Theatre of the Absurd seems a natural development. Hildesheimer regards the Theatre of the Absurd, as he has pointed out in a brilliantly argued lecture on the subject,[1] as a theatre of parables. Admittedly,

the story of the prodigal son is also a parable. But it is a parable of a different kind. Let us analyse the difference – the story of the prodigal

1. Wolfgang Hildesheimer, '*Erlanger Rede über das absurde Theater*', *Akzente*, Munich, no. 6, 1960.

son is a parable deliberately conceived to allow an indirect statement (that is, to give the opportunity to reach a conclusion by analogy), while the 'absurd' play becomes a parable of life precisely through the intentional omission of any statement. For life, too, makes no statement.[1]

Hildesheimer's collected volume of the plays that illustrate his conception of the Theatre of the Absurd has the title *Spiele in denen es dunkel wird* (*Plays in Which Darkness Falls*).[2] This is literally the case. As each of the three plays unfolds, the light fades. In *Pastorale oder Die Zeit für Kakao* (*Pastoral or Time for Cocoa*), some elderly characters disport themselves in a strange syncopation of dialogue concerned with business matters and stock-exchange deals, with artistic and poetic overtones (a mixture very characteristic of the tone of West German society today). As the light grows darker, summer turns into autumn and winter, and death overtakes the president of a big company, a consul, and a mining engineer.

In *Landschaft mit Figuren* (*Landscape with Figures*), a painter is shown at work painting the portraits of a group of equally empty and pretentious characters – a great but ageing lady, her gigolo, and an elderly tycoon. Here too the characters pass from middle to old age before our eyes until they die, are neatly packed into boxes, and sold to a collector – so that the characters themselves have become their own portraits. As this work proceeds, a glazier is putting new panes of glass into the studio windows. It is through them that the light gradually becomes dark. But at the end the painter and his wife are as young as they were in the beginning, and as they are left alone, the mauve panes of glass fall to the ground and the stage is once more bathed in light.

The glazier appears again in *Die Uhren* (*The Clocks*), but this time the panes of glass he puts into the windows of a room in-

1. ibid.
2. Hildesheimer, *Spiele in denen es dunkel wird* (Pfullingen: Neske, 1958).

habited by a man and wife are jet black and impenetrable. As the work proceeds, the couple relive scenes from their life together; towards the end a salesman comes who sells them a profusion of clocks of all kinds. And at the final curtain the man and his wife are inside the clocks, making ticking noises.

These dramatic parables are impressive poetic statements, even though they are far from being free from rather obviously drawn analogies and somewhat facile conclusions.

GÜNTER GRASS

Hildesheimer's parable plays are gentle and elegant. The theatre of Günter Grass (born in 1927) is of a far rougher texture. Grass also started his career as a painter. His plays are like the canvases of Bosch or Goya brought to life – violent and grotesque. In *Onkel, Onkel* (*Uncle, Uncle*), we meet Bollin, a young man single-mindedly dedicated to murder, who is always shown as failing because his intended victims display no fear of him. The little girl under whose bed he has hidden takes no notice of him when he emerges, but merely asks him to help her with her crossword puzzle; the gamekeeper he traps in the woods continues to instruct two city children in the botany of forest trees and methods of escape; the film star whom he wants to kill in her bathtub drives him away with her foolish chatter; and in the end two children steal Bollin's revolver and shoot *him* dead.

In *Zweiunddreissig Zähne* (*Thirty-two Teeth*), we meet a schoolmaster as single-minded as Bollin – for him tooth hygiene overrides all other passions. *Hochwasser* (*The Flood*) shows a family fleeing from the rising water on to the top floor of their house and then to the roof, where they encounter a pair of philosophical rats. As the waters recede and they return to routine lives in a ruined home, they regret losing the excitement and the corrupt figures of fantasy they met during the emergency.

The short play *Noch zehn Minuten bis Buffalo* (*Ten Minutes to Buffalo*) presents an ancient toy locomotive passing through a nonsense landscape accompanied by nautical conversation and never getting to Buffalo at all.

Günter Grass's most interesting play, however, *Die Bösen Köche* (*The Wicked Cooks*), is an ambitious attempt to transmute a religious subject into poetic tragicomedy. Cooks proliferate on the stage – there are two rival factions of cooks, and they are after the secret of a mysterious grey soup consisting of ordinary cabbage soup with the addition of a special kind of ashes. The holder of this secret is known as the Count, although his real name is the very ordinary one of Herbert Schymanski. The cooks make a bargain with the Count. He can marry Martha, the nurse, if he promises to let them in on his secret. But when they demand that he keep his part of the bargain, the Count has forgotten the recipe. 'I have told you often enough, it is not a recipe but an experience, living knowledge, continuous change. You should be aware of the fact that no cook has ever succeeded in cooking the same soup twice. . . . The last months, this life with Martha . . . has made this experience superfluous. I have forgotten it.'[1] Unable to fulfil their part of the bargain, the Count and Martha kill themselves. There can be little doubt that an analogy to the Passion pervades the play. Martha washes the Count's feet shortly before he dies, and there is an association between the mysterious food and the Eucharist, which, after all, was instituted in the course of, and is symbolized by, a meal.

Günter Grass wrote most of his plays before 1957. He has since then achieved major success with a number of vast and grotesquely exuberant novels including, *Die Blechtrommel* (1959), *Hundejahre* (1963), and *The Flounder* (1977). His play *Die Plebejer proben den Aufstand* (1966) deals with an episode in the life of Brecht and uses a Brechtian convention of drama.

1. Günter Grass, *Die Bösen Köche*, stage ms., p. 101.

ROBERT PINGET

Another notable novelist who also started his career as a painter and who has also ventured into the field of the Theatre of the Absurd is Robert Pinget (born in 1919). Pinget is a native of Geneva who now lives in Paris. He studied law, painted, taught French in England for a while, and became one of the leading figures in the group of 'new novelists' around Alain Robbe-Grillet. Pinget is a close friend of Samuel Beckett and his play *Lettre Morte* (*Dead Letter*) shared the bill with Beckett's *Krapp's Last Tape* at the Théâtre Récamier in the spring of 1960.

Lettre Morte takes up the theme of Pinget's novel *Le Fiston* (1959), which is in the form of a letter addressed by an abandoned father to his prodigal son; the father does not know where his son has gone, so the letter cannot be sent off and remains a 'dead letter'. *Le Fiston* tries to reproduce the rambling, ill-organized shape of an endless epistle, added to from day to day; the book lacks even pagination, thus increasing the reader's illusion that he is reading a real letter composed by a besotted old man. The play, *Lettre Morte*, puts that same old man, Monsieur Levert, on the stage. It is as though the author had become so obsessed with the reality of the long letter that he had to see the man who wrote it before his eyes in the flesh. We see Monsieur Levert in two situations – in the bar, opening his heart to the bartender, and in the post office, trying to persuade the clerk behind the counter to have another good look to see whether there isn't somewhere, after all, a letter from his lost son that might have gone astray. But the bartender and the post-office clerk are played by the same actor, the counter of the post office is the same as that of the bar. The old man is waiting without real hope, like the tramps in *Waiting for Godot*. He is continually racking his brain to find the reason why his son has left him, what he has done wrong to lose his affection. Outside, a funeral passes. Monsieur Levert is waiting for death. In a short *scherzo* in this symphony of melancholy and regret two of the actors of an itinerant company come into the bar and playfully repeat passages from the sentimental bedroom farce they have been performing that night. The play is called *The Prodigal Son*, and it deals with a father who writes letters to his son, imploring him to return. Whereupon he *does* return. Here the worn-out convention of boulevard theatre, where everything happens as it should, is cruelly confronted with that of the Theatre of the Absurd, where nothing happens at all and where the lines of dialogue do not flit wittily to and fro like ping-pong balls but are as repetitious and inconclusive as in real life – and hence as absurd as reality in a meaningless world is bound to be.

Pinget's second attempt at the dramatic form is a short radio play, *La Manivelle* (translated under the title *The Old Tune* by Samuel Beckett, and first broadcast in the B.B.C.'s Third Programme on 23 August 1960), in which the absurdity of real speech is carried to the extreme: two old men, an organ-grinder and his friend, are talking about the past. The conversation rambles from subject to subject, and each of the old men comes out with some choice bit of his past life. The trouble is that the other immediately contradicts the truth of that information, so that each one's recollection of his own past life is called into question. The past of each of these two old men mutually cancels out the other. What are they left with? Was their past life a mere illusion? As the two stand talking in the street, the sounds of modern traffic almost drown their recollections. Eventually, however, the handle of the barrel organ that had jammed (hence the title of the French original) turns again, and the old tune rises triumphantly above the traffic, perhaps a symbol that the old tune of memory, however rickety and uncertain, still prevails.

This short radio play, brilliantly translated by Beckett into an Irish idiom, creates, out of fragments that in their strict naturalness are incoherent to the point of imbecility, a strange texture of nostalgic associations and lyrical beauty. For there is no real contradiction between a meticulous reproduction of reality and a literature of the Absurd. Quite the reverse. Most real conversation, after all, is incoherent, illogical, ungrammatical, and elliptical. By transcribing reality with ruthless accuracy, the dramatist arrives at the disintegrating language of the Absurd. It is the strictly logical dialogue of the rationally constructed play that is unrealistic and highly stylized. In a world that has become absurd, transcribing reality with meticulous care is enough to create the impression of extravagant irrationality.

In a volume which appeared in 1961, Pinget published three further plays, one full-length and two one-act: *Ici ou Ailleurs*, in three acts, is, like *Lettre Morte*, closely related to one of Pinget's novels, *Clope au Dossier*. The hero, Clope, lives in a leaf-hut on the platform of a railway station, earns his livelihood by telling people's fortune from the cards and is haunted by something in his past. A young man, Pierrot, who passes by on his way to catch a train, strikes up a friendship with Clope. It looks as though he might stay with him but then, one day, his yearning to catch a train wins and he is gone. The image of the sedentary and contemplative type who tries to build up a lasting relationship in the hustle and bustle of travellers and trains is a striking one.

Architruc, the first of the shorter plays in the volume, concerns a bored, incompetent and childish king and his minister, trying to while away the time with empty games – rather like the two tramps in *Waiting for Godot*. In the end Death arrives and takes the king's life. *L'Hypothèse*, the other one-act play in the volume, is far more interesting and original. Mortin, the only character, is seen composing a lecture or speech about a manuscript that was found at the bottom of a well and trying to evolve a hypothesis about how it could have got there – how and why a writer might have been driven to throw his manuscript down a well. As the hypothesis grows wilder and more curious, an image of Mortin, which has occasionally been projected on to a screen at the back, takes over his musings and speaks instead of him. Mortin grows more and more agitated and in the end it looks as though he were about to give up and throw away the manuscript on which we have seen him working – so perhaps the hypothesis concerns himself and his own manuscript. . . .

In the massive novel *L'Inquisitoire* (1962) Pinget fuses his work as a dramatist and as a novelist: it is in the form of questions and answers, a long and mysterious examination and cross-examination. Here the Theatre of the Absurd coalesces with the *nouveau roman*.

NORMAN FREDERICK SIMPSON

If Pinter's plays transmute realism into poetic fantasy, the work of Norman Frederick Simpson (born in 1919) is philosophical fantasy strongly based on reality. N. F. Simpson, an adult-education lecturer who lives in London, first came into prominence by winning one of the prizes in the *Observer*'s 1957 play-writing competition with *A Resounding Tinkle* (first performed in a much shortened version at the Royal Court Theatre, London, on 1 December 1957). Although Simpson's work is extravagant fantasy in the vein of Lewis Carroll, and is compared by the author himself to a regimental sergeant-major reciting 'Jabberwocky' over and over again through a megaphone,[1] it is nevertheless firmly based in the English class system. If Pinter's world is one of tramps and junior clerks, Simpson's is unmistakably suburban.

A Resounding Tinkle takes place in the living-room of the bungalow inhabited by Mr and Mrs Paradock (the Paradocks, in fact), and the action, however wild and extravagant it becomes, always remains firmly rooted in the world of the English suburban lower middle class. The Paradocks have ordered an elephant from the store, but they don't like it

---

1. N. F. Simpson, *A Resounding Tinkle*, in *New English Dramatists 2* (Penguin Books, 1960), p. 81. First published in *The Observer Plays*, ed. Kenneth Tynan (London: Faber & Faber, 1958).

because it is several sizes too large for a private house ('It's big enough for a hotel'), so they exchange it for a snake ('You can have them lengthened but we shan't bother') – two transactions only slightly more absurd than the pointless buying and exchanging of furniture practised in these circles.

The Paradocks invite some comedians to entertain them at home – which is only slightly more extravagant than getting them on the television. Their son Don comes home, but has turned into a young woman ('Why, you've changed your sex') – but then sex is not all that important in the restrained world of the suburbs. The Paradocks and their guests, the two comedians, get drunk on nectar and ambrosia. They listen to a religious service on the radio which comes from the 'Church of the Hypothetical Imperative in Brinkfall'[1] but is delivered in 'a voice of cultured Anglican fatuity'[2] while enjoining listeners to 'make music, water, love, and rabbit hutches'[3] and making them pray:

Let us laugh with those we tickle. . . . Let us weep with those we expose to tear gas. Let us throw back our heads and laugh at reality, which is an illusion caused by mescalin deficiency; at sanity, which is an illusion caused by alcohol deficiency; at knowledge, which is an illusion caused by certain biochemical changes in the human brain structure during the course of human evolution. . . . Let us laugh at thought, which is a phenomenon like any other. At illusion, which is an illusion, which is a phenomenon like any other. . . .[4]

Nonsense and satire mingled with parody, but the serious philosophical intent is again and again brought into the open. The two comedians learnedly discuss Bergson's theory of laughter ('We laugh every time a person gives us the impression of being a thing'), and Mr Paradock promptly puts the theory to the test by having himself plugged into the electricity

1. *A Resounding Tinkle* (short version), in *The Hole and Other Plays and Sketches* (London: Faber & Faber, 1964), p. 88.
2. *A Resounding Tinkle*, in *New English Dramatists 2*, p. 99.
3. ibid., p. 100.   4. ibid.

supply and converting himself into a mechanical brain, which, however, in spite of being fed with data, fails to produce the correct results – because of a short circuit.

The author appears from time to time, apologizing for the shortcomings of the play, which came to him in Portuguese, a language that unfortunately he does not know too well. 'I lay claim,' he announces, 'to no special vision, and my own notions as to what I have in mind here may well fall pitifully short of your own far better notions. No. I am the dwarf in the circus – I give what scope I can to such deficiencies as I have.'[1] And in the final summing up of 'an odd evening', the author draws the attention of the public to the comforting fact that 'the retreat from reason means precious little to anyone who has never caught up with reason in the first place. It takes a trained mind to relish a *non sequitur*.'[2] And so it does. N. F. Simpson's plays are highly intellectual entertainments. They lack the dark obsessiveness of Adamov, the manic proliferation of things in Ionesco, or the anxiety and menace of Pinter. They are spontaneous creations that often rely on free association and a purely verbal logic ('The small of my back is too big, Doctor') and lack the formal discipline of Beckett. As Simpson himself put it in one progamme note, 'From time to time parts of the play may seem about to become detached from the main body. No attempt, well intentioned or not, should be made from the audience to nudge these back into position while the play is in motion. They will eventually drop off and are quite harmless.'[3]

But for all this looseness of construction and spontaneity, Simpson's world bears the mark of the fantasies of an eminently sane, intelligent man with deep learning and a delicious sense of humour. 'I think life is excruciatingly funny,' he once said. 'People travelling every day on the tube and doing things which are a means to an end but become ends in themselves,

1. ibid., p. 130.   2. ibid., p. 140.
3. Simpson, quoted by Penelope Gilliatt, 'Schoolmaster from Battersea', *Manchester Guardian*, 14 April 1960.

like buying cars to get about at weekends and spending every weekend cleaning them.'[1]

The prayers and responses in the short, one-act version of *A Resounding Tinkle* seem to sum up the purpose of Simpson's endeavours:

PRAYER: Give us light upon the nature of our knowing. For the illusions of the sane man are not the illusions of the lunatic, and the illusions of the flagellant are not the illusions of the alcoholic, and the illusions of the delirious are not the illusions of the love-sick, and the illusions of the genius are not the illusions of the common man:

RESPONSE: Give us light that we may be enlightened.

PRAYER: Give us light that, sane, we may attain to a distortion more acceptable than the lunatic's and call it truth:

RESPONSE: That, sane, we may call it truth and know it to be false.

PRAYER: That, sane, we may know ourselves, and by knowing ourselves may know what it is we know.

RESPONSE: Amen.[2]

There could hardly be a better statement of the objectives not merely of Simpson himself but of the Theatre of the Absurd.

The exploration of the relativity of our vision of the world, according to the individual's preoccupations, obsessions, and circumstances, is the subject of Simpson's second play, *The Hole* (performed in a double bill at the Royal Court, with the shortened version of *A Resounding Tinkle*, in December 1957). Here a group of characters congregates around a hole in the street, discussing what it might be, each of them in turn seeing different things happening in its dark opening.

The crowd gradually congregates round a 'visionary' who has settled down on a camp stool with blankets and a supply of food to watch for an unspecified event of religious connotation, which he says is imminent down there – the solemn unveiling of a great window whose many-coloured glass will stain the

1. Simpson, quoted in *Daily Mail*, 25 February 1960.
2. *A Resounding Tinkle* (short version), pp. 87–8.

white radiance of eternity. The visionary admits that it was once his ambition 'to have a queue stretching away from me in every direction known to the compass',[1] but he has now toned down his expectations; he will be satisfied if he becomes the nucleus of a more modest queue.

Other, more commonplace characters arrive and watch the hole, projecting in turn their preoccupations – the whole content of their minds – on to the blank darkness of the mysterious opening. The discussion around the hole thus becomes a survey of the fantasy life of an English suburb. It starts with sports, ranging from dominoes to cricket, boxing, and golf; proceeds to nature, turning the hole into an aquarium housing a variety of species of fish that can be discussed with expertise; then turns to crime and punishment and violent demands for torture, execution, and revenge; and, having aroused the emotions of all concerned, culminates in fantasies of a political nature – the violence of both chauvinism and revolutionary action. After all this, a workman emerges from the hole and informs the bystanders that it contains a junction box of the electricity supply.

The intellectual among the crowd, Cerebro, is ready to accept this sobering fact and consoles himself with the thought that, after all, something is positively known about junction boxes. But his antagonist, Soma, who plays Stalin to Cerebro's Marx, seeing the potentialities of power and mass emotion, accuses him of wanting 'to take away all the mystery, all the poetry, all the enchantment'. Gradually the sober, positive truth is reinvested with metaphysical significance. Even Cerebro indulges in pseudo-logical speculations on whether one should speak of the cables going into, or coming out of, the junction box, while Soma turns the crowd into a meeting celebrating the religious rites of a cult of electrical generation. The technological facts have been turned back into vague emotional mumbo-jumbo. The visionary alone remains on the

1. Simpson, *The Hole*, in *The Hole and Other Plays and Sketches*, p. 11.

scene, still waiting for the coloured glass that will stain the white radiance of eternity.

The Hole is a philosophical fable. In his third play, *One Way Pendulum*, Simpson combines this theme with the suburban nonsense world of *A Resounding Tinkle*. When asked for the meaning of the title, he is reported to have replied that it is merely a name, like London or Simpson. In fact it is a kind of signpost indicating that the contents of the play are paradoxical. During its first run at the Royal Court Theatre, where it opened (after a try-out in Brighton) on 22 December 1959, the play was subtitled 'An evening of high drung and slarrit'. When it was transferred to the West End, this somewhat esoteric description was replaced by the more readily understandable 'A farce in a new dimension'.

As in *The Hole*, a group of characters is presented, each of whom is preoccupied with a private world of fantasy. As Simpson himself put it in a radio interview, 'In these plays each man is an island. The whole point about the relationship in the family is that everyone is in fact preoccupied with his own interests and makes very little contact, except superficially, with the other characters in the play.'[1] The family in question are the Groomkirbys. Arthur Groomkirby, the father of the family, earns his living as a private-enterprise keeper of parking meters, a highly appropriate profession to choose in present-day Britain. Like all good suburban fathers he has a hobby. He combines an interest in the law with a passion for do-it-yourself carpentry, and constructs, in the course of the play, a very life-like replica of the court at the Old Bailey in his own living-room.

Arthur's son, Kirby Groomkirby, who has trained himself by the Pavlov method and is unable to have a meal without having heard first the bell of a cash register, is engaged on a gigantic educational enterprise – he wants to teach five hundred

1. Simpson, interview B.B.C. General Overseas Service, 6 March 1960.

'speak-your-weight' weighing machines to sing the 'Halle-lujah' chorus from the *Messiah*. Being of a logical mind, he argues that if these machines can speak, they must be capable of learning to sing as well. And he is making progress. Once he has taught the machines to sing, he hopes to transport them to the North Pole, where they would attract large crowds of people eager to hear them. These multitudes might then be induced to jump all at the same moment, thereby tilting the axis of the earth, and causing an ice age in Britain, which would lead to the death of many people. Kirby needs many deaths, for he likes to wear black, but, being logical, he needs deaths to give him an opportunity to don his mourning attire.

The teenage daughter of the family, Sylvia, is also pre-occupied with death, or rather she wants to be, having been given a skull as a *memento mori*. But she finds that the skull does not work; it fails to remind her of death. On the other hand, Sylvia is deeply dissatisfied with the human condition. She can-not understand why her arms are not long enough to reach her knees; she cannot see the logic of the construction of human bodies. There is an old aunt who sits in a wheel-chair and is, on Bergsonian principles, treated as a thing rather than a human being. Only the mother of the family, Mabel, is wholly matter-of-fact, not surprised by anything that goes on around her, and herself highly eccentric in her sanity. The charwoman she employs, Myra Gantry, is used by her to eat up surplus food, which is hard work, since much is left over.

In the second act, the home-made Old Bailey at the Groom-kirbys' house suddenly fills with judge, prosecutor, and defence counsel, and while the household goes on with its routine, a trial develops. Arthur Groomkirby is called as a witness and sub-jected to a fantastic cross-examination, which undermines his alibi by proving that there are millions of places he has *not* been to at a given moment, making the probability that he has not been in a particular place so small as to be negligible. After a nightmare game of three-handed whist with the judge, Arthur

Groomkirby returns to the proceedings. Only now is it announced that the accused is his own son, who has killed forty-three people in order to be able to wear mourning for them. Although it is proved that he has committed these murders, he is acquitted because, as a mass murderer could be sentenced for only one crime, this would mean cheating the law of its retribution for the others. Hence he is discharged.

The play ends with Arthur Groomkirby preparing himself to act as the judge in his own courtroom – apparently with little chance of success.

One Way Pendulum owed its considerable success with the public to the sustained inventiveness of its nonsense and, in particular, to the brilliant parody of British legal procedure and language in the court scene, which occupies almost the whole of the second act. In fact, however, the play is far less amiable than it appears at first sight. What seems little more than a harmless essay in upside-down logic is essentially a ferocious comment on contemporary British life.

The play portrays a suburban family living so wrapped up in its private fantasies that each of its members might be inhabiting a separate planet. It also hints at the connection between the reticences – the mutual tolerance that allows each of the Groomkirbys to plant his weird preoccupations in the middle of the living-room – and the deep undercurrents of cruelty and sadism that lie behind such a society. Kirby's Pavlovian self-conditioning is a key image of the play; it stands for the automatism induced by habit on which the suburban commuting world rests. To lead an emotional life, Kirby has to stun himself into unconsciousness; only then can he indulge in sex. When awakened from one of these stupors by his Pavlovian cash-register bell, he angrily exclaims, 'I might have been dreaming. . . . Might have stopped me stone dead in the middle of an orgasm!'[1]

1. Simpson, *One Way Pendulum* (London: Faber & Faber, 1960), p. 50.

Habit and social convention are the great deadeners of the inauthentic society. To find a social justification for wearing black, Kirby turns into a mass murderer. Repression and habit, however, are always accompanied by guilt, hence the appearance of the courtroom in the middle of the Groomkirbys' suburban world. The proceedings may be hilarious parody, but the trial that is being conducted has its affinities with Kafka's trial of another guilty petty bourgeois. In the eerie three-handed whist game during the recess, the judge assumes an almost satanic tinge. Mr Groomkirby faces him with earplugs in his ears. When sent out by the judge to see if it is light, he reports back that he kept his eyes shut, as he does not intend 'to be blinded suddenly by the sunrise'. At one point he loses the power of speech, and when the judge savagely asks him, 'Are you dentally fit?', he has no answer. No wonder that after this nightmare orgy of guilt, he greets the dawn with 'monumental relief'.

The actual proceedings of the court are, in comparison, reassuring. They may express deep feelings of guilt, but at the same time they provide a lightning-conductor in their total irrelevance to life, through the formalism of reasoning in a vacuum. Here Simpson needed only a minimum supply from his rich comic invention to turn reality into satire. On one level, his Old Bailey is a fantasy of guilt in a suburban world of respectability; on another level it is a powerful satirical image of tradition running down in formalistic irrelevance. *One Way Pendulum* portrays a society that has become absurd because routine and tradition have turned human beings into Pavlovian automata. In that sense, Simpson is a more powerful social critic than any of the social realists. His work is proof that the Theatre of the Absurd is by no means unable to provide highly effective social comment.

EDWARD ALBEE

The work we have surveyed in this chapter shows that the
Theatre of the Absurd has had its impact on writers in France,
Italy, Spain, Germany, Switzerland, and Great Britain.
The relative absence of dramatists of the Absurd in the United
States, however, is puzzling, particularly in view of the fact
that certain aspects of American popular art have had a decisive
influence on the dramatists of the Absurd in Europe (see the
following chapter).

But the reason for this dearth of examples of the Theatre of
the Absurd in the United States is probably simple enough – the
convention of the Absurd springs from a feeling of deep disil-
lusionment, the draining away of the sense of meaning and
purpose in life, which has been characteristic of countries like
France and Britain in the years after the Second World War.
In the United States there has been no corresponding loss of
meaning and purpose. The American dream of the good life is
still very strong. In the United States the belief in progress that
characterized Europe in the nineteenth century has been maintained into the middle of the twentieth. It is only since the
events of the 1970's – Watergate and defeat in Vietnam –
that this optimism has received some sharp shocks.

It is certainly significant that such a notable work of the
American avant-garde as Robert Hivnor's *Too Many Thumbs*,
which has been compared to the fantasies of Ionesco, is in fact
an affirmation of a belief in progress and the perfectibility of
man. It shows a chimpanzee compressing his evolution to the
status of man – and far beyond that, to complete spirituality –
into a matter of months. The fantasy is there, but certainly no
sense of the futility and absurdity of human endeavour.

On the other hand, Edward Albee (born in 1928) comes into
the category of the Theatre of the Absurd precisely because his

work attacks the very foundations of American optimism. His first play, *The Zoo Story* (1958), which shared the bill at the Provincetown Playhouse with Beckett's *Krapp's Last Tape*, already showed the forcefulness and bitter irony of his approach. In the realism of its dialogue and in its subject matter – an outsider's inability to establish genuine contact with a dog, let alone any human being – *The Zoo Story* is closely akin to the world of Harold Pinter. But the effect of this brilliant one-act duologue between Jerry, the outcast, and Peter, the conformist bourgeois, is marred by its melodramatic climax; when Jerry provokes Peter into drawing a knife and then impales himself on it, the plight of the schizophrenic outcast is turned into an act of sentimentality, especially as the victim expires in touching solicitude and fellow-feeling for his involuntary murderer.

But after an excursion into grimly realistic social criticism (the one-act play *The Death of Bessie Smith*, a re-creation of the end of the blues singer Bessie Smith in Memphis in 1937; she died after a motor accident because hospitals reserved for whites refused to admit her), Albee produced a play that clearly takes up the style and subject-matter of the Theatre of the Absurd and translates it into a genuine American idiom. *The American Dream* (1959–60; first performed at the York Playhouse, New York, on 24 January 1961) fairly and squarely attacks the ideals of progress, optimism, and faith in the national mission, and pours scorn on the sentimental ideals of family life, togetherness, and physical fitness; the euphemistic language and unwillingness to face the ultimate facts of the human condition that in America, even more than in Europe, represent the essence of bourgeois assumptions and attitudes. *The American Dream* shows an American family – Mommy, Daddy, Grandma – in search of a replacement for the adopted child that went wrong and died. The missing member of the family arrives in the shape of a gorgeous young man, the embodiment of the American dream, who admits that he consists only of muscles and a healthy exterior, but is dead inside, drained of genuine feeling and the capacity for experience. He will do anything for money – so he will even consent to become a member of the family. The language of *The American Dream* resembles that of Ionesco in its masterly combination of clichés. But these clichés, in their euphemistic, baby-talk tone, are as characteristically American as Ionesco's are French. The most disagreeable verities are hidden behind the corn-fed cheeriness of advertising jingles and family-magazine unctuousness. There are very revealing contrasts in the way these writers of different nationalities use the clichés of their own countries – the mechanical hardness of Ionesco's French platitudes; the flat, repetitive obtuseness of Pinter's English nonsense dialogue; and the oily glibness and sentimentality of the American cliché in Albee's promising and brilliant first example of an American contribution to the Theatre of the Absurd.

With his first full-length play *Who's Afraid of Virginia Woolf?* (first performed in New York on 14 October 1962) Albee achieved his breakthrough into the first rank of contemporary American playwrights. On the surface this is a savage marital battle in the tradition of Strindberg and the later O'Neill. George, the unsuccessful academic, his ambitious wife, and the young couple they are entertaining, are realistic characters; their world, that of drink-sodden and frustrated university teachers, is wholly real. But a closer inspection reveals elements which clearly still relate the play to Albee's earlier work and the Theatre of the Absurd. George and Martha (there are echoes there of George and Martha Washington) have an imaginary child which they treat as real, until in the cold dawn of that wild night they decide to 'kill' it by abandoning their joint fantasy. Here the connection to *The American Dream* with its horrid dream-child of the ideal all-American boy becomes clear; thus there are elements of dream and allegory in the play (is the dream child which cannot become real among people torn by ambition and lust something like the American ideal itself?); and there is also a Genet-like ritualistic element in its structure as a sequence of three rites: act I – 'Fun and Games'; act II – '*Walpurgisnacht*'; act III – 'Exorcism'.

With *Tiny Alice* (1963) Albee broke new ground in a play which clearly tried to evolve a complex image of man's search for truth and certainty in a constantly shifting world, without ever wanting to construct a complete allegory or to offer any solutions to the questions he raised. Hence the indignant re-action of some critics seems to have been based on a profound misunderstanding. The play shows its hero buffeted between the church and the world of cynical wisdom and forced by the church to abandon his vocation for the priesthood to marry a rich woman who made a vast donation dependent on his decision. Yet immediately the marriage is concluded the lady and her staff depart, leaving the hero to a lonely death. The central image of the play is the mysterious model of the great mansion, in which the action takes place, that occupies the centre of the stage. Inside this model every room corresponds to one in the real house, and tiny figures can be observed repeating the movements of the people who occupy it. Everything that happens in the macrocosm is exactly repeated in the microcosm of the model. And no doubt inside the model there is another smaller model, which duplicates everything that happens on an even tinier scale, and so on *ad infinitum*, upwards and downwards on the scale of being. It is futile to search for the philosophical meaning of such an image. What it communicates is a mood, a sense of the mystery, the im-penetrable complexity of the universe. And that is precisely what a dramatic poet is after.

With *A Delicate Balance* (1966) Albee returned to a more realistic setting which, however, is also deeply redolent of mystery and nameless fears.

JACK GELBER

Jack Gelber's *The Connection* (1959) skilfully blends jazz with Beckett's theme of waiting. The image of the drug addicts waiting for the arrival of the messenger carrying their drug is a powerful conception. The presence of a jazz quartet improvising onstage lends the play a fascinating element of spontaneity, and the dialogue has a lyricism of pointlessness that equals much of the best writing in the Theatre of the Absurd. But the play is marred by a laborious superstructure of pretence at realism. Author and director appear, and go to great lengths to convince the audience that they are seeing real drug addicts; two film cameramen who are supposed to record the events of the evening are involved in the action, and one is actually seduced into drug-taking. And, finally, the strange, spontaneous, poetic play culminates in a plea for a reform of the drug laws. *The Connection*, brilliant as it is in parts, founders in its uncertainty as to which convention it belongs to – the realist theatre of social reform or the Theatre of the Absurd. In a later play *The Apple* (1961) Gelber moved closer to a theatre of improvisation, or prearranged improvisation, half-way between Pirandello and the Happening.

ARTHUR L. KOPIT

How difficult it seems in America to use the convention of the Theatre of the Absurd is also illustrated by Arthur L. Kopit's intriguing play *Oh Dad, Poor Dad, Mamma's Hung You in the Closet and I'm Feeling So Sad* (1960), performed in London in 1961. This play takes the oblique approach of parody. Described as 'A pseudo-classical tragifarce in a bastard French tradition', the play projects a young man's feelings about a dominating mother who tries to deprive him of contact with the outside world. But by treating the horrible mother, who travels with her stuffed dead husband in a coffin, and the retarded son, who finally strangles the girl who is ready to make love to him, with a parodistic snigger that deprives the playwright of the possibility of introducing genuine tragicomic effects (like those used by Ionesco in *Jacques*, or Adamov in *As We Were*), the author merely underlines the painfully Freudian aspects of his fantasy. In seeming to say, 'Don't take this seriously, I am only piling on the horror for the sake of fun!' Kopit spoils his opportunity to transmute his material into a grotesque poetic image. On the other hand, there is enough evidence of his genuine concern with the problem of the play to prevent it from being a mere parodistic joke.

THE THEATRE OF THE ABSURD IN EASTERN EUROPE

In the early 1950's, at the time of the controversy between Kenneth Tynan and Ionesco, it appeared as though the Theatre of the Absurd – introspective, oblivious of social problems and their remedies – was the very antithesis of the political theatre as preached by Brecht and his followers, or by the official arbiters of the arts in the Soviet Union and her bloc. It is one of the ironies of the cultural history of our times that, after the thaw had set in in Eastern Europe, it was precisely the theatre of Ionesco which provided the model for an extremely vigorous and barbed kind of political theatre in some of the countries concerned.

Indeed, the very nature of the convention of the Theatre of the Absurd can, on some reflection, be seen to predestine it for such a role. For, essentially, the theatre of Beckett or Ionesco is an instrument for the communication of human predicaments portrayed, not in their outward and accidental circumstances, but all the more effectively for being confined to the essentials of the mood, the basic psychological dilemmas or frustrations involved. It had, for example, long been an accepted truth of literary criticism that Kafka's novels, by exploring the perplexity of man confronted with a soulless, over-mechanized, over-organized world, had not only forecast the essentials of developments such as the concentration camps or the bureaucratic tyrannies of totalitarianism, but had in fact described their essence more accurately and more truthfully than any purely naturalistic novel could have done. When *Waiting for Godot* – a totally apolitical play in Britain or America – was first performed in Poland at the time of the thaw of 1956, the audience there immediately understood it as a portrayal of the frustration of life in a society which habitually explains away the hardships of the present by emphasizing that one day the millennium of plenty is bound to come. And it soon became clear that a theatre of such concretized images of psychological dilemmas and frustrations which transmuted moods into myths was extremely well suited to deal with the realities of life in Eastern Europe, with the added advantage that, concentrating on the psychological essentials of the situation in a setting of myth and allegory, it had no need to be openly political or topical by referring to politics or social conditions as such.

In Poland, the country which was the first to achieve a certain measure of freedom for artists, a number of extremely gifted dramatists turned to the new type of play. The fact that a tradition of Surrealist drama of this kind had existed before the war[1] undoubtedly had its influence on this development but so, undoubtedly also, had a growing awareness of what was happening in the theatre in France and Britain.

1. For a brief account of the work of Witkiewicz and Gombrowicz, see the next chapter, pp. 392–5.

SLAWOMIR MROZEK

Mrozek (born 1930) has become the best known among these Polish avant-garde dramatists. His first play, *Policja* (*The Police*, first performed in Warsaw on 27 June 1958), is a characteristically Kafkaesque parable. It describes the situation in a mythical country where the secret police have been so successful that all opposition to the ruling tyrannical regime has disappeared. There is only one suspect left, who has held out for years and still refuses to admit the error of his ways. When he too, to the dismay of the policemen, finally declares himself converted to the ruling ideology, the secret police has lost its *raison d'être*. Rather than allow the loss of the livelihood of so many staunch men who have devoted their lives to the cause, the police chief decides to keep the force in being by ordering one of his own men to commit political crimes.

In *Na Pelnym Morzu* (*Out at Sea*, 1961) three men, a fat one, a thin one, and one of medium build, are shipwrecked on a raft and faced with the necessity that one of them must be eaten by the others. They try all types of political method to determine who the victim should be – elections, discussion, scientific attempts to establish who has had the best life and therefore will lose least by dying before his time. But whatever method is used, for some mysterious reason it is always the thin castaway, the weakest of the three, who emerges as the potential victim. Yet he refuses to accept his fate. Only when the fat man persuades him that his death is a heroic, altruistic act, does the thin man finally consent to die. At this moment, in rummaging for the salt, the medium-sized castaway finds a tin of baked beans and sausages. Now it is no longer necessary to kill the thin man. But the fat man orders his minion to hide the tin away. 'I don't want baked beans,' he mutters, 'and anyway. . . . Can't you see? He's happy as he is!'

In *Strip-tease* (1961) two men are pushed into an empty room. They are highly indignant at this treatment. Then a huge hand appears and gradually strips them of their clothes. They decide that the best course would be to apologize to the hand. They make an abject speech asking the hand for its forgiveness, and kiss it. Another hand appears, 'wholly clad in a red glove. It beckons both and crowns them with dunce's hats which plunge them in total darkness.' The two men nevertheless are ready to go where the red hand bids them. 'If one is called, one must go,' says one of them ...

These, and a number of other short plays (*The Martyrdom of Peter Ohey, Charlie, Enchanted Night*) are fairly obvious, sharply pointed political allegories. *Zabawa* (*The Party*, 1963) is a short play with a more ambitious aim. Three men have been invited, or think they have been invited, to a party. They arrive in an empty place looking for the fun. But there is no party. So, in order to have one, they persuade one among them to hang himself, just to provide some action. As they are about to carry out the execution distant music is heard. So perhaps there *is* a party somewhere else. The play ends with one of the three turning to the audience and asking *them*: 'Ladies! Gentlemen! Where is the party?' There are echoes of *Waiting for Godot* here, unmistakably, but the atmosphere is that of Polish folklore and folk-culture, with its village bands and strange dancing masks.

Mrozek's most ambitious play hitherto is *Tango* (first performed in Belgrade, January 1965; in Polish at Bydgoszcz in June 1965; yet its triumphant opening on 7 July 1965 at Erwin Axer's Teatr Wspolczesny in Warsaw must be reckoned its real opening night). The impact of the Warsaw opening of *Tango* has been characterized as the most explosive event in the theatrical history of Poland for half a century.

Tango is a complex play. It has been described as a parody or paraphrase of *Hamlet* in that it shows a young man horrified by the behaviour of his parents, deeply ashamed by his mother's promiscuity and his father's complacency. It is also, clearly, a bitter attack by a young man on the previous generation which has plunged his country into war, occupation, and devastation. Arthur, the young hero of the play, has grown up in a world without values. His father is a feckless would-be artist who spends his time in futile avant-garde experiments. His mother sleeps with the boorish proletarian Eddie, who hangs around the untidy and dishevelled apartment which the family calls home. There is a grandmother who is occasionally ordered to lie in her late husband's coffin, which somehow has never been removed. And there is an aristocratic uncle with gentlemanly manners and an addled head. Arthur longs for standards, rules of conduct, respectability, order. He tries to persuade his cousin Ala to marry him in the old-fashioned way. Ala cannot understand the need for ceremony and respectability. If he wants to sleep with her, she is quite willing to let him do it without any ceremonial. But Arthur insists. When he gets hold of his father's gun, he stages a revolution and forces the family into decent clothes, makes them tidy up the cluttered apartment and prepares himself for the wedding. And yet he is unable to go through with it. When he realizes that the old order cannot be imposed by force, he gets drunk. The values of the past are destroyed and cannot be restored by force. What remains? Only force itself. 'I ask you: when there is nothing left and even revolt has become impossible, what can we then bring into being out of nothingness? . . . Only power! Only power can be created out of nothingness. It exists, even if nothing else exists. . . . All that matters is to be strong and resolute. I am strong. . . . Power, after all, is also revolt! It is revolt in the form of order . . .'

To prove his point Arthur is resolved to kill his old uncle. Ala tries to distract his attention and cries out that she, Arthur's bride, has slept with Eddie on the very morning of their wedding. Arthur is shaken. He is too human to be an exponent of the doctrine of naked power. Eddie seizes the opportunity. He fells Arthur with a savage blow. Now naked power really has triumphed. The other members of the family submit to

Eddie's rule. The play ends with Eddie and the old uncle, the representative of aristocratic tradition, dancing a tango over Arthur's dead body.

The tango here is the symbol of what the original impulse to revolt was about. For when the tango was a new and daring dance, the generation of Arthur's parents was fighting for their right to dance the tango. At the end of the road, when the revolt against traditional values has destroyed all values and nothing is left except naked power – Eddie's power, the power of the brainless mass – the tango *is* being danced, on the ruins of the civilized world.

The implications of this exercise in the dialectics of revolt are clear enough: the cultural revolt leading to the destruction of all values and thus to the attempt by intellectual idealists to restore these values; the realization on the part of the intellectuals that values, once destroyed, cannot be reconstituted and that thus only naked power remains; and finally, because the intellectuals are not ruthless enough to exercise naked power, its assumption by the Eddies of this world. It would be wrong to think that *Tango* has relevance only for the Communist sphere. The destruction of values, the invasion of the seats of power by vulgar mass man, can after all also be detected in the West. *Tango* is a play of far wider importance. It is brilliantly constructed, full of invention and extremely funny.

TADEUSZ RÓZEWICZ

Mrozek started life as a cartoonist and writer of grotesques. Rózewicz (born 1921) began as, and has essentially remained, a lyrical poet. An atmosphere of dream and nightmare pervades his plays, and passages of sardonic verse punctuate the action. Having fought with the partisans during the war and continuing to live, by choice rather than necessity, in the heart of the gloomy Upper Silesian industrial agglomeration – at Gliwice – Rózewicz constantly remains aware of the precariousness of life in our 'normalized' times. His first play *Kartoteka* (*The Card Index*, first performed at Warsaw on 25 March 1960) presents his hero, whose name changes almost from line to line, simultaneously lying in bed and out of it at various stages of his life which constantly merge into each other – at one moment he is a schoolboy of seventeen, at the next a bureaucrat of forty, and then a schoolboy again – just as one's own memories of oneself at different times of one's life coexist in one's consciousness.

> An empty place
> I hoped to find,
> the place I had left.
> Now I know:
> There are no gaps.
> Life
> like flowing water
> fills cracks and crannies
> more than enough.
>
> I have sunk like a stone
> Down into the depth.
> I lie on the seabed
> And I feel
> As though I had never existed

These lines from the poem that opens the play and which has the title 'The Prodigal Son – after a painting of Hieronymus Bosch' convey the elegiac feeling that underlies the grotesque action of *The Card Index*.

In *Grupa Laokoona* (*The Laocoon Group*, 1962) Rózewicz has become a somewhat more conventional satirist. The play ridicules the travel fever that came over the inhabitants of Eastern European countries when the thaw had made it easier to go abroad for holidays. But in his third play Rózewicz returned to his dreamlike, lyrical vein. *Swadkowie czyli Nasza Mala Stabilizacja* (*The Witnesses* or *We are almost back to normal*, 1963) is built in three movements rather like a sonata. Each movement is self-contained, yet the three together produce the total desired effect of variations on a basic theme, interrelated images. The first movement is a poem, recited by a man and a woman, a string of images of the precariousness of the newly won peace-time normality. The second movement presents a married couple, seemingly happy and spouting Ionesco-like clichés of novellettish endearment, yet very worried because the wife's mother is coming to live with them and they do not have sufficient room; and throughout their dialogue they casually report to each other what they can see through the window: children chasing a kitten and finally brutally mal-treating it and burying it alive. The third movement shows two men who are sitting in armchairs, back to back. They talk to each other, try to visualize each other, but are unable to catch a glimpse of each other because they cannot leave their chairs, which we are made to understand they have at last succeeded in occupying after dire struggles, so that nothing will induce them to move away and leave them free for anyone else. Throughout their dialogue they are concerned with something lying in the road which one of them can see. Is it a bundle of rags, a dead dog or perhaps a human being in need? The horrible thing comes nearer and in the end it seems indeed likely that it is a dying man. But to help him would mean leaving their armchairs and that is plainly out of the question. *The Witnesses* is a little masterpiece of lyrical drama, a telling concretized metaphor of the brutality and callousness that underlie the thin crust of the post-war world's normality.

Impatient with the conventions of the theatre, even those of the avant-garde as they exist today, Rózewicz is a tireless ex-perimenter. In *Smieszny Staruszek* (*The Ridiculous Old Man*, 1964) the central character, an old man accused of molesting little girls, addresses a tribunal of judges who are represented by tailor's dummies, while live children play around the stage taking no notice of the old man and his tribunal. Another short play, *Akt pzerwany* (*The Interrupted Act*), subtitled a 'Non-scenic comedy' (i.e. a play not to be staged – it *was* staged at Ulm in 1965), introduces the author trying to finish a play which he restarts several times. Here finally the author's mind itself has become the scene of the action.

In Czechoslovakia the thaw came later than in Poland, but when it finally came, it went even further initially, at least in the theatre. An avant-gardist theatre in Prague, *Divadlo na Zabradli*, the Theatre at the Balustrade, embarked on productions of *Waiting for Godot* and *Ubu Roi*.

VACLAV HAVEL

Vaclav Havel (born 1936), assistant to the artistic director of this theatre, the brilliant critic and director Jan Grossmann, gradually evolved into the '*dramaturg*' and resident playwright of the tightly knit group. His first success *Zahradni Slavnost* (*The Garden Party*, 1963) displays a mixture of hard-hitting political satire, Schweykian humour and Kafkaesque depths which are highly characteristic of Havel's work. The play takes place in a country where the regime has decided to abolish the Office for Liquidation and a more positively oriented ministry, the Office for Inauguration, is charged with this task. But the Office for Liquidation insists that this is impossible. As long as there is something to be liquidated, only the Office for Liquidation can be competent. The hero, a young careerist, rises to high rank thanks to his brilliant contribution to the arguments and intrigues which this dilemma brings into being.

Havel's second success, *Vyrozumeny* (*The Memorandum*, 1965), also delves into the tortuous world of bureaucracy. It shows an organization of uncertain purpose but vast complexity which suddenly finds itself confronted with the fact that someone has introduced a new official language in which all business must henceforth be transacted. This language, Ptydepe, is designed to make all misunderstandings impossible and is therefore of unimaginable complexity. The manager of the organization, Gross, is unable to get the first memorandum he finds written in Ptydepe translated. For although a translation department has been established, the regulations that have to be followed to get a translation authorized are so complex that it is in practice impossible to get one done. Balas, Gross's sinister deputy, who clearly is behind the introduction of the new language, takes advantage of his discomfiture, displaces him and has him demoted to a menial position. A girl typist in the translation department, who admires Gross and has taken pity on him, finally decides to break the rule and to translate the memorandum for him. It says that the new language is harmful and should never have been introduced. Armed with this disclosure Gross gets back into office. Balas is demoted but manages to remain as Gross's deputy by abjectly confessing his sins. Gross, although back in power, has been deeply demoralized. And when he discovers that another new language is being introduced – this time an idiom of such simplicity that the same word can have almost infinite meanings – he is determined not to suffer again. So when Maria, the typist who has been dismissed for breaking the rule in translating the memorandum for Gross, comes to ask him for help, he makes an impassioned speech in defence of human values and refuses to help her. After all she *did* break a rule in helping *him* . . .

The theory of the new languages discussed in the play is brilliantly worked out (Prague after all is the home of modern structural linguistics and Havel uses the terminology of redundancy and information theory to great effect) and their value as a metaphor of the situation in a country where life and death have in the past depended on the exact interpretation given by the individual to sacred Marxist texts, is clearly immense. The construction of the action is completely symmetrical, each scene on Gross's downward path exactly corresponding to one on his renewed rise to power. Havel is a master of the ironical, inverted repetition, of almost identical

7

THE TRADITION OF THE ABSURD

IT may seem strange that the chapter that tries to trace an outline of the tradition on which the Theatre of the Absurd is based should follow rather than precede the account of its present exponents. But the history of ideas, like most other history, is essentially a search for the origins of the present, and hence changes as the configurations of the present change. We cannot look for the germs of a current phenomenon like the Theatre of the Absurd without first having defined its nature sufficiently to be able to discern from which of the recurring elements that combine and recombine in the kaleidoscopic patterns of changing tastes and outlooks it is made up. Avant-garde movements are hardly ever entirely novel and unprecedented. The Theatre of the Absurd is a return to old, even archaic, traditions. Its novelty lies in its somewhat unusual combination of such antecedents, and a survey of these will show that what may strike the unprepared spectator as iconoclastic and incomprehensible innovation is in fact merely an expansion, revaluation, and development of procedures that are familiar and completely acceptable in only slightly different contexts.

It is only from the set expectations of the naturalistic and narrative conventions of the theatre that the man in the stalls will find a play like Ionesco's *The Bald Prima Donna* shocking and incomprehensible. Let the same man sit in a music hall, and he will find the equally nonsensical cross-talk of the comedian and his stooge, which is equally devoid of plot or narrative content, perfectly acceptable. Let him take his children to one of the ever-available dramatizations of *Alice in Wonderland*, and he will find a venerable example of the traditional Theatre of the

Absurd, wholly delightful and not in the least obscure. It is only because habit and fossilized convention have so narrowed the public's expectation as to what constitutes theatre proper that attempts to widen its range meet with angry protests from those who have come to see a certain closely defined kind of entertainment and who lack the spontaneity of mind to let a slightly different approach make its impact on them.

The age-old traditions that the Theatre of the Absurd displays in new and individually varied combinations – and, of course, as the expression of wholly contemporary problems and preoccupations – might perhaps be classed under the headings of:

'Pure' theatre; i.e. abstract scenic effects as they are familiar in the circus or revue, in the work of jugglers, acrobats, bullfighters, or mimes

Clowning, fooling, and mad-scenes

Verbal nonsense

The literature of dream and fantasy, which often has a strong allegorical component.

These headings often overlap; clowning relies on verbal nonsense as well as on abstract scenic effects, and such plotless and abstract theatrical spectacles as *trionfi* and processions are often charged with allegorical meaning. But the distinctions between them serve to clarify the issue in many instances and are useful in isolating the different strands of development.

The element of 'pure', abstract theatre in the Theatre of the Absurd is an aspect of its anti-literary attitude, its turning away from language as an instrument for the expression of the deepest levels of meaning. In Genet's use of ritual and pure, stylized action; in the proliferation of things in Ionesco; the music-hall routines with hats in *Waiting for Godot*; the externalization of the characters' attitudes in Adamov's earlier plays; in Tardieu's attempts to create theatre from movement and sound alone; and in the ballets and mimeplays of Beckett and Ionesco, we find a return to earlier non-verbal forms of theatre.

Theatre is always more than mere language. Language alone can be read, but true theatre can become manifest only in performance. The entry of the bullfighters into the arena, the procession of the participants at the opening of the Olympic Games, the state drive of the sovereign through the streets of his capital, the meaningful actions of the priest in celebrating the Mass – all these contain powerful elements of pure, abstract theatrical effects. They have deep, often metaphysical meaning and express more than language could. These are the elements that distinguish any stage performance from the reading of a play, elements that exist independent of words, as in the performance of Indian jugglers that made Hazlitt marvel at the possibilities of man and gave him an insight into his nature: 'Is it then a trifling power we see at work, or is it not something next to miraculous? It is the utmost stretch of human ingenuity, which nothing but the bending of the faculties of body and mind to it from the tenderest infancy, with incessant, ever-anxious application up to manhood, can accomplish, or make even a slight approach to. Man, thou art a wonderful animal, and thy ways past finding out! Thou canst do strange things, but thou turnest them to little account!'[1] This is the strange metaphysical power of the concreteness and skill in theatrical performance, which Nietzsche spoke of in *The Birth of Tragedy*: 'The myth by no means finds its adequate objectification in the spoken word. The structure of the scenes and the visible imagery reveal a deeper wisdom than that which the poet himself is able to put into words and concepts.'[2]

There has always been a close relationship between the per-

1. William Hazlitt, 'The Indian jugglers', *Table Talk* (London and New York: Everyman's Library), p. 78.
2. Friedrich Nietzsche, *Die Geburt der Tragödie*, in *Werke*, vol. I, ed. Schlechta (Munich: Hanser, 1955), p. 94.

formers of wordless skills – jugglers, acrobats, tightrope walkers, aerialists, and animal trainers–and the clown. This is a powerful and deep secondary tradition of the theatre, from which the legitimate stage has again and again drawn new strength and vitality. It is the tradition of the *mimus*, or mime, of antiquity, a form of popular theatre that coexisted with classical tragedy and comedy and was often far more popular and influential. The *mimus* was a spectacle containing dancing, singing, and juggling, but based largely on the broadly realistic representation of character types in semi-improvised spontaneous clowning.

Hermann Reich, the great historian and partial rediscoverer of the *mimus* from obscure sources, tried to trace the line of succession from the Latin *mimus* through the comic characters of medieval drama to the Italian *commedia dell'arte* and to Shakespeare's clowns. And while much of his evidence for the *direct* handing on of the tradition has been discredited since the publication of his monumental work, the deep *inner* connection of all these forms remains a self-evident fact.

In the mimeplay of antiquity, the clown appears as the *moros* or *stupidus*; his absurd behaviour arises from his inability to understand the simplest logical relations. Reich quotes the character[1] who wants to sell his house and carries one brick about with himself to show as a sample – a gag which is also attributed to the Arlecchino of the *commedia dell'arte*. Another such character wants to teach his donkey the art of going without food. When the donkey finally dies of starvation, he says, 'I have suffered a grievous loss; when my donkey had learned the art of going without food, it died.'[2] Another such moronic character dreams that he stepped on a nail and hurt his foot. Thereupon he puts a bandage round his foot. His friend asks him what has happened and when told that he had only dreamed he stepped on a nail, he replies, 'Indeed, we are

1. Hermann Reich, *Der Mimus*, vol. I (Berlin, 1903), p. 459.
2. ibid., p. 460.

rightly called fools! Why do we go to sleep in bare feet?'[1]

Such grotesque characters appeared in the *mimus* within a crudely realistic convention, but, characteristically, these plays, which were often half improvised, were not bound by any of the strict rules of the regular tragedy or comedy. There was no limitation on the number of characters; women appeared and played leading parts; the unities of time and place were not observed. Apart from plays with prearranged plots (*hypotheses*), there were shorter performances that remained without plot and consisted of animal imitations, dances, or juggling tricks (*paegnia*). In later antiquity, fantastic plots with dreamlike themes became prevalent. Reich quotes Apuleius as saying, '*Mimus hallucinatur*,' and adds:

We shall have to think not only of the lower meaning of *hallucinari* as 'talking at random, talking nonsense', but also of its more elevated meaning of 'dreaming, to talk and think strange things'. Indeed, with all its realism, the *mimus* not infrequently contained curious dreams and hallucinations, as in the plays of Aristophanes. In a gloss to Juvenal, the mimes are called *paradoxi*. And in fact everything fantastic is paradoxical, as are also the *mimicae ineptiae*, clowning and foolery. The expression probably refers to both these aspects. Thus, in the *mimus*, high and low, serious, even horrifying matters are miraculously mingled with the burlesque and humorous; flat realism with highly fantasticated and magical elements.[2]

Little of the *mimus* has been preserved. Most of its plays were improvised and even those that were written down were not thought respectable enough to be copied and handed on. In the dramatic literature of antiquity that has come down to us, only the theatre of Aristophanes contains the same freedom of imagination and the mixture of fantasy and broad comedy that characterized the wild and vulgar mimeplays. Yet for all their brilliance of invention, the plays of Aristophanes have had little impact on the development of at least the regular, literary

1. ibid.
2. ibid., pp. 595–6.

drama. If their spirit lived on, it did so in that other stream of the tradition of the theatre – the anti-literary, improvised folk-theatre, which was always equally unfettered in its topical comment, equally irreverent and extravagant.

It is this stream of tradition that was kept alive throughout the Middle Ages – while the schoolmen copied the comedies of Plautus and Terence – by itinerant *ioculatores* and clowns, who were the direct descendants of the Roman mimes. Their clowning and fooling reappear in the comic characters, often as Devils and personified vices, of French and English mystery plays; in the numerous farces of French medieval literature; and in the German *Fastnachtsspiele*.

Another descendant of the *mimus* of antiquity was the court jester: 'The long stick he carries was the wooden sword of the comic actor in ancient times.'[1] And both clowns and court jesters appear in the comic characters of Shakespeare's theatre. This is not the place for a detailed study of Shakespearean clowns, fools, and ruffians as forerunners of the Theatre of the Absurd. Most of us are too familiar with Shakespeare to notice how rich his plays are in precisely the same type of inverted logical reasoning, false syllogism, free association, and the poetry of real or feigned madness that we find in the plays of Ionesco, Beckett, and Pinter. This is not to make any claim that these latter-day playwrights should be compared to Shakespeare, but merely to point out that both the fantastic and the nonsensical have quite a respectable and generally accepted tradition.

These elements in Shakespeare are merely parts of the whole, embedded in a rich amalgam of the poetic and literary, the popular and the vulgar, but they are present nevertheless – in the earthy vulgarity of the low type of moron like Bernardine in *Measure for Measure* who refuses to attend his own execution because he has a hangover; in the naïve stupidity of Launce in *Two Gentlemen of Verona*; in the childishness of Launcelot

1. E. Tietze-Conrat, *Dwarfs and Jesters in Art* (London: Phaidon, 1957), p. 7.

Gobbo, the melancholy madness of Feste, or the Fool in *King Lear*. There is also in Shakespeare the personification of the subconscious part of man in great archetypal characters like Falstaff or Caliban, and the exalted madness of Ophelia, Richard II, and Lear – real descents into the realms of the irrational. Again, in a play like *A Midsummer Night's Dream*, there is the savage parody of conventional poetic language in the artisans' play, and Bottom's transformation into an ass is used to reveal his true animal nature. But, above all, there is in Shakespeare a very strong sense of the futility and absurdity of the human condition. This is particularly apparent in the tragicomic plays like *Troilus and Cressida*, where both love and heroism are cruelly deflated, but it underlies most of Shakespeare's conception of life:

> As flies to wanton boys, are we to the gods;
> They kill us for their sport.

If in Shakespeare's theatre elements of a vulgar, spontaneous, and in many ways irrational folk-tradition broke into literature (though the presence of these very elements delayed Shakespeare's acceptance as a serious, regular poet for a very long time), the tradition of spontaneous drama outside the realm of literature continued and flourished in Italy in the *commedia dell'arte*. Whether Reich's contention that there is a direct link between the *mimus* and the improvised *commedia dell'arte* – with the Roman Sannio appearing as Zanni (in English popular drama – Zany) and Scapin – is correct or not, the deep affinity between the two genres is evident. They meet the same very human demand for fooling, the release of inhibitions in spontaneous laughter. Many of the traditional *lazzi* – the verbal and non-verbal gags of the *commedia dell'arte* – bear a close family resemblance to those of the *mimus*. Here again we have the stupid simpleton who cannot understand the meaning of the most common terms and becomes entangled in endless semantic speculations and misunderstandings. The recurring types of the sly and lecherous servant, the braggart, the glutton, the senile old man, and the spurious scholar project the basic urges of the human subsconscious on to the stage in images as powerful as they are coarse. Basically simple, this theatre depends a great deal on the sheer professional skill of the performers. As Joseph Gregor points out, 'Only if we imagine these, in themselves hackneyed, motifs presented in an almost superhuman confusion; the jokes, in themselves stupid enough, delivered with superhuman dexterity of tongue; the acrobatics performed with superhuman skill, can we get an idea of this theatre.'[1]

So strong was the appeal of the *commedia dell'arte* that it has, in various guises, survived into the present. In France it was absorbed into legitimate drama through the work of such dramatists as Molière and Marivaux. But, in an unliterary form, it also persisted in the pantomimes of the *funambules*, where Debureau created his archetypal figure of the silent, pale, lovesick Pierrot. In England, it was the harlequinade that kept the tradition of the *commedia dell'arte* alive well into the nineteenth century, when it reached a peak in the inspired clowning of Grimaldi. The harlequinade formed the basis of the later English pantomime, which, in a somewhat modified shape, continues to this day as an irrepressible form of truly vulgar folk-theatre.

Other elements of the harlequinade merged into the tradition of the English music hall and American vaudeville, with its cross-talk comedians, tap-dancers, and comic songs. The greatest performers of this genre reached heights of tragicomic pathos that left much of the contemporary legitimate theatre far behind. One of the greatest of these was Dan Leno, of whom Max Beerbohm wrote:

That face puckered with cares . . . that face so tragic, with all the tragedy that is writ on the face of a baby monkey, yet ever liable to

1. Joseph Gregor, *Weltgeschichte des Theaters* (Vienna: Phaidon, 1933), p. 212.

relax its mouth into a sudden wide grin and to screw up its eyes to vanishing point over some little triumph wrested from Fate, the tyrant; that poor little personage, so 'put upon' yet so plucky with his squeaking voice and his sweeping gestures; bent but not broken; faint but pursuing; incarnate of the will to live in a world not at all worth living in – surely all hearts went always out to Dan Leno.[1]

Dan Leno's patter sometimes contained passages of almost philosophical nonsense strongly reminiscent of the Theatre of the Absurd – when, for example, he asked, 'Ah, what is man? Wherefore does he why? Whence did he whence? Whither is he withering?'[2]

And so the line from the *mimus* of antiquity, through the clowns and jesters of the Middle Ages and the Zanni and Arlecchini of the *commedia dell'arte*, emerges in the comedians of music hall and vaudeville, from which the twentieth century derived what will in all probability be regarded as its only great achievement in popular art – the silent film comedy of the Keystone Cops, Charlie Chaplin, Buster Keaton, and a host of other immortal performers. The type of gag and the fast-and-furious timing of the grotesque comedy of the silent cinema stems directly from the clowning and acrobatic dancing of music hall and vaudeville. But the superhuman dexterity of movement of which Gregor spoke in describing the effect of the *commedia dell'arte* is even further and more miraculously enhanced by the magic of the screen.

The silent film comedy is without doubt one of the decisive influences on the Theatre of the Absurd. It has the dreamlike strangeness of a world seen from outside with the uncomprehending eyes of one cut off from reality. It has the quality of nightmare and displays a world in constant, and wholly purposeless, movement. And it repeatedly demonstrates the deep poetic power of wordless and purposeless action. The

1. Max Beerbohm, *Around Theatres* (London: Rupert Hart-Davis, 1953), p. 350.
2. Quoted by Colin McInnes, *Spectator*, London, 23 December 1960.

great performers of this cinema, Chaplin and Buster Keaton, are the perfect embodiments of the stoicism of man when faced with a world of mechanical devices that have got out of hand,

The coming of sound in the cinema killed the tempo and fantasy of that heroic age of comedy, but it opened the way for other aspects of the old vaudeville tradition. Laurel and Hardy, W. C. Fields, and the Marx Brothers also exercised their influence on the Theatre of the Absurd. In Ionesco's *The Chairs* the old man impersonates the month of February by 'scratching his head like Stan Laurel',[1] and Ionesco himself told the audience at the American première of *The Shepherd's Chameleon* that the French Surrealists had 'nourished' him but that the three biggest influences on his work had been Groucho, Chico, and Harpo Marx.[2]

With the speed of their reactions, their skill as musical clowns, Harpo's speechlessness, and the wild Surrealism of their dialogue, the Marx Brothers clearly bridge the tradition between the *commedia dell'arte* and vaudeville, on the one hand, and the Theatre of the Absurd, on the other. A scene like the famous one in *A Night at the Opera* in which more and more people stream into a tiny cabin on an ocean liner has all the mad proliferation and frenzy of Ionesco. Yet the Marx Brothers are clearly recognizable representatives of the ancient and highly skilled tribe of itinerant clowns. They belong to the same category as the great W. C. Fields, also a brilliant Surrealist comedian and at the same time a skilled juggler, and the equally great Grock, who was both an acrobat and an astonishingly accomplished musician.

In the cinema at present only one worthy representative of this art is still active, and he, if anything, is too conscious and sophisticated an artist and thus lacks some of the glorious naïveté and vulgarity of his predecessors. Still, Jacques Tati's Monsieur Hulot is a figure helplessly enmeshed in the heartless

1. Ionesco, *The Chairs*, p. 115.
2. *Time*, New York, 12 December 1960.

mechanical civilization of our time. Tati's approach is closely related to that of the Theatre of the Absurd, particularly in his deflation of language, by using dialogue mostly as an indistinct background murmur, and his subtle introduction of highly charged symbolical imagery, as in the masterly final scene of *Mon Oncle*, where his departure from an insanely mechanized and busy airport is subtly raised into an image of death.

The tradition of the *commedia dell'arte* reappears in a number of other guises. Its characters have survived in the puppet theatre and the Punch and Judy shows, which also, in their own way, have influenced the writers of the Theatre of the Absurd.

In Central Europe, the tradition of the *commedia dell'arte* merged with that of the clowns and ruffians of Elizabethan England to produce a long line of Pickelherrings, Hans Wursts, and other coarse comic characters who dominated the folk-theatre of the seventeenth and eighteenth centuries. In the Austrian folk-theatre, this tradition fused with another line of development, that of the baroque spectacle play and the allegorical drama of the Jesuits, to produce a genre combining clowning with allegorical imagery that foreshadows many elements of the Theatre of the Absurd. This is the genre of which Schikaneder's libretto for Mozart's *The Magic Flute* is an undistinguished example, and which found its greatest master in the Viennese actor-playwright Ferdinand Raimund (1790–1836). In Raimund's theatre, which has remained relatively unknown outside Austria, owing to the strongly local colour of its language, we find scenes in which broad comedy merges into naïve poetic allegory. In *Der Bauer als Millionär* (*The Peasant as Millionaire*), the vulgar, broadly comical new-rich millionaire Wurzel is confronted with his own youth, in the shape of a lovely boy who ceremoniously takes leave of him, whereupon Old Age is heard knocking at the door and, when refused entry, breaks it down. Here, as in the best examples of the Theatre of the Absurd, the human condition is presented to us as a concrete poetic image that has become flesh on the stage and that is at the same time broadly comic and deeply tragic.

Raimund's successor as the dominant figure of the Viennese folk-theatre, Johann Nestroy (1801–62), also wrote allegorical tragicomedies in this vein, but he excelled as a master of linguistic absurdity and as a ruthless parodist of pretentious drama, thus also anticipating some of the characteristics of the Theatre of the Absurd. Most of Nestroy's dialogue is un-translatable, since it is in broad dialect, full of local allusions, and based on elaborate multiple puns. But in a short passage like the following from his *Judith und Holofernes* (1849 – a parody of Hebbel's *Judith*), it might be possible to get a glimpse of his Surrealist quality:

> I am nature's most brilliant piece of work [boasts the great warrior Holofernes]; I have yet to lose a battle; I am the virgin among generals. One day I should like to pick a fight with myself, just to see who is stronger – I or I?[1]

On a more literary level, the traditions of the *commedia dell'arte* and that of Shakespeare's clowns unite in another forebear of the Theatre of the Absurd, Georg Büchner (1813–1837), one of the greatest dramatists of the German-speaking world. Büchner's delightful comedy *Leonce und Lena* (1836), which is inscribed with a motto from *As You Like It*:

> O that I were a fool,
> I am ambitious for a motley coat . . .[2]

deals with the futility of human existence that can be relieved only by love and the ability to see oneself as absurd. As Valerio says, in language derived from that of Shakespeare's fools:

> The sun looks like an inn sign and the fiery clouds above it like an

1. Johann Nestroy, *Judith und Holofernes*, scene 3, in *Sämtliche Werke*, vol. IV, ed. Brukner and Rommel (Vienna: Schroll), p. 167.
2. Shakespeare, *As You Like It*, II, 7.

inscription – Tavern of the Golden Sun. The earth and the water below are like a table on which wine has been spilled, and we lie on it like playing-cards with which God and the Devil play, out of boredom, and you are a playing-card king and I a playing-card knave, and all that is lacking is a queen, a beautiful Queen with a gingerbread heart on her breast.[1]

The same Büchner who wrote this gently resigned comedy of autumnal clowning is also one of the pioneers of another type of the Theatre of the Absurd – the violent, brutal drama of mental aberration and obsession. *Woyzeck*, which he left unfinished when he died, at the age of twenty-three, in 1837, is one of the first plays of world literature to make a tormented creature, almost feeble-minded and beset by hallucinations, the hero of a tragedy. In the grotesque nightmare figures that torture the helpless Woyzeck (above all the doctor who subjects him to scientific experiments), and in the violence and extravagance of its language, *Woyzeck* is one of the first modern plays – the germ of much of Brecht, German Expressionism, and of the dark strain of the Theatre of the Absurd exemplified by Adamov's early plays.

Büchner's contemporary, Christian Dietrich Grabbe (1801–1836), may not have had Büchner's genius, but he too belongs in the group of the *poètes maudits* who have influenced the Theatre of the Absurd. His comedy *Scherz, Satire, Ironie und tiefere Bedeutung* (*Joke, Satire, Irony and Deeper Meaning*), in which the Devil visits the earth and is mistaken for a maiden-lady novelist, is a masterpiece of *humour noir* and was translated into French by Alfred Jarry himself (under the title *Les Silènes*).

From Grabbe and Büchner, the line of development leads straight to Wedekind, the Dadaists, German Expressionism, and the early Brecht.

But before we turn to these and other direct antecedents of the Theatre of the Absurd, we must take up the story of another

1. Georg Büchner, *Leonce und Lena*, act II, scene 2.

of the strains that have contributed to the peculiar quality of its plays – the literature of verbal nonsense.

'Delight in Nonsense', says Freud in his study of the sources of the comic,[1] 'has its root in the feeling of freedom we enjoy when we are able to abandon the straitjacket of logic.' At the time Freud wrote his essay, he hastened to add that this delight is 'covered up in serious life almost to the point of disappearance', so that he had, to find evidence for it in the child's delight in stringing words together without having to bother about their meaning or logical order, and in the fooling of students in a state of alcoholic intoxication. It is certainly significant that today, when the need to be rational in 'serious, adult life' has become greater than ever, literature and the theatre are in increasing measure giving room to that liberation through nonsense which the stiff bourgeois world of Vienna before the First World War would not admit in any guise.

Yet nonsense literature and nonsense poetry have provided lustful release from the shackles of logic for many centuries. Robert Benayoun opens his fascinating *Anthologie du Nonsense* with French scholastic nonsense poetry of the thirteenth century. And so we read in the *Fatrasies* of Philippe de Rémi, Sire de Beaumanoir (1250–96), of a sour herring that laid siege to the city of Gisor, and of an old shirt that wanted to plead in court:

> *Une vieille chemise*
> *Avait pris à tâche*
> *De savoir plaider,*
> *Mais une cerise*
> *Devant elle s'est mise*
> *Pour la vilipender.*
> *Sans une vieille cuillère*
> *Qui avait repris haleine*
> *En apportant un vivier,*

1. Freud, *Der Witz und seine Beziehung zum Unbewussten* (1905), paperback edition (Frankfurt: Fischer, 1958), p. 101.

Toute l'eau de la Tamise
Fût entrée en un panier.[1]

Though this may be among the earliest preserved examples of nonsense verse, we can be sure that nonsense rhymes have been sung to children and chanted by adults since the earliest times. There is a magic about nonsense, and magic formulas often consist of syllables that still have rhyme or rhythm but have lost any sense they may originally have contained.

The nursery rhymes of most nations include a large number of nonsense verses. In their *Oxford Dictionary of Nursery Rhymes*, Iona and Peter Opie produce evidence for versions of that great nonsense rhyme 'Humpty Dumpty' from as far afield as Germany, Denmark, Sweden, France, Switzerland, and Finland. And in their study *The Lore and Language of School Children*, the same authors have collected nonsense rhymes still being handed on by word of mouth among British schoolchildren – proof that the need for liberation from the constraints of logic is as powerful now as it was in Freud's day or in the thirteenth century.

The literature of verbal nonsense expresses more than mere playfulness. In trying to burst the bounds of logic and language, it batters at the enclosing walls of the human condition itself. This is the impulse behind the exuberant vision of perhaps the greatest of the masters of nonsense prose and verse, François Rabelais, when he imagined a world of giants with superhuman appetites, a world he described in language so rich and extravagant that it transcends the relative poverty of the real world and opens up a glimpse into the infinite. To the poverty of sense and its restrictions, Rabelais opposed a vision of infinite freedom, which goes far beyond the rule of his humanist Abbaye de Thélème, '*Fay ce que vouldras*', but includes the freedom to create new concepts and new worlds of the imagination.

Verbal nonsense is in the truest sense a metaphysical en-

1. Robert Benayoun, *Anthologie du Nonsense* (Paris: Pauvert, 1957), p. 36.

deavour, a striving to enlarge and to transcend the limits of the material universe and its logic:

> Like to the mowing tones of unspoke speeches
> Or like two lobsters clad in logick breeches;
> Or like the grey fleece of a crimson catt,
> Or like the moone-calf in a slipshodd hatt;
> Or like the shadow when the sun is gone,
> Or like a thought that nev'r was thought upon:
>> Even such is man who never was begotten
>> Untill his children were both dead and rotten. . . .[1]

sang Richard Corbet (1582–1635), Ben Jonson's friend and at one time Bishop of Oxford. And it is precisely the desire to grasp the shadow when the sun is gone, or to hear the tones of the unspoken speeches of mankind, that lies behind the impulse to speak nonsense. It is thus no coincidence that the greatest masters of English nonsense should have been a logician and mathematician, Lewis Carroll, and a naturalist, Edward Lear. These two fascinating writers offer infinite material for aesthetic, philosophical, and psychological inquiry. In our context here, it will be enough if attention is drawn to the connection between language and being in their work.

Both Lear and Carroll are great inventors of unheard-of creatures that receive their existence from their *names*. Lear's *Nonsense Botany*, for example, contains flowers like the 'Tickia Orologica', with blossoms in the form of pocket watches; or the 'Shoebootia Utilis', which grows boots and shoes; or the 'Nasticreechia Krorluppia', which consists of a stem up which nasty creatures crawl. Yet these inventions pale before the poetry of Lear's greatest nonsense songs, like 'The Dong with a Luminous Nose', who lives by the great Gromboolian Plain and was once visited by the Jumblies, who went to sea in a sieve; or the Yonghy-Bonghy-Bo, who inhabits the 'Coast of Coromandel where the early pumpkins blow', or the Pobble,

1. Richard Corbet, '*Epilogus incerti authoris*', in *Comic and Curious Verse*, ed. J. M. Cohen (Penguin Books, 1952), p. 217.

who has no toes – all the spontaneous creations of fantasy freed from the shackles of reality and therefore able to create by the act of naming.

There is, of course, also a destructive, brutal streak in Lear. Countless characters in his Limericks are being smashed, devoured, killed, burned, and otherwise annihilated:

> There was an Old Person of Buda,
> Whose conduct grew ruder and ruder;
> Till at last, with a hammer, they silenced his clamour,
> By smashing that Person of Buda.

In a universe freed from the shackles of logic, wish-fulfilment will not be inhibited by considerations of human kindness. Yet here too the fate of the characters is ruled by the names of the places they inhabit. If the old person of Buda had to die because of rudeness, this was entirely a geographical accident. For

> There was an Old Person of Cadiz
> Who was always polite to all ladies,

which, incidentally, did not prevent him from being drowned in the exercise of his good manners. As in the Theatre of the Absurd, and, indeed, as in the vast world of the human sub-conscious, poetry and cruelty, spontaneous tenderness and destructiveness, are closely linked in the nonsense universe of Edward Lear.

But is the arbitrariness of a world determined by the assonance of names less cruel than the real world, which determines the fate of its inhabitants by the accidents of birth, race, or environment?

> There was an old man of Cape Horn
> Who wished he had never been born;
> So he sat on a chair, till he died of despair,
> That dolorous Man of Cape Horn.

That is why, in Lewis Carroll's nonsense world, there are creatures that try to break the determinism of meaning and significance, which cannot be shaken off in reality:

343

'When I use a word,' Humpty Dumpty said, in rather a scornful tone, 'it means just what I choose it to mean – neither more nor less.'

'The question is,' said Alice, 'whether you *can* make words mean so many different things.'

'The question is,' said Humpty Dumpty, 'which is to be master – that's all.'

This mastery over the meaning of words can be lost when the inexpressible is encountered. That is what happened to the Banker in *The Hunting of the Snark* when he met a Bandersnatch:

> To the horror of all who were present that day
> He uprose in full evening dress,
> And with senseless grimaces endeavoured to say
> What his tongue could no longer express.
>
> Down he sank in his chair – ran his hands through his hair –
> And chanted in mimsiest tones
> Words whose utter inanity proved his insanity,
> While he rattled a couple of bones.

The Hunting of the Snark is an expedition into the unknown – to the limits of being. When the hero of the poem, the Baker, finally encounters a Snark, it *is* a Boojum, and contact with a Boojum means that one vanishes away into nothingness. There is, in Lewis Carroll, a curious yearning for the void where both being and language cease.

As Miss Elizabeth Sewell suggests in her fascinating study of Lear and Carroll, *The Field of Nonsense*, one of the most significant passages in *Through the Looking-Glass* is Alice's adventure in the wood where things have no names. In that wood, Alice herself forgets her own name: 'Then it really *has* happened, after all! And now, who am I? I *will* remember, if I can! I'm determined to do it!' But she has forgotten her name and thus her identity. She encounters a fawn that has also forgotten its identity and

so they walked on together through the wood, Alice with her arms clasped lovingly round the soft neck of the fawn, till they came out into another open field, and here the fawn gave a sudden bound into the air, and shook itself free from Alice's arm. 'I'm a fawn!' it cried out in a voice of delight. 'And, dear me! You're a human child!' A sudden look of alarm came into its beautiful brown eyes, and in another moment it had darted away at full speed.

Miss Sewell comments, 'There is a suggestion here that to lose your name is to gain freedom in some way, since the nameless one would be no longer under control. . . . It also suggests that the loss of language brings with it an increase in loving unity with living things.'[1] In other words, individual identity defined by language, having a name, is the source of our separateness and the origin of the restrictions imposed on our merging in the unity of being. Hence it is through the destruction of language – through nonsense, the arbitrary rather than the contingent naming of things – that the mystical yearning for unity with the universe expresses itself in a nonsense poet like Lewis Carroll.

This metaphysical impulse is even more clearly visible in Christian Morgenstern (1871–1914), the German nonsense poet. More openly philosophical than Lear or Carroll, Morgenstern's nonsense verse is frequently based on his taking all concepts as equally real. In 'Der Lattenzaun' ('The Wooden Fence'), for example, an architect takes the spaces between the boards of the fence and uses this material to build a house:

> The fence was utterly dumbfounded:
> Each post stood there with nothing round it.
>
> A sight most terrible to see.
> (They charged it with indecency.)[2]

There is also a strong streak of *humour noir* in Morgenstern's *Galgenlieder* (*Songs from the Gallows*), with their grotesque mixture of punning and cosmic fear – a knee wandering

1. Elizabeth Sewell, *The Field of Nonsense* (London: Chatto & Windus, 1952), p. 128.
2. Christian Morgenstern, 'Der Lattenzaun', trans. R. F. C. Hull, in *More Comic and Curious Verse*, ed. J. M. Cohen (Penguin Books, 1956), p. 49.

through the world on its own, since the man to whom it once belonged was destroyed all around it in some war; a dead man's shirt crying in the wind; or a piece of sandwich paper that, lying in a lonely wood in the snow,

> ... Commenced, from fright, there is no doubt,
> To think, commenced, began, set out
>
> To think just think, what here combined,
> Received (by fear) – a thinking mind ...[1]

thereby anticipating Heidegger's philosophy of being (the poem was first published in 1916) but being eaten by a bird in the end.

Like Edward Lear, Morgenstern was an inveterate inventor of new species of animals; like Lewis Carroll, he attempted to write poetry in a language wholly his own:

> Kroklowafzi? Sen͞emem͞i!
> Seiokronto – prafriplo:
> Bifzi, bafzi; hulalem͞i:
> quasti, basti bo ...
> Lalu lalu lalu la![2]

Edward Lear, Lewis Carroll, and Christian Morgenstern are the most important among a host of poets who have found an outlet in nonsense. A surprising number of major, otherwise wholly serious, poets have occasionally written nonsense verse; they range from Samuel Johnson and Charles Lamb to Keats and Victor Hugo. The limits of nonsense verse are fluid. Do the outrageously witty rhymes of Byron's *Don Juan* belong to nonsense, or the fantastic puns and assonances of Thomas Hood? Do the brilliantly illustrated verse stories of Wilhelm Busch, that static anticipator of the cartoon film, rank as nonsense? Or the cruel verses that accompany *Struwwelpeter*? Or Hilaire Belloc's *Cautionary Tales*? All these contain some of

1. Morgenstern, '*Das Butterbrotpapier*', trans. A. E. W. Eitzen, *Das Mondschaft* (Wiesbaden: Insel, 1953), p. 19.

2. Morgenstern, '*Das Grosse Lalulā*', *Alle Galgenlieder* (Wiesbaden: Insel, 1950), p. 23.

the elements of the true nonsense universe – its exuberance or its cruelty, which is also an outstanding feature of Harry Graham's *Ruthless Rhymes* or Joachim Ringelnatz's *Kuttel-Daddeldu* and *Kinder-Verwirr-Buch*.

The field of nonsense prose is equally large, extending from Laurence Sterne to the aphorisms of Lichtenberg, from Charles Nodier to Mark Twain and Ambrose Bierce. There are also the delightful nonsense playlets of Ring Lardner (1885–1933), which Edmund Wilson has compared to the work of the Dadaists but which nevertheless basically belong to the Anglo-Saxon tradition of nonsense prose. Though written in dramatic form, and even occasionally performed, these miniature masterpieces of the art of gentle *non sequitur* are not really plays. Some of their funniest lines occur in the stage directions, so that the little plays become more effective when read than when seen. How, for example, is a stage direction like the following, in *Clemo-Uti* (*The Water Lilies*), to be acted?

[Mama enters from an exclusive waffle parlour. She exits as if she had had waffles.]

For all its amiable inconsequence, the dialogue of these short plays, like most writing based on free association, has its psychological relevance in returning again and again to basic human relations. In *The Tridget of Griva*, one of the characters (who are sitting in rowboats pretending to fish) asks another, 'What was your mother's name before she was married?' and receives the reply, 'I didn't know her then.' In *Dinner Bridge*, one of the characters reveals that his first wife is dead. He is asked, 'How long were you married to her?' and retorts, 'Right up to the time she died.' In *I Gaspiri* (*The Upholsterers*), one stranger asks another, 'Where was you born?' and is told, 'Out of wedlock,' whereupon the first stranger comments, 'That's might pretty country around there.' When asked, in turn, whether *he* is married, he answers, 'I don't know. There's a woman living with me, but I can't place her.'

Ring Lardner's nonsense is closely related to the nonsense monologues of Robert Benchley. Another among the large number of brilliant American practitioners of nonsense prose is S. J. Perelman, who was responsible for some of the best dialogue in the Marx Brothers films and who has therefore directly influenced the Theatre of the Absurd.

Most nonsense verse and prose achieve their liberating effect by expanding the limits of sense and opening up vistas of freedom from logic and cramping convention. There is, however, another kind of nonsense, which relies on a contraction rather than an expansion of the scope of language. This procedure, much used in the Theatre of the Absurd, rests on the satirical and destructive use of cliché – the fossilized débris of dead language.

The foremost pioneer of this type of nonsense is Gustave Flaubert, who was greatly preoccupied with the problem of human stupidity and composed a dictionary of cliché and automatic responses, the *Dictionnaire des Idées Reçues*, which appeared as an appendix to his posthumously published novel *Bouvard et Pécuchet*. Additional entries have since come to light, and the dictionary now contains no fewer than nine hundred and sixty-one articles, listing in alphabetical order the most common clichés, conventional misconceptions, and accepted associations of ideas of the nineteenth-century French bourgeois: 'Money – the root of all evil', as well as 'Diderot – always followed by d'Alembert', or 'Jansenism – one does not know what it is, but it is very chic to talk about it.'

James Joyce followed Flaubert in working a whole encyclopedia of English clichés into the Gertie McDowell–Nausikaa episode of *Ulysses*. And the Theatre of the Absurd, from Ionesco to Pinter, continues to tap the inexhaustible resources of comedy discovered by Flaubert and Joyce in the storehouse of clichés and ready-made language.

Equally basic among the age-old traditions present in the

Theatre of the Absurd is the use of mythical, allegorical, and dreamlike modes of thought – the projection into concrete terms of psychological realities. For there is a close connection between myth and dream; myths have been called the collective dream images of mankind. The world of myth has almost entirely ceased to be effective on a collective plane in most rationally organized Western societies (it was most effectively in evidence in Nazi Germany, and remains so in the countries of totalitarian Communism), but, as Mircea Eliade points out, 'at the level of *individual experience* it has never completely disappeared; it makes itself felt in the dreams, the fantasies, and the longings of modern man.'[1] These are longings the Theatre of the Absurd seeks to express. As Ionesco put it in one of his impassioned pleas for his kind of theatre:

The value of a play like Beckett's *Endgame* ... lies in its being nearer to the Book of Job than to the boulevard theatre or the *chansonniers*. That work has found again, across the gulf of time, across the ephemeral phenomena of history, a less ephemeral archetypal situation, a primordial subject from which all others spring. ... The youngest, the most recent works of art will be recognized by, and will speak to, all epochs. Yes, it is King Solomon who is the leader of the movement I follow; and Job, that contemporary of Beckett.[2]

The literature of dreams has always been strongly linked with allegorical elements; after all, symbolic thought is one of the characteristics of dreaming. *Piers Plowman*, Dante's *Divine Comedy*, Bunyan's *Pilgrim's Progress*, and William Blake's prophetic visions are essentially allegorical dreams. The allegorical element can often become mechanically intellectualized and pedantic, as in some of the *autos sacramentales* of the

1. Mircea Eliade, *Myths, Dreams and Mysteries* (London: Harvill Press, 1960), p. 27.
2. Ionesco, '*Lorsque j'écris*', *Cahiers des Saisons*, Paris, no. 15, Winter 1959, p. 211.

Spanish baroque theatre, or it can retain its poetic quality while maintaining its meticulously worked-out correspondences, as does Spenser's *Faerie Queene*.

In the theatre it is not always easy to trace the dividing line between the poetic representation of reality and the opening up of a dream world. Shakespeare's *A Midsummer Night's Dream* deals with dreams and delusions, Bottom's metamorphosis, and the lovers' bewitchment, but at the same time the whole play is itself a dream. The plot of *A Winter's Tale* appears impossibly laboured and mannered if taken as real, but will immediately fall into place and become moving poetry, if the play is seen as a dream of guilt redeemed in a glorious fantasy of wish-fulfilment. In fact, the Elizabethan theatre in some ways shares Genet's conception of the hall of mirrors, in that it sees the world as a stage and life as a dream. If Prospero says, 'We are such stuff as dreams are made on, and our little life is rounded with a sleep,' he himself is part of a fairy-tale play of dreamlike quality. If the world is a stage, and the stage presents dreams, it is a dream within a dream.

The same idea appears in the theatre of Calderón, not only in a play like *La Vida Es Sueño*, in which life is equated with a dream, but also in a great allegorical vision like *El Gran Teatro del Mundo*, which presents the world as a stage on which each character plays the part assigned to him by the Creator, the author of the world. The characters enact their life upon the stage of the world as in a dream from which death is the awakening into the reality of eternal salvation or damnation. Calderón's play is said to be based on a text by Seneca (*Epistolae LXXVI* and *LXXVII*) in which occurs the image of the great of this world being no better than actors who have to return their insignia of power after leaving the stage.

In another great allegorical drama of the baroque period, *Cenodoxus* by the German Jesuit Jakob Bidermann (1635), which shows devils and angels fighting for the hero's soul, the choir sings in the hour of death:

Vita enim hominum
Nihil est, nisi somnium.

The baroque plays of extravagant cruelty, of which the tragedies of John Webster, and Cyril Tourneur's *The Revenger's Tragedy* are the best-known examples, are dreams of another kind – savage nightmares of suffering and revenge.

With the decline of the fashion for allegory, the element of fantasy begins to dominate – in such satirical fantasies as Swift's *Gulliver's Travels* or in Gothic novels like Walpole's *The Castle of Otranto*, in which a mysterious helmet crashes into the castle with the dreamlike inevitability of the growing corpse invading Amédée's apartment in Ionesco's play. If the dream world of baroque allegory was symbolical but strictly rational, the dream literature of the eighteenth and early nineteenth centuries makes increasing use of fluid identities, sudden transformations of characters, and nightmarish shifts of time and place. E. T. A. Hoffmann, Gérard de Nerval, and Barbey d'Aurevilly are the masters of this genre. Their fantastic tales may have appeared to their contemporaries as a kind of science fiction; today they are seen to be essentially dreams and fantasies, projections of aggression, guilt, and desire. The extravagant, orgiastic fantasies of the Marquis de Sade are even more clearly projections of a psychological reality in the form of literary fantasy.

In dramatic literature, the dream motif also appears, in the form of real events that are made to look like a dream to the simpleton who is put through them – on the lines of Sly's adventure in the frame-plot of *The Taming of the Shrew*, or in such great and savagely ruthless comedies as Ludvig Holberg's *Jeppe paa Bjerget* (1722). The drunken peasant Jeppe is first made to believe, when waking in the Baron's castle, that he is in Paradise, but later he has another awakening – on the gallows. Goethe ventured into a dream world in the two Walpurgis Night scenes in the first and second parts of *Faust*, and there are scenes of dreamlike fantasy in Ibsen's *Peer Gynt*;

Madach's *The Tragedy of Man*, one of the masterpieces of Hungarian drama, centres on Adam's dream of the coming history and extinction of mankind; but the first to put on the stage a dream world in the spirit of modern psychological thinking was August Strindberg. The three parts of *To Damascus* (1898–1904), *A Dream Play* (1902), and *The Ghost Sonata* (1907) are masterly transcriptions of dreams and obsessions, and direct sources of the Theatre of the Absurd.

In these plays the shift from the objective reality of the world of outside, surface appearance to the subjective reality of inner states of consciousness – a shift that marks the watershed between the traditional and the modern, the representational and the Expressionist projection of mental realities – is finally and triumphantly accomplished. The central character in *To Damascus* is surrounded by archetypal figures – the woman, who represents the female principle in his life; the other man, who is his eternal, primordial enemy – as well as by emanations of his own personality: the tempter, who represents his evil tendencies; the confessor and the beggar, who stand for the better sides of his self. In the same way, the stage space that encloses these figures is a mere emanation of the hero's, or the author's, mental states – the sumptuous banquet at which he is entertained by the government as a great inventor suddenly turns into an assembly of disreputable outcasts who mock him because he cannot pay the bill. As Strindberg says in the introductory note to *A Dream Play*:

In this dream play, as in his former dream play *To Damascus*, the author has sought to reproduce the disconnected but apparently logical form of a dream. Anything can happen; everything is possible and probable. Time and space do not exist. On a slight groundwork of reality, imagination spins and weaves new patterns made up of memories, experiences, unfettered fancies, absurdities, and improvisations. The characters are split, double, and multiply; they evaporate, crystallize, scatter, and converge. But a single consciousness holds sway over them all – that of the dreamer. For him there are no secrets, no incongruities, no scruples and no law . . .[1]

While *To Damascus* leads up to a solution of religious faith and consolation, *A Dream Play* and *The Ghost Sonata* show a world of grim hopelessness and despair. Indra's daughter, in *A Dream Play*, learns that to live is to do evil, while the world of *The Ghost Sonata* is a charnel-house of guilt, obsessions, madness, and absurdity.

It is a significant and somewhat paradoxical fact that the development of the psychological subjectivism that manifested itself in Strindberg's Expressionist dream plays was the direct and logical development of the movement that had led to naturalism. It is the desire to represent reality, all of reality, that at first leads to the ruthlessly truthful description of surfaces, and then on to the realization that objective reality, surfaces, are only part, and a relatively unimportant part, of the real world. This is where the novel takes the leap from the meticulous descriptions of Zola to the even more meticulous and microscopic description of the world, as reflected in the mind of one observer, in the work of Proust. In the same way, Strindberg's development led from his early historical plays to the romantic dramas of the eighties to the ruthless naturalism of obsessive pictures of reality like *The Father*, and from there to the Expressionistic dream plays of the first decade of the new century.

The development of James Joyce was analogous on a different plane. In his youth he learned Norwegian to be able to read Ibsen in the original, and in his early play *Exiles*, and in his meticulously observed Dublin stories, he tried to capture the surface of the real world, until he decided that he wanted to record an even more total reality in *Ulysses*. The Nighttown episode in this novel, written in the form of a dream play, is one

1. August Strindberg, *A Dream Play*, in *Six Plays of Strindberg*, trans. Sylvia Sprigge (New York: Doubleday Anchor Books, 1955), p. 193.

of the great early examples of the Theatre of the Absurd. Bloom's dream of grandeur and degradation, and Stephen's dream of guilt, are here merged in swiftly changing scenes of grotesque humour and heartbreaking anguish.

It is no coincidence that almost forty years after Joyce completed *Ulysses*, there should have been several, by no means unsuccessful attempts to stage *Ulysses*, and the Nighttown sequence in particular.[1] For by that time the success of Beckett and Ionesco had made it possible to stage Joyce's scenes, which not only anticipate the Theatre of the Absurd but in many ways surpass it in boldness of conception and originality of invention.

Joyce's *Finnegans Wake* also anticipates the Theatre of the Absurd's preoccupation with language, its attempt to penetrate to a deeper layer of the mind, closer to the subconscious matrix of thought. But here too Joyce has in many respects gone further and probed deeper than a later generation.

If the dream allegories of the Middle Ages and the baroque period expressed a stable and generally accepted body of belief and thus concretized the acknowledged myths of their age, writers like Dostoevski, Strindberg, and Joyce, by delving into their own subconscious, discovered the universal, collective significance of their own private obsessions. This is also true of Franz Kafka, whose impact on the Theatre of the Absurd has been as powerful and direct as that of Strindberg and Joyce.

Kafka's short stories and unfinished novels are essentially meticulously exact descriptions of nightmares and obsessions – the anxieties and guilt feelings of a sensitive human being lost in a world of convention and routine. The images of Kafka's own sense of loss of contact with reality, and his feelings of guilt at being unable to regain it – the nightmare of K accused of a crime against a law he has never known; the predicament of

1. James Joyce, *Ulysses in Nighttown*, adapted by Marjorie Barkentin under supervision of Padraic Colum; first perf. New York, 5 June 1958 (New York: Random House Modern Library Paperbacks, 1958). Also *Bloomsday*, another dramatization of *Ulysses*, by Alan MacClelland.

that other K, the surveyor, who has been summoned to a castle he cannot penetrate – have become the supreme expression of the situation of modern man. As Ionesco observes in a short but illuminating essay on Kafka:

This theme of man lost in a labyrinth, without a guiding thread, is basic . . . in Kafka's work. Yet if man no longer has a guiding thread, it is because he no longer wants to have one. Hence his feeling of guilt, of anxiety, of the absurdity of history.[1]

Although Kafka is known to have been greatly attracted by the theatre, only one short dramatic fragment by him is extant, *Der Gruftwächter* (*The Guardian of the Crypt*), the opening scene of an unfinished play, in which a young prince summons the old guardian of the mausoleum where his ancestors are buried, and is told by the old man about the terrifying fight he has each night with the spirits of the departed, who want to leave the prison of their tomb and to invade the world of the living.

Yet even if Kafka's own modest attempt to write a play came to nothing, the directness of his narrative prose, the concrete clarity of its images and its mystery and tension, have proved a constant temptation to adapters who felt that it was ideal material for the stage. Perhaps most important among a whole series of such adaptations of Kafka's novels and stories was *The Trial* by André Gide and Jean-Louis Barrault, which opened at the Théâtre de Marigny on 10 October 1947.

This was a production that deeply stirred its public. It came at a peculiarly propitious moment – shortly after the nightmare world of the German occupation had vanished. Kafka's dream of guilt and the arbitrariness of the powers that rule the world was more for the French audience of 1947 than a mere fantasy. The author's private fears had become flesh, had turned into the collective fear of nations; the vision of the world as absurd,

1. Ionesco, '*Dans les armes de la ville*', *Cahiers de la Compagnie Madeleine Renaud–Jean-Louis Barrault*, Paris, no. 20, October 1957, p. 4.

arbitrary, and irrational had been proved a highly realistic assessment.

The Trial was the first play that fully represented the Theatre of the Absurd in its mid-twentieth-century form. It preceded the performances of the work of Ionesco, Adamov, and Beckett, but Jean-Louis Barrault's direction already anticipated many of their scenic inventions and united the traditions of clowning, the poetry of nonsense, and the literature of dream and allegory. As one bewildered critic put it at the time, 'This is not a play, so much as a sequence of images, phantoms, hallucinations.' Or, in the words of another, 'This is cinema, ballet, pantomime, all at once. It reminds one of film montage, or of the illustrations in a picture book.'[1]

In using a free, fluid, and grotesquely fantastic style of production, Jean-Louis Barrault fused Kafka's work with a style in which he himself had been nurtured and which is in the direct literary and stage lineage of the Theatre of the Absurd – the tradition of the iconoclasts: Jarry, Apollinaire, the Dadaists, some of the German Expressionists, the Surrealists, and the prophets of a wild and ruthless theatre, like Artaud and Vitrac.

This was the movement that began on that memorable evening of 10 December 1896, when Jarry's *Ubu Roi* opened at Lugné-Poë's Théâtre de l'Œuvre and provoked a scandal as violent as the famous battle at the first night of Victor Hugo's *Hernani*, in 1830, which opened the great dispute about Romanticism in the French theatre.

Alfred Jarry (1873–1907) is one of the most extraordinary and eccentric figures among the *poètes maudits* of French literature; when he died he was regarded as little more than one of those bizarre specimens of the Paris *Bohème* who merge their lives and their poetry by turning their own personalities into grotesque

1. Quoted by André Franck, '*Il y a dix ans . . .*', *Cahiers de la Compagnie Madeleine Renaud – Jean-Louis Barrault*, no. 20, October 1957, p. 35.

characters of their own creation that disappear when they perish, as Jarry did, from over-indulgence in absinthe and dissipation. Yet Jarry left an *œuvre* that has been exerting growing influence ever since he died.

Wild, extravagant, and uninhibited in his use of language, Jarry belongs to the school of Rabelais, but his imagery also owes much to the dark, brooding, haunted dream world of that other perverse and unhappy *poète maudit*, Isidore Ducasse, who called himself the Comte de Lautréamont (1846–70) and was the author of that masterpiece of the Romantic agony, *Les Chants de Maldoror*, which later became the inspiration of the Surrealists. Jarry also owes much to Verlaine, Rimbaud, and, above all, Mallarmé, in whose writings on the theatre there are a number of scattered pleas for a revolt against the rational, well-made play of the *fin de siècle*. As early as 1885, Mallarmé demanded a theatre of myth that would be wholly un-French in its irrationality, with a story 'freed of place, time, known characters', for 'the century, or our country that exalts it, has dissolved the myths by thought. Let us remake them!'[1]

Ubu Roi certainly created a mythical figure and a world of grotesque archetypal images. Originally the play had been a schoolboy prank aimed at one of the teachers at the *lycée* in Rennes where Jarry was a pupil. This teacher, Hébert, was the butt of much ridicule and had been nicknamed Père Héb or Père Hébé, and later Ubu. In 1888, when Jarry was fifteen, he wrote a puppet play about the exploits of Père Ubu and performed it for the benefit of his friends.

Ubu is a savage caricature of a stupid, selfish bourgeois seen through the cruel eyes of a schoolboy, but this Rabelaisian character, with his Falstaffian greed and cowardice, is more than mere social satire. He is a terrifying image of the animal nature of man, his cruelty and ruthlessness. Ubu makes himself King of Poland, kills and tortures all and sundry, and is finally chased

1. Stéphane Mallarmé, '*Richard Wagner, rêverie d'un poète français*', in *Œuvres* (Paris: Pléiade, 1945), pp. 544–5.

out of the country. He is mean, vulgar, and incredibly brutal, a monster that appeared ludicrously exaggerated in 1896, but was far surpassed by reality by 1945. Once again, an intuitive image of the dark side of human nature that a poet had projected on to the stage proved prophetically true.

Jarry consciously intended his monstrous puppet play, which was acted by a cast clad in highly stylized, wooden-looking costumes, in a décor of childish naïveté, to confront a bourgeois audience with the horror of its own complacency and ugliness:

I wanted the stage to stand, as soon as the curtain went up, before the public like one of those mirrors in the fairy tales of Madame Leprince de Beaumont, where the vicious villain sees himself with bull's horns and a dragon's body, the exaggerations of his own vicious nature. And it is by no means astonishing that the public was stupefied at the sight of its ignoble double, which had never before been presented to it in its entirety, made up, as M. Catulle Mendés has excellently put it, 'of the eternal imbecility of man, his eternal lubricity, his eternal gluttony, the baseness of instinct raised to the status of tyranny; of the coyness, the virtue, the patriotism, and the ideals of the people who have dined well'.[1]

The public was indeed stupefied. As soon as Gémier, who played Ubu, had uttered the opening line ' *Merdre!* ', the storm broke loose. It was fifteen minutes before silence could be re-established, and the demonstrations for and against continued throughout the evening. Among those present were Arthur Symons, Jules Renard, W. B. Yeats, and Mallarmé. Arthur Symons has left a description of the décor and production:

The scenery was painted to represent, by a child's convention, indoors and out of doors, and even the torrid, temperate, and arctic zones at once. Opposite you, at the back of the stage, you saw apple trees in bloom, under a blue sky, and against the sky a small closed window and a fireplace ... through the very midst of which ... trooped in and out the clamorous and sanguinary persons of the

1. Alfred Jarry, ' *Questions de théâtre* ', in *Ubu Roi* (Lausanne: Henri Kaeser, 1948), p. 158.

drama. On the left was painted a bed, and at the foot of the bed a bare tree and snow falling. On the right there were palm trees ... a door opened against the sky, and beside the door a skeleton dangled. A venerable gentleman in evening dress ... trotted across the stage on the points of his toes between every scene and hung the new placard [with the description of the place where the action was laid] on its nail.[1]

Yeats rightly sensed that the scandalous performance he attended marked the end of an era in art. In his autobiography, *The Trembling of the Veil*, he left an exact description of what he felt when confronted with Jarry's grotesque drama, with its stark colours and deliberate rejection of delicate nuances:

The players are supposed to be dolls, toys, marionettes, and now they are all hopping like wooden frogs, and I can see for myself that the chief personage, who is some kind of King, carries for a sceptre a brush of the kind that we use to clean a closet. Feeling bound to support the most spirited party, we have shouted for the play, but that night at the Hôtel Corneille I am very sad, for comedy, objectivity, has displayed its growing power once more. I say: 'After Stéphane Mallarmé, after Paul Verlaine, after Gustave Moreau, after Puvis de Chavannes, after our own verse, after all our subtle colour and nervous rhythm, after the faint mixed tints of Conder, what more is possible? After us the Savage God.'[2]

Yet Mallarmé, whom Yeats invoked as one of the masters of subtle nuance, congratulated Jarry:

You have put before us, with a rare and enduring glaze at your finger-tips, a prodigious personage and his crew, and this as a sober and sure dramatic sculptor. He enters into the repertoire of high taste and haunts me.[3]

1. Arthur Symons, *Studies in Seven Arts*, quoted in Roger Shattuck, *The Banquet Years* (London: Faber & Faber, 1959), p. 161.

2. W. B. Yeats, *Autobiographies* (London: Macmillan, 1955), pp. 348–9.

3. Mallarmé, undated letter to Jarry, in Mallarmé, *Propos sur la Poésie*, ed. H. Mondor, quoted in J. Robichez, *Le Symbolisme au Théâtre* (Paris: L'Arche, 1957), pp. 359–60.

Another among those present on that memorable first night was the French playwright Henri Ghéon. Almost half a century later he summed up the significance of the event:

... in my view the chief claim of the Théâtre de l'Œuvre to the gratitude of the friends of the art of the theatre [lies in] the presentation of *Ubu Roi* in a cacophony of birdcalls, whistles, protests, and laughter. . . . The schoolboy Jarry, to mock a professor, had without knowing it created a masterpiece in painting that sombre and over-simplified caricature with brushstrokes in the manner of Shakespeare and the puppet theatre. It has been interpreted as an epic satire of the greedy and cruel bourgeois who makes himself a leader of men. But whichever sense is attributed to the piece, *Ubu Roi* . . . is 'hundred per cent theatre', what we to-day would call 'pure theatre', synthetic and creating, on the margin of reality, a reality based on symbols.[1]

And so a play that had only two performances in its first run and evoked a torrent of abuse appears, in the light of subsequent developments, as a landmark and a forerunner.

Jarry himself more and more assumed the manner of speaking of Ubu, who makes an appearance in a number of his subsequent works (as indeed he had in the earlier *Les Minutes de Sable Mémorial* and *César–Antechrist*, a strange cosmic fantasy that mixes mystical and heraldic elements with Ubu's kingship of Poland in its third, terrestrial act). In 1899, 1901, and 1902, Jarry published Almanachs of Père Ubu, while a full-scale sequel to *Ubu Roi, Ubu Enchaîné*, appeared in 1900. In this play, Ubu has arrived in exile in France, where, in order to be different in a country of free men, he turns himself into a slave.

Some of Jarry's most important works appeared only after his death, notably *Gestes et Opinions du Docteur Faustroll* (1911), an episodic novel modelled on Rabelais in which the hero, whose nature is indicated by his name, is half Faust, half troll (Jarry knew the Scandinavian nature sprite from Ibsen's *Peer*

1. Henri Ghéon, *L'Art du Théâtre* (Montreal: Editions Serge, 1944), p. 149.

Gynt), and is the chief spokesman of the science of pataphysics. Originally it was Ubu who professed himself a doctor of pataphysics (in his first appearance in *Les Minutes de Sable Mémorial*), simply because Hébert had been a physics teacher. But what had started as a mere burlesque of science later turned into the basis of Jarry's own aesthetics. As defined in *Faustroll*, pataphysics is

. . . the science of imaginary solutions, which symbolically attributes the properties of objects, described by their virtuality, to their lineaments.[1]

In effect, the definition of a subjectivist and expressionist approach that exactly anticipates the tendency of the Theatre of the Absurd to express psychological states by objectifying them on the stage. And so Jarry, whose memory is kept green by the College of Pataphysics, of which Ionesco, René Clair, Raymond Queneau, and Jacques Prévert are leading members and in which the late Boris Vian played an important part, must be regarded as one of the originators of the concepts on which a good deal of contemporary art, and not only in literature and the theatre, is based.

Something of the verve and extravagance of *Ubu* can be found in another play that caused an almost comparable scandal nearly twenty years later – Guillaume Apollinaire's *Les Mamelles de Tirésias* (*Tiresias's Breasts*), staged at the Théâtre Maubel in Montmartre on 24 June 1917. In his preface to the play, Apollinaire claims that most of it was written much earlier, in 1903. Apollinaire, who knew Jarry well, was a friend of the young painters of genius who founded the Cubist school and became one of its most influential critics and theoreticians. He labelled *Les Mamelles de Tirésias* '*drame surréaliste*', and can thus claim to have been the first to invent a term that later became the hallmark of one of the important aesthetic movements of the century.

However, Apollinaire's use of the term is quite different from

1. Jarry, *Gestes et Opinions du Docteur Faustroll* (Paris: Fasquelle, 1955), p. 32, trans. in *Evergreen Review*, New York, no. 13, 1960, p. 131.

the meaning it was given in the writings of André Breton, which defined Surrealism in its later sense. Here is Apollinaire's explanation of the term:

> To characterize my drama, I have used a neologism, for which I hope to be forgiven, as it does not happen often that I do such a thing, and I have coined the adjective 'Surrealist', which does not mean symbolical ... but rather well defines a tendency of art that, if it is no newer than anything else under the sun, has at least never been utilized to formulate an artistic or literary creed. The idealism of the dramatists who succeeded Victor Hugo sought likeness to nature in a conventional local colour that corresponds to the *trompe-l'œil* naturalism of the comedies of manner. ... To attempt, if not a renovation of the theatre, at least a personal effort, I thought one should return to nature itself, but without imitating her in the manner of the photographers. When man wanted to imitate the action of walking, he created the wheel, which does not resemble a leg. He has thus used Surrealism without knowing it. ...[1]

Surrealism for Apollinaire was an art more real than reality, expressing essences rather than appearances. He wanted a theatre that would be 'modern, simple, rapid, with the shortcuts and enlargements that are needed to shock the spectator'.[2]

Les Mamelles de Tirésias is a grotesque vaudeville that purports to have a serious political message – it advocates the radical re-population of France, decimated by war and the emancipation of women. The Tiresias of the title starts out as a woman called Thérèse, who wants to enter politics, the arts, and a number of other masculine occupations and decides to turn into a man – an operation accomplished by the release of her breasts, which float into the air as coloured toy balloons. Her husband thereupon decides to fulfil the function of Thérèse, who has now become Tiresias. In act II, he has succeeded in producing forty thousand and forty-nine children, simply by wanting them

1. Guillaume Apollinaire, Preface to *Les Mamelles de Tirésias*, in *Œuvres Poétiques* (Paris: Pléiade, 1956), pp. 865–6.
2. ibid., p. 868.

very hard. In the end, his wife returns to him. All this takes place in Zanzibar, in front of the people of Zanzibar, represented by a single actor who never says a word but sits by a table equipped with all kinds of instruments suitable for the production of noises – from guns, drums, and castanets to pots and pans that can be broken with a bang. The play is preceded by a prologue in which the director of the company of actors presenting it sums up Apollinaire's dramatic creed:

> For the theatre should not be a copy of reality
> It is right that the dramatist should use
> All the mirages at his disposal . . .
> It is right that he should let crowds speak inanimate objects
> If he so pleases
> And that he no longer should reckon with time
> Or space
> His universe is the play
> Within which he is God the Creator
> Who disposes at will
> Of sounds gestures movements masses colours
> Not merely in order
> To photograph what is called a slice of life
> But to bring forth life itself in all its truth . . .[1]

Apollinaire's play *Couleur du Temps* (*The Colour of Time*), which was in rehearsal when he died of Spanish influenza on 9 November 1918 (the day of the collapse of Germany), though very different from *Les Mamelles de Tirésias*, also creates its own universe. It is a curious verse play in which a group of aviators escape from the war; arrive at the South Pole, where they want to find eternal peace; discover a beautiful woman frozen into the ice; and kill each other fighting for her – another allegorical dream that, coming from the author of *Tirésias*, testifies to the close connection between the grotesque nonsense of that play and the atmosphere of myth in this.

The Paris *Bohème* of Jarry and Apollinaire was a world in

1. ibid., p. 882.

which painting, poetry, and theatre mingled, and the efforts to find a modern art overlapped. The décor for *Ubu Roi* had been painted by Jarry himself with the aid of Pierre Bonnard, Vuillard, Toulouse-Lautrec, and Sérusier.[1] Apollinaire was the advocate and propagandist of the Cubist movement, and a friend and companion of Matisse, Braque, and Picasso. The fight to transcend the conception of art as mere mimesis, imitation of appearances, was carried forward on a broad front, and the Theatre of the Absurd is as much indebted to the collages of Picasso or Juan Gris and the paintings of Klee (the titles of which are often little nonsense poems) as to the work of its literary forebears.

The Dada movement, which began in Zürich during the war, among French, German, and other European refugees and conscientious objectors, and which thus merged a Parisian with a Central European tradition, also mingled writers, painters, and sculptors. On 2 February 1916, the Zürich papers announced the formation of the Cabaret Voltaire. On 5 February, the first evening's entertainment was provided by Tristan Tzara (1896–1963), the young Rumanian poet, reading his own work. Hugo Ball (1886–1927) and his wife, Emmy Hennings (1885–1948); Richard Huelsenbeck (1892–1974); Hans Arp, the sculptor and poet (1887–1966); and the painter Marcel Janco, another Rumanian (born in 1895), were the other founder-members of the movement, which owed its name to a lucky dip into a French dictionary. Huelsenbeck and Ball, looking for a name for a singer in the cabaret, came across the word '*dada*' – hobbyhorse. The aim of the Dadaists was the destruction of art, or at least the conventional art of the bourgeois era that had produced the horrors of war.

The programme of the Cabaret Voltaire at No. 1 Spiegelgasse, in the old town of Zürich – right opposite house No. 6, inhabited by Lenin, who must have been disturbed every evening by the noisy goings on there – was on a modest scale: songs,

1. Shattuck, op. cit., p. 161.

recitations of poetry, short sketches, an occasional play. Here the tradition of the literary cabarets of Munich, where Wedekind and his circle had cultivated an impertinent and witty kind of chanson, merged with the French tradition of popular song that had produced Yvette Guilbert and Aristide Bruant. Hugo Ball's diary lists readings of poems by Kandinsky, songs by Wedekind and Bruant, music by Reger and Debussy. Arp read from *Ubu Roi;* Huelsenbeck, Tzara, and Janco performed a *Poème Simultan*, a simultaneous recitation of three different poems, producing an indistinct and inarticulate murmur, 'showing the struggle of the *vox humana* with a threatening, entangling, and destroying universe whose rhythm and sequence of noise is inescapable'.[1] In June 1916, the Dadaists published what remained the only number of a periodical, *Cabaret Voltaire*, which included contributions by Apollinaire, Picasso, Kandinsky, Marinetti, Blaise Cendrars, and Modigliani.

The first play performed at a Dada soirée, in new and larger premises, was *Sphinx und Strohmann* by the Austrian painter Oskar Kokoschka (born in 1886). Marcel Janco was responsible for directing the play, and he designed the masks. Hugo Ball, who played one of the leading parts, has described the strange performance in his diary under the date of 14 April 1917:

The play was acted . . . in tragic body-masks; mine was so large that I could comfortably read my part inside it. The head of the mask was lit up electrically, and it must have made a rather strange effect in the darkened auditorium, with light coming from the eyes. . . . Tzara, in the back room, was responsible for thunder and lightning as well as having to say 'Anima, sweet Anima' as the voice of the parrot. But he was also looking after entrances and exits, thundered and lightninged in the wrong places, and gave the impression that this was a special effect intended by the director, an intended confusion of backgrounds. . .[2]

1. Hugo Ball, '*Dada Tagebuch*', in Arp/Huelsenbeck/Tzara, *Die Geburt des Dada* (Zürich: Arche, 1957), p. 117.
2. ibid., p. 139.

Kokoschka's play, labelled by the author 'a curiosity', is a remarkable example of early Expressionism (it had already been given an improvised performance at the Vienna School of Arts and Crafts in 1907). Its plot revolves around Mr Firdusi, who is in love with Anima, the female soul. Kautschukmann (Rubber Man), a 'snake man' and obviously the embodiment of evil, pretends he is a doctor who can cure Firdusi of his love. Firdusi's head is turned by love, which means that it is actually turned backwards on his straw body. So even when he is face to face with Anima, he cannot see her. The cure of love is death. Kautschukmann makes Firdusi jealous by letting the parrot call on sweet Anima, and as he cannot turn his head to see what is really happening, he dies of grief. A chorus of top-hatted gentlemen with holes instead of faces quickly pronounces a series of nonsense aphorisms, and Death, who alone among all the characters has the appearance and costume of an entirely ordinary human being, leaves with Anima, whom he 'attempts to console, with good results'.[1]

Tzara noted in his diary, 'This performance decided the role of our theatre, which will leave the direction to the subtle invention of the explosive wind [of spontaneity], with the scenario in the auditorium, visible direction, and grotesque means – the Dadaist theatre.'[2] But in spite of these high hopes for Dada in the theatre, the movement never produced a real impact on the stage. And this is not surprising. Dada was essentially destructive and so radical in its nihilism that it could hardly be expected to be creative in an art form that necessarily relies on constructive cooperation. As Georges Ribemont-Dessaignes, one of the leading French exponents of Dada, recognized in his autobiography, 'Dada consisted of opposing, incompatible, explosive tendencies. To destroy a world so as to put another in its place

1. Oskar Kokoschka, *Sphinx und Strohmann*, in *Schriften 1907–1955* (Munich: Albert Langen, 1956), p. 167.
2. Tristan Tzara, '*Chronique Zurichoise*', in *Die Geburt des Dada*, p. 173.

in which nothing more exists, that was, in fact, the watchword of Dada.'[1]

The plays the Dadaists produced and largely performed themselves are essentially nonsense poems in dialogue form, accompanied by equally nonsensical business and decorated with bizarre masks and costumes. The Dada manifestation at the Théâtre de l'Œuvre in Paris (which had become the centre of Dada after the end of the war) on 27 March 1920, presented a selection of plays that included *La Première Aventure Céleste de M. Antipyrine* (*The First Celestial Adventure of M. Antipyrine*), by Tzara, in which a 'parabola' recites verses that contain lines like:

This bird has come white and feverish as
from which regiment comes the clock? from that music humid as
M. Cricri receives the visit of his fiancée at the hospital
in the Jewish cemetery the graves rise like snakes
Mr Poet was an archangel – really
he said that the druggist resembled the butterfly
and our Lord and that life is simple like a bumbum
like the bumbum of his heart.[2]

Ribemont-Dessaignes's *Le Serin Muet* (*The Dumb Canary*), which was performed on the same occasion by André Breton, Philippe Soupault, and Mlle A. Valère, had one of the characters perched on top of a ladder, while another was a Negro who believes he is the composer Gounod and has taught all his compositions to his mute canary, who sings them most beautifully without uttering a sound. Similarly bizarre and largely improvised plays performed at this manifestation were *S'Il Vous Plaît* (*If You Please*), by Breton and Soupault, and *Le Ventriloque Désaccordé* (*The Out of Tune Ventriloquist*), by Paul Dermée. Lugné-Poë, the director of the Œuvre, who had performed *Ubu* twenty-five years earlier, was so delighted with the *succès de*

1. Georges Ribemont-Dessaignes, *Déjà Jadis* (Paris: Julliard, 1958).
2. Tzara, *Première Aventure Céleste de M. Antipyrine* (Collection Dada, Zürich, 1916); extract in Tzara, *Morceaux Choisis* (Paris: Bordas, 1947).

scandale of this Dada manifestation that he asked for more Dada plays. Ribemont-Dessaignes was the only one who responded to the offer. He composed a play called *Zizi de Dada,* 'of which the manuscript is lost. The Pope was in it, enclosed in a chalk circle from which he could not leave . . . but what happened? Even the memory of it is lost!'[1] Lugné-Poë gave the piece careful consideration, but rejected it in the end as being somewhat improper.

At a second Dada manifestation at the Salle Gaveau, on 26 May 1920, the programme included another play by Tzara, *La Deuxième Aventure Céleste de M. Antipyrine (M. Antipyrine's Second Celestial Adventure)*; another sketch by Breton and Soupault, *Vous M'Oublierez (You Will Forget Me)*; a piece by Aragon, *Système DD*; and *Vaseline Symphonique*, by Tzara, a cacophony of inarticulate sounds, performed by an ensemble advertised as twenty strong, that aroused the protests of Breton, who did not like being reduced to the role of a musical instrument. Among the other participants in that evening's entertainment were Picabia and Eluard.

Most successful among the Dadaist plays was Tzara's three-act piece *Le Cœur à Gaz (The Gas Heart)*, first performed 10 June 1921, at the Studio des Champs-Elysées, a weird re-citation by characters representing parts of the body – the ear, the neck, the mouth, the nose, and the eyebrow. Ribemont-Dessaignes confessed that he could not remember the perform-ance because, clearly, he did not see it. Yet he appeared in the play in the part of the mouth, together with Soupault, Aragon, Benjamin Péret, and Tzara himself, in the part of the eyebrow. *Le Cœur à Gaz* is a piece of 'pure theatre' that derives its impact almost entirely from the subtle rhythms of its otherwise non-sensical dialogue, which, in the use of the clichés of polite conversation, foreshadows Ionesco.

Tzara himself called the play 'the biggest swindle of the cen-tury in three acts', which 'will make happy only the industrial-

1. Ribemont-Dessaignes, op. cit., p. 73.

ized imbeciles who believe in the existence of men of genius. The actors are asked to give to this piece the attention due to a masterpiece of the power of *Macbeth* or *Chantecler*, but to treat the author, who is not a genius, with little respect and to note the lack of seriousness of the text, which contributed nothing new to the technique of the theatre.'[1] A revival of *Le Cœur à Gaz* with professional actors at the Théâtre Michel on 6 July 1923 led to one of the most memorable battles of the declining years of Dadaism, with Breton and Eluard jumping on to the stage and being thrown out after hand-to-hand fighting.

More substantial than any of these short plays, whose main function was to shock a bourgeois audience, are two works by Ribemont-Dessaignes that really try to create a poetic universe with validity on the stage. They are *L'Empereur de Chine* (*The Emperor of China*), written in 1916, and *Le Bourreau du Pérou* (*The Executioner of Peru*), published in 1928.

The first of these deals with the themes of sexuality, violence, and war. The heroine, Onane, Princess of China, is a wilful and cruel sex-kitten; her father Espher, who becomes Emperor of China, a sadistic tyrant. Onane is accompanied by two slaves, Ironique and Equinoxe, who arrive in the opening scene in cages, as presents from the Emperor of the Philippines. They are eccentrically dressed in top hats, kilts, and dinner jackets. Ironique has his left eye bandaged, Equinoxe his right eye, so that they have to look at the world together. War and torture play a great part in the action. The Minister of Peace takes up the study of strategy and becomes Minister of War, and scenes of rape and violence follow. Only those women who drink the blood of those already killed will be spared by the soldiers. In the end, the bureaucrat Verdict kills Onane, who is in love with him. The final scene is a duet of nonsense words by the two slaves. The final lines are:

IRONIQUE: When love dies ...
EQUINOXE: Urine.

1. Tzara, *Le Cœur à Gaz* (Paris: GLM, 1946), p. 8.

VOICE OF VERDICT [*in the shadows*]: God.
IRONIQUE: Constantinople.
EQUINOXE: An old woman died of starvation yesterday in Saint-Denis.[1]

L'Empereur de Chine is a powerful play that combines the elements of nonsense and violence which characterize the Theatre of the Absurd. Its weakness lies in the insufficient blending of its elements into an organic whole, and in the length of its somewhat rambling design.

Le Bourreau du Pérou expresses preoccupations similar to those of the earlier play. The government abdicates and hands the sacred seals of state to the hangman, and a period of gratuitous murder and execution ensues. Here again, in a curious way, the free flow of the imagination and the release of the subconscious fantasies of a poet assume a prophetic content. The outbreak of violence in the era of the Second World War is exactly forecast by *L'Empereur de Chine* and even more drastically by *Le Bourreau du Pérou*. It is as though the destructiveness of the Dadaists was a sublimated release of the same secular impulse toward aggression and violence that found expression in the mass murders of the totalitarian movements.

While Dadaism had shifted its centre of gravity to Paris after the end of hostilities, other members of the Zürich circle went back to Germany, transplanting the movement to Berlin and Munich, where it merged and coexisted with the powerful stirrings of German Expressionism. The dramatic products of the Expressionist movement were on the whole too idealistic and politically conscious to rank as forerunners of the Theatre of the Absurd, with which, however, they share the tendency to project inner realities and to objectify thought and feeling. The only major writer among the Expressionists who definitely belongs to the antecedents of the Theatre of the Absurd is Yvan Goll (1891–1950), who, born in the disputed territory of

1. Ribemont-Dessaignes, *L'Empereur de Chine, suivi de Le Serin Muet* (Paris: Sans Pareil, Collection Dada, 1921), p. 127.

Alsace-Lorraine, had gone to Switzerland at the outbreak of the war. There he met Arp and other members of the Dadaist circle. Later he went to Paris. Goll, who described himself as without a homeland, 'Jewish by destiny, born in France by chance, described as a German by a piece of stamped paper',[1] became a bilingual poet who sometimes wrote in French, sometimes in German.

Goll's dramatic work during his Expressionist-Dadaist period was written in German. Clearly under the influence of Jarry and Apollinaire, Goll was also greatly impressed with the possibilities of the cinema. *Die Chaplinade* (1920), which he describes as a 'film poem', is a highly imaginative combination of poetry and film images. Charlie Chaplin's little tramp is its hero. Chaplin's image comes to life on a poster, escapes from the billsticker, who tries to pin him back, and floats through a series of dreamlike, filmlike adventures, accompanied by a doe (which turns into a beautiful girl and is killed by a huntsman). He is involved in revolutions and riots and finally returns to his poster. This is a beautiful work, probably the first to recognize the poetry and poetic potentialities of the cinema.

During the same year, 1920, Goll published two plays under the joint title *Die Unsterblichen* (*The Immortals*), which he subtitled *Überdramen*, or superdramas, in the sense in which Apollinaire used the term *drame surréaliste* in his subtitle for *Tirésias*. In his preface, Goll explains his conception of a new kind of theatre. In Greek drama, the gods measured themselves against human beings; theatre was a vast enlargement of reality on to a superhuman scale. But in the nineteenth century, plays sought to be nothing but 'interesting, challenging in the manner of an advocate [of a cause] or simply descriptive, imitative of life, not creative'.[2] The dramatist of the new age must again

1. Yvan Goll, autobiographical note, in K. Pinthus, *Menschheitsdämmerung* (Berlin: Rowohlt, 1920), p. 292.

2. Goll, Preface to *Die Unsterblichen*, in *Dichtungen* (Neuwied: Luchterhand, 1960), p. 64.

find a way to penetrate behind the surface of reality:

> The poet must again know that there are worlds quite different from that of the five senses: a superworld (*Überwelt*). He must come to grips with it. This will by no means be a relapse into the mystical or the romantic or the clowning of the music hall, although it has something in common with all of these – the probing into a world beyond the senses. ... It has been quite forgotten that the stage is nothing but a magnifying glass. Great drama has always known this – the Greeks walked on the cothurnus; Shakespeare spoke with giant spirits of the dead. It has been quite forgotten that the first symbol of the theatre is the mask. ... In the mask there lies a law and this is the law of the theatre – the unreal becomes fact. For a moment it is proved that the most banal can be unreal and 'divine' and that precisely in this there lies the greatest truth. Truth is not contained in reason; it is found by the poet, not the philosopher. ... The stage must not only work with 'real' life; it becomes 'surreal' when it is aware of the things behind the things. Pure realism was the greatest lapse in all literature.[1]

The theatre must not be just a means to make the bourgeois comfortable, it must frighten him, turn him into a child again. 'The simplest means is the grotesque, but without inciting to laughter. The monotony and stupidity of human beings are so enormous that they can be adequately represented only by enormities. Let the new drama be an enormity.'[2] To create the effect of masks in our technical age, the stage must use the techniques of recording, electrical posters, megaphones. The characters must be caricatures in masks and on stilts.

This is an impressive manifesto, which accurately describes many of the features and the aims of the Theatre of the Absurd. Yet the two plays in which Goll sought to translate these ideas into action are disappointing. *Der Unsterbliche*, in two acts, shows a musician of genius who loses his mistress to a tycoon and sells his soul to him for a large sum of money. His soul is abstracted in the process of filming it, making him immortal.

1. ibid., pp. 64–5.   2. ibid., p. 65.

In the second act, the musician's mistress desperately seeks him, but flirts with the bridegroom of a newly married couple who come to be photographed by her tycoon-husband. In the end, Sebastian, the musician, comes to life again – on film, crying out for her – but she finally departs with an officer. Although the play uses the technique of projected stills and film, and some of the characters appear as grotesque masks, its contents are, after all, the old romantic, sentimental clichés of the artist who loses his soul to commerce and the beloved woman who cannot resist money or power.

The second *Überdrama*, *Der Ungestorbene* (*The Not Yet Dead*), deals with the very similar dilemma of the philosopher who wants to improve the world and lectures on eternal peace. This time his wife, who sits at the box office of the lecture hall, is seduced by a journalist who battens on the thinker, and persuades him, for the sake of sensationalism, to die in public, to prove that he is serious about progress. But after his public death for humanity is advertised, the philosopher fails to die. Nevertheless, the newspaper still proclaims that he has died for humanity. In the end, his wife returns and he launches a new series of lectures, this time on 'The hygienic conditions of bed-bugs in hotels'. Again a good many technical devices are used by Goll to translate his ideas into stage reality – the mad dance of modern publicity is expressed in a dance of advertising columns, the public at the hero's lectures is represented by a monstrous giant figure, a student throws his brain on the floor and later picks it up again and puts it back in his head – but again the Surrealist devices cannot hide the lack of originality of the basic idea, the commercialization of idealism by the press.

The same discrepancy between the modernity of the means of expression employed and the tameness of the content characterizes Goll's most ambitious attempt in this genre, the 'satirical drama' *Methusalem, oder Der Ewige Bürger* (*Methusalem, or The Eternal Bourgeois*). Again the theoretical preface is far more original than the play itself:

The modern satirist must seek new means of provocation. He has found them in 'Surrealism' (*Überrealismus*) and in 'a-logic'. Surrealism is the strongest negation of realism. The reality of appearance is unmasked in favour of the truth of being. 'Masks' – rough, grotesque, like the emotions of which they are the expression. ... A-logic is the most spiritual form of humour, and thus the best weapon against the clichés that dominate our whole life. ... So as not to be a tearful pacifist or salvationist, the poet must perform a few somersaults to make you into children again. For this is his aim – to give you some dolls, to teach you to play and then to throw the sawdust of the broken doll into the wind.[1]

But *Methusalem*, witty and charming though it is, proves to be little more than the conventional satire against the *Spiessbürger* with his shoe factory and his greedy, businesslike son, who instead of a mouth has the mouthpiece of a telephone, whose eyes are five-mark pieces, and whose forehead and hat consist of a typewriter topped by radio aerials. Again there is the student idealist who is a poet and a revolutionary and seduces Methusalem's daughter, and who in one scene appears split into three parts – his 'I', his 'Thou', and his 'He'. The student is killed in a duel with Methusalem's son, but in the last scene he is alive again; has married the daughter, who has given birth to his child; and is on the point of becoming a bourgeois himself. For revolutions end 'when the others no longer have villas', and new revolutions start 'when we have got one'. And the outcome of all the romantic love is the young mother's cry: 'If only [our son] would not piss so much!'

Again Goll uses film in a sequence of Methusalem's dreams. In another dream sequence, the animals that adorn his household, alive or dead, call for a revolution against the tyranny of man. Dead characters come to life to show that life always goes on in one form or another, and that the theatre can never furnish valid, final solutions. But the most successful parts of this

1. Goll, *Methusalem*, in *Schrei und Bekenntnis*, ed. K. Otten (Neuwied: Luchterhand, 1959), pp. 426–7.

ambitious play, which was published with illustrations by Georg Grosz, the leading German Dadaist painter, and performed in 1924 in masks designed by him, are the dialogues of the bourgeois and his guests, which consist entirely of clichés, and thus anticipate Ionesco. This fact, surely, reveals Goll's mistake: he, who was a great and sensitive lyric poet and a master of language, fell victim to the seduction of new techniques, and, in subordinating his imagination to the demands of masks and film, he failed to transmute his material into the new poetry of the Absurd, which he had so clearly foreseen and so effectively formulated in theory. Perhaps Goll was too tender and gentle a soul to be able to live up to the harshness of his satirical objectives.

Among Goll's German contemporaries, the one who came nearest to the realization of a theatre as cruel and grotesque as the one Goll had postulated was Bertolt Brecht, who hailed Goll's first published plays in a review published in December 1920, calling him the Courteline of Expressionism. In the course of his development from anarchic poetic drama, in the style of Büchner and Wedekind, toward the austerity of the Marxist didacticism of his later phase, Brecht wrote a number of plays that come extremely close to the Theatre of the Absurd, both in their use of clowning and music-hall knockabout humour and in their preoccupation with the problem of the identity of the self and its fluidity.

Brecht was deeply influenced by the great Munich beerhall comedian Karl Valentin, an authentic heir of the harlequins of the *Commedia dell'arte*. In Brecht's one-act farce *Die Hochzeit* (*The Wedding*), written *circa* 1923, the collapse of pieces of furniture externalizes the rottenness of the family in which the wedding takes place, in exactly the way that objects express inner realities in the plays of Adamov and Ionesco while, at the same time, giving an opportunity for broad music-hall gags.

In a far more serious vein, Brecht's most enigmatic play, and one of his greatest, *Im Dickicht der Städte* (*In the Jungle of Cities*), written 1921-3, foreshadows the Theatre of the Absurd in its deliberate rejection of motivation. The play shows a fight to the death between two men, Garga and Shlink, who are linked in a strange relationship of love-hatred. It opens with Shlink's attempt to buy Garga's opinion of a book. He offers Garga, who is employed in a lending library, a large sum of money to make him declare that he likes a book for which he has expressed a dislike. From this point, the fight develops; it is always a matter of making the one man acknowledge the other's superiority through forcing him into either gratitude or aggression. All this takes place in a grotesque Chicago of gangsters and lynching mobs.

Im Dickicht der Städte deals not only with the impossibility of knowing the motivation of human beings in their actions (thus anticipating the techniques of Pinter), it also presents the problem of communication between human beings, which preoccupies Beckett, Adamov, and Ionesco. The fight between Shlink and Garga is essentially an attempt to achieve contact. At the end they recognize the impossibility of such contact, even through conflict. 'If you crammed a ship full of human bodies till it burst, the loneliness inside it would be so great that they would turn to ice . . . so great is our isolation that even conflict is impossible.'[1]

The 'comedy' *Mann ist Mann* (*Man Equals Man*), written 1924-5, describes the transformation of a meek little man into a ferocious soldier. Here again Brecht uses the techniques of the music hall. The transformation scene, in which the victim is induced to commit what he believes to be a crime, is tried, sentenced, and made to think that he has been shot (after which he is resurrected in his new personality), is presented like a variety act – a series of conjuring tricks. In productions of this play Brecht used stilts and other devices to turn the British colonial soldiers who perform the transformation into huge

1. Bertolt Brecht, *Im Dickicht der Städte*, in *Stücke I* (Frankfurt: Suhrkamp, 1953), pp. 291-2.

monsters. *Mann ist Mann* anticipates the Theatre of the Absurd in its thesis that human nature is not a constant, and that it is possible to transform one character into another in the course of a play.

The recent publication of a hitherto unpublished poem by Brecht has thrown an interesting light on the connection between *Mann ist Mann* and his earlier *Im Dickicht der Städte*. This poem comes from an early draft-play, *Der Grüne Garraga* (*Green Garraga*), and deals with a citizen, Galgei, who was turned into another human being. Thus Galy Gay, the victim of *Mann ist Mann*, was originally identical with Garga, the victim of aggression in *Im Dickicht der Städte*. And in fact Shlink's attempt to buy Garga's opinion is an attempt to rob him of his personality, just as Galy Gay is robbed of his personality in the later play. Both plays are about the appropriation of human personality by a stronger personality – the stealing of one's identity, as a form of rape. And this is one of the themes of the Theatre of the Absurd as well: Ionesco's *Jacques ou La Soumission* is a clear case in point.

Brecht's short interlude, *Das Elephantenkalb* (*The Baby Elephant*), was written to be performed in the entr'acte of *Mann ist Mann* in 1924–5. In it the automatic writing of Surrealism is as much anticipated as the problem of shifting identity. A baby elephant, accused of having murdered its mother, can prove that the mother is not dead at all and is not its mother in any case. Yet the case is proved and the baby elephant found guilty. This is pure anti-theatre, and dramatizes its author's subconscious mind as ruthlessly as Adamov's early plays project *his* neurosis.

Like Adamov, Brecht later rejected this phase of his artistic development. Like Adamov, he turned towards a socially committed and, at least in outward intention, fully rational theatre. Yet Brecht's case also shows that the irrational Theatre of the Absurd and the highly purposeful politically committed play are not so much irreconcilable contradictions as, rather, the obverse and reverse side of the same medal. In Brecht's case, the neurosis and despair that were given free rein in his anarchic and grotesque period continued as actively and as powerfully behind the rational façade of his political theatre, and provide most of its poetic impact.

In fact, Kenneth Tynan in quoting Brecht to Ionesco as an example of his socially committed ideal, and Ionesco in attacking Brecht as the embodiment of the arid ideological theatre, are both equally wide of the mark. Brecht was one of the first masters of the Theatre of the Absurd, and his case shows that the *pièce à thèse* stands or falls not by its politics but by its poetic truth, which is beyond politics, since it proceeds from far deeper levels of the author's personality. Brecht's personality contained a strong element of anarchy and despair. Hence even in his politically committed period, the picture he presented of the capitalist world was essentially negative and absurd: the universe of *The Good Woman of Setzuan* is ruled by imbecile gods, that of *Puntila* is modelled on a Chaplinesque formula of slapstick, and in *The Caucasian Chalk Circle* justice is done only by the unlikeliest of accidents.

While in Germany the impulse behind Dadaism and Expressionism had flagged into the *Neue Sachlichkeit* by the middle twenties, and the whole modern movement was swallowed up in the intellectual quicksands of the Nazi period in the thirties, the line of development continued unbroken in France. The destructiveness of Dadaism had cleared the air. Dada was reborn in a changed form in the Surrealist movement. Where Dada was purely negative, Surrealism believed in the great positive, healing force of the subconscious mind. As André Breton put it in his famous definition of the word in the first Surrealist manifesto of 1924, Surrealism was a 'pure psychic automatism by which it is proposed to express, verbally, in writing, or in any other way, the real functioning of thought.' This is not the place to trace in detail the fascinating story of the struggles and internal conflicts of the Surrealist movement or its achievements in poetry or painting. In the theatre, the harvest of Surrealism proved a meagre one. The stage is far too deliberate an art form to allow complete automatism in the composition of plays. It is most unlikely that any of the plays we can today class as Surrealist were written in the way Breton ideally wanted them composed.

Louis Aragon's volume *Le Libertinage* (1924) contains two such plays. *L'Armoire à Glace un Beau Soir* (*The Mirror-Wardrobe One Beautiful Evening*) is a charming sketch. In the prologue we meet an assortment of fantastic characters. A soldier meets a nude woman, the President of the Republic appears with a Negro general, Siamese twin sisters appeal to the President for permission to marry separately. A man on a tricycle passes; his nose is so long that he has to lift it when he wants to speak; Théodore Fraenkel (a member of the Surrealist circle) introduces a fairy. The play proper opens with the familiar scene of a husband returning home, while his wife nervously eyes the wardrobe, implores him not to go near it, and gives every indication that her lover is hidden inside it. After suspense and jealousy have been built up into an atmosphere of sexual excitement, the couple disappear into the next room. Finally, after a long and charged pause, the husband returns with his clothes in disorder and opens the cupboard. Out march all the fantastic characters of the prologue in solemn procession. The President of the Republic sings a nonsense song.

Au Pied du Mur (*At the Foot of the Wall*), Aragon's second play in *Le Libertinage*, uses the same method – a fairly conventional action interrupted by Surrealist interludes. The main plot is romantic to the point of ridiculousness. A young man, who has been left by his mistress, forces the maid in the country inn where he has sought refuge to kill herself to prove her love for him. In the second act, the young hero, Frédéric, and his mistress roam the high mountains of the Alps, and finally Frédéric faces the narrator of the framework scenes as his own double.

The appearance of fairies and Parisian workmen in overalls cannot disguise the fact that basically this is a romantic play in the vein of Musset or Victor Hugo, revealing, through its modernistic trappings, Aragon's essential traditionalism, which later also emerged in his beautiful wartime poetry and his monumental social novels.

Aragon and Breton jointly wrote a play, *Le Trésor des Jésuites* (*The Treasure of the Jesuits*), from which they both dissociated themselves after Aragon's break with the Surrealist movement, and which has therefore never been republished. One of the most remarkable features of this play is that, more than ten years before, it forecast the outbreak of the Second World War in 1939, lending force to Breton's claim that the Surrealist method of automatic writing awakens powers of prophecy and clairvoyance.

More important than most of the dramatic production within the Surrealist movement was the work some of its members produced after they had left, or been expelled from it. Antonin Artaud (1896–1948), one of the finest of the Surrealist poets and also a professional actor and director who became the most powerful seminal influence on the modern French theatre, and Roger Vitrac (1899–1952), the ablest dramatist to emerge from Surrealism, were both banished from the circle by Breton because they had yielded to unworthy commercial instincts, to the extent of wanting to produce Surrealist plays in the framework of the professional theatre. Artaud and Vitrac were proscribed by Breton toward the end of 1926. They became associates in a venture appropriately named the Théâtre Alfred Jarry, which opened on 1 June 1927, with a programme that included a one-ct play by Artaud, *Ventre Brûlé, ou La Mère Folle* (*Upset tomach, or The Mad Mother*), and Vitrac's *Les Mystères de l'Amour* (*The Mysteries of Love*).

Les Mystères de l'Amour (three acts, five scenes) is probably the most sustained effort to write a truly Surrealist play. It could well be the product of automatic writing, consisting, as it does, largely of the tender and sadistic fantasies of two lovers. The author himself appears at the close of the first scene. He has tried to commit suicide by shooting himself, and enters bathed in blood but shaking with helpless laughter. At the end, he re-appears, none the worse for his experience. Lloyd George and Mussolini also form part of the cast, and Lloyd George in particular appears in a gruesome light – he is sawing off heads and trying to dispose of fragments of corpses. The sets are modelled on Surrealist paintings. Thus, the fourth scene represents, at the same time, a railway station, a dining-car, the seashore, a hotel hall, a draper's shop, and the main square of a provincial town. Past, present, and future merge in dreamlike fashion, the actual and the potential are inextricably interwoven. Yet in this chaos there are passages of remarkable poetic power. At one point, in a dialogue between the hero, Patrice, and the author, the basic theme of the Theatre of the Absurd, the problem of language, is squarely faced:

THE AUTHOR: Your words make everything impossible, my friend.
PATRICE: Then make a theatre without words.
THE AUTHOR: But, my dear sir, have I ever wanted to do anything else?
PATRICE: You have: you have put words of love into my mouth.
THE AUTHOR: You ought to have spat them out.
PATRICE: I tried, but they changed into shots or vertigo.
THE AUTHOR: That is not my fault. Life is like that.[1]

Vitrac's second Surrealist play, *Victor, ou Les Enfants au Pouvoir* (*Victor, or Power to the Children*), first performed under Artaud's direction on 24 December 1924, has already left the chaos of pure automatism behind and adopts the convention of the farcical and fantastic drawing-room comedy we find again in Ionesco's work. Victor is a boy of nine, seven feet tall and with the intelligence of an adult. He and his six-year-old girl-friend Esther are the only rational beings in a family of mad

1. Roger Vitrac, *Les Mystères de l'Amour* in *Théâtre II* (Paris: Gallimard, 1948), p. 56.

puppetlike adults. Victor's father has an affair with Esther's mother, but the children expose the lovers, and Esther's father hangs himself. One of the characters is a woman of breathtaking beauty but disconcerting carminative incontinence. In the end, Victor dies of a stroke on his ninth birthday and his parents commit suicide. As the maid rightly points out in the last line of the play, '*Mais, c'est un drame!*'[1]

Victor anticipates Ionesco in many ways: the banality of a cliché-laden language is parodied when one of the characters reads genuine extracts from *Le Matin* of 12 September 1909; there is a similar mixture of the parody of the conventional theatre and pure absurdity. Yet Vitrac's play lacks the sense of form and the poetry that gives Ionesco's madness its method – and its charm. Here the blending of the elements is not complete, the nightmare alternates with the students' rag.

Vitrac's later plays return to a more traditional form, but some of them still bear traces of his Surrealist experience. Even so sociological and political a play as *Le Coup de Trafalgar* (a picture of a slice of Parisian society before, during, and after the First World War, first performed in 1934) shows traces of a delightful crazy humour, while in *Le Loup-Garou* (*The Werewolf*), a comedy that takes place in a fashionable mental hospital, the author's Surrealist experience is clearly detectable in his mastery of the technique of lunatic dialogue.

Antonin Artaud directed Vitrac's Surrealist plays and is the author of one or two remarkable dramatic sketches, but his real importance for the Theatre of the Absurd lies in his theoretical writings and in his practical experiments as a producer. One of the most extraordinary men of his age, actor, director, prophet, blasphemer, saint, madman – and a great poet – Artaud's imagination may have outrun his practical achievement in the theatre. But his vision of a stage of magic beauty and mythical power remains, to this day, one of the most active leavens in the

1. Vitrac, *Victor, ou Les Enfants au Pouvoir*, in *Théâtre I* (Paris: Gallimard, 1946), p. 90.

theatre. Although he had worked under Dullin and had directed the performances of the short-lived Théâtre Alfred Jarry, Artaud's revolutionary conception of the theatre crystallized only after he had seen the Balinese dancers at the Colonial Exhibition of 1931. He formulated his ideas in a series of impassioned manifestos later collected in the volume *Le Théâtre et Son Double* (1938).

Diagnosing the confusion of his time as springing from the 'rupture between things and words, between things and the ideas that are their representation'[1] and rejecting the psychological and narrative theatre, with its 'preoccupation with personal problems',[2] Artaud passionately called for a return to myth and magic, for a ruthless exposure of the deepest conflicts of the human mind, for a 'Theatre of Cruelty'. 'Everything that acts is a cruelty. It is upon this idea of extreme action, pushed beyond all limits, that the theatre must be rebuilt.'[3] By confronting the audience with the true image of their internal conflicts, a poetic, magical theatre would bring liberation and release. 'The theatre restores to us all our dormant conflicts and all their powers, and gives these powers names we hail as symbols – and behold! Before our eyes is fought a battle of symbols ... for there can be theatre only from the moment when the impossible really begins and when the poetry that occurs on the stage sustains and superheats the realized symbols.'[4]

This amounts to a complete rejection of realism and a demand for a theatre that would project collective archetypes:

The theatre will never find itself again ... except by furnishing the spectator with the truthful precipitate of dreams, in which his taste for crime, his erotic obsessions, his savagery, his chimeras, his utopian sense of life and matter, even his cannibalism pour out on a level not counterfeit and illusory, but interior. In other terms, the theatre must pursue by all its means a reassertion not only of all the

1. Antonin Artaud, *The Theatre and its Double*, trans. Mary Caroline Richards (New York: Grove Press, 1958), p. 7.

2. ibid., p. 42.　　　3. ibid., p. 85.　　　4. ibid., p. 28.

aspects of the objective and descriptive external world but of the internal world; that is, of man considered metaphorically.[1]

Under the influence of the powerful impression made on him by the subtle and magical poetry of the Balinese dancers, Artaud wanted to restore the language of gesture and movement, to make inanimate things play their part in the action, and to relegate dialogue (which 'does not belong specifically to the stage, it belongs to books')[2] to the background. Quoting the music hall and the Marx Brothers as well as the Balinese dancers, he called for a true language of the theatre, which would be a wordless language of shapes, light, movement, and gesture:

The domain of the theatre is not psychological but plastic and physical. And it is not a question of whether the physical language of theatre is capable of achieving the same psychological resolutions as the language of words, whether it is able to express feelings and passions as well as words, but whether there are not attitudes in the realm of thought and intelligence that words are incapable of grasping and that gestures and . . . a spatial language attain with more precision.[3]

The theatre should aim at expressing what language is incapable of putting into words. 'It is not a matter of suppressing speech in the theatre but of changing its role, and especially of reducing its position.'[4]

Behind the poetry of the texts, there is the actual poetry, without form and without text.[5] . . . For I make it my principle that words do not mean everything, and that by their nature and defining character, fixed once and for all, they arrest and paralyse thought instead of permitting it and fostering its development. . . . I am adding another language to the spoken language, and I am trying to restore to the language of speech its old magic, its essential spellbinding power.[6]

In theory, Artaud had formulated some of the basic tendencies of the Theatre of the Absurd by the early 1930s. But he lacked the opportunity either as dramatist or as a director

1. ibid. p. 93.　　2. ibid., p. 37.　　3. ibid., p. 71.
4. ibid., p. 73.　　5. ibid., p. 78.　　6. ibid., pp. 110–11.

to put these ideas into practice. His only chance to achieve his aims came in 1935, when he found backers for a performance of his *théâtre de la cruauté*. He decided to make his own adaptation of the gruesome story of the Cenci which Stendhal had written as a story and which Shelley had made into a tragedy. But in spite of some beautiful points of detail, the performance was a failure. Artaud himself played the part of Count Cenci. His ritual chanting of the text was intriguing, but it did not convince the audience. Financial failure followed and played its part in driving Artaud into abject poverty, despair, and long spells of insanity. Jean-Louis Barrault, then twenty-five years old, acted as the secretary of the production, and Roger Blin, one of the most important directors in the Theatre of the Absurd, assisted Artaud as director and played the part of one of the hired assassins.

Artaud, who made his debut as an actor under Lugné-Poë at the Théâtre de l'Œuvre; who knew and acted with Gémier, the first Ubu; who appeared in 1924 in Yvan Goll's *Methusalem* when it was performed in Paris; Artaud, who was befriended by Adamov in the period of his mental illness, forms the bridge between the pioneers and today's Theatre of the Absurd. Outwardly his endeavours ended in utter failure and mental collapse. And yet in some sense, he triumphed.

Another important poet who emerged from the Surrealist movement was Robert Desnos (1900–45), the author of elegiac and nonsense verse, recorder of delicate and dreadful dreams, and writer of numerous Surrealist film scenarios that were never made into films. His only dramatic work is *La Place de l'Etoile*, written as early as 1927, revised shortly before his arrest and deportation in 1944, and published after his tragic death in the concentration camp of Theresienstadt, where he was found emaciated and dying at the end of hostilities.

La Place de l'Etoile is a punning title; it refers not to the Paris landmark but to the starfish, which is the poetic symbol of the dreams and desires of its hero, Maxime. People ask Maxime to give them his starfish, and he refuses. But when he does give it away to the woman he loves, not only does a policeman come almost immediately to bring it back, having found it in the street below his window, but groups of people come and bring him more and more starfish. Twelve waiters enter with twelve starfish on silver platters, and the streets of the town are so full of starfish that one can barely walk.

La Place de l'Etoile is also a romantic love-story of Maxime and two women, Fabrice and Athénais, but in its dreamlike atmosphere, in the conversations of drinkers in a bar, which provide a kind of Greek chorus, the play foreshadows much of the Theatre of the Absurd. Desnos gave the play the sub-title Antipoème, and thus anticipated Ionesco's anti-pièce.

So strong was the tendency of the times and the influence of the pioneers of abstract art in painting and sculpture that even outside the Surrealist movement attempts were made to break the conventions of the naturalistic theatre. Jean Cocteau experimented with a theatre of pure movement. Parade, devised by Cocteau with décor by Picasso and music by Satie (who was a master of humour noir in his own right), and performed by the Diaghilev Ballet Russe in 1917, is a return to the circus and music hall, while Cocteau's Le Bœuf sur le Toit (The Ox on the Roof, 1920), with décor by Dufy and music by Milhaud, was performed by such famous music-hall actors as the three Fratellinis. Les Mariés de la Tour Eiffel (The Married Couple of the Eiffel Tower, 1921) is a mimeplay and ballet accompanied by narration spoken by actors in the costumes of giant phonographs.

Although most of Cocteau's later work oscillates between the heavily romantic and the merely playful, it bears the stamp of his preoccupation with some of the basic elements of an abstract and dreamlike theatre, most clearly perhaps in his poetic and haunting films, from Le Sang d'un Poète (The Blood of a Poet) to La Belle et la Bête (Beauty and the Beast); Orphée with its brilliantly realized images of the land of the dead; and the final

Testament d'Orphée. Ionesco has paid tribute to Cocteau for precisely his playfulness and baroque taste:

I think Jean Cocteau has been reproached for having merely touched upon grave problems lightly. I feel that this is wrong; he raises them in a moon-struck, enchanted décor. He has been reproached for an impurity of style, his fairyland of cardboard stage sets. It is precisely his confetti that I love, his serpentine, his baroque fairground sphinxes. As everything is but a mirage and life a fairground, it is not amiss that there should be sphinxes and that there should be a kind of fair. Nothing expresses better than these itinerant and precarious festivities the precariousness of life, the fragility of beauty, evanescence.[1]

A play that clearly anticipates Ionesco's onslaught on the bourgeois family and that originated in Cocteau's circle is *Les Pélicans* (*The Pelicans*, 1921), by that precocious genius Raymond Radiguet (1903–23). In two short acts we meet the Pelican family, anxious to do great deeds to make their name so famous that it will no longer sound ridiculous. The lady of the house comes riding in on the back of her swimming teacher, who does not know how to swim but has an affair with her. The son tries to become a jockey, and the daughter, wanting to commit suicide, wins a skating trophy on the frozen Seine. The play ends with a grotesque family group.

At about this time, Armand Salacrou, who later became a leading playwright in a robust stage idiom, wrote some delicate near-Surrealist plays intended to be read rather than acted. Most of these are lost, but *Les Trente Tombes de Judas* (*The Thirty Tombs of Judas*) and *Histoire de Cirque* (*Circus Story*) escaped destruction and were reprinted in 1960.[2] Set in a dance hall and a circus, these little plays combine the traditions of clowning and the dream – oranges spout blood, strange plants grow

1. Ionesco, '*Pour Cocteau*', *Cahiers des Saisons*, no. 12, October 1957.
2. Armand Salacrou, *Pièces à Lire*, in *Les Œuvres Libres*, Paris, no. 173, October 1960.

before our eyes, and the circus tent vanishes to let the love sick youth die in a snowstorm.

In 1924, while still boys at school, René Daumal (1908–44) and Roger Gilbert-Lecomte (1907–43) composed a series of miniature playlets, in a truly Jarryesque spirit, which have been published under the auspices of the Collège de Pataphysique, with the title *Petit Théâtre*. They are delightful nonsense and wholly beyond interpretation. Both authors developed into considerable poets. Daumal carried his exploration of the dark regions of the soul to the point of repeatedly committing a kind of controlled suicide by inhaling toxic fumes so that he could reach the frontiers of life. He is regarded as one of the most authentic followers of Jarry, and his memory is cultivated by the Collège de Pataphysique.

Even more important as a nonsense dramatist among the pataphysical heroes is Julien Torma (1902–33), another poetic vagabond and *poète maudit* who drifted through life with sovereign unconcern until he disappeared in the Austrian Alps, walking out of his hotel never to return. Torma, who despised the Surrealists for their publicity-seeking and exploitation of their personalities, wrote some extraordinary nonsense plays. *Coupures (Cuts)*, 'a tragedy in nine scenes', and the one-act play *Lauma Lamer* appeared during his lifetime in a limited edition of two hundred copies. His most ambitious play, *Le Bétrou*, was posthumously published by the Collège de Pataphysique.

Coupures is remarkable chiefly for a character who speaks all the stage directions and is presented as a god who arbitrarily dominates the action. He is called Osmur and evidently represents fate in all its absurdity. After the play has ended, Osmur is pulled offstage on a wheeled platform and revealed as a mere mechanism. In accordance with this, the action itself, dictated by a mechanical and senseless mechanism, cannot make sense, except that it shows images of eroticism and violence. *Lauma Lamer* is a nautical nonsense play. The hero of *Le Bétrou* (which is in four acts, numbered backward from minus three to zero) is a strange creature who inspires his numerous wives with terror. The Bétrou speaks in inarticulate stammers and has his utterances interpreted by an astronomer. At the end of the second act (or, rather, act minus 2), practically all the characters have been killed by the Bétrou, but they are resuscitated in the next act (minus 1), to be killed again; they are again alive and kicking in the final act (zero), in which the action reaches its appointed end – the quantity of nothingness.

There is an element of suspense here – the Bétrou is being taught to speak and reaches a point where he can imitate certain animal noises. This, however, somehow seems to diminish his power. He flees in disorder, and the play ends in chaos. As the learned pataphysical editors explain, 'The essential element of the play is in the psychological paralysis that reigns everywhere and in the "*phraséolalie*", or, if one wanted to put it like that, in the verbal material which dominates everything and which is fate itself.'[1] This is analogous to the dominance of language over fate in nonsense poets like Lewis Carroll, Edward Lear, and Christian Morgenstern.

Torma explained his ideas in clearer language in a slim little volume of aphorisms, *Euphorismes* (1926), a remarkable book the copy of which in the Bibliothèque Nationale is inscribed by Torma with a dedication to Max Jacob: 'If God existed, you could not invent him!' Some of the aphorisms probe into the ethics of homosexuality, but others contain a resolute rejection of language. 'As soon as one speaks, there is a stink of the social',[2] or even more drastically, 'To express oneself . . . the word itself borrows the scatosociological urge and consecrates it as the model of elocution'[3], so that language becomes 'cacophony'. Hence Torma's endeavour to 'give back to thought

1. J. H. Sainmont, H. Robillot, A. Templenul, Introduction to J. Torma, *Le Bétrou* (Paris: Collège de Pataphysique, year 83 of the pataphysical era 1956), p. 14.

2. Torma, *Euphorismes* (Paris, 1926), p. 37.

3. ibid., p. 36.

the fundamental and *unthinkable* ambiguity, which, however, *is* reality – to deossify language and to *leave* literature'.[1]

Torma, who knew and corresponded with Daumal and Desnos, is a writer's writer and will probably never be read outside a narrow circle of enthusiastic connoisseurs of poetic nonsense. He did not want to have an impact or to be taken seriously: 'I am neither a man of letters nor a poet. I do not even pretend to be interested, I just amuse myself. . . . For me even the admission of tragic silences is too much. I don't have any confessions to make, I do nothing in particular – just as I have perpetrated these poems, lightly.'[2] He was one of the few who had the courage to take their recognition of the absurdity of the human condition to its logical conclusion – he refused to take anything seriously, least of all himself. The casual manner of his death shows that this attitude was anything but a pose.

As strange and eccentric as Torma and, in his own peculiar way, as influential on contemporary writing, was Raymond Roussel (1877–1933). Immensely rich, he travelled all over the world without taking the trouble to look at it. Having arrived at Peking, he drove once through the town and then locked himself in his hotel room. When the ship he travelled on lay in the harbour of Tahiti, he remained in his cabin, writing, not even looking out of the porthole. In his writings as well, Roussel aimed at excluding the real world completely. He wanted to construct a world entirely his own and based, like that of Torma or the nonsense poets, on the logic of assonance and verbal association.

Some of Roussel's novels are constructed on the principle of two cornerstone sentences, similar in sound but different in sense, which he made into the opening and closing phrases of the book and then tried to link by a chain of propositions that would constitute an unbroken sequence of such verbal logic – a logic of metaphor, pun, homonym, association of ideas, and anagrams. The same internal logical mechanisms actuate his

1. ibid., p. 39.　　　　2. ibid.

plays, *L'Etoile au Front* (*The Star on the Forehead*, 1924) and *La Poussière de Soleils* (*Sun Dust*, 1926).

These long and complicated plays, which he had produced at his own expense and which were performed to gales of derisive laughter, must be among the most undramatic dramas ever written. They consist almost exclusively of chains of very complicated and fantastic stories that the characters tell each other in a curiously static, stilted language. Roussel's theatre is more truly 'epic' than Brecht's and infinitely more antitheatrical than anything that Ionesco has ever written. At the same time, the incredible fantasy of Roussel's invention, combined with an involuntary primitivism that makes him the Douanier Rousseau of the theatre, gives his work an almost hypnotic power and has made him the idol of Surrealists and pataphysicians. Roussel committed suicide – in Florence – in 1933.

From Apollinaire to the Surrealists and beyond, an extremely close link has always existed between the pioneers of painting and sculpture and the avant-garde of poets and dramatists. Beckett has written a sensitive study of the abstract painter Bram van Velde,[1] and Ionesco is a friend of Max Ernst and Dubuffet. The influence of some of the leading painters of the age on the Theatre of the Absurd is clearly discernible in the imagery and décor of its plays (*vide* the girl with three noses in Ionesco's *Jacques*).

Moreover, a good many of the painters and sculptors of our time have ventured into the field of avant-garde poetry or drama. We have already referred to Kokoschka's pioneering Dadaist play, which he followed up with a number of other dramatic experiments. The great German Expressionist sculptor Ernst Barlach (1870–1938) also wrote a series of haunting plays that anticipate some of the dreamlike, mythical features of the Theatre of the Absurd. And Picasso was the author of

1. Beckett/Georges Duthuit/Jacques Putman, *Bram van Velde* (New York: Grove Press, 1960).

two avantgardist plays, *Le Désir Attrapé par la Queuee Desire Caught by the Tail*, 1941) and *The Four Little Girls* (1952).

The first of these, which was given a public reading on 19 March 1944, under the direction of Albert Camus and with the participation of Simone de Beauvoir, Jean-Paul Sartre, Michel Leiris, Raymond Queneau, and other distinguished personalities of the world of literature and the arts, consists, like Tzara's *Le Cœur à Gaz*, of dialogues between disembodied feet (some of which monotonously complain of chilblains) and other dehumanized characters. There is little plot, but the action reflects wartime worries in its preoccupation with images of cold and of food shortages. In its mixture of humour and grimness, the little play says what one of Picasso's paintings would say if it came to life for a moment and could speak. It has the playfulness and the sensuality of its master's style.

The same applies to *The Four Little Girls*, from which Roland Penrose quotes in his biography of Picasso, and which contains stage directions like, 'Enter an enormous winged white horse dragging its entrails, surrounded by wings, an owl perched on its head; it stands for a brief moment in front of the little girl, and then disappears at the other end of the stage.'[1]

The modern movement in painting and the Theatre of the Absurd meet in their rejection of the discursive and narrative elements, and in their concentration on the poetic image as a concretization of the inner reality of the conscious and subconscious mind and the archetypes by which it lives.

The connection between the modern movement in painting and new experimental trends in drama is also strikingly demonstrated by Stanislaw Ignacy Witkiewicz (1885–1939), one of the most brilliant figures of the European avant-garde of his time, whose importance is only now being discovered outside his native Poland. Witkiewicz – who did much of his work under

1. R. Penrose, *Picasso: His Life and Work* (London: Gollancz, 1955), p. 335.

the pseudonym Witkacy – began his career as a painter and developed an aesthetic of 'pure form' which ultimately postulated the complete independence of the artist from nature and external reality.

In his work as a dramatist – which received scant attention in his lifetime – Witkiewicz explored the worlds of dream, madness, parody, and political satire. Grotesque nightmares merge into the visions of madmen, political parables turn into hilarious parodies of the Polish classics. Clearly a good deal of the effectiveness of Witkiewicz's *œuvre* must depend on a thorough knowledge of the political background of his time and of Polish literature. Nevertheless a number of his plays have recently been translated into German and into English. They reveal a playwright of tremendous inventiveness, undoubtedly a major figure. The two-volume edition of Witkiewicz's plays which appeared in Warsaw in 1962 contains twenty plays, a rich mine for exploration and re-discovery. A proud lonely figure and an eccentric, Witkiewicz committed suicide on 18 September 1939, the day after the entry of Soviet troops into Poland sealed the doom of his country's independence.

Another Polish writer of world importance, who has largely been active as a novelist, Witold Gombrowicz (1904–1969), must be regarded as a precursor and at the same time as a mature master of the Theatre of the Absurd. Gombrowicz, who left Poland in 1939, settled in the Argentine and spent the rest of his life in exile. His play *Iwona, Ksieczniczka Burgunda* (*Yvonne, Princess of Burgundy*, 1935) takes us into a grotesque, romantic fairytale world – the court of a King which resembles that in Büchner's *Leonce and Lena* or those in the fairy tales of Hans Christian Andersen. The Prince, bored and dissipated, is introduced to an ugly and stupid Princess who never utters a word. And it is this speechlessness of hers which allows him to imagine her inner life for himself without any interference from her and makes him fall in love with the girl. Until, that is, he tires of her and she is murdered by being made to eat a fish so rich in bones that she is bound to choke to death. Gombrowicz's second play *Slub* (*The Wedding*, written 1945, first published 1950, first performed in Paris 1963) is a dream play of great impact. The hero Henryk, vaguely aware that he is serving as a soldier in a war somewhere in northern France, sees himself transported back to his native country with his best friend Wladzio. But the house where he lived has turned into a low tavern, his father and mother into publicans, his fiancée into a whore. And then again father and mother appear as a king and queen and Henryk himself as a prince who is about to marry a princess. And yet dimly he remains aware that his fiancée is a whore after all, and the two worlds merge into each other. Henryk frequently lapses into verse. He is aware of the unnaturally solemn mode of his speech and yet cannot help speaking in that manner. This is a brilliant transposition of a dream situation.

> Well, I have said it.
> But again this saying
> Sounded so solemn and changes into *explanation*.
> And sinks like a stone
> In this silence. . . . Ah, now I know, why
> I am not speaking, but explaining. You are not here
> And I am alone, alone, alone. . . . Speaking
> To no one and have to be artificial,
> For speaking to no one and yet speaking I have to be
> Artificial . . .

The nightmare seems to reflect Henryk's fear of marriage. He is determined to go through with it, yet can't. Involved in conspiracies and revolution, he throws his father into prison and makes himself dictator of his country. Jealous of rumours that Wladzio has deceived him with his bride, he asks Wladzio to commit suicide as a token of his friendship for him. And so, as the wedding proceeds, Wladzio kills himself with the knife Henryk has given him. The wedding has turned into a funeral.

The continued presence of several different levels of consciousness in the dreamer's mind is brilliantly suggested by Gombrowicz. For Gombrowicz reality is problematic and man not autonomous but the product of the situation in which he finds himself, a product of the language which arises out of a given situation:

> ... each of us says
> Not what he wants to say, but what is seemly. Words
> Conspire treacherously behind our backs
> And it is not we who speak the words, the words speak us
> And betray our thoughts which also
> Betray our treacherous feelings ...

Here, then, as in the nonsense world of Lewis Carroll and Edward Lear, language has become autonomous. In a world that has lost the objective criteria of reality, thought has become omnipotent, but thought in turn is the slave of language and its conventions.

The younger generation of dramatists of the Absurd in the Poland of the 1960s clearly owed a great deal to, and continued the tradition of surrealist drama created by Witkiewicz and Gombrowicz.

In Spain – the homeland of Picasso and Goya, the country of the allegorical *autos sacramentales* and the baroque poetry of Quevedo and Góngora – some of the tendencies of the Surrealists found their literary parallels in the work of two important dramatists.

Ramón del Valle-Inclán (1866–1936), a great novelist and dramatist practically unknown outside Spain, from about 1920 onwards developed a style of dramatic writing that he called *esperpento* (the grotesque or ridiculous) in which the world is depicted as inhabited by tragicomic, almost mechanically actuated marionettes. As Valle-Inclán explained it, the artist can see the world from three different positions. He can look upwards, as if on his knees before it, and present an idealized, reverent picture of reality; he can confront it standing on the same level, which will lead to a realistic approach; or he can see the world from above – and from this distant vantage point it will appear ridiculous and absurd, for it will be seen as through the eyes of a dead man who looks back on life. Valle-Inclán's *esperpentos*, notably *Las Galas del Defunto* (*The Gala of Death*) and *Los Cuernos de Don Friolera* (*The Horns of Don Friolera*), written about 1925, are bitter caricatures of life in which deformed and ugly lovers are pursued by witless and ridiculous husbands while the rules and mannerisms of society appear as mechanical and dehumanized as machines gone mad and functioning in a void. Among the younger dramatists of the Absurd, Arrabal acknowledges Valle-Inclán as an important influence on his work.

In a gentler and more poetic mood, some of the plays of Federico García Lorca clearly show the influence of the French Surrealists. Less well known and earlier than Lorca's great realistic tragedies, these include the charming short scenes of *Teatro Breve* (*Short Theatre*, 1928), one of which, *El Paseo de Buster Keaton* (*Buster Keaton's Walk*), openly derives from the American silent film (like Goll's *Chaplinade*). They also include the puppet play *Retablillo de Don Cristobal* (*The Little Altar Piece of Don Cristobal*, 1931), with its charming brand of slapstick and outspokenness derived from Andalusian folk entertainment; the more intellectualized Surrealism of *Asi que Pasen Cinco Años* (*So Pass Five Years*, 1931), a legend of time, in a dream idiom; and the two scenes from an unfinished play *El Publico* (*The Public*, 1933) that are very near to the Theatre of the Absurd, especially the first, in which a Roman emperor is confronted with two non-human characters, one wholly covered in vines, the other wholly covered in golden bells.

In the English-speaking theatre, the influence of Dadaism and Surrealism has been slight. Gertrude Stein wrote a number of pieces she described as 'plays', but most of them are short abstract prose poems in which single sentences or short paragraphs are labelled act I, act II, and so on. Even a work like *Four Saints in Three Acts*, which has been staged successfully as a ballet opera (with choreography by Frederick Ashton and music by Virgil Thomson), is essentially an abstract prose poem on which elements of 'pure theatre' can be imposed in a more or less arbitrary fashion. When, towards the end of her life, Gertrude Stein wrote a play with a plot and dialogue, *Yes Is for a Very Young Man*, it turned out to be a fascinating but essentially traditional piece of work about the French Resistance and an American expatriate lady's unspoken affection for a young French Resistance fighter, written in a mildly Steinian idiom.

In some ways, F. Scott Fitzgerald's play *The Vegetable*, which was staged, and failed dismally, in November 1922, must be regarded as an early example of the Theatre of the Absurd, at least in its middle part, which gives a grotesque nonsense version of life at the White House. But this satirical sequence of scenes is laboriously motivated in the first act by making the hero, Jerry Frost, drunk on bootleg liquor so as to justify the satire as an alcoholic nightmare; in the third act the action is laboriously brought back to earth. *The Vegetable* is an attempt to leave the naturalistic convention, and fails by remaining firmly anchored within it.

This pitfall has been brilliantly avoided in E. E. Cummings' *him* (1927), one of the most successful plays in the Surrealist style, and far more integrated as an artistic whole than the majority of the French Surrealist plays of the period. Here a spiritual odyssey of a man and a woman is embedded in a dreamlike sequence of fairground scenes and fantastic incidents. Eric Bentley has given an ingenious interpretation of the play as the fantasy of the heroine, Me, 'who is lying under an anaesthetic awaiting the birth of a child',[1] so that the play revolves around the story of Me and Him, 'a young American

1. Eric Bentley, Notes to *him*, in *From the Modern Repertoire*, series II (Indiana University Press, 1957), p. 478.

couple and their quest for reality'. The chorus of weird sisters talking a nonsense language; the vaudeville scenes of fairground barkers and soap-box salesmen; the skits on gangster films, popular ballads, Americans in Europe, and Mussolini's Italy, all fit beautifully into this interpretation. Bentley, however, also quotes Cummings' dialogue between the Author and the Public, in which the author says, '. . . so far as you are concerned "life" is a verb of two voices, active, to do, and passive, to dream. Others believe doing to be only a kind of dreaming. Still others have discovered (in a mirror surrounded with mirrors) something harder than silence but softer than falling: the third voice of "life" which believes itself and which cannot mean because it is.'[1]

This, surely, is a perfect statement of the philosophy of the Theatre of the Absurd, in which the world is seen as a hall of reflecting mirrors, and reality merges imperceptibly into fantasy.

The Theatre of the Absurd is part of a rich and varied tradition. If there is anything really new in it it is the unusual way in which various familiar attitudes of mind and literary idioms are interwoven. Above all, it is the fact that for the first time this approach has met with a wide response from a broadly based public. This is a characteristic not so much of the Theatre of the Absurd as of its epoch. Surrealism admittedly lacked the qualities that would have been needed to create a real Surrealist drama; but this may have been due as much to the lack of a real need for such a theatre on the part of the public as to a lack of interest or application on the part of the writers concerned. They were ahead of their time; now the time has caught up with the avant-garde of the twenties and thirties, and the theatre Jarry and Cummings created has found its public.

1. e. e. cummings, quoted by Bentley, op. cit., p. 487.

8

THE SIGNIFICANCE OF THE ABSURD

WHEN Nietzsche's Zarathustra descended from his mountains to preach to mankind, he met a saintly hermit in the forest. This old man invited him to stay in the wilderness rather than go into the cities of men. When Zarathustra asked the hermit how he passed his time in his solitude, he replied; 'I make up songs and sing them; and when I make up songs I laugh, I weep, and I growl; thus do I praise God.' Zarathustra declined the old man's offer and continued on his journey. But when he was alone, he spoke thus to his heart: 'Can it be possible! This old saint in the forest has not yet heard that God is dead!'[1]

Zarathustra was first published in 1883. The number of people for whom God is dead has greatly increased since Nietzsche's day, and mankind has learned the bitter lesson of the falseness and evil nature of some of the cheap and vulgar substitutes that have been set up to take his place. And so, after two terrible wars, there are still many who are trying to come to terms with the implications of Zarathustra's message, searching for a way in which they can, with dignity, confront a universe deprived of what was once its centre and its living purpose, a world deprived of a generally accepted integrating principle, which has become disjointed, purposeless – absurd.

The Theatre of the Absurd is one of the expressions of this search. It bravely faces up to the fact that for those to whom the world has lost its central explanation and meaning, it is no longer possible to accept art forms still based on the continuation of standards and concepts that have lost their validity; that is, the possibility of knowing the laws of conduct and ultimate

1. Nietzsche, *Also Sprach Zarathustra*, in *Werke*, vol. II (Munich: Hanser, 1955), p. 279.

values, as deducible from a firm foundation of revealed certainty about the purpose of man in the universe.

In expressing the tragic sense of loss at the disappearance of ultimate certainties the Theatre of the Absurd, by a strange paradox, is also a symptom of what probably comes nearest to being a genuine religious quest in our age: an effort, however timid and tentative, to sing, to laugh, to weep – and to growl – if not in praise of God (whose name, in Adamov's phrase, has for so long been degraded by usage that it has lost its meaning), at least in search of a dimension of the Ineffable; an effort to make man aware of the ultimate realities of his condition, to instil in him again the lost sense of cosmic wonder and primeval anguish, to shock him out of an existence that has become trite, mechanical, complacent, and deprived of the dignity that comes of awareness. For God is dead, above all, to the masses who live from day to day and have lost all contact with the basic facts – and mysteries – of the human condition with which, in former times, they were kept in touch through the living ritual of their religion, which made them parts of a real community and not just atoms in an atomized society.

The Theatre of the Absurd forms part of the unceasing endeavour of the true artists of our time to breach this dead wall of complacency and automatism and to re-establish an awareness of man's situation when confronted with the ultimate reality of his condition. As such, the Theatre of the Absurd fulfils a dual purpose and presents its audience with a two-fold absurdity.

In one of its aspects it castigates, satirically, the absurdity of lives lived unaware and unconscious of ultimate reality. This is the feeling of the deadness and mechanical senselessness of half-unconscious lives, the feeling of 'human beings secreting inhumanity', which Camus describes in *The Myth of Sisyphus*:

> In certain hours of lucidity, the mechanical aspect of their gestures, their senseless pantomime, makes stupid everything around them. A man speaking on the telephone behind a glass partition – one cannot hear him but observes his trivial gesturing. One asks oneself, why is

he alive? This malaise in front of man's own inhumanity, this incalculable letdown when faced with the image of what we are, this 'nausea', as a contemporary writer calls it, also is the Absurd.[1]

This is the experience that Ionesco expresses in plays like *The Bald Prima Donna* or *The Chairs*, Adamov in *La Parodie*, or N. F. Simpson in *A Resounding Tinkle*. It represents the satirical, parodistic aspect of the Theatre of the Absurd, its social criticism, its pillorying of an inauthentic, petty society. This may be the most easily accessible, and therefore most widely recognized, message of the Theatre of the Absurd, but it is far from being its most essential or most significant feature.

In its second, more positive aspect, behind the satirical exposure of the absurdity of inauthentic ways of life, the Theatre of the Absurd is facing up to a deeper layer of absurdity – the absurdity of the human condition itself in a world where the decline of religious belief has deprived man of certainties. When it is no longer possible to accept complete closed systems of values and revelations of divine purpose, life must be faced in its ultimate, stark reality. That is why, in the analysis of the dramatists of the Absurd in this book, we have always seen man stripped of the accidental circumstances of social position or historical context, confronted with the basic choices, the basic situations of his existence: man faced with time and therefore waiting, in Beckett's plays or Gelber's, waiting between birth and death; man running away from death, climbing higher and higher, in Vian's play, or passively sinking down toward death, in Buzzati's; man rebelling against death, confronting and accepting it, in Ionesco's *Tueur Sans Gages*; man inextricably entangled in a mirage of illusions, mirrors reflecting mirrors, and forever hiding ultimate reality, in the plays of Genet; man trying to establish his position, or to break out into freedom, only to find himself newly imprisoned, in the parables of Manuel de Pedrolo; man trying to stake out a modest place for him-

1. Camus, *Le Mythe de Sisyphe* (Paris: Gallimard, 1942), p. 29.

self in the cold and darkness that envelops him, in Pinter's plays; man vainly striving to grasp the moral law forever beyond his comprehension, in Arrabal's; man caught in the inescapable dilemma that strenuous effort leads to the same result as passive indolence – complete futility and ultimate death – in the earlier work of Adamov; man forever lonely, immured in the prison of his subjectivity, unable to reach his fellow-man, in the vast majority of these plays.

Concerned as it is with the ultimate realities of the human condition, the relatively few fundamental problems of life and death, isolation and communication, the Theatre of the Absurd, however grotesque, frivolous, and irreverent it may appear, represents a return to the original, religious function of the theatre – the confrontation of man with the spheres of myth and religious reality. Like ancient Greek tragedy and the medieval mystery plays and baroque allegories, the Theatre of the Absurd is intent on making its audience aware of man's precarious and mysterious position in the universe.

The difference is merely that in ancient Greek tragedy – and comedy – as well as in the medieval mystery play and the baroque *auto sacramental*, the ultimate realities concerned were generally known and universally accepted metaphysical systems, while the Theatre of the Absurd expresses the absence of any such generally accepted cosmic system of values. Hence, much more modestly, the Theatre of the Absurd makes no pretence at explaining the ways of God to man. It can merely present, in anxiety or with derision, an individual human being's intuition of the ultimate realities as he experiences them; the fruits of one man's descent into the depths of his personality, his dreams, fantasies, and nightmares.

While former attempts at confronting man with the ultimate realities of his condition projected a coherent and generally recognized version of the truth, the Theatre of the Absurd merely communicates one poet's most intimate and personal intuition of the human situation, his own *sense of being*, his individual vision of the world. This is the *subject-matter* of the Theatre of the Absurd, and it determines its *form*, which must, of necessity, represent a convention of the stage basically different from the 'realistic' theatre of our time.

As the Theatre of the Absurd is not concerned with conveying information or presenting the problems or destinies of characters that exist outside the author's inner world, as it does not expound a thesis or debate ideological propositions, it is not concerned with the representation of events, the narration of the fate or the adventures of characters, but instead with the presentation of one individual's basic situation. It is a theatre of situation as against a theatre of events in sequence, and therefore it uses a language based on patterns of concrete images rather than argument and discursive speech. And since it is trying to present a sense of being, it can neither investigate nor solve problems of conduct or morals.

Because the Theatre of the Absurd projects its author's personal world, it lacks objectively valid characters. It cannot show the clash of opposing temperaments or study human passions locked in conflict, and is therefore not dramatic in the accepted sense of the term. Nor is it concerned with telling a story in order to communicate some moral or social lesson, as is the aim of Brecht's narrative, 'epic' theatre. The action in a play of the Theatre of the Absurd is not intended to tell a story but to communicate a pattern of poetic images. To give but one example: things happen in *Waiting for Godot*, but these happenings do not constitute a plot or story; they are an image of Beckett's intuition that *nothing really ever happens* in man's existence. The whole play is a complex poetic image made up of a complicated pattern of subsidiary images and themes, which are interwoven like the themes of a musical composition, not, as in most well-made plays, to present a line of development, but to make in the spectator's mind a total, complex impression of a basic, and static, situation. In this, the Theatre of the Absurd is analogous to a Symbolist or Imagist poem, which also presents a pattern of images and associations in a mutually interdependent structure.

While the Brechtian epic theatre tries to widen the range of drama by introducing narrative, epic elements, the Theatre of the Absurd aims at concentration and depth in an essentially lyrical, poetic pattern. Of course, dramatic, narrative, and lyrical elements are present in all drama. Brecht's own theatre, like Shakespeare's, contains lyrical inserts in the form of songs; even at their most didactic, Ibsen and Shaw are rich in purely poetic moments. The Theatre of the Absurd, however, in abandoning psychology, subtlety of characterization, and plot in the conventional sense, gives the poetical element an incomparably greater emphasis. While the play with a linear plot describes a development in time, in a dramatic form that presents a concretized poetic image the play's extension in time is purely incidental. Expressing an *intuition in depth*, it should ideally be apprehended *in a single moment*, and only because it is physically impossible to present so complex an image in an instant does it have to be spread over a period of time. The formal structure of such a play is, therefore, merely a device to express a complex total image by unfolding it in a sequence of interacting elements.

The endeavour to communicate a total sense of being is an attempt to present a truer picture of reality itself, reality as apprehended by an individual. The Theatre of the Absurd is the last link in a line of development that started with naturalism. The idealistic, Platonic belief in immutable essences – ideal forms that it was the artist's task to present in a purer state than they could ever be found in nature – foundered in the philosophy of Locke and Kant, which based reality on perception and the inner structure of the human mind. Art then became mere imitation of external nature. Yet the imitation of surfaces was bound to prove unsatisfying and this inevitably led to the next step – the exploration of the reality of the mind. Ibsen and Strindberg exemplified that development during the span of their own lifetimes' exploration of reality. James Joyce began with minutely realistic stories and ended up with the vast multiple structure of *Finnegans Wake*. The work of the dramatists of the Absurd continues the same development. Each of these plays is an answer to the questions 'How does this individual feel when confronted with the human situation? What is the basic mood in which he faces the world? What does it feel like to be he?' And the answer is a single, total, but complex and contradictory poetic image – one play – or a succession of such images, complementing each other – the dramatist's *œuvre*.

In apprehending the world at any one moment, we receive simultaneously a whole complex of different perceptions and feelings. We can only communicate this instantaneous vision by breaking it down into different elements which can then be built up into a sequence in time, in a sentence or series of sentences. To convert our perception into conceptual terms, into logical thought and language, we perform an operation analogous to that of the scanner that analyses the picture in a television camera into rows of single impulses. The poetic image, with its ambiguity and its simultaneous evocation of multiple elements of sense association, is one of the methods by which we can, however imperfectly, communicate the reality of our intuition of the world.

The highly eccentric German philosopher Ludwig Klages – who is almost totally unknown, and quite unjustly so, in the English-speaking world – formulated a psychology of perception based on the recognition that our senses present us with images (*Bilder*) built up of a multitude of simultaneous impressions that are subsequently analysed and disintegrated in the process of translation into conceptual thinking. For Klages, this is part of the insidious action of critical intellect upon the creative element of the mind – his philosophical *magnum opus* is called *Der Geist als Widersacher der Seele* (*The Intellect as Antagonist of the Soul*) – but however misguided his attempt to turn this opposition into a cosmic battle between the creative and the analytical may have been, the basic idea that conceptual and discursive thought impoverishes the ineffable fullness of the perceived image remains valid, at least as an illustration of the problem of what it is that is being communicated in poetic imagery.

And it is in this striving to communicate a basic and as yet undissolved totality of perception, an intuition of being, that we can find a key to the devaluation and disintegration of language in the Theatre of the Absurd. For if it is the translation of the total intuition of being into the logical and temporal sequence of conceptual thought that deprives it of its pristine complexity and poetic truth, it is understandable that the artist should try to find ways to circumvent this influence of discursive speech and logic. Here lies the chief difference between poetry and prose: poetry is ambiguous and associative, striving to approximate to the wholly unconceptual language of music. The Theatre of the Absurd, in carrying the same poetic endeavour into the concrete imagery of the stage, can go further than pure poetry in dispensing with logic, discursive thought, and language. The stage is a multidimensional medium; it allows the simultaneous use of visual elements, movement, light, and language. It is, therefore, particularly suited to the communication of complex images consisting of the contrapuntal interaction of all these elements.

In the 'literary' theatre, language remains the predominant component. In the anti-literary theatre of the circus or the music hall, language is reduced to a very subordinate role. The Theatre of the Absurd has regained the freedom of using language as merely one – sometimes dominant, sometimes submerged – component of its multidimensional poetic imagery. By putting the language of a scene in contrast to the action, by reducing it to meaningless patter, or by abandoning discursive logic for the poetic logic of association or assonance, the Theatre of the Absurd has opened up a new dimension of the stage.

In its devaluation of language, the Theatre of the Absurd is in tune with the trend of our time. As George Steiner pointed out in two radio talks entitled *The Retreat from the Word*, the devaluation of language is characteristic not only of the development of contemporary poetry or philosophical thought but, even more, of modern mathematics and the natural sciences. 'It is no paradox to assert', Steiner says, 'that much of reality now begins *outside* language.[1] . . . Large areas of meaningful experience now belong to non-verbal languages such as mathematics, formulae, and logical symbolism. Others belong to "anti-languages", such as the practice of non-objective art or atonal music. The world of the word has shrunk.'[2] Moreover, the abandonment of language as the best instrument of notation in the spheres of mathematics and symbolic logic goes hand in hand with a marked reduction in the popular belief in its practical usefulness. Language appears more and more as being in contradiction to reality. The trends of thought that have the greatest influence on contemporary popular thinking all show this tendency.

Take the case of Marxism. Here a distinction is made between *apparent* social relations and the social *reality* behind them. Objectively, an employer is seen as an exploiter, and therefore an enemy, of the working class. If an employer therefore says to a worker, 'I have sympathy with your point of view,' he may himself believe what he is saying, but objectively his words are meaningless. However much he asserts his sympathy for the worker, he remains his enemy. Language here belongs to the realm of the purely subjective, and is thus devoid of objective reality.

The same applies to modern depth psychology and psychoanalysis. Every child today knows that there is a vast gap between what is consciously thought and asserted and the

1. George Steiner, 'The retreat from the word: I', *Listener*, London, 14 July 1960.
2. Steiner, 'The retreat from the word: II', loc. cit., 21 July 1960.

psychological reality behind the words spoken. A son who tells his father that he loves and respects him is objectively bound to be, in fact, filled with the deepest Oedipal hatred of his father. He may not know it, but he means the opposite of what he says. And the subconscious has a higher content of reality than the conscious utterance.

The relativization, devaluation, and criticism of language are also the prevailing trends in contemporary philosophy, as exemplified by Wittgenstein's conviction, in the last phase of his thinking, that the philosopher must endeavour to disentangle thought from the conventions and rules of grammar, which have been mistaken for the rules of logic.

A *picture* held us captive. And we could not get outside it, for it lay in our language, and language seemed to repeat it to us inexorably. ... Where does our investigation get its importance from, since it seems only to destroy everything interesting; that is, all that is great and important? (As it were, all the buildings, leaving behind only bits of stone and rubble.) What we are destroying is nothing but houses of cards, and we are clearing up the ground of language on which they stand.[1]

By a strict criticism of language, Wittgenstein's followers have declared large categories of statements to be devoid of objective meaning. Wittgenstein's 'word games' have much in common with the Theatre of the Absurd.

But even more significant than these tendencies in Marxist, psychological, and philosophical thinking is the trend of the times in the workaday world of the man in the street. Exposed to the incessant, and inexorably loquacious, onslaught of the mass media, the press, and advertising, the man in the street becomes more and more sceptical toward the language he is exposed to. The citizens of totalitarian countries know full well that most of what they are told is double-talk, devoid of

1. Ludwig Wittgenstein, *Philosophical Investigations: I* (Oxford: Blackwell, 1958), pp. 48–48e.

real meaning. They become adept at reading between the lines; that is, at guessing at the reality the language conceals rather than reveals. In the West, euphemisms and circumlocutions fill the press or resound from the pulpits. And advertising, by its constant use of superlatives, has succeeded in devaluing language to a point where it is a generally accepted axiom that most of the words one sees displayed on billboards or in the coloured pages of magazine advertising are as meaningless as the jingles of television commercials. A yawning gulf has opened between language and reality.

Apart from the general devaluation of language in the flood of mass communications, the growing specialization of life has made the exchange of ideas on an increasing number of subjects impossible between members of different spheres of life which have each developed their own specialized jargons. As Ionesco says, in summarizing, and enlarging on, the views of Antonin Artaud:

As our knowledge becomes separated from life, our culture no longer contains ourselves (or only an insignificant part of ourselves), for it forms a 'social' context into which we are not integrated. So the problem becomes that of bringing our life back into contact with our culture, making it a living culture once again. To achieve this, we shall first have to kill 'the respect for what is written down in black and white' . . . to break up our language so that it can be put together again in order to re-establish contact with 'the absolute', or, as I should prefer to say, 'with multiple reality'; it is imperative to 'push human beings again towards seeing themselves as they really are'.[1]

That is why communication between human beings is so often shown in a state of breakdown in the Theatre of the Absurd. It is merely a satirical magnification of the existing state of affairs. Language has run riot in an age of mass communication. It must be reduced to its proper function – the expression of authentic content, rather than its concealment.

1. Ionesco, 'Ni un dieu, ni un démon', Cahiers de la Compagnie Madeleine Renaud – Jean-Louis Barrault, Paris, nos. 22–3, May 1958, p. 131.

But this will be possible only if man's reverence toward the spoken or written word as a means of communication is restored, and the ossified clichés that dominate thought (as they do in the limericks of Edward Lear or the world of Humpty Dumpty) are replaced by a living language that serves it. And this, in turn, can be achieved only if the limitations of logic and discursive language are recognized and respected, and the uses of poetic language acknowledged.

The means by which the dramatists of the Absurd express their critique – largely instinctive and unintended – of our disintegrating society are based on suddenly confronting their audiences with a grotesquely heightened and distorted picture of a world that has gone mad. This is a shock therapy that achieves what Brecht's doctrine of the 'alienation effect' postulated in theory but failed to achieve in practice – the inhibition of the audience's identification with the characters on the stage (which is the age-old and highly effective method of the traditional theatre) and its replacement by a detached, critical attitude.

If we identify ourselves with the main character in a play, we automatically accept his point of view, see the world in which he moves with *his* eyes, feel *his* emotions. From the standpoint of a didactic, Socialist theatre, Brecht argued that this time-honoured psychological link between the actor and the audience must be broken. How could an audience be made to see the actions of the characters in a play *critically* if they were made to adopt their points of view? Hence Brecht, in his Marxist period, tried to introduce a number of devices designed to break this spell. Yet he never completely succeeded in achieving his aim. The audience, in spite of the introduction of songs, slogans, nonrepresentational décor, and other inhibiting devices, continues to identify with Brecht's brilliantly drawn characters and therefore often tends to miss the critical attitude Brecht wanted it to assume toward them. The old magic of the theatre is too strong; the pull toward identification, which springs from a basic psychological characteristic of human nature, is overwhelming. If we see Mother Courage weep for her son, we cannot resist feeling her sorrow and therefore fail to condemn her for her acceptance of war as a business, which inevitably leads to the loss of her children. The finer the characterization of a human being on the stage, the more inevitable is this process of identification.

In the Theatre of the Absurd, on the other hand, the audience is confronted with characters whose motives and actions remain largely incomprehensible. With such characters it is almost impossible to identify; the more mysterious their action and their nature, the less human the characters become, the more difficult it is to be carried away into seeing the world from their point of view. Characters with whom the audience fails to identify are inevitably comic. If we identified with the figure of farce who loses his trousers, we should feel embarrassment and shame. If, however, our tendency to identify has been inhibited by making such a character grotesque, we laugh at his predicament. We see what happens to him from the outside, rather than from his own point of view. As the incomprehensibility of the motives, and the often unexplained and mysterious nature of the characters' actions in the Theatre of the Absurd effectively prevent identification, such theatre is a comic theatre in spite of the fact that its subject-matter is sombre, violent, and bitter. That is why the Theatre of the Absurd transcends the category of comedy and tragedy and combines laughter with horror.

But, by its very nature, it cannot provoke the thoughtful attitude of detached social criticism that was Brecht's objective. It does not present its audience with sets of social facts and examples of political behaviour. It presents the audience with a picture of a disintegrating world that has lost its unifying principle, its meaning, and its purpose – an absurd universe. What is the audience to make of this bewildering confrontation with a truly alienated world that, having lost its rational principle, has in the true sense of the word gone mad?

Here we are face to face with the central problem of the effect, the aesthetic efficacy and validity, of the Theatre of the Absurd. It is an empirical fact that, in defiance of most of the accepted rules of drama, the best plays of this kind are effective as theatre – the convention of the Absurd *works*. But *why* does it work? To some extent, the answer has been given in the foregoing account of the nature of comic and farcical effects. The misfortunes of characters we view with a cold, critical, unidentified eye *are* funny. Stupid characters who act in mad ways have always been the butt of derisive laughter in the circus, the music hall, and the theatre. But such comic characters usually appeared in a rational framework, and were set off by positive characters with whom the audience could identify. In the Theatre of the Absurd, the whole of the action is mysterious, unmotivated, and at first sight nonsensical.

The alienation effect in the Brechtian theatre is intended to activate the audience's critical, intellectual attitude. The Theatre of the Absurd speaks to a deeper level of the audience's mind. It activates psychological forces, releases and liberates hidden fears and repressed aggressions, and, above all, by confronting the audience with a picture of disintegration, it sets in motion an active process of integrative forces in the mind of each individual spectator.

As Eva Metman says in her remarkable essay on Beckett:

In times of religious containment, [dramatic art] has shown man as protected, guided, and sometimes punished by [archetypal] powers, but in other epochs it has shown the visible tangible world, in which man fulfils his destiny, as permeated by the demonic essences of his invisible and intangible being. In contemporary drama, a new, third orientation is crystallizing in which man is shown not in a world into which the divine or demonic powers are projected but alone with them. This new form of drama forces the audience out of its familiar orientation. It creates a vacuum between the play and the audience so that the latter is compelled to experience something itself, be it a reawakening of the awareness of archetypal powers or a reorientation of the ego, or both . . .[1]

One need not be a Jungian or use Jungian categories to see the force of this diagnosis. Human beings who in their daily lives confront a world that has split up into a series of disconnected fragments and lost its purpose, but who are no longer aware of this state of affairs and its disintegrating effect on their personalities, are brought face to face with a heightened representation of this schizophrenic universe. 'The vacuum between what is shown on the stage and the onlooker has become so unbearable that the latter has no alternative but either to reject and turn away or to be drawn into the enigma of the plays in which nothing reminds him of any of his purposes in and reactions to the world around him.'[2] Once drawn into the mystery of the play, the spectator is compelled to come to terms with his experience. The stage supplies him with a number of disjointed clues that he has to fit into a meaningful pattern. In this manner, he is forced to make a creative effort of his own, an effort at interpretation and integration. The time has been made to appear out of joint; the audience of the Theatre of the Absurd is being compelled to set it right, or, rather, by being made to see that the world has become absurd, in acknowledging that fact takes the first step in coming to terms with reality.

The madness of the times lies precisely in the existence, side by side, of a large number of unreconciled beliefs and attitudes – conventional morality, for example, on the one hand, and the values of advertising on the other; the conflicting claims of science and religion; or the loudly proclaimed striving of all sections for the general interest when in fact each is pursuing very narrow and selfish particular ends. On each page of his newspaper, the man in the street is confronted with a different and contradictory pattern of values. No wonder that the art of

1. Eva Metman, 'Reflections on Samuel Beckett's plays', *Journal of Analytical Psychology*, London, January 1960, p. 43.
2. ibid.

such an era shows a marked resemblance to the symptoms of schizophrenia. But it is not, as Jung pointed out in an essay on Joyce's *Ulysses*, the artist who is schizophrenic: 'The medical description of schizophrenia offers only an analogy, in that the schizophrenic has apparently the same tendency to treat reality as if it were strange to him, or, the other way around, to estrange himself from reality. In the modern artist, this tendency is not produced by any disease in the individual but is a manifestation of our time.'[1]

The challenge to make sense out of what appears as a senseless and fragmented action, the recognition that the fact that the modern world has lost its unifying principle is the source of its bewildering and soul-destroying quality, is therefore more than a mere intellectual exercise; it has a therapeutic effect. In Greek tragedy, the spectators were made aware of man's forlorn but heroic stand against the inexorable forces of fate and the will of the gods – and this had a cathartic effect upon them and made them better able to face their time. In the Theatre of the Absurd, the spectator is confronted with the madness of the human condition, is enabled to see his situation in all its grimness and despair. Stripped of illusions and vaguely felt fears and anxieties, he can face this situation consciously, rather than feeling it vaguely below the surface of euphemisms and optimistic illusions. By seeing his anxieties formulated he can liberate himself from them. This is the nature of all the gallows humour and *humour noir* of world literature, of which the Theatre of the Absurd is the latest example. It is the unease caused by the presence of illusions that are obviously out of tune with reality that is dissolved and discharged through liberating laughter at the recognition of the fundamental absurdity of the universe. The greater the anxieties and the temptation to indulge in illusions, the more beneficial is this therapeutic effect – hence the success of *Waiting for Godot* at San Quentin. It was a relief for the convicts to be made to recognize

1. Jung, 'Ulysses', quoted by Metman, loc. cit., p. 53.

in the tragicomic situation of the tramps the hopelessness of their own waiting for a miracle. They were enabled to laugh at the tramps – and at themselves.

As the reality with which the Theatre of the Absurd is concerned is a psychological reality expressed in images that are the outward projection of states of mind, fears, dreams, nightmares, and conflicts within the personality of the author, the dramatic tension produced by this kind of play differs fundamentally from the suspense created in a theatre concerned mainly with the revelation of objective characters through the unfolding of a narrative plot. The pattern of exposition, conflict, and final solution mirrors a view of the world in which solutions are possible, a view based on a recognizable and generally accepted pattern of an objective reality that can be apprehended so that the purpose of man's existence and the rules of conduct it entails can be deduced from it.

This is true even of the lightest type of drawing-room comedy, in which the action proceeds on a deliberately restricted view of the world – that the sole purpose of the characters involved is for each boy to get his girl. And even in the darkest pessimistic tragedies of the naturalistic or Expressionist theatres, the final curtain enables the audience to go home with a formulated message or philosophy in their minds: the solution may have been a sad one, but it was a rationally formulated conclusion nevertheless. This, as I pointed out in the introduction, applies even to the theatre of Sartre and Camus, which is based on a philosophy of the absurdity of human existence. Even plays like *Huis Clos*, *Le Diable et le Bon Dieu* (*Lucifer and the Lord*), and *Caligula* allow the audience to take home an intellectually formulated philosophical lesson.

The Theatre of the Absurd, however, which proceeds not by intellectual concepts but by poetic images, neither poses an intellectual problem in its exposition nor provides any clear-cut solution that would be reducible to a lesson or an apophthegm. Many of the plays of the Theatre of the Absurd have a circular structure, ending exactly as they began; others progress merely by a growing intensification of the initial situation. And as the Theatre of the Absurd rejects the idea that it is possible to motivate all human behaviour, or that human character is based on an immutable essence, it is impossible for it to base its effect on the suspense that in other dramatic conventions springs from awaiting the solution of a dramatic equation based on the working out of a problem involving clearly defined quantities introduced in the opening scenes. In most dramatic conventions, the audience is constantly asking itself the question 'What is going to happen next?'

In the Theatre of the Absurd, the audience is confronted with actions that lack apparent motivation, characters that are in constant flux, and often happenings that are clearly outside the realm of rational experience. Here, too, the audience can ask, 'What is going to happen next?' But then *anything* may happen next, so that the answer to this question cannot be worked out according to the rules of ordinary probability based on motives and characterizations that will remain constant throughout the play. The relevant question here is not so much what is going to happen next but what *is* happening? 'What does the action of the play represent?'

This constitutes a different, but by no means less valid, kind of dramatic suspense. Instead of being provided with a *solution*, the spectator is challenged to formulate the *questions* that he will have to ask if he wants to approach the meaning of the play. The total action of the play, instead of proceeding from point A to point B, as in other dramatic conventions, gradually builds up the complex pattern of the *poetic image* that the play expresses. The spectator's suspense consists in waiting for the gradual completion of this pattern which will enable him to see the image as a whole. And only when that image is assembled – after the final curtain – can he *begin* to explore, not so much its meaning as its structure, texture, and impact.

It is certainly arguable that this new kind of suspense represents a higher level of dramatic tension and evokes a more satisfying, because more challenging, aesthetic experience in the audience. Of course, the poetic qualities of great drama, of Shakespeare, Ibsen, and Chekhov, have always provided the audience with a deeply complex pattern of poetic association and significance; however simple the motivations may appear to be on the surface, the profound intuition with which the characters are drawn, the multiple planes on which the action proceeds, the complex quality of truly poetic language combine in a pattern that transcends any attempt at a simple and rational apprehension of the action or its solution. The suspense in a play like *Hamlet* or *The Three Sisters* does *not* lie in an anxious expectation of how these plays will *end*. Their eternal freshness and power lie in the inexhaustible quality of the poetic and infinitely ambiguous image of the human condition they present. In a play like *Hamlet*, we do indeed ask, 'What is happening?' And the answer clearly is that it is not just a dynastic conflict or a series of murders and sword fights. We are confronted with a projection of a psychological reality and with human archetypes shrouded in perpetual mystery.

This is the element that the Theatre of the Absurd has tried to make the core of its dramatic convention (without making any claim at reaching the heights the greatest dramatists have attained by their intuition and the richness of their creative capacity). If Ionesco, in seeking to trace the tradition to which he belongs, singles out the scenes of Richard II's loneliness and degradation, it is because they are such poetic images of the human condition:

All men die in solitude; all values are degraded in a state of misery: that is what Shakespeare tells me. . . . Perhaps Shakespeare wanted to relate the story of Richard II: if he had narrated merely that, the *story of another human being*, it would not have moved me. But Richard II's prison is not a truth that has been overtaken by the flow of history. Its invisible walls still stand, while so many philosophies, so many ideologies have crumbled forever. All this endures because this language is the language of living evidence, and not that of discursive and demonstrative thought. It is the theatre which provides this eternal and living presence; it corresponds, without doubt, to the essential structure of the tragic truth, of stage reality. ... This is a matter of archetypes of the theatre, of the essence of the theatre, of the language of the theatre.[1]

It is this language of stage images that embody a truth beyond the power of mere discursive thought which the Theatre of the Absurd places at the centre of its endeavour to build a new dramatic convention, subordinating all other elements of stagecraft to it.

But if the Theatre of the Absurd concentrates on the power of stage imagery, on the projection of visions of the world dredged up from the depth of the subconscious; if it neglects the rationally measurable ingredients of the theatre – the highly polished carpentry of plot and counterplot of the well-made play, the imitation of reality which can be measured against reality itself, the clever motivation of character – how can it be judged by rational analysis, how can it be subjected to criticism by objectively valid standards? If it is a purely subjective expression of its author's vision and emotion, how can the public distinguish the genuine, deeply felt work of art from mere impostures?

These are the old questions that have been asked about each phase in the development of modern art and literature. That they are questions of real relevance is clear to anyone who has seen the bewildered attempts of professional critics to come to terms with works in any of these new conventions – the art critics who miss the quality of 'classical beauty' in Picasso's grimmer pictures, as well as the drama critics who dismiss Ionesco or Beckett because their characters lack verisimilitude or transgress the rules of polite behaviour that are to be expected in drawing-room comedy.

1. Ionesco, 'Expérience du théâtre', Nouvelle Revue Française, Paris, 1 February 1958, p. 226.

But all art is subjective, and the standards against which the critics measure success or failure are always worked out *a posteriori* from an analysis of accepted and empirically successful works. In the case of a phenomenon like the Theatre of the Absurd, which is the outcome not of the conscious pursuit of a collectively worked-out programme or theory (as the Romantic movement was, for example) but of an unpremeditated response by a number of independent authors to tendencies inherent in the general movement of thought in a period of transition, we have to analyse the works themselves and find the tendencies and modes of thought they express, in order to gain a picture of their artistic purpose. And once we have gained a clear idea of their general tendency and aim, we can arrive at a perfectly valid judgement of how they measure up to what they have set out to do.

If in the course of this book, therefore, we have established that the Theatre of the Absurd is concerned essentially with the evocation of concrete poetic images designed to communicate to the audience the sense of perplexity that their authors feel when confronted with the human condition, we must judge the success or failure of these works by the degree to which they succeed in communicating this mixture of poetry and grotesque, tragicomic horror. And this in turn will depend on the quality and power of the poetic images evoked.

How can we assess the quality of a poetic image or a complex pattern of such images? Of course, as in the criticism of poetry, there will always be a subjective element of taste or personal responsiveness to certain associations, but on the whole it is possible to apply objective standards. These standards are based on such elements as suggestive power, originality of invention, and the psychological truth of the images concerned; on their depth and universality; and on the degree of skill with which they are translated into stage terms. The superiority of complex images like the tramps waiting for Godot, or the proliferation of chairs in Ionesco's masterpiece, over some of the more childish pranks of the early Dadaist theatre is as evident as the superiority of Eliot's *Four Quartets* over the doggerel on a Christmas card, and for the same self-evident and purely objective reasons – higher complexity, greater depth, more brilliant and sustained invention, and infinitely greater craftsmanship. Adamov himself rightly puts a play like *Le Professeur Taranne* above a play on a similar subject like *Les Retrouvailles* because the former sprang from a genuine dream image while the latter was artificially contrived. The criterion here is that of psychological truth, and even if we did not have the author's own evidence, we could deduce the greater psychological truth, and hence the greater validity, of *Le Professeur Taranne* from an analysis of its imagery. It is clearly more organic, less symmetrical, and less mechanically constructed, far more intense and coherent, than the imagery of the later play.

Touchstones of judgement such as these – depth, originality of invention, psychological truth – may not perhaps be reducible to quantitative terms, but they are no less objective than the same criteria applied to making the distinction between a Rembrandt and a mannerist painting, or between a poem of Pope's and one of Settle's.

Valid criteria certainly exist to assess the success of works within the category of the Theatre of the Absurd. It is more difficult to place the best works in this convention into a general hierarchy of dramatic art as a whole, but this, in any case, is an impossible task. Is Raphael a greater painter than Brueghel, Miró a greater painter than Murillo? While it is clearly futile to argue, as is so often done in discussing abstract painting or the works of the Theatre of the Absurd, whether such apparently effortless products of the imagination deserve the title of works of art simply because they lack the sheer effort and ingenuity that go into a group portrait or a well-made play, it is worthwhile to refute some of these popular misconceptions.

It is *not* true that it is infinitely more difficult to construct a rational plot than to summon up the irrational imagery of a play of the Theatre of the Absurd, just as it is quite untrue that any child could draw as well as Klee or Picasso. There is an immense difference between artistically and dramatically valid nonsense and just nonsense. Anyone who has seriously tried to write nonsense verse or to devise a nonsense play will confirm the truth of this assertion. In constructing a realistic plot, as in painting from a model, there is always reality itself and the writer's own experience and observation to fall back on – characters one has known, events one has witnessed. Writing in a medium in which there is complete freedom of invention, on the other hand, requires the ability to *create* images and situations that have no counterpart in nature while, at the same time, establishing a world of its own, with its own inherent logic and consistency, which will be instantly acceptable to the audience. Mere combinations of incongruities produce mere banality. Anyone attempting to work in this medium simply by writing down what comes into his mind will find that the supposed flights of spontaneous invention have never left the ground, that they consist of incoherent fragments of reality that have not been transposed into a valid imaginative whole. Unsuccessful examples of the Theatre of the Absurd, like unsuccessful abstract paintings, are usually characterized by the transparent way in which they still bear the mark of the fragments of reality from which they are made up. They have not undergone that sea change through which the merely *negative* quality of *lack* of logic or verisimilitude is transmuted into the *positive* quality of a new world that makes imaginative sense in its own right.

Here we have one of the real hallmarks of excellence in the Theatre of the Absurd. Only when its invention springs from deep layers of profoundly experienced emotion, only when it mirrors real obsessions, dreams, and valid images in the subconscious mind of its author, will such a work of art have that quality of truth, of instantly recognized general, as distinct from merely private, validity that distinguishes the vision of a poet from the delusions of the mentally afflicted. This quality of depth and unity of vision is instantly recognizable and beyond trickery. No degree of technical accomplishment and mere cleverness can here, as in the sphere of representational art or drama, cover up the poverty of the inner core of the work in question.

To write a well-made problem play or a witty comedy of manners may therefore be more laborious or require a higher degree of ingenuity or intelligence. On the other hand, to invent a generally valid poetic image of the human condition requires unusual depth of feeling and intensity of emotion, and a far higher degree of genuinely creative vision – in short, inspiration. It is a widespread but vulgar fallacy that bases a hierarchy of artistic achievement on the mere difficulty or laboriousness of the process of composition. If it were not futile from the outset to argue in terms of position on a scale of values, such a scale could be based only on the quality, the universal validity, the depth of vision and insight of the work itself, whether or not it was produced in decades of patient plodding or in a flash of inspiration.

The criteria of achievement in the Theatre of the Absurd are not only the quality of invention, the complexity of the poetic images evoked, and the skill with which they are combined and sustained but also, and even more essentially, the *reality* and *truth* of the vision these images embody. For all its freedom of invention and spontaneity, the Theatre of the Absurd is concerned with communicating an experience of being, and in doing so it is trying to be uncompromisingly honest and fearless in exposing the reality of the human condition.

This is the consideration from which it is possible to resolve the controversy between the 'realistic' theatre and the Theatre of the Absurd. Kenneth Tynan rightly argued in his debate with Ionesco that he expected what an artist communicated *to be true*. But Ionesco, in asserting that he was concerned with communicating *his personal vision*, in no way contradicted Tynan's postulate. Ionesco also strives to tell the truth – the truth about his intuition of the human condition. The truthful exploration of a psychological, inner reality is in no way less true than the exploration of an outward objective reality. Indeed, the reality of vision is more immediate and nearer to the core of experience than any description of an objective reality. Is a painting of a sunflower by van Gogh less real, less objectively true, than a picture of a sunflower in a textbook of botany? In some senses, perhaps, but certainly not in others. And the van Gogh painting will have a higher level of truth and reality than any scientific illustration, even if van Gogh's sunflower has the wrong number of petals.

Realities of vision and perception are as real as quantitatively verifiable external realities. There is no real contradiction between what claims to be a theatre of objective reality and a theatre of subjective reality. Both are equally realistic – but concerned with different aspects of reality in its vast complexity.

This also disposes of the apparent conflict between an ideological, politically oriented theatre and the seemingly apolitical, anti-ideological Theatre of the Absurd. A *pièce à thèse* on, say, as important a subject as capital punishment will try to present a set of arguments and circumstances to illustrate its case. If the circumstances presented are *true*, the play will be convincing. If they are obviously biased and manipulated, it will fail. But the test of the truth of the play must lie ultimately in its ability to communicate the truth of the *experience* of the characters involved. And here the test of its truth and realism will ultimately coincide with its *inner reality*. However correct the statistics and descriptive details of the play may be, its dramatic truth will depend on the author's ability to convey the victim's fear of death, the human reality of his predicament. And here, too, the test of truth will lie in the creative ability, the poetic imagination of the author. And this is precisely the criterion by which we can judge the truth of the wholly subjective creations of a theatre not concerned with social realities.

The contradiction does not lie between realistic and unrealistic, objective and subjective, theatre but merely between poetic vision, poetic truth, and imaginative reality on the one hand, and arid, mechanical, lifeless, poetically untrue writing on the other. A *pièce à thèse* written by a great poet like Brecht is as true as an exploration of private nightmares like Ionesco's *The Chairs*. And paradoxically some play by Brecht in which the poet's truth has proved stronger than the thesis may be *politically* less effective than that very play by Ionesco, which does attack the absurdities of polite society and bourgeois conversation.

In trying to deal with the ultimates of the human condition not in terms of intellectual understanding but in terms of communicating a metaphysical truth through a living experience, the Theatre of the Absurd touches the religious sphere. There is a vast difference between *knowing* something to be the case in the conceptual sphere and *experiencing* it as a living reality. It is the mark of all great religions that they not only possess a body of knowledge that can be taught in the form of cosmological information or ethical rules but that they also communicate the essence of this body of doctrine in the living, recurring poetic imagery of ritual. It is the loss of the latter sphere, which responds to a deep inner need in all human beings, that the decline of religion has left as a deeply felt deficiency in our civilization. We possess at least an approximation to a coherent philosophy in the scientific method, but we lack the means to make it a living reality, an experienced focus of men's lives. That is why the theatre, a place where men congregate to experience poetic or artistic insights, has in many ways assumed the function of a substitute church. Hence the immense importance placed upon the theatre by totalitarian creeds, which are fully aware of the need to make their doctrines a living, experienced reality to their followers.

The Theatre of the Absurd, paradoxical though this may appear at first sight, can be seen as an attempt to communicate the metaphysical experience behind the scientific attitude and, at the same time, to supplement it by rounding off the partial view of the world it presents, and integrating it in a wider vision of the world and its mystery.

For if the Theatre of the Absurd presents the world as senseless and lacking a unifying principle, it does so merely in the terms of those philosophies that start from the idea that human thought *can* reduce the totality of the universe to a complete, unified, coherent system. It is only from the point of view of those who cannot bear a world where it is impossible to know why it was created, what part man has been assigned in it, and what constitutes right actions and wrong actions, that a picture of the universe lacking all these clear-cut definitions appears deprived of sense and sanity, and tragically absurd. The modern scientific attitude, however, rejects the postulate of a wholly coherent and simplified explanation that must account for all the phenomena, purposes, and moral rules of the world. In concentrating on the slow, painstaking exploration of limited areas of reality by trial and error – by the construction, testing, and discarding of hypotheses – the scientific attitude cheerfully accepts the view that we must be able to live with the realization that large segments of knowledge and experience will remain for a long time, perhaps forever, outside our ken; that ultimate purposes cannot, and never will be, known; and that we must therefore be able to accept the fact that much that earlier metaphysical systems, mythical, religious, or philosophical, sought to explain must forever remain unexplained. From this point of view, any clinging to systems of thought that provide, or purport to provide, complete explanations of the world and man's place in it must appear childish and immature, a flight from reality into illusion and self-deception.

The Theatre of the Absurd expresses the anxiety and despair that spring from the recognition that man is surrounded by areas of impenetrable darkness, that he can never know his true nature and purpose, and that no one will provide him with ready-made rules of conduct. As Camus says in *The Myth of Sisyphus:*

The certainty of the existence of a God who would give meaning to life has a far greater attraction than the knowledge that without him one could do evil without being punished. The choice between these alternatives would not be difficult. But there is no choice, and that is where the bitterness begins.[1]

But by facing up to anxiety and despair and the absence of divinely revealed alternatives, anxiety and despair can be overcome. The sense of loss at the disintegration of facile solutions and the disappearance of cherished illusions retains its sting only while the mind still clings to the illusions concerned. Once they are given up, we have to readjust ourselves to the new situation and face reality itself. And because the illusions we suffered from made it more difficult for us to deal with reality, their loss will ultimately be felt as exhilarating. In the words of Democritus that Beckett is fond of quoting, 'Nothing is more real than Nothing.'

To confront the limits of the human condition is not only equivalent to facing up to the philosophical basis of the scientific attitude, it is also a profound mystical experience. It is precisely this experience of the ineffability, the emptiness, the nothingness at the basis of the universe that forms the content of Eastern as well as Christian mystical experience. For if Lao-tzu says, 'It was from the nameless that Heaven and Earth sprang, the named is but the mother that rears the ten thousand creatures, each after its kind',[2] St John of the Cross speaks of the soul's intuition 'that it cannot comprehend God at all',[3] and Meister Eckhart expresses the same experience in the words,

1. *Le Mythe de Sisyphe*, p. 94.
2. Lao-tzu, quoted in Aldous Huxley, *The Perennial Philosophy* (London: Chatto & Windus, 1946), p. 33.
3. St John of the Cross, quoted in Huxley, op. cit.

'The Godhead is poor, naked, and empty, as though it were not; it has not, wills not, wants not, works not, gets not. . . . The Godhead is as void as though it were not.'[1] In other words, in facing man's inability ever to comprehend the meaning of the universe, in recognizing the Godhead's total transcendence, his total otherness from all we can understand with our senses, the great mystics experienced a sense of exhilaration and liberation. This exhilaration also springs from the recognition that the language and logic of cognitive thought cannot do justice to the ultimate nature of reality. Hence a profoundly mystical philosophy like Zen Buddhism bases itself on the rejection of conceptual thinking itself:

> The denying of reality is the asserting of it,
> And the asserting of emptiness is the denying of it.[2]

The recent rise of interest in Zen in Western countries is an expression of the same tendencies that explain the success of the Theatre of the Absurd – a preoccupation with ultimate realities and a recognition that they are not approachable through conceptual thought alone. Ionesco has been quoted as drawing a parallel between the method of the Zen Buddhists and the Theatre of the Absurd,[3] and in fact the teaching methods of the Zen masters, their use of kicks and blows in reply to questions about the nature of enlightenment and their setting of nonsense problems, closely resemble some of the procedures of the Theatre of the Absurd.

Seen from this angle the dethronement of language and logic forms part of an essentially mystical attitude toward the basis of reality as being too complex and at the same time too unified, too much of one piece, to be validly expressed by the analytical means of orderly syntax and conceptual thought. As

1. Meister Eckhart, quoted in Huxley, op. cit.
2. Seng-t'san, 'On believing in mind', quoted in Suzuki, *Manual of Zen Buddhism* (London: Rider, 1950), p. 77.
3. Ionesco, quoted in Towarnicki, *Spectacles*, Paris, no. 2, July 1958.

the mystics resort to poetic images, so does the Theatre of the Absurd. But if the Theatre of the Absurd presents analogies with the methods and imagery of mysticism, how can it, at the same time, be regarded as expressing the scepticism, the humble refusal to provide an explanation of absolutes, that characterize the scientific attitude?

The answer is simply that there is no contradiction between recognizing the limitations of man's ability to comprehend all of reality in a single system of values and recognizing the mysterious and ineffable oneness, beyond all rational comprehension, that, once experienced, gives serenity of mind and the strength to face the human condition. These are in fact two sides of the same medal – the mystical experience of the absolute otherness and ineffability of ultimate reality is the religious, poetic counterpart to the rational recognition of the limitation of man's senses and intellect, which reduces him to exploring the world slowly by trial and error. Both these attitudes are in basic contradiction to systems of thought, religious or ideological (e.g. Marxism), that claim to provide complete answers to all questions of ultimate purpose and day-to-day conduct.

The realization that thinking in poetic images has its validity side by side with conceptual thought and the insistence on a clear recognition of the function and possibilities of each mode does not amount to a return to irrationalism; on the contrary, it opens the way to a truly rational attitude.

Ultimately, a phenomenon like the Theatre of the Absurd does not reflect despair or a return to dark irrational forces but expresses modern man's endeavour to come to terms with the world in which he lives. It attempts to make him face up to the human condition as it really is, to free him from illusions that are bound to cause constant maladjustment and disappointment. There are enormous pressures in our world that seek to induce mankind to bear the loss of faith and moral certainties by being drugged into oblivion – by mass entertainments, shallow material satisfactions, pseudo-explanations of reality, and cheap ideologies. At the end of that road lies Huxley's Brave New World of senseless euphoric automata. Today, when death and old age are increasingly concealed behind euphemisms and comforting baby talk, and life is threatened with being smothered in the mass consumption of hypnotic mechanized vulgarity, the need to confront man with the reality of his situation is greater than ever. For the dignity of man lies in his ability to face reality in all its senselessness; to accept it freely, without fear, without illusions – and to laugh at it.

That is the cause to which, in their various individual, modest, and quixotic ways, the dramatists of the Absurd are dedicated.

9

BEYOND THE ABSURD

THE major dramatists dealt with in this book emerged into the theatre in the late 1940's and early 1950's; by the late fifties and early sixties they had become famous, successful and established and exerted considerable influence on younger playwrights.

By the middle sixties the situation was bound to change. Had the Theatre of the Absurd spent itself, had it become no more than yesterday's fashion?

In so far as it was a fashion, this is certainly so. And undoubtedly any new approach generates a fashion among audiences, critics, and indeed among writers. At any given time the manuscripts which reach producers and publishers clearly show the mark of the prevailing fashion. There is nothing discreditable about this: the movement of fashions in art as well as in clothes is one of society's mechanisms by which changes in basic attitudes are spread throughout its ranks. From some points of view *every* artistic movement or style has at one time or another been the prevailing fashion. If it was no more than that, it disappeared without a trace. If it had a genuine content, if it contributed to an enlargement of human perception, if it created new modes of human expression, if it opened up new areas of experience, however, it was bound to be absorbed into the main stream of development.

And this is what happened with the Theatre of the Absurd which, apart from having been in fashion, undoubtedly *was* a genuine contribution to the permanent vocabulary of dramatic expression.

New theatrical devices, new approaches to language, character, plot and construction of plays are necessary to the continued vitality of the theatre. Surprise, shock, the gasp of incomprehension are among the most powerful weapons in the armoury of the stage. But the more astonishing and surprising such devices are, the more quickly they use themselves up. Already the audience of the second performance of *Waiting for Godot* could not entirely relive the shock of novelty which the first-night audience had experienced, because many members of that second-night audience must already have heard about the play or read about it in the newspapers. (Hence first nights have been regarded as something special ever since the beginning of theatre.) It is therefore quite natural that many of the devices and inventions of the dramatists of the Absurd no longer appear as shocking and surprising. They have indeed become part of the everyday vocabulary of playwriting in general. If a playwright like John Osborne, who usually works in a quite different convention, quite naturally starts a play like *Inadmissible Evidence* (1964) with a dream-sequence and no one in the audience is shocked or surprised by such a device, this illustrates the degree to which the innovations of the dramatists of the Absurd have become integrated into the mainstream of dramatic technique. The playwrights of the mid-sixties were in a position to make use of the dramatic vocabulary developed by the Absurdists, the audiences of the mid-sixties had learned to understand and to accept that vocabulary, as indeed they had learned to respond to the dramatic vocabulary of the epic theatre of Brecht, which had been as unusual and as shocking at an earlier date.

The Brechtian theatre, intent on making the stage into a platform for social research and experimentation, had developed a valid new vocabulary for presenting the *external* reality of our world, more efficiently perhaps than the photographic illusionism of the post-naturalistic theatre would have been capable of presenting it; the Absurdists on the other hand developed a vocabulary and a stage convention capable of putting on to the stage an *internal psychological* reality, an inscape of the mind. For those who experience them, dreams, daydreams, fantasies, nightmares and hallucinations are realities as significant, as terrifying, as decisive for their lives as any external realities. And insights into the working of other people's dreams and fantasies can be as emotionally satisfying, as fascinating and as cathartic as insights into the external circumstances of their lives.

The playwrights of the post-Brechtian and the post-Absurdist era have at their disposal, then, a uniquely enriched vocabulary of dramatic technique. They can use these devices freely, separately and in an infinite variety of combinations, together with those bequeathed to them by other dramatic conventions of the past.

Far from being finished or spent, therefore, the Theatre of the Absurd is being absorbed into the mainstream of the tradition from which, as I have tried to show in this book, it had never been entirely absent, and out of which, when the time was propitious, it had emerged in this specific form at a specific moment in time.

Of the acknowledged masters of the Absurd, Beckett, Ionesco, and Pinter remain active and continue to explore new areas of expression and content. Genet is silent and Adamov has died. And while it is difficult to claim that any of the younger generation of playwrights who have emerged since the 1950's would wholly fit into the category of the Theatre of the Absurd, it can equally be stated that none of them is entirely free of its influence; just as it is impossible to say that any of them is free from the impact of the theories or practice of Brecht. In a play like Peter Weiss's *Marat/Sade* (1964) there are many subtle alienation effects which clearly derive from, and even go far beyond, Brecht: the fact, for example, that a historical play is being shown as performed by inmates of a lunatic asylum, with scenes supposedly of romantic love being acted out by a sex maniac who has to be calmed down by being doused with cold water, is an extreme case of Brechtian alienated acting. But, at the same time, the play's use of the fantasies of the insane and its essential quality as a metaphor of the human condition itself, equally clearly owes a good deal to Beckett, Ionesco, and Genet. Its style, it has been said, is derived from Artaud's Theatre of Cruelty, and that is certainly correct. But Artaud was also one of the main inspirations of the Theatre of the Absurd. Moreover, in its subject matter, the *Marat/Sade* actually deals with a debate between the Brechtian and Absurdist world view. Marat, the social revolutionary, believes that violence has to be used to make man good, by creating a just society, even through terror; while de Sade, the author of the most cruel fantasies of torture, having looked so deeply inside himself, has come to the conclusion that only if man faces his own cruelty on an individual basis, and thus gains insight into the corruption of his nature, can a non-violent and just world be established; this is the way of introspection, the way of Ionesco rather than Brecht.

The work of a major playwright like John Arden equally shows traces of the Brechtian manner and influence, allied to elements of fantasy and introspection which derive from the Theatre of the Absurd. The ritual of the expulsion of the guilty politician as the town's scapegoat in *The Workhouse Donkey* (1963) has a Genet-like flavour, the tree in *Armstrong's Last Goodnight* (1965) with Armstrong's corpse dangling from it has the stark simplicity of a Beckettian image, and the fantasy treatment of the playwright's own predicament in *The Bagman* (1970) shows many interesting parallels with the work of Ionesco.

A similar merging of epic and absurdist elements characterizes the work of another major English post-Absurdist playwright, Edward Bond. His *Lear* (1971) has the epic sweep of a Brechtian parable play, but the treatment of Lear's madness through the materialization of his thoughts in the figure of the dead boy who accompanies him has all the hallmarks of an absurdist approach.

The plays of Tom Stoppard also clearly show the impact of

the Theatre of the Absurd, in spite of the obvious difference in other aspects of their approach and the tradition – that of English high comedy – which they represent. *Rosencrantz and Guildenstern are Dead* (1966) uses structural elements of *Waiting for Godot*, while *Jumpers* (1972) concludes its brilliant and zany-absurdist exploration of the problem of good and evil in human existence with a direct paraphrase of famous lines from *Waiting for Godot*: 'At the graveside the undertaker doffs his top hat and impregnates the prettiest mourner.' To which the character of Archie, and surely the author of the play also, adds: 'Wham, bam, thank you Sam.' The play's debt to Samuel Beckett could not have been more clearly emphasized.

In the United States the all-pervasive influence of the Absurdists is only too evident in the work of the best of the younger generation of playwrights like Israel Horovitz or Sam Shepard, to name but two of the most prominent.

In France Romain Weingarten and Roland Dubillard – two of the outstanding playwrights in a period which represents a relative lull in the development of French drama – continue the tradition, while in the German-speaking world the Austrian avant-garde movement also can be seen to derive from the experiments and innovations of Beckett, Ionesco, and Genet. Peter Handke, whose play *Kaspar* (1968) is one of the major contributions of Central Europe to the drama of our time, is an extreme exponent of the critique of language initiated by the Absurdists; Wolfgang Bauer, in plays like *Magic Afternoon* (1968) and *Change* (1969), transfers the basic situation of *Waiting for Godot* into a grotesquely satirized naturalistic milieu of existential boredom; while the plays of Thomas Bernhard clearly derive from Beckett in their preoccupation with deformity, death and disease.

If certain aspects of the Theatre of the Absurd have thus naturally and smoothly reintegrated themselves into the main stream of the tradition, others have clearly contributed to the negative and disruptive trends which tend towards the destruction of the tradition itself and its replacement by new and as yet unheard-of forms. The rejection of traditional concepts of plot and character in the Theatre of the Absurd, the devaluation of dialogue and language itself, have undoubtedly played their part in helping to formulate the far more radical negations or the creators of such revolutionary concepts of an art beyond the theatre itself as that of the Happening. It is as yet too early to pass judgement on the validity of these efforts, on their potential as sources of a new art form. But it would be foolish to dismiss them out of hand, merely because some – not by any means all – of the earliest experiments were childish or amateurish in their execution.

Far from being a sign of decadence or foolish faddism, the search for innovation, for new methods and techniques, the experiments with new modes of expression in our time, are, in my opinion, an indication of the theatre's vitality, its awareness of the boundless opportunities of a world rapidly transforming itself under the impact of a new technologies. Under such conditions no art can survive which complacently falls back on past traditions and standards – least of all the theatre, which is the most social of the arts and most directly responds to social change. The Theatre of the Absurd was the expression of such impulses, a response to the cultural and social changes of our epoch. That is why it could not and did not harden into just another rigid convention, why the driving force behind it continues to manifest itself in the manifold strivings of a Protean avant-garde.

BIBLIOGRAPHY

I. THE DRAMATISTS OF THE ABSURD

ADAMOV, ARTHUR

PLAYS

Théâtre, 4 vols., Paris: Gallimard, vol. I, 1953, vol. II, 1955, vol. III, 1966, vol. IV, 1968.

> Vol. I contains: *La Parodie, L'Invasion, La Grande et la Petite Manœuvre, Le Professeur Taranne, Tous Contre Tous. (Le Professeur Taranne* trans. by A. Bermel in *Four Modern French Comedies*, New York: Capricorn Press, 1960; by Peter Meyer in *Absurd Drama*, Harmondsworth: Penguin Books, 1965)

> Vol. II contains: *Le Sens de la Marche, Les Retrouvailles, Le Ping-Pong. (Le Ping-Pong* trans. by Richard Howard, New York: Grove Press, 1959)

> Vol. III contains: *Paolo Paoli, La Politique des Restes, Sainte Europe*

> Vol. IV contains: *M. le Módéré, Le Printemps '71*

Separately published plays

La Parodie, L'Invasion, précédées d'une lettre d'André Gide, et de témoignages de René Char, Jacques Prévert, Henri Thomas, Jacques Lemarchand, Jean Vilar, Roger Blin, Paris: Charlot, 1950

Paolo Paoli, Paris: Gallimard 1957 (English trans. by Geoffrey Brereton, London: Calder, 1959)

Les Ames Mortes, d'après le poème de Nicolas Gogol, Paris: Gallimard, 1960

Comme Nous Avons Eté, Paris: *Nouvelle Revue Française*, March 1953 (trans. by Richard Howard, *As We Were*, New York: *Evergreen Review*, I, 4, 1957)

Théâtre de Société. Scènes d'Actualité, Paris: Les Editeurs Français Réunis, 1958, contains three short sketches by Adamov: *Intimité, Je ne Suis pas Français, La Complainte du Ridicule.*

En Fiacre (radio play), unpublished ms., 1959

Le Printemps '71, Paris: Gallimard, 1961

Si l'Été Revenait, Paris: Gallimard, 1970

437

BIBLIOGRAPHY

OTHER WRITINGS

L'Aveu, Paris: Sagittaire, 1946 (one section of this autobiographical confession trans. by Richard Howard, 'The endless humiliation', New York: *Evergreen Review*, II, 8, 1959)

'Assignation', Paris: *L'Heure Nouvelle*, no. II, 1945

'Le Refus', Paris: *L'Heure Nouvelle*, no. II, 1946

Auguste Strindberg, Dramaturge, Paris: L'Arche, 1955

'Théâtre, argent et politique', Paris: *Théâtre Populaire*, no. 17, 1956

'Parce que je l'ai beaucoup aimé . . .' (on Artaud), Paris: *Cahiers de la Compagnie M. Renaud – J.-L. Barrault*, nos. 22–3, May 1958

Anthologie de la Commune (ed. Adamov), Paris: Editions Sociales, 1959

Ici et Maintenant (collected essays), Paris: Gallimard, 1964

L'Homme et l'Enfant (diaries), Paris: Gallimard, 1968

Je . . . Ils (reissue of *L'Aveu* and new memoirs), Paris: Gallimard, 1969

TRANSLATIONS BY ADAMOV

RILKE, *Le Livre de la Pauvreté et de la Mort*, Algiers: 1941

BÜCHNER, *Théâtre Complet*, trans. by Adamov and Marthe Robert

DOSTOEVSKY, *Crime et Châtiment*

JUNG, *Le Moi et l'Inconscient*, Paris: 1938

GOGOL, *Les Ames Mortes*, Lausanne: La Guilde du Livre

CHEKHOV, *L'Esprit des Bois*, Paris: Gallimard (in the series 'Le Manteau d'Arlequin')

CHEKHOV, *Théâtre*, Paris: Club Français du Livre

STRINDBERG, *Le Pélican*, Paris: *Théâtre Populaire*, no. 17, 1956

STRINDBERG, *Père*, Paris: L'Arche, 1958

KLEIST, *La Cruche Cassée*, Paris: *Théâtre Populaire*, no. 6, 1954

GORKI, *Théâtre*, Paris: L'Arche

ON ADAMOV

GAUDY, RENÉ, *Arthur Adamov*, Paris: Stock, 1971

LYNES, CARLOS, JR, 'Adamov or "*le sens littéral*" in the theatre', *Yale French Studies*, no. 14, Winter 1954–5

REGNAUT, MAURICE, '*Arthur Adamov et le sens du fétichisme*', Paris: *Cahiers de la Compagnie M. Renaud – J.-L. Barrault*, nos. 22–3, May 1958

ALBEE, EDWARD

The Zoo Story (written 1958), New York: *Evergreen Review*, no. 12, March–April 1960; also in *Absurd Drama*, Harmondsworth: Penguin Books, 1965

The American Dream, A play, New York: Coward-McCann, 1961; London: Cape, 1962; also in *New American Drama*, Harmondsworth: Penguin Books, 1966

The Zoo Story, The Sandbox, The Death of Bessie Smith, published in one volume, New York: Coward-McCann, 1960

Who's Afraid of Virginia Woolf? A play, New York: Atheneum, 1963; London: Cape, 1964; Harmondsworth: Penguin Books, 1965

Tiny Alice, London: Cape, 1966

A Delicate Balance, London: Cape, 1968

Box and Quotations from Chairman Mao Tse-tung, New York: Atheneum, 1969

All Over, New York, Atheneum, 1971

Seascape, London: Cape, 1976

ON ALBEE

BIGSBY, C. W. E., *Albee*, Edinburgh: Oliver & Boyd. 1969

COHN, RUBY, *Edward Albee*, Minneapolis: University of Minnesota Press, 1969

KERJEAN, LILIANE, *Albee*, Paris: Seghers, 1971

KERJEAN, LILIANE, Le Théâtre d'Edward Albee, Paris: Klincksieck, 1978

ARRABAL, FERNANDO

Théâtre, Paris: Christian Bourgois, 12 vols.

Vol. I contains: *Oraison, Les Deux Bourreaux, Fando et Lis, Le Cimetière des Voitures*

Vol. II contains: *Guernica, Le Labyrinthe, Le Tricycle, Pique-nique en Campagne, La Bicyclette du Condamné*

Vol. III contains: *Le Grand Cérémonial, Cérémonie pour un Noir Assassiné*

Vol. IV contains: *Le Couronnement, Concert dans un Œuf*

Vol. V (Théâtre Panique) contains: *Théâtre Panique, L'Architecte et L'Empereur d'Assyrie*

Vol. VI contains: *Le Jardin des Délices, Bestialité Érotique, Une Tortue Nommée Dostoievski*

Vol. VII (Théâtre de guerilla) contains: *Et Ils Passèrent des Menottes aux Fleurs, L'Aurore Rouge et Noire*

Vol. VIII (Deux opéras paniques) contains: *Ars Amandi, Dieu Tenté par les Mathématiques*

Vol. IX contains: *Le Ciel et la Merde, La Grande Revue du XXe Siècle*

Vol. X contains: *Bella Ciao, La Guerre de Mille Ans*

Vol. XI contains: *La Tour de Babel, La Marche Royale, Une Orange sur le Mont de Vénus, La Gloire en Images*

Vol. XII contains: *Vole-moi un Petit Millard, Le Pastaga des Loups ou Ouverture Orang-Outan, Punk et Punk et Colégram*

Plays not included in the collected Theatre: *Sur le Fil, Jeunes Barbares d'Aujourd'hui*

ON ARRABAL

GILLE, BERNARD, *Fernando Arrabal*, Paris: Seghers, 1970

MORRISSETT, ANN, 'Dialogue with Arrabal', New York: *Evergreen Review*, no. 15, November–December 1960

SCHIFRES, ALAIN, *Entretiens avec Arrabal*, Paris: Pierre Belfond, 1969

SERREAU, GENEVIÈVE, '*Un nouveau style comique: Arrabal*', Paris: *Les Lettres Nouvelles*, no. 65, November 1958 (trans. New York: *Evergreen Review*, no. 15, November–December 1960)

BECKETT, SAMUEL

PLAYS

En Attendant Godot, Paris: Editions de Minuit, 1952 (trans. by author, *Waiting for Godot* – U.S. edition, New York: Grove Press, 1954; English edition, London: Faber & Faber, 1955)

Fin de Partie, suivi de Acte Sans Paroles, Paris: Editions de Minuit, 1957 (trans. by author, *Endgame, followed by Act Without Words* – U.S. edition, New York: Grove Press, 1958; English edition, London: Faber & Faber, 1958)

All That Fall, London: Faber & Faber, 1957 [U.S. edition, see below]

Krapp's Last Tape and Embers, London: Faber & Faber, 1959

Krapp's Last Tape and Other Dramatic Pieces, New York: Grove Press, 1960, contains *Krapp's Last Tape, All That Fall, Embers, Act Without Words I, Act Without Words II*

Happy Days, New York: Grove Press, 1961 (trans. by author, *Oh les Beaux Jours*, Paris: Editions de Minuit, 1963)

Play and Two Short Pieces for Radio, London: Faber & Faber, 1964, contains: *Play, Words and Music, Cascando* (trans. by author)

Comédie et Actes Divers, Paris: Editions de Minuit, 1966, contains: *Comédie* (*Play* trans. by author); *Va et Vient, Dramaticule* (*Come and Go* trans. by author); *Cascando, Pièce radiophonique pour musique et voix*; *Paroles et Musique, Pièce radiophonique* (*Words and Music* trans. by author); *Dis Joe, Pièce pour la télévision* (*Eh Joe* trans. by author); *Acte Sans Paroles II, pour deux personnages et un aiguillon* (*Act Without Words II* trans. by author)

Come and Go (English original) first published in *Samuel Beckett, Aus einem aufgegebenen Werk und kurze Spiele* (a collection of short prose works and plays in the original language and German trans.), Frankfurt: Suhrkamp, 1966 (no. 145 in 'Edition Suhrkamp'); separate publication, London: Calder & Boyars, 1967

Eh Joe and Other Writings, London: Faber & Faber, 1967, contains *Eh Joe, Act Without Words II, Film*

Breath and Other Shorts, London: Faber & Faber, 1971, contains: *Breath, Come and Go, Act Without Words I, Act Without Words II, From an Abandoned Work*

Not I, London: Faber & Faber, 1973

Footfalls, London: Faber & Faber, 1976

That Time, London: Faber & Faber, 1976

End and Odds. Plays and Sketches, London: Faber & Faber, 1977, contains: *Not I, That Time, Footfalls, Ghost Trio, . . . but the clouds . . ., Theatre I, Theatre II, Radio I, Radio II*

Film. Complete Scenario; Illustrations; Production shots, New York: Grove Press, 1969

NARRATIVE PROSE

More Pricks than Kicks, London: Chatto & Windus, 1934; one story, 'Dante and the lobster', New York: *Evergreen Review*, I, I

Murphy, London: Routledge, 1938; new edition, New York: Grove Press, n.d.

Watt, Paris: Olympia Press, 1958

Molloy, Paris: Editions de Minuit, 1951

Malone Meurt, Paris: Editions de Minuit, 1951

L'Innommable, Paris: Editions de Minuit, 1953

Three Novels, London: Calder, 1959, contains: *Molloy*, trans. by Patrick Bowles, *Malone Dies* and *The Unnamable*, trans. by author

Nouvelles et Textes pour Rien, Paris: Editions de Minuit, 1955 (a story trans. by Richard Seaver and author, 'The end', New York: *Evergreen Review*, no. 15, November–December 1960)

Text for Nothing I, trans. by author, New York: *Evergreen Review*, no. 9, Summer 1959

From an Abandoned Work, London: Faber & Faber, 1957; New York: *Evergreen Review*, I, 3, 1957

Comment C'Est, Paris: Editions de Minuit, 1961 (trans. by author, *How It Is*, New York: Grove Press, 1964; London: Calder, 1964); an extract from an earlier version of this novel, '*L'image*', London: X, no. 1, November 1959 (another extract trans. by author, 'From an unabandoned work', New York: *Evergreen Review*, no. 14, September–October 1960)

Imagination Morte Imaginez, Paris: Editions de Minuit, 1965 (trans. by author, *Imagination Dead Imagine*, London: Calder, 1965)

assez, Paris: Editions de Minuit, 1966

bing, Paris: Editions de Minuit, 1966

No's Knife, Collected Shorter Prose 1947–1966, London: Calder & Boyars, 1967, contains: *Stories, Texts for Nothing, From an Abandoned Work, Enough, Imagination Dead Imagine, Ping*

Premier Amour, Paris: Editions de Minuit, 1970

Le Dépeupleur, Paris: Editions de Minuit, 1970 (trans. by author, *The Lost Ones*, London: Calder & Boyars, 1972)

VERSE

Whoroscope, Paris: The Hours Press, 1930

Echo's Bones, Paris: Europe Press, 1935

'*Trois poèmes*', Paris: *Cahiers des Saisons*, no. 2, October 1955

Poems in English, London: Calder, 1961

Gedichte (bilingual edition of *Echo's Bones* followed by other poems in English and French, with German parallel translation), Wiesbaden: Limes, 1959

ESSAYS

Proust, London: Chatto & Windus, 1931 (Dolphin series); reprinted New York: Grove Press, n.d.
Proust, Three Dialogues, London: Calder, 1965
'Dante ... Bruno. Vico ... Joyce', in *Our Exagmination round his Factification for Incamination of Work in Progress*, Paris: Shakespeare & Co., 1929
Bram van Velde, New York: Grove Press, 1960

ON BECKETT

ABEL, LIONEL, 'Joyce the father, Beckett the son', New York: *The New Leader*, 14 December 1959

BENTLEY, ERIC, *What is Theatre?*, Boston: Beacon Press, 1956

CALDER, JOHN (ed.), *Beckett at Sixty* (essays by 24 contributors), London: Calder & Boyars, 1967

COE, RICHARD N., *Beckett*, Edinburgh and London: Oliver & Boyd, 1964 (in the series 'Writers and Critics')

COHN, RUBY, *Samuel Beckett: The Comic Gamut*, New Brunswick, N. J.: Rutgers University Press, 1962

——*Back to Beckett*, Princeton, N. J.: Princeton University Press, 1973

——(ed.), *Samuel Beckett. A Collection of Criticism*, New York: McGraw-Hill, 1975

——*Play Beckett*, Princeton, N. J.: Princeton University Press, 1979

ELLMAN, RICHARD, *James Joyce*, New York and London: Oxford University Press, 1959

ESSLIN, MARTIN, 'Samuel Beckett', in *The Novelist as Philosopher*, ed. John Cruickshank, London: Oxford University Press, 1962

ESSLIN, MARTIN (ed.), *Samuel Beckett, A Collection of Critical Essays*, Englewood Cliffs, N.J.: Prentice-Hall, 1965 (in the series 'Twentieth-Century Views')

FEDERMAN, RAYMOND, *Journey to Chaos, Samuel Beckett's Early*

Fiction, Berkeley and Los Angeles: University of California Press, 1965

FEDERMAN, RAYMOND and FLETCHER, JOHN, *Samuel Beckett: His Work and His Critics, An Essay in Bibliography*, Berkeley and Los Angeles: University of California Press, 1970

FLETCHER, JOHN, *The Novels of Samuel Beckett*, London: Chatto & Windus, 1964

——*Samuel Beckett's Art*, London: Chatto & Windus, 1967

FLETCHER, JOHN and SPURLING, JOHN, *Beckett. A Study of his Plays*, London: Eyre Methuen, 1972

FLETCHER, JOHN; FLETCHER, BERYL S.; SMITH, BARRY; BACHEM, WALTER, *A Student's Guide to the Plays of Samuel Beckett*, London: Faber & Faber, 1978

FRIEDMAN, M. J. (ed.), *Samuel Beckett*, Paris: Minard, 1964 ('Configuration Critique' no. 8)

GESSNER, N., *Die Unzulänglichkeit der Sprache*, Zürich: Juris, 1957
'Godot gets around', New York: *Theatre Arts*, July 1958

GUGGENHEIM, PEGGY, *out of this century, the informal memoirs of peggy guggenheim*, New York: the dials press, 1946

——*Confessions of an Art Addict*, London: André Deutsch, 1960

HARVEY, LAWRENCE E., *Samuel Beckett. Poet and Critic*, Princeton, N.J.: Princeton University Press, 1970

HOBSON, HAROLD, 'Samuel Beckett, dramatist of the year', *International Theatre Annual*, no. 1, London: Calder, 1956

JACOBSEN, JOSEPHINE and MÜLLER, WILLIAM R., *The Testament of Samuel Beckett*, New York: Hill & Wang, 1964

JANVIER, LUDOVIC, *Pour Samuel Beckett*, Paris: Editions de Minuit, 1966

JOYCE, JAMES, *Letters* (ed. Stuart Gilbert), London: Faber & Faber, 1957

KENNER, HUGH, *Samuel Beckett, A Critical Study*, New York: Grove Press, 1961; London: Calder, 1962

——*The Stoic Comedians: Flaubert, Joyce and Beckett*, London: W. H. Allen, 1964

KERN, EDITH, 'Drama stripped for inaction: Beckett's *Godot*', *Yale French Studies*, no. 14, Winter 1954–5

LEVY, ALAN, 'The long wait for Godot', New York: *Theatre Arts*, August 1956

MARISSEL, ANDRÈ, *Beckett*, Paris: Editions Universitaires, 1963

MAURIAC, CLAUDE, *La Littérature Contemporaine*, Paris: Albin Michel, 1958

MELESE, PIERRE, *Beckett*, Paris: Seghers, 1966 (in the series 'Théâtre de Tous les Temps')

MERCIER, VIVIAN, *Beckett/Beckett*, New York: Oxford University Press, 1977

——'Messenger of Gloom' (profile), London: *Observer*, 9 November 1958

METMAN, EVA, 'Reflections on Samuel Beckett's plays', London: *Journal of Analytical Psychology*, January 1960

——*San Quentin News*, San Quentin, Cal., vol. XVII, no. 24, 28 November 1957

SCHNEIDER, ALAN, 'Waiting for Beckett', New York: *Chelsea Review*, Autumn 1958

SCHOELL, KONRAD, *Das Theater Samuel Becketts*, Munich: Wilhelm Fink, 1967

SCOTT, NATHAN A., *Samuel Beckett*, London: Bowes & Bowes, 1965 (in the series 'Studies in Modern European Thought and Literature')

BUZZATI, DINO

Un Caso Clinico, Commedia in 2 tempi e 13 quadri, Milan: Mondadori, 1953 (no. 85 in the series 'La Medusa degli Italiani')

Un Verme al Ministero, Turin: *Il Dramma*, no. 283

D'ERRICO, EZIO

La Foresta, Turin: *Il Dramma*, no. 278

Tempo di Cavalette, Turin: *Il Dramma*, no. 261

Il Formicaio, stage ms.

ON D'ERRICO

TRILLING, OSSIA, 'Ezio d'Errico – a new Pirandello?', London: *Theatre World*, April 1958

FRISCH, MAX

Biedermann und die Brandstifter, Berlin and Frankfurt: Suhrkamp, 1958. This is the stage version, based on an earlier radio play, *Herr Biedermann und die Brandstifter*, first broadcast by Bayrischer Rundfunk, Munich, 1953; published Hamburg: Hans Bredow Institut, sixth edition, 1959. (Stage version trans. by Michael Bullock, *The Fire Raisers*, in *Three Plays*, London: Methuen, 1962)

ON FRISCH

BÄNZIGER, HANS, *Frisch und Dürrenmatt*, Berne: Francke, 1960
ZISKOVEN, WILHELM, 'Max Frisch', in *Zur Interpretation des modernen Dramas* (ed. Rolf Geissler), Frankfurt: Diesterweg, 1960
These two exhaustive studies also contain bibliographical data on Frisch's numerous other plays which do not fall into the category of the Theatre of the Absurd.

GELBER, JACK

The Connection (with Introduction by Kenneth Tynan), New York: Grove Press, 1960
The Apple, New York: Grove Press, 1961

GENET, JEAN

PLAYS

Haute Surveillance, Paris: Gallimard, 1949 (trans. by B. Frechtman, *Deathwatch*, in *The Maids/Deathwatch*, New York: Grove Press, 1954; English edition, *Deathwatch*, London: Faber & Faber, 1961)
Les Bonnes, Décines: L'Arbalète, 1948; a new edition, *Les Bonnes, Les deux versions précédées d'une lettre de l'auteur*, containing the first version (as performed at the Athénée in 1946) and the revised version (as performed at the Théâtre de la Huchette in 1954); the second version also reprinted in *Les Bonnes–L'Atelier d'Alberto Giacometti*, Décines: L'Arbalète, 1958, further containing 'L'enfant criminel'

(a suppressed radio talk) and '*Le funambule*' (prose reflections); (*Les Bonnes*, second version, trans. by B. Frechtman, *The Maids*, in *The Maids/Deathwatch*, New York: Grove Press, 1954; English edition, London: Faber & Faber, 1957)

Le Balcon (first version, 13 scenes), Décines: L'Arbalète, 1956; (second version, 9 scenes), Décines: L'Arbalète, 1960 (second version trans. by B. Frechtman, *The Balcony*, New York: Grove Press, 1960; English edition, London: Faber & Faber, 1960)

Les Nègres, Clownerie, Décines: L'Arbalète, 1958; second edition with photographs of the Paris performance and an introductory note by Genet, 1960 (trans. by B. Frechtman, *The Blacks, A clown show*, New York: Grove Press, 1960; English edition, London: Faber & Faber, 1960)

Les Paravents, Décines: Marc Barbézat (L'Arbalète), 1961 (trans. by B. Frechtman, *The Screens*, London: Faber & Faber, 1963)

OTHER WRITINGS

Journal du Voleur, Paris: Gallimard, 1949 (trans. by B. Frechtman, *The Thief's Journal*, Paris: Olympia Press, 1954; London: Anthony Blond, 1965; Harmondsworth: Penguin Books, 1967)

Œuvres Complètes, vol. II, Paris: Gallimard, 1951, contains: *Notre-Dame-des-Fleurs, Le Condamné à Mort, Miracle de la Rose, Un Chant d'Amour*

Œuvres Complètes, vol. III, Paris: Gallimard, 1953, contains: *Pompes Funèbres, Le Pêcheur de Suquet, Querelle de Brest*

Poèmes, Décines: Marc Barbézat (L'Arbalète), 1962

Lettres à Roger Blin (letters to the director of production of *The Screens* at the Odéon in 1966), Paris: Gallimard, 1966

ON GENET

ABEL, LIONEL, 'Metatheater', New York: *Partisan Review*, Spring 1960

BATAILLE, GEORGES, *La Littérature et le Mal*, Paris: Gallimard, 1957

DUVIGNAUD, JEAN, '*Roger Blin aux prises avec Les Nègres de Jean Genet*', Paris: *Les Lettres Nouvelles*, 28 October 1959

SARTRE, JEAN-PAUL, *Saint Genet, Comédien et Martyr* (vol. I of Genet, *Œuvres Complètes*), Paris: Gallimard, 1952

GRASS, GÜNTER

PLAYS

Die Bösen Köche, in *Modernes deutsches Theater I*, Neuwied: Luchterhand, 1961

Onkel, Onkel, Berlin: Wagenbach, 1965

Noch zehn Minuten bis Buffalo, stage ms.

Zweiunddreissig Zähne, Frankfurt: Suhrkamp, 1963

Hochwasser, stage ms.

Die Plebejer proben den Aufstand, Neuwied: Luchterhand, 1966

English translations

Four Plays, trans. Ralph Manheim, London: Secker & Warburg, 1968, contains: *Still Ten Minutes to Buffalo; Uncle, Uncle; The Flood; The Wicked Cooks.*

The Plebeians Rehearse the Uprising, A German Tragedy, trans. by Ralph Manheim, London: Secker & Warburg, 1967

OTHER WRITINGS

Die Vorzüge der Windühner (poems and prose sketches), Neuwied: Luchterhand, 1956

Die Blechtrommel (novel), Neuwied: Luchterhand, 1959 (trans. by Ralph Manheim, *The Tin Drum*, London: Secker & Warburg, 1962; Harmondsworth: Penguin Books, 1965)

Gleisdreieck (poems), Neuwied: Luchterhand, 1960

Katz und Maus (novel), Neuwied: Luchterhand, 1961 (trans. by Ralph Manheim, *Cat and Mouse*, London: Secker & Warburg, 1963; Harmondsworth: Penguin Books, 1966)

Hundejahre (novel), Neuwied: Luchterhand, 1963 (trans. by Ralph Manheim, *Dog Years*, London: Secker & Warburg, 1965; Harmondsworth: Penguin Books 1969)

Ausgefragt (poems), Neuwied: Luchterhand, 1967

Selected Poems, trans. by Michael Hamburger and Christopher Middleton, have been published by Secker & Warburg, 1966; Harmondsworth: Penguin Books, 1969

Der Butt (novel) Neuwied: Luchterhand, 1977 (trans. by Ralph Manheim, *The Flounder*, London: Secker & Warburg, 1978)

ON GRASS

TANK, KURTH LOTHAR, *Günter Grass*, Berlin: Colloquium, 1963

HAVEL, VACLAV

Protokoly (collected writings, including the two plays *The Garden Party* and *The Memorandum*), Prague: Mlada Fronta, 1966 (*The Memorandum*, trans. by Vera Blackwell, London: Cape, 1967)

HILDESHEIMER, WOLFGANG

PLAYS

Spiele in denen es dunkel wird, Pfullingen: Neske, 1958, contains: *Pastorale oder Die Zeit für Kakao, Landschaft mit Figuren, Die Uhren.* Hildesheimer's radio plays include: *Das Ende kommt nie, Begegnung im Balkanexpress, Prinzessin Turandot* (stage version, *Der Drachenthron*), *An den Ufern der Plotinitza, Das Atelierfest, Die Bartschedelidee, Herrn Walsers Raben.*

OTHER WRITINGSS

'*Erlanger Rede über das absurde Theater*', Munich: *Akzente*, no. 6, 1960

IONESCO, EUGÈNE

PLAYS

[*for collected editions see p. 452*]

La Cantatrice Chauve (written 1948, first performance 1950), in *Théâtre I* [Arcanes]; also in *Théâtre I* [Gallimard] (trans. by Donald M. Allen, *The Bald Soprano*, in *Plays*, vol. I [New York: Grove Press]; trans. by Donald Watson, *The Bald Prima Donna*, in *Plays*, vol. I [London: Calder])

La Leçon (written 1950, first performance 1951), in *Théâtre I* [Arcanes]; also in *Théâtre I* [Gallimard] (trans. *The Lesson*, by Donald M.

Allen in *Plays*, vol. I [New York: Grove Press]; by Donald Watson in *Plays*, vol. I [London: Calder], and in *Penguin Plays*, 1962)

Jacques, ou La Soumission (written 1950, first performance 1955), in *Théâtre I* [Arcanes]; also in *Théâtre I* [Gallimard] (trans. by Donald M. Allen, *Jack or the Submission*, in *Plays*, vol. I [New York: Grove Press]; trans. by Donald Watson, *Jacques or Obedience*, in *Plays*, vol. I [London: Calder])

Les Chaises (written 1951, first performance 1952), in *Théâtre I* [Gallimard] (trans., *The Chairs*, by Donald M. Allen in *Plays*, vol. I [New York: Grove Press]; by Donald Watson in *Plays*, vol. I [London: Calder], and in *Penguin Plays*, 1962)

Le Salon de l'Automobile (first performance 1953), in *Théâtre I* [Arcanes]; also in *Théâtre IV* (trans. by Sasha Moorsom, *The Motor Show*, London: 3 *Arts Quarterly*, no. 2, Summer 1960)

L'Avenir est dans les Œufs ou Il faut de tout pour faire un monde (written 1951, first performance 1957), in *Théâtre II* (trans. by Derek Prouse, *The Future is in Eggs or It takes all sorts to make a world*, in *Plays*, vol. IV)

Victimes du Devoir (written 1952, first performance 1953), in *Théâtre I* [Gallimard] (trans. by Donald Watson, *Victims of Duty*, in *Plays*, vol. II)

Amédée ou Comment s'en débarrasser (written 1953, first performance 1954), in *Théâtre I* [Gallimard] (trans. by Donald Watson, *Amédeé or How to get rid of it*, in *Plays*, vol. II, and in *Absurd Drama*, Harmondsworth: Penguin Books, 1965)

Le Nouveau Locataire (written 1953, first performance 1955), in *Théâtre II* (trans. by Donald Watson, *The New Tenant*, in *Plays*, vol. II)

Les Grandes Chaleurs (first performance 1953), based on a play by Caragiale, unpublished

La Jeune Fille à Marier (first performance 1953), in *Théâtre II* (trans. by Donald Watson, *Maid to Marry*, in *Plays*, vol. III)

Le Maitre (first performance 1953), in *Théâtre II* (trans. by Derek Prouse, *The Leader*, in *Plays*, vol. IV)

Le Connaissez-Vous? (first performance 1953), unpublished

La Nièce-Epouse (first performance 1953), unpublished

Le Rhume Onirique (first performance 1953), unpublished

Le Tableau (first performance 1955), *Dossiers Acénonètes de Collège de Pataphysique*, no. 1, 1958; also in *Théâtre III* (trans. by Donald

Watson, *The Picture*, broadcast in B.B.C. Third Programme, 11 March 1957; in *Plays*, vol. VII)

L'Impromptu de l'Alma ou Le Caméléon du Berger (written 1955, first performance 1956), in *Théâtre II* (trans. by Donald Watson, *Improvisation or The Shepherd's Chameleon*, in *Plays*, vol. III)

Impromptu pour la Duchesse de Windsor (written 1957, first performance 1957), unpublished (trans. by Donald Watson, unpublished)

Tueur Sans Gages (written 1957, first performance 1959), in *Théâtre II* (trans. by Donald Watson, *The Killer*, in *Plays*, vol. III)

[Le] Rhinocéros [the definite article on the title page is an error by the publishers] (written 1958, first performance 1959), Paris: Gallimard, 1959 (in the series 'Le Manteau d'Arlequin'); also in *Théâtre III* (trans. by Derek Prouse, *Rhinoceros*, in *Plays*, vol. IV, and in *Penguin Plays*, 1962)

Scène à Quatre (written 1959, first performance 1959), *Cahiers du Collège de Pataphysique*, *Dossier 7*, 1959; also Paris: *Avant-Scène* no. 210, 15 December 1959; also in *Théâtre III* (trans. by Donald M. Allen, *Foursome*, New York: *Evergreen Review*, no. 13, May–June 1960)

Apprendre à Marcher, Ballet (first performance 1960), in *Théâtre IV*

Les Salutations (opening scene of an as yet uncompleted play, *Scène à Sept*), Paris: *Les Lettres Françaises*, no. 805, 31 December 1960; also in *Théâtre III*

Le Roi se Meurt (written 1962, first performance 1962), Paris: Gallimard, 1963; also in *Théâtre IV* (trans. by Donald Watson, *Exit the King*, in *Plays*, vol. V)

Le Piéton de l'Air (written 1962, first performance 1963), in *Théâtre III* (trans. by Donald Watson, *A Stroll in the Air*, in *Plays*, vol. VI)

Délire à Deux . . . à tant qu'on veut (written 1962, first performed 1962), in *Théâtre III* (trans. by Donald Watson, *Frenzy for Two*, in *Plays*, vol. VI)

La Soif et la Faim (written 1965, first performance 1966), in *Théâtre IV* (trans. by Donald Watson, *Hunger and Thirst*, in *Plays*, vol. VII)

Jeux de Massacre, Paris: Gallimard 1970

Macbett, Paris: Gallimard, 1972

L'Homme aux Valises suivi de Ce Formidable Bordel, Paris: Gallimard, 1975 (trans. adapted by Israel Horovitz, *Man with Bags,* New York: Grove Press, 1977)

Collected editions

Théâtre I, Paris: Arcanes, 1953 (in the series 'Locus Solus'), contains: *La Cantatrice Chauve, La Leçon, Jacques ou La Soumission, Le Salon de l'Automobile*

[A second volume of the above edition, announced as being in preparation in 1953, did not appear. It was to contain: *Les Chaises, Victimes du Devoir, La Nièce-Epouse, La Jeune Fille à Marier*]

Théâtre I, Paris: Gallimard, 1954, contains: *Préface* by Jacques Lemarchand, *La Cantatrice Chauve, La Leçon, Jacques, ou La Soumission, Les Chaises, Victimes du Devoir, Amédée*

Théâtre II, Paris: Gallimard, 1958, contains: *L'Impromptu de l'Alma, Tueur Sans Gages, Le Nouveau Locataire, L'Avenir est dans les Œufs, Le Maître, La Jeune Fille à Marier*

Théâtre III, Paris: Gallimard, 1963, contains: *Rhinocéros, Le Piéton de l'Air, Délire à Deux, Le Tableau, Scène à Quatre, Les Salutations, La Colère*

Théâtre IV, Paris: Gallimard, 1966, contains: *Le Roi se Meurt, La Soif et la Faim, La Lacune, Le Salon de l'Automobile, L'Œuf Dur, Le Jeune Homme à Marier, Apprendre à Marcher*

Théâtre V, Paris: Gallimard, 1974, contains: *Jeux de Massacre, Macbett, La Vase, Exercices de conversation et de diction Françaises pour étudiants Américains*

English translations

[Ionesco's plays have been published by Grove Press, New York, and John Calder, London. The first volume of these editions differs; the others are identical]

Vol. I [U.S. edition], trans. by Donald M. Allen, contains: *The Bald Soprano, The Lesson, Jack or The Submission, The Chairs*

Vol. I [English edition], trans. by Donald Watson, contains: *The Lesson, The Chairs, The Bald Prima Donna, Jacques or Obedience*

Vol. II, trans. by Donald Watson, contains: *Amédée or How to get rid of it, The New Tenant, Victims of Duty*

Vol. III, trans. by Donald Watson, contains: *The Killer, Improvisation or The Shepherd's Chameleon, Maid to Marry*

Vol. IV, trans. by Derek Prouse, contains: *Rhinoceros, The Leader, The Future is in Eggs*

Vol. V, trans. by Donald Watson, contains: *Exit the King, The Motor Show, Foursome*

Vol. VI, trans. by Donald Watson, contains: *A Stroll in the Air, Frenzy for Two*

Vol. VII, trans. by Donald Watson, contains: *Hunger and Thirst, The Picture, Greetings, Anger*

Vol. VIII, trans. by Donald Watson, contains: *Here Comes a Chopper (Jeux de massacre), The Oversight (La Lacune), The Foot of the Wall*

Vol. IX, trans. by Donald Watson, contains: *Macbett, The Mire, Learning to Walk*

Vol. X, trans. by Donald Watson, contains: *Oh What a Bloody Circus, The Hardboiled Egg*

NARRATIVE PROSE

Une Victime du Devoir (written 1952), Paris: *Medium*, January 1955; Paris: *Cahiers des Saisons*, no. 24, Winter 1961 [basis of *Victimes de Devoir*]

Oriflamme, Paris: *Nouvelle Revue Français*, February 1964 [basis of *Amédée*] (trans., *Flying High*, New York: *Mademoiselle*, 1957)

La Photo du Colonel, Paris: *Nouvelle Revue Française*, November 1955 [basis of *Tueur Sans Gages*] (trans. by Stanley Read, *The Photograph of the Colonel*, *Evergreen Review*, I, 3, 1957)

Rhinocéros, Paris: *Les Lettres Nouvelles*, September 1957; Paris: *Cahiers de la Compagnie M. Renaud – J.-L. Barrault*, no. 29, February 1960 (trans. by Donald M. Allen, New York: *Mademoiselle*, March 1960)

La Photo du Colonel, Récits (collected short stories), Paris: Gallimard, 1962

The Colonel's Photograph (collected stories in English), trans. by Jean Stewart and John Russell, London: Faber & Faber, 1967

Le Solitaire. Roman, Paris: Mercure de France, 1973

ESSAYS AND OTHER PROSE WRITINGS

'*L'invraisemblable, l'insolite, mon univers ...*', Paris: *Arts*, 14 August 1953; also Paris: *Cahiers des Saisons*, no. 15, Winter 1959, under the title '*Je n'ai jamais réussi ...*'

'*Le point du départ*', Paris: *Cahiers des Quatre Saisons*, no. 1, August 1955 [this periodical changed its title to *Cahiers des Saisons* from no. 2, October 1955] (trans. by L. C. Pronko, New York: *Theatre Arts*, June 1958; by Donald Watson in *Plays*, vol. I[London: Calder])

'*Théâtre et anti-théâtre*', Paris: *Cahiers des Saisons*, no. 2, October 1955 (trans. by L. C. Pronko, New York: *Theatre Arts*, June 1958)

'*Mes pièces ne prétendent pas sauver le monde*', Paris: *L'Express*, 15–16 October 1955

'*Mes critiques et moi*', Paris: *Arts*, 22 February 1956

'*Gammes*' (nonsense aphorisms), Paris: *Cahiers des Saisons*, no. 7, September 1956

'There is no avant-garde theatre', trans. by Richard Howard, New York: *Evergreen Review*, I, 4, 1957

'The world of Ionesco', *International Theatre Annual*, no. 2, ed. Harold Hobson, London: Calder, 1957; *Tulane Drama Review*, October 1958

'*Olympie*' (prose poem), Paris: *Cahiers des Saisons*, no. 10, April–May 1957

'*Pour Cocteau*', Paris: *Cahiers des Saisons*, no. 12, October 1957

'The theatre', talk on B.B.C. Third Programme, July 1957 [an early version of '*Expérience du théâtre* – see below]

'*Dans les armes de la ville*' (on Kafka), Paris: *Cahiers de la Compagnie M. Renaud – J.-L. Barrault*, no. 20, October 1957

'*Qu'est-ce que l'avant-garde en 1958?*', Paris: *Les Lettres Françaises*, 10 April 1958; also Paris: *Cahiers des Saisons*, no. 15, Winter 1959, under the title '*Lorsque j'écris . . .*'

'*Expérience du théâtre*', Paris: *Nouvelle Revue Française*, February 1958 (trans. by L. C. Pronko, 'Discovering the theatre', *Tulane Drama Review*, September 1959)

'*Ni un dieu ni un démon*' (on Artaud), Paris: *Cahiers de la Compagnie M. Renaud–J.-L. Barrault*, nos. 22–3, May 1958

'Reality in depth', London: *Encore*, May–June 1958

'The playwright's role', London: *Observer*, 29 June 1958 (The entire controversy with Kenneth Tynan is reproduced as '*Controverse londonienne*' in *Cahiers des Saisons*, no. 15, Winter 1959)

'*La tragédie du langage*', Paris: *Spectacles*, no. 2, July 1958 (trans. by Jack Undank, 'The tragedy of language', *Tulane Drama Review*, Spring 1960)

'*Préface*' to *Les Possédés*, adapted from the novel by Dostoevsky by Akakia Viala and Nicolas Bataille, Paris: Emile-Paul, 1959

'*Le cœur n'est pas sur la main*' (reply to Kenneth Tynan not published by the *Observer*), Paris: *Cahiers des Saisons*, no. 15, Winter 1959

'*Naissance de* La Cantatrice', Paris: *Cahiers des Saisons*, no. 15, Winter 1959

'*La démystification par l'humour noir*', Paris: *Avant-Scène*, 15 February 1959

'*Eugène Ionesco ouvre le feu*' (with parallel English translation), Paris: *World Theatre*, vol. VIII, no. 3, Autumn 1959

Interview with Claude Sarraute, Paris: *Le Monde*, 17 January 1960

Interview with himself, Paris: *France-Observateur*, 21 January 1960; reprinted *Cahiers du Collège de Pataphysique, Dossiers 10–11*, 1960

Interview, Paris: *L'Express*, 28 January 1960

'*Pages de journal*', Paris: *Nouvelle Revue Française*, February 1960

'*Printemps 1939. Les débris du souvenir. Pages de journal*', *Cahiers de la Compagnie M. Renaud – J.-L. Barrault*, no. 29, February 1960

'*Propos sur mon théâtre et sur les propos des autres*', Brussels: *L'VII*, no. 3, 1960

'*Le* Rhinocéros *à New York*', Paris: *Arts*, February 1961

'Some recollections of Brancusi', trans. by John Russell, *London Magazine*, April 1961

Notes et Contre-notes (collected critical writings), Paris: Gallimard, 1962 (trans. by Donald Watson, *Notes and Counter-Notes*, London: Calder, 1965)

Journal en miettes, Paris: Mercure de France, 1967

Présent passé, Passé présent, Paris: Mercure de France, 1968

Découvertes, Geneva: Skira, 1969

Antidotes, Paris: Gallimard, 1977

ON IONESCO

Das Abenteuer Ionesco. Beiträge zum Theater von Heute (with contributions by Ionesco, A. Schulze Vellinghausen and Rudolf Sellner), Zürich: Verlag H. R. Stauffacher, 1958

ANOUILH, JEAN, '*Du chapitre des* Chaises', Paris: *Le Figaro*, 23 April 1956

BIBLIOGRAPHY

BATAILLE, NICOLAS, 'La bataille de La Cantatrice', Paris: Cahiers des Saisons, no. 15, Winter 1969

BENMUSA, SIMONE, Eugène Ionesco, Paris: Seghers, 1956 (in the series 'Théâtre de Tous les Temps')

BENTLEY, ERIC, 'Ionesco, playwright of the fifties', New York: Columbia Daily Spectator, 11 March 1958

BONNEFOY, CLAUDE, Entretiens avec Eugène Ionesco, Paris: Belfond, 1966

BOSQUET, ALAIN, 'Le théâtre d'Eugène Ionesco, ou les 36 recettes du comique', Paris: Combat, 17 February 1955

COE, RICHARD, Ionesco, Edinburgh and London: Oliver & Boyd, 1961 (no. 5 in the series 'Writers & Critics')

DOUBROVSKY, SERGE, 'Ionesco and the comedy of the absurd', Yale French Studies, no. 23, Summer 1959; also Paris: Nouvelle Revue Française, February 1960, under the title 'Le rire d'Eugène Ionesco'

DUVIGNAUD, JEAN, 'La dérision', Paris: Cahiers de la Compagnie M. Renaud – J.-L. Barrault, no. 29, February 1960

FRANCUEIL, BERNARD, 'Digression automobile & Dilectus quemadmodum filius unicornium' (review of Rhinocéros), Cahiers du Collège de Pataphysique, Dossiers 10–11, 1960

LAUBREAUX, R., 'Situation de Ionesco', Paris: Théâtre d'Aujourd'hui, January–February 1959

LAUBREAUX, R. (ed.), Les Critiques de notre temps et Ionesco, Paris: Garnier, 1973

LERMINIER, GEORGES, 'Clés pour Ionesco', Paris: Théâtre d'Aujourd' hui, September–October 1957

LUTEMBI, 'Contribution à une étude de La Cantatrice Chauve', Cahiers du Collège de Pataphysique, nos. 8–9, 1953

MARCEL, GABRIEL, 'La crise du théâtre et le crépuscule de l'humanisme', Paris: Revue Théâtrale, no. 39

ROBBE-GRILLET, ALAIN, 'Notes', Paris: Critique, January 1953

ROUD, RICHARD, 'The opposite of sameness', London: Encore, June–July 1957

SAROYAN, WILLIAM, 'Ionesco', New York: Theatre Arts, July 1958

SAUREL, RENÉE, 'Ionesco ou Les blandices de la culpabilité', Paris: Les Temps Modernes, no. CIII, 1954

'A school of vigilance', London: The Times Literary Supplement, 4 March 1960

SENART, PHILIPPE, *Ionesco*, Paris: Editions Universitaires, 1964

TOBI, SAINT, *Eugène Ionesco ou La Recherche du paradis perdu*, Paris: Gallimard, 1973

TOUCHARD, P. A., 'La loi du théâtre', Paris: *Cahiers des Saisons*, no. 15, Winter 1959

—— 'Un nouveau favuliste', Paris: *Cahiers de la Compagnie M. Renaud–J.-L. Barrault*, no. 29, February 1960

TOWARNICKI, F., 'Des Chaises vides . . . à Broadway', Paris: *Spectacles*, no. 2, July 1958

VERNOIS, PAUL, *La Dynamique théâtrale d'Eugène Ionesco*, Paris: Klingsieck, 1972

KOPIT, ARTHUR L.

Oh Dad, Poor Dad, Mamma's Hung You in the Closet and I'm Feeling So Sad. A pseudo-classical tragifarce in a bastard French tradition, New York: Hill & Wang, 1960; London: Methuen, 1961

MROZEK, SLAWOMIR

The original texts of Mrozek's plays can be found in the monthly journal *Dialog*, published in Warsaw, *passim* 1958–67.

A COLLECTION IN GERMAN

Stücke, vol. I, Berlin: Henssel, 1963, contains: *Die Polizei, Auf hoher See, Striptease, Karol, Das Martyrium des Peter Ohey, Racket Baby, Der Hirsch*

Stücke, vol. II, Berlin: Henssel, 1965, contains: *Eine wundersame Nacht, Zabawa, Tango*

ENGLISH TRANSLATIONS

Six Plays, trans. by Nicholas Bethell, London: Cape, 1967, contains: *The Police, The Martyrdom of Peter Ohey, Out at Sea, Charlie, The Party, Enchanted Night*

Tango, trans. by Nicholas Bethell, London: Cape, 1968

BIBLIOGRAPHY

PEDROLO, MANUEL DE

Cruma, in *Premi Joan Santamaria 1957*, Barcelona: Editorial Nereida, 1958

Homes i No, Barcelona: *Quaderns de Teatre A.D.B.*, no. 2, 1960

PINGET, ROBERT

Lettre Morte, Paris: Editions de Minuit, 1959

La Manivelle, Pièce radiophonique (with parallel trans. by Samuel Beckett, *The Old Tune*), Paris: Editions de Minuit, 1960

Ici ou Ailleurs, suivi de Architruc et de L'Hypothèse, Paris: Editions de Minuit, 1961

PINTER, HAROLD

The Birthday Party and Other Plays, London: Methuen, 1960, contains: *The Room, The Dumb Waiter, The Birthday Party. The Dumb Waiter* also in *Penguin New English Dramatists 2* and *Penguin Plays*, Harmondsworth: Penguin Books, 1961 and 1964

The Caretaker, London: Methuen 1960

A Slight Ache and Other Plays, London: Methuen, 1961, contains: *A Slight Ache, A Night Out, The Dwarfs*, and some revue sketches

The Collection and The Lover, London: Methuen, 1963

The Homecoming, London: Methuen, 1965

Tea Party and Other Plays, London: Methuen, 1967, contains the three television plays *Tea Party, The Basement, Night School*

Landscape and Silence, London: Methuen, 1969

Old Times, London: Methuen, 1971

Five Screen Plays, London: Methuen, 1971

No Man's Land, London: Eyre Methuen, 1975

Poems and Prose, London: Eyre Methuen, 1978

The Proust Screenplay, London: Eyre Methuen, 1978

Betrayal, London: Eyre Methuen, 1978

BIBLIOGRAPHY

ON PINTER

DUKORE, BERNARD F., *Where Laughter Stops. Pinter's Tragicomedy*, Columbia: University of Missouri Press, 1976

ESSLIN, MARTIN, *Pinter. A Study of his Plays*, 3rd expanded edition, London: Eyre Methuen, 1977

GANZ, ARTHUR, (ed.), *Pinter. A Collection of Critical Essays*, in the series 'Twentieth-Century Views', Englewood Cliffs, N.J.: Prentice-Hall, 1972

HINCHCLIFFE, ARNOLD P., *Harold Pinter*, New York: Twayne, 1967

IMHOF, RUDIGER, *Pinter. A Bibliography*, 2nd revised edition, London: TQ Publications, 1976

KERR, WALTER, *Harold Pinter*, New York: Columbia University Press, 1967

SIMPSON, NORMAN FREDERICK

PLAYS

A Resounding Tinkle, in *The Observer Plays* (anthology of prize-winning entries in a playwriting competition), London: Faber & Faber, 1958; also in *New English Dramatists 2*, Harmondsworth: Penguin Books, 1960, and in *Penguin Plays 1*, 1964; shorter stage version as performed at the Royal Court Theatre, London, 1 December 1957, in *The Hole and Other Plays and Sketches*, London: Faber & Faber, 1964

One Way Pendulum, A farce in a new dimension, London: Faber & Faber, 1960

The Hole and Other Plays and Sketches, London: Faber & Faber, 1964, contains: *The Hole, A Resounding Tinkle* (shorter version), *The Form, Gladly Otherwise, Oh, One Blast and Have Done*

The Cresta Run, London: Faber & Faber, 1966

OTHER WRITINGS

The Overcoat (short story), London: *Man About Town*, December 1960

459

TARDIEU, JEAN

Théâtre de Chambre I, Gallimard, 1955, contains: *Qui Est Là?*, *La Politesse Inutile*, *Le Sacre de la Nuit*, *Le Meuble*, *La Serrure*, *Le Guichet*, *Monsieur Moi*, *Faust et Yorick*, *La Sonate et les Trois Messieurs ou Comment Parler Musique*, *La Société d' Apollon ou Comment Parler des Arts*, *Oswald et Zenaïde ou Les Apartés*, *Ce Que Parler Veut Dire ou Le Patois des Familles*, *Il y Avait Foule au Manoir ou Les Monologues*, *Eux Seuls le Savent*, *Un Geste pour un Autre*, *Conversation-Sinfonietta*

Théâtre II: Poèmes à Jouer, Paris: Gallimard, 1960, contains: *L'A.B.C. de Notre Vie*, *Rhythme à Trois Temps ou Le Temple de Ségeste*, *Une Voix Sans Personne*, *Les Temps du Verbe ou Le Pouvoir de la Parole*, *Les Amants du Métro*, *Tonnerre Sans Orage ou Les Dieux Inutiles*

Théâtre III: Une Soirée en Province, Paris: Gallimard, 1975, contains: *Une Soirée en Province ou le mot et le cri*, *Cinq Divertissements*, *Candide*, *Livrets d'opéras de chambre*

ON TARDIEU

JACOTTET, PHILIPPE, 'Note à propos de Jean Tardieu', Paris: *Nouvelle Revue Française*, July 1960

VIAN, BORIS

For a full bibliography of Vian's numerous writings, see *Cahiers du Collège de Pataphysique*, Dossier 12, 1960

PLAYS

L'Equarrissage pour Tous (also containing extracts from notices of the performance, 'Salut à Boris Vian' by Cocteau, and a second short play, *Le Dernier des Métiers*, *Saynètes pour Patronages*), Paris: Toutain, 1950; *L'Equarrissage pour Tous* reprinted in *Paris Théâtre*, no. 66, 1952

Les Bâtisseurs d'Empire ou Le Schmürz, *Cahiers du Collège de Pataphysique*, Dossier 6, 1959; Paris: L'Arche, 1959 (in the series 'Collection du Répertoire du TNP')

Théâtre, Paris: Pauvert, 1965, contains: *Les Bâtisseurs d'Empire, Le Goûter des Généraux, L'Equarrissage pour Tous*

ON VIAN

Cahiers du Collège de Pataphysique, Dossier 12, 1960, contains critical and biographical studies

2. BACKGROUND AND HISTORY OF THE THEATRE OF THE ABSURD

GENERAL WORKS

BARNES, HAZEL, *The Literature of Possibility*, Lincoln, Nebraska: University Press, 1959

BEIGBEDER, MARC, *Le Théâtre en France depuis la Libération*, Paris: Bordas, 1959

BERGEAUD, JEAN, *Je choisis ... mon théâtre. Encyclopédie du Théâtre Contemporain*, Paris: Odilis, 1956

BERGSON, HENRI, *Le Rire. Essai sur la Signification du Comique*, in *Œuvres*, Paris: Presses Universitaires de France, 1959

BOISDEFFRE, PIERRE DE, *Une Histoire Vivante de la Littérature d'Aujourd'hui*, Paris: Le Livre Contemporain

CAMUS, ALBERT, *Le Mythe de Sisyphe*, Paris: Gallimard, 1942

CRUICKSHANK, JOHN, *Albert Camus and the Literature of Revolt*, London and New York: Oxford University Press, 1959

Dictionnaire des Hommes de Théâtre Français Contemporains (tome I: Directeurs, Animateurs, Historiens, Critiques), Paris: Librairie Théâtrale, 1957

ECO, UMBERTO, 'L'Œuvre ouverte ou La poétique de l'indétermination', Paris: *Nouvelle Revue Française*, July and August 1960

EVREINOV, NIKOLAI, *The Theatre of the Soul, Monodrama*, trans. by M. Potapenko and C. St John, London, 1915

FOWLIE, WALLACE, *Dionysus in Paris. A Guide to Contemporary French Theatre*, New York: Meridian, 1960; London: Gollancz, 1961

FREUD, SIGMUND, *Der Witz und seine Beziehung zum Unbewussten* (1905), paperback reprint, Frankfurt: S. Fischer, 1958

461

GREGOR, JOSEPH, *Weltgeschichte des Theaters*, Vienna: Phaidon, 1932

GROSSVOGEL, DAVID, *The Selfconscious Stage in Modern French Drama*, New York: Columbia University Press, 1958

HUXLEY, ALDOUS (ed.), *The Perennial Philosophy*, London: Chatto & Windus, 1946

MALLARMÉ, STÉPHANE, *Crayonné au Théâtre*, in *Œuvres Complètes*, Paris: Pléiade, 1945

NIETZSCHE, *Die Geburt der Tragödie* and *Also sprach Zarathustra*, in *Werke*, ed. Schlechta, Munich: Hanser, vols. I and II, 1955

POUND, EZRA, *Literary Essays*, ed. T. S. Eliot, London: Faber & Faber, 1954

SARTRE, JEAN-PAUL, *L'Etre et le Néant*, Paris: Gallimard, 1943

STEINER, GEORGE, 'The retreat from the word', London: *Listener*, 14 and 21 July 1960

SUZUKI, D., *Manual of Zen Buddhism*, London: Rider, 1950

Théâtre Populaire, '*Du côté de l'avant-garde*' (special number on the avant-garde theatre), no. 18, May 1956

WITTGENSTEIN, LUDWIG, *Philosophical Investigations*, Oxford: Blackwell, 1958

PURE THEATRE, CLOWNING, COMMEDIA DELL'ARTE, MUSIC HALL, ETC.

BEERBOHM, MAX, 'Dan Leno', in *Around Theatres*, London: Hart-Davis, 1953

BÜCHNER, GEORG, *Werke und Briefe*, Leipzig: Insel, 1958
——*Woyzeck*, trans. by John Holmstrom, in *Three German Plays*, Harmondsworth: Penguin Books, 1963

CRICHTON, KYLE, *The Marx Brothers*, London: Heinemann, 1951

DISHER, WILLSON, *Clowns and Pantomimes*, London: Constable, 1925

GRABBE, CHRISTIAN DIETRICH, *Werke*, ed. Wukadinowic, 2 vols., Berlin: Bong, n.d.

HAZLITT, WILLIAM, 'The Indian jugglers', *Table Talk*, London and New York: Everyman's Library

HOLZER, RUDOLF, *Die Wiener Vorstadtbühnen*, Vienna: 1951

LEA, K. M., *Italian Popular Comedy. A Study in the Commedia dell'Arte*, London: Oxford University Press, 1934

MACINNES, COLIN, 'Wherefore does he why?' (on Dan Leno), London: *Spectator*, 23 December 1960

MCKECHNIE, SAMUEL, *Popular Entertainment through the Ages*, London: Sampson Low, n.d.

NESTROY, JOHANN, *Sämtliche Werke*, ed. Bruckner and Rommel, Vienna: Schroll, 15 vols., 1924–30.

RAIMUND, FERDINAND, *Werke*, ed. Castle, Leipzig: Hesse & Becker, n.d.

REICH, HERMANN, *Der Mimus*, vol. I (in two tomes) [no further volumes appeared], Berlin: Weidmann, 1903

TIETZE-CONRAT, E., *Dwarfs and Jesters in Art*, London: Phaidon, 1957

WOOD, J. HICKORY, *Dan Leno*, London: Methuen, 1905

NONSENSE POETRY AND NONSENSE PLAYS

BELLOC, HILAIRE, *Cautionary Verses*, London: Duckworth, 1940

BENAYOUN, R., *Anthologie du Nonsense*, Paris: Pauvert, 1957

BRETON, ANDRÉ, *Anthologie de l'Humour Noir*, Paris: Sagittaire, 1950

BUSCH, WILHELM, *Sämtliche Werke*, Gutersloh: Bertelsmann, 2 vols., n.d.

CARROLL, LEWIS, *Complete Works*, London: Nonesuch; New York: Random House, 1939

COHEN, J. M., *Comic and Curious Verse*, Harmondsworth: Penguin Books, 1952

COHEN, J. M., *More Comic and Curious Verse*, Harmondsworth: Penguin Books, 1956

FLAUBERT, GUSTAVE, *Dictionnaire des idées Reçues* (augmented with newly discovered entries), Paris: Aubier, 1951

LARDNER, RING
Nonsense Plays
  The Tridget of Griva, unpublished (extract in ELDER [see below])
  Dinner Bridge, New York: *New Republic*, 20 July 1927; also in *First and Last*, New York: Scribner, 1934
  I Gaspiri (The Upholsterers), *Chicago Literary Times*, 15 February 1924; also in *What of It?*, New York: Scribner, 1925
  Clemo-Uti/The Water Lilies, in *What of It?*, New York: Scribner, 1925

Cora or Fun at the Spa, New York: *Vanity Fair*, June 1925

Quadroon. A Play in Four Pelts which May All Be Attended in One Day or Missed in a Group, The New Yorker, 19 December 1931

Abend di Anni Nouveau, New York: *The Morning Telegraph*, 1928

On Lardner

ELDER, DONALD, *Ring Lardner*, New York: Doubleday, 1956

LEAR, EDWARD, *The Complete Nonsense of Edward Lear*, ed. Holbrook Jackson, London: Faber & Faber, 1947

MORGENSTERN, CHRISTIAN, *Alle Galgenlieder*, Wiesbaden: Insel, 1950

——*Das Mondschaf, Deutsch und englisch* (English versions by A. E. W. Eitzen), Wiesbaden: Insel, 1953

OPIE, IONA and PETER, *The Oxford Dictionary of Nursery Rhymes*, London: Oxford University Press, 1951

——*The Lore and Language of Schoolchildren*, London: Oxford University Press, 1959

RINGELNATZ, JOACHIM, *Kinder-Verwirr-Buch*, Berlin: Rowohlt, 1931

——*Turngedichte*, Munich: Kurt Wolff, 1923

——*Kuttel-Daddeldu*, Berlin: Rowohlt, 1930

SEWELL, E., *The Field of Nonsense*, London: Chatto & Windus, 1952

DREAM PLAYS AND ALLEGORIES

BIDERMANN, JAKOB, *Cenodoxus der Doktor von Paris*, in *Deutsche Dichtung des Barock*, ed. Edgar Hederer, Munich: Hanser, n.d.

CALDERÓN DE LA BARCA, PEDRO, *Autos Sacramentales*, vol. III of *Obras Completas*, Madrid: Aguilar, 1945–52

ELIADE, MIRCEA, *Myths, Dreams and Mysteries*, London: Harvill, 1960

GREGOR, JOSEPH, *Das Spanische Welttheater*, Vienna: Reichner, 1937

HOLBERG, *Comoedierne*, ed. Bull, Kristiania: 1922–5

HONIG, EDWIN, *Dark Conceit. The Making of Allegory*, Chicago: Northwestern University Press, 1959; London: Faber & Faber, 1960

JOYCE, JAMES, *Stage adaptations of* Ulysses

Ulysses in Nighttown, adapted by Marjorie Barkentin under the supervision of Padraic Colum, New York: Random House, Modern Library Paperbacks, 1958

Bloomsday, adapted by Alan MacClelland

KAFKA, FRANZ, *Der Gruftwächer* (dramatic fragment), in *Beschreibung eines Kampfes*, New York: Schocken, 1946

Kafka, Franz, adapted by GIDE, ANDRÉ and BARRAULT, JEAN-LOUIS, *Le Procès*, Paris: Gallimard, 1947

Franz Kafka du Procès *au* Château, special number of *Cahiers de la Compagnie M. Renaud – J.-L. Barrault*, no. 20, October 1957

LOPE DE VEGA, *Obras Escogidas*, 3 vols., Madrid: Aguilar, 1952-5, contains Lope's principal *Autos sacramentales*

MADACH, IMRE, *Az Ember Tragédiája*, Budapest: Franklin, n.d.

STRINDBERG, AUGUST, *Samlade Skrifter*, 55 vols., Stockholm: Bonnier, 1911-21

——*A Dream Play* and *The Ghost Sonata*, in *Six Plays of Strindberg*, trans. by E. Sprigge, New York: Doubleday (Anchor Books), 1955

DADAISM, SURREALISM, PATAPHYSICIANS, AND THEIR FORERUNNERS AND FOLLOWERS

APOLLINAIRE, GUILLAUME

Les Mamelles de Tirésias/*Couleur du Temps*, in *Œuvres Poétiques*, Paris: Pléiade, 1956

ARAGON, LOUIS

L'Armoire à Glace un Beau Soir and *Au Pied du Mur*, in *Le Libertinage*, Paris: Gallimard, 1924

with BRETON, ANDRÉ, *Le Trésor des Jésuites*, Brussels: *Variétés*, June 1929

ARTAUD, ANTONIN

Œuvres Complètes, vols. I–XIV, Paris: Gallimard, 1956-78 [further volumes in preparation]

Le Théâtre et son Double, Paris: Gallimard, 1938 (trans. by C. Richards, *The Theatre and its Double*, New York: Grove Press, 1958)

Lettres à Jean-Louis Barrault (with a study of Artaud's theatre by Paul Arnold), Paris: Bordas, 1952

ARNOLD, PAUL study of Artaud's theatre in *Lettres à Jean-Louis Barrault* [see above]

BIBLIOGRAPHY

Antonin Artaud et le Théâtre de Notre Temps, Paris: special issue of *Cahiers de la Compagnie M. Renaud – J.-L. Barrault*, nos. 22–3, May 1958

Antonin Artaud ou La Santé des Poètes, Jarnac: special number of *La Tour du Feu*, December 1959

ESSLIN, MARTIN, *Antonin Artaud*, London: Fontana, 1976

BARLACH, ERNST

Das Dichterische Werk, Band I, Munich: Piper, 1956

BRECHT, BERTOLT

Stücke, 14 vols., Frankfurt: Suhrkamp, 1954–67

COCTEAU, JEAN

Les Mariés de la Tour Eiffel, in *Théâtre I*, Paris: Gallimard, 1948

Parade and *Le Bœuf sur le Toit*, in *Nouveau Théâtre de Poche*, Monaco: Editions du Rocher, 1960

Orphée, Paris: Stock, 1927

Le Sang d'un Poète (film), Paris: Marin, 1948

CUMMINGS, E. E.

him in *From the Modern Repertoire, Series Two*, ed. Eric Bentley, Indiana University Press, 1957

    BENTLEY, ERIC, Notes to *him*, ibid.

    NORMAN, CHARLES, *The Magic Maker*, New York: Macmillan, 1958

DADA

ARP/HUELSENBECK/TZARA, *Die Geburt des Dada*, Zürich: Arche, 1957

MEHRING, WALTER, *Berlin Dada*, Zürich: Arche, 1959

HUELSENBECK, RICHARD, *Mit Witz, Licht und Grütze*, Wiesbaden: Limes, 1957

DAUMAL, RENÉ and GILBERT-LECOMTE, ROGER, *Petit Théâtre*, Paris: Collège de Pataphysique, 1957

DESNOS, ROBERT

La Place de l'Etoile, Antipoème, Rodez: Collection Humour, 1945

Domaine Publique (collected poems), Paris: Gallimard, 1953

    BERGER, PIERRE, *Robert Desnos* (essay on Desnos with anthology of his work), Paris: Seghers, 1960 (no. 16 in the series 'Poètes d'Aujourd'hui')

Expressionismus. Literatur und Kunst, 1910–1923 (catalogue of an exhibition at the Schiller Museum, Marbach, West Germany, 8

May-31 October 1961, ed. B. Zeller, containing a very full bibliography of Expressionism, with biographical notes on all important authors), Marbach: 1960

FITZGERALD, F. SCOTT

The Vegetable or From President to Postman, New York: Scribner, 1923

    MIZENER, ARTHUR, *This Side of Paradise*, London: Eyre & Spottiswoode, 1951

GOLL, YVAN

Dichtungen, ed. Claire Goll, Neuwied: Luchterhand, 1960, reprints *Die Chaplinade, Die Unsterblichen, Zwei Überdramen* (1. *Der Unsterbliche*, 2. *Der Ungestorbene*), *Melusine*

Methusalem, in *Schrei und Bekenntnis. Expressionistisches Theater* (anthology of Expressionist plays), ed. K. Otten, Neuwied: Luchterhand, 1959

    ROMAINS, JULES/BRION, MARCEL/CARMODY, F./EXNER, R., *Yvan Goll* (anthology and critical essays), Paris: Seghers, 1956 (no. 50 in the series 'Poètes d'Aujourd'hui')

GOMBROWICZ, WITOLD

The Marriage, trans. by Louis Iribarne, London: Calder & Boyars, 1970

Princess Ivona, trans. by Krystyna Griffith and Catherine Robins, London: Calder & Boyars, 1969

Operetta, trans. by Louis Iribarne, London: Calder & Boyars, 1971

JARRY, ALFRED

Œuvres Complètes, Monte Carlo and Lausanne: 1948

Ubu Roi, Ubu Enchaîné, Paralipomènes d'Ubu, Questions de Théâtre, Les Minutes de Sable Mémorial, César-Antéchrist, Poésies, L'Autre Alceste, Lausanne: Henri Kaeser, 1948 (colllection of all Ubuesque writings)

Tout Ubu (another collection of Ubuesque writings), Paris: Le Livre de Poche, 1962

Ubu Roi, trans. by Barbara Wright, in *Four Modern French Comedies*, New York: Capricorn Books, 1961

Ubu, Version pour la scène (acting edition of *Ubu Roi* and *Ubu Enchaîné* adapted for performance as one play at the Théâtre Nationale Populaire), Paris: L'Arche, 1958

Gestes et Opinions du Docteur Faustroll, Paris: Fasquelle, 1955 (trans., New York: *Evergreen Review*, no. 13, 1960, p. 131)

BIBLIOGRAPHY

KOKOSCHKA, OSKAR
Schriften 1907–1955, Munich: Langen, 1956

LAUTRÉAMONT, COMTE DE (ISIDORE DUCASSE)
Œuvres Complètes, Paris: Corti, 1946

LORCA, FEDERICO GARCÍA
Obras Completas, Madrid: Aguilar, 1955

NADEAU, MAURICE
Histoire du Surréalisme, Paris: Editions du Seuil, 1945

PICASSO, PABLO
Le Désir Attrapé par la Queue, Paris: Messages II, 1944; also, in book form, Paris: Gallimard, 1949 (no. 23 of the collection 'Metamorphoses') (trans. by B. Frechtman, *Desire Caught by the Tail*, London: Rider, 1950)

> PENROSE, ROLAND, *Picasso, His Life and Work*, London: Gollancz, 1955

PINTHUS, KURTH
Menschheitsdämmerung (one of the first anthologies of Expressionist poetry), Berlin: Rowohlt, 1920; reissue (with new introduction and bibliographical material), Hamburg: Rowohlt, 1959

RADIGUET, RAYMOND
Les Pélicans, Pièce en deux actes, in *Œuvres Complètes*, vol. I, Paris: Club des Libraires de France, 1959

RIBEMONT-DESSAIGNES, GEORGES
Théâtre, Paris: Gallimard, 1966
Déjà Jadis (memoirs), Paris: Julliard, 1958

ROBICHEZ, J.
Le Symbolisme au Théâtre, Lugné-Poë et les Débuts de l'Œuvre, Paris: L'Arche, 1957

ROUSSEL, RAYMOND
L'Etoile au Front, Paris: Lemerre, 1925
La Poussière de Soleils, Paris: Lemerre, 1927

> ROUSSELOT, JEAN, *Raymond Roussel et la Toute-Puissance du Langage*, Paris: *La Tour St Jacques*, March–April 1957
> HEPPENSTALL, RAYNER, *Raymond Roussel, a critical guide*, London: Calder & Boyars, 1966

SALACROU, ARMAND
  Surrealist playlets
  Pièces à Lire: Les Trente Tombes de Judas, Histoire de Cirque, Paris:
  Les Œuvres Libres, no. 173, October 1960

SHATTUCK, ROGER
  The Banquet Years (containing outstanding studies of Apollinaire
  and Jarry), London: Faber & Faber, 1959

SOKEL, WALTER H.
  *The Writer in Extremis: Expressionism in Twentieth-Century German
  Literature*, Stanford University Press, 1959

STEIN, GERTRUDE
  Four Saints in Three Acts, New York: Random House, 1934
  Geography and Plays, Boston: Four Seas, 1922
  Doctor Faustus Lights the Lights
  In Savoy or Yes Is for a Very Young Man, London: Pushkin Press,
  1946

TORMA, JULIEN
  Coupures, Tragédie, suivi de Lauma Lamer, Paris: Pérou, 1926
  Euphorismes, no publisher indicated, 1926
  Le Bétrou, Drame en IV actes, Paris: Collège de Pataphysique, 1956
      Hommage à Torma (biographical, bibliographical, and critical
      studies by various hands), *Cahiers du Collège de Pataphysique*,
      no. 7, 1952

TZARA, TRISTAN
  La Première Aventure Céleste de M. Antipyrine, Zürich: Collection
  Dada, 1916
  La Deuxième Aventure Céleste de M. Antipyrine, Paris: Réverbère,
  1938
  Le Cœur à Gaz, Paris: GLM, 1946
  La Fruite, Paris: Gallimard, 1947

VALLE-INCLÁN, RAMÓN DEL
  Martes de Carnaval, Esperpentos, in *Opera Omnia*, vol. 24, Madrid:
  Editorial Rua Nueva, 1943, contains: *Las Galas del Difunto,
  Los Cuernos de Don Friolera, La Hija del Capitan*

VITRAC, ROGER
  Théâtre, 4 vols., Paris: Gallimard, 1946, 1964

WITKIEWICZ, STANISLAW

   Dramaty, 2 vols. ed. Konstanty Puzyna, Warsaw: Panstwowy Instytut Wydawniczy, 1962

Plays available in English are contained in:

   The Madman and the Nun and Other Plays, trans. and ed. by Daniel C. Gerould and C. S. Durer, Seattle: University of Washington Press, 1968, contains: *The Madman and the Nun, The Water Hen, The Crazy Locomotive, The Mother, They, The Shoemakers*

and

   Tropical Madness. Four Plays, trans. by Daniel and Eleanor Gerould, New York: Winter House, 1972, contains: *The Pragmatists, Mr Price or: Tropical Madness, Gyubal Wahazar, Metaphysics of a Two-Headed Calf*

YEATS, W. B.

   Autobiographies, London: Macmillan, 1955

INDEX

Abel, Lionel, 68

Absurd, the definition of term, 23–4
(*see also* Theatre of the Absurd)

Adamov, Arthur, 15, 17, 21, 24, 27,
92–127, 128, 153, 170–71, 172,
189, 197, 228, 233, 265–6, 268,
274, 290, 304, 328, 339, 356,
375–7, 385, 402, 432, 437–8
Biographical data, 92–8, 101,
103–18, 121–7
Les Ames Mortes (Dead Souls), 120,
437
L'Aveu, 93–4, 96, 109, 125, 126, 438
*Comme Nous Avons Été (As We
Were)*, 112–13, 316, 437
En Fiacre, 125, 437
Je . . . Ils . . ., 127
La Grande et la Petite Manœuvre,
104–7, 121–2, 437
L'Homme et l'Enfant, 127
L'Invasion, 101–4, 116, 437
Paolo Paoli, 118–24, 127, 437
La Parodie, 99–101, 104, 109–10,
114, 121, 123, 401, 437
Le Ping-Pong, 113–17, 119, 121–2,
127, 437
La Politique des Restes, 126, 437
Le Printemps, 125–6, 437
Le Professeur Taranne, 108–12, 121,
420, 437
Les Retrouvailles, 112–13, 420, 437
M. le Modéré, 126
Off Limits, 126
Sainte Europe, 126, 437
Si l'Été Revenait, 126, 437
Le Sens de la Marche, 107–8, 111,
437
Théâtre de Société, 124, 437
Tous Contre Tous, 111, 437

Aeschylus, 198

Albee, Edward, 311–14, 439
The American Dream, 312–13, 439

*Box and Quotations from Chairman
Mao Tse-tung*, 439
The Death of Bessie Smith, 312, 439
A Delicate Balance, 314, 439
The Sandbox, 439
Seascape, 439
Tiny Alice, 314, 439
Who's Afraid of Virginia Woolf?,
313, 439
The Zoo Story, 312, 439

Alienation effect, 142, 410–12

Allegory, 328, 349–56

Anderson, Lindsay, 131

Anouilh, Jean, 24, 40, 153

Apollinaire, Guillaume, 26, 275, 356,
361–5, 371, 391
Couleur du Temps, 363
Les Mamelles de Tirésias, 275,
361–3, 371

Apuleius, Lucius, 331

Aragon, Louis, 368, 379–80

Arden, John, 433

Arghezi, Tudor, 135

Aristophanes, 331

Arp, Hans, 364–5

Arrabal, Fernando, 17, 285–92, 396,
402, 439
L'Architecte et l'Empereur d'Assyrie,
291–2, 439
Ars amandi, 440
L'Aurore Rouge et Noire, 440
Bella Ciao, 440
Bestialité Érotique, 440
La Bicyclette du Condamné, 439
Cérémonie pour un Noir Assassiné,
439
Le Ciel et la Merde, 440
*Le Cimetière des Voitures (The Auto-
mobile Graveyard)*, 288–9, 439
Concert dans un Œuf, 439
Le Couronnement, 439

Les Deux Bourreaux (*The Executioners*), 287, 439
Dieu Tenté par les Mathematiques, 440
Et Ils Passèrent des Menottes aux Fleurs, 440
Fando et Lis, 287–8, 439
La Gloire en Images, 440
Le Grand Cérémonial, 439
La Grande Revue du XXe Siècle, 440
Guernica, 439
La Guerre de Mille Ans, 440
Le Jardin des Délices, 440
La Marche Royale, 440
Oraison, 286–7, 439
Une Orange sur le Mont de Vénus, 440
Orchestration Théâtrale, 290
Le Pastaga des Loups en Ouverture Orang-Outan, 440
Pique-nique en Campagne, 286, 439
Punk et Punk et Colégram, 440
Théâtre Panique, 439
La Tour de Pontil, 440
Le Tricycle, 439
Vote-moi un Petit Millard, 440
Artaud, Antonin, 127, 356, 380–85, 409, 433, 465–6
Atkinson, Brooks, 179
Audiberti, Jacques, 25, 153
Austrian folk-theatre, 337
Autos sacramentales, 349, 395, 402

Ball, Hugo, 364–5
Balzac, Honoré de, 49–50, 92
Bänziger, Hans, 294, 446
Barbey d'Aurevilly, Jules, 351
Barbu, Ion, 135
Barlach, Ernst, 391
Barrault, Jean-Louis, 27, 139, 180, 184, 230, 355–6, 385
Bataille, Nicolas, 27, 139, 144
Baudelaire, Charles, 136, 233
Baver, Wolfgang, 434
Beckett, John, 40, 42
Beckett, Samuel, 12, 15, 17, 24, 27, 29–91, 153, 158, 173, 189, 197,

264, 265–6, 299–300, 304, 315, 316, 329, 332, 354, 356, 376, 391, 401, 412, 418, 426, 432–3, 434, 440–45
Biographical data, 29–44
Act Without Words I, 40, 74–5, 440
Act Without Words II, 441
All That Fall, 41, 76–7, 84, 87, 440
assez (*Enough*), 442
bing (*Ping*), 442
Breath, 441
Cascando, 42, 80–82, 441
Come and Go (*Va et Vient*), 41, 83, 441
Comment C'Est, 41, 442
'Dante . . . Bruno. Vico . . . Joyce', 30, 443
Echo's Bones, 33, 442
Eh Joe (*Dis Joe*), 42, 83–4, 441
Eleutheria, 35, 37, 67
Embers, 41, 76, 79–80, 84, 87, 89, 441
Endgame (*Fin de Partie*), 37, 40–41, 44, 62–78, 80, 86–7, 89, 151, 349, 440
Film, 42, 81, 441
Footfalls, 43, 89–90, 441
From an Abandoned Work, 41, 441–2
Ghost Trio, 43, 90
Happy Days (*Oh les Beaux Jours*), 41, 82–3, 441
Imagination Morte Imaginez (*Imagination Dead Imagine*), 442
Le Dépeupleur (*The Lost One*), 442
L'Innommable (*The Unnamable*), 37, 41, 442
Krapp's Last Tape, 41, 44, 64, 76–9, 87, 90, 299, 312, 441
Malone Meurt (*Malone Dies*), 37, 41, 442
Mercier et Camier, 37
Molloy, 36–7, 39, 41, 442
More Pricks than Kicks, 33, 441
Murphy, 29, 33, 35, 39, 73–4, 85, 442
Not I, 43, 441

Nouvelles et Textes pour Rien, 37, 442

Play (Comédie), 41, 44, 82, 441

Premier Amour, 442

Proust, 32–3, 50–51, 59, 68, 70, 79, 443

That Time, 43, 90, 441

Waiting for Godot (En Attendant Godot), 11, 19–21, 36–7, 39–40, 44–62, 69–71, 75–6, 77–8, 80, 85–7, 280, 282, 290, 299, 301, 317, 319, 324, 328, 403, 414, 419, 431, 434, 440

Watt, 37, 62, 442

Whoroscope, 31–2, 442

Words and Music (Paroles et Musique), 42, 80, 441

Beerbohm, Sir Max, 334

Belloc, Hilaire, 346

Benayoun, Robert, 340

Benchley, Robert, 348

Bentley, Eric, 17, 49, 387–8, 456

Bérard, Christian, 213

Berger, John, 130

Bergson, Henri, 303, 308

Bernhard, Thomas, 434

Bidermann, Jakob, 350

Bierce, Ambrose, 347

Blake, William, 349

Blau, Herbert, 17, 19, 38

Blin, Roger, 27, 39–40, 104, 228, 230, 385, 447

Bond, Edward, 433

Bonnard, Pierre, 364

Bosch, Hieronymus, 135, 297

Bosquet, Alain, 195

Boulez, Pierre, 173

Braque, Georges, 364

Brecht, Bertolt, 118, 123, 129–30, 141–2, 170, 172, 185, 221, 292, 339, 375–8, 391, 403–4, 410–12, 424, 431–3

Im Dickicht der Städte (In the Jungle of Cities), 375–7

Das Elephantenkalb (The Baby Elephant), 377

Die Hochzeit, 375

Mann ist Mann (Man Equals Man), 376–7

Breton, André, 176, 362, 367–9, 378–80

Brook, Peter, 216, 229

Bruant, Aristide, 365

Brueghel, Pieter, the Elder, 135

Büchner, Georg, 103, 118, 127, 198, 338–9, 375, 462

Busch, Wilhelm, 346

Buzzati, Dino, 277–9, 401, 445

Un Caso Clinico, 277–9, 445

Un Verme al Ministero, 279, 445

Byron, George Gordon, Lord, 346

Cabaret Voltaire (Zürich), 364–5

Calderón de la Barca, Pedro, 350

Camus, Albert, 23–4, 277, 392, 415

Le Mythe de Sisyphe (The Myth of Sisyphus), 23, 400–401, 426

Carroll, Lewis, 302, 342, 343–6, 389

Alice in Wonderland, 327

The Hunting of the Snark, 344

Through the Looking Glass, 344–5

Castle of Otranto, The (Horace Walpole), 351

Cendrars, Blaise, 365

Chagall, Marc, 27, 184

Chaplin, Charles, 174, 335–6, 371

Char, René, 104

Chavannes, Puvis de, 359

Chekhov, Anton, 103, 116, 118, 127, 128, 417

Circus, 47, 168, 194, 328, 412

Claudel, Paul, 104, 106

Clowns and clowning, 328–31, 336–7, 387

Cocteau, Jean, 198, 213, 275, 386–7

Comedy and tragedy, 191–2, 411

Commedia dell'arte, 330, 333–7, 375

Communism, 97–8

Copeau, Jacques, 27

Corbet, Richard, 342

Corneille, Pierre, 198

Court jesters, 335

cummings, e. e., 27, 397-8, 466
  him, 397-8
Cuvelier, Marcel, 147

Dada, 339, 347, 356, 364-71, 378, 420, 465
Daumal, René, 388, 390
Debureau, Jean-Gaspard, 334
Defoe, Daniel, 185
Democritus, 73, 426
Dermée, Paul, 367
d'Errico, Ezio, 279-81, 445
Desnos, Robert, 385-6, 390, 466-7
Devine, George, 41, 130
Dhomme, Sylvain, 27, 152
Divine Comedy, The, 349
Donner, Clive, 261
Dostoevski, Fyodor, 127, 144, 354
Doubrovsky, Serge, 156-7
Dream literature, 328, 349-57, 387-8, 393-4
Dubillard, Roland, 434
Dubuffet, Jean, 391
Dullin, Charles, 27, 383
Dumas, Alexandre, fils, 198
Dumesnil, Suzanne, 43
Dürrenmatt, Friedrich, 292

Eckhart, Meister 25, 426-7
Eliade, Mircea, 349
Ellmann, Richard, 31, 33-4
Eluard, Paul, 93, 368-9
Ernst, Max, 391
Eveinov, Nikolai, 65
Ewell, Tom, 40
Existentialism, 25, 61, 93, 156, 170, 201
Expressionism, 100, 339, 356, 366, 370-71, 466-7

Faerie Queene, The (Edmund Spenser), 350
Feydeau, Georges 189
Fields, W. C., 336
Fitzgerald, F. Scott, 397, 467
  The Vegetable, 397, 467

Flaubert, Gustave, 348
Frechtman, Bernard, 215, 446, 468
Freud, Sigmund, 157, 340
Frisch, Max, 292-5, 446
  Biedermann und die Brandstifter, 292-5, 446

Gautier, Jean-Jacques, 153
Gelber, Jack, 315, 401, 446
  The Apple, 315, 446
  The Connection, 315, 446
Genet, Jean, 12, 15, 24, 200-233, 265-6, 268, 274, 328, 350, 401, 432-3, 434, 446-7
  Biographical data, 201-3, 205, 212-15, 227-32
  Adam Miroir, 200
  Le Balcon (*The Balcony*), 214-24, 233, 447
  Les Bonnes (*The Maids*), 207-14, 222, 226, 233, 446
  Un Chant d'Amour, 213
  Haute Surveillance (*Deathwatch*), 205-9, 214, 219, 222, 446
  Journal du Voleur (*The Thief's Journal*), 200-204, 447
  Lettres à Roger Blin, 447
  Mademoiselle, 230
  Les Nègres (*The Blacks*), 223-9, 233, 447
  Les Paravents (*The Screens*), 228-30, 447
  Poèmes, 447
Gessner, Niklaus, 47, 85, 87
Ghelderode, Michel de, 25
Gide, André, 103-4, 355
Gilbert-Lecomte, Roger, 388
Giraudoux, Jean, 24, 169, 198
Goethe, Johann Wolfgang von, 351
Gogol, Nikolai, 120, 127
Goll, Yvan, 370-75, 467
  Die Chaplinade, 371, 396
  Methusalem, 373-4, 385
  Die Unsterblichen, 371-3
Gombrowicz, Witold, 393-5, 467
Gorki, Maxim, 127, 128, 172

Grabbe, Christian Dietrich, 339
Graham, Harry, 347
Grass, Günter, 297-8, 448-9
Greek drama, 402, 414
Gregor, Joseph, 334-5
Grimaldi, Joseph, 334
Gris, Juan, 26, 364
Grock, 336
Grossman, Jan, 324, 326
Grosz, Georg, 375
Guggenheim, Peggy, 34-5
Guilbert, Yvette, 365
Gulliver's Travels (Jonathan Swift),
    351

Hall, Donald, 261
Handke, Peter, 434
Happening, 435
Havel, Vaclav, 324-6, 449
Hazlitt, William, 329
Heidegger, Martin, 346
Hennings, Emmy, 364
Hildesheimer, Wolfgang, 295-7, 449
Hirsch, Robert, 184
Hivnor, Robert, 311
Hobson, Harold, 29n.
Hoffmann, E. T. A., 351
Holberg, Ludvig, 351
Hood, Thomas, 346
Horovitz, Israel, 434
Huelsenbeck, Richard, 364-5
Huet, Henri-Jacques, 140
Hugo, Victor, 198, 346, 356, 362, 380
Huxley, Aldous, 426n., 427n., 429

Ibsen, Henrik, 139, 198, 351, 353,
    360, 404, 417
Ionesco, Eugène, 12, 15, 17, 21, 23-4,
    27, 42, 128-99, 211, 233, 238,
    265-6, 268, 274, 304, 313, 316,
    328-9, 332, 336, 348-9, 354-6,
    361, 368, 375-6, 378, 381-2,
    386-7, 391, 409, 417-19, 422-3,
    432-3, 434, 449-57
    Biographical data, 133-40, 144-5,
        150-54, 158-9, 164-7, 168-74,
        180-81, 184-5
    Methods of work, 143, 170, 174,
        186-8, 196-7
    Views on art and the theatre,
        129-33, 136-7, 141-2, 152-6,
        159-60, 167, 169-71, 188-93,
        195-9, 417-18
    Amédée ou Comment s'en débarrasser
        (*Amédée or How to get rid of it*),
        160-64, 174, 178, 195, 351, 450,
        452
    Anger, 453
    Apprendre à Marcher, 451-2
    Ce Formidable Bordel, 186
    L'Avenir est dans les Œufs (*The
        Future is in Eggs*), 149-50, 182,
        197, 450, 452-3
    La Cantatrice Chauve (*The Bald
        Soprano, The Bald Prima Donna*),
        139-45, 148-9, 167-8, 172, 184,
        187, 189-90, 195, 266-7, 294,
        327, 401, 449, 452
    Les Chaises (*The Chairs*), 26, 128,
        150-53, 158, 160, 171-2, 190,
        195, 197, 336, 401, 419, 424, 450,
        452
    La Colère, 452
    Délire à Deux (*Frenzy for Two*),
        451-2
    Greetings, 453
    L'Homme aux Valises, 186, 451
    *L'Impromptu de l'Alma ou Le
        Caméléon du Berger* (*Improvisation
        or The Shepherd's Chameleon*),
        169-71, 336, 451-2
    *Impromptu pour la Duchesse de
        Windsor*, 173, 451
    Jacques, ou La Soumission (*Jack or
        The Submission, Jacques or Obedi-
        ence*), 148-50, 153, 165, 190, 195,
        197-8, 294, 316, 377, 391, 450,
        452
    Jeux de Massacre, 185, 451, 453
    La Jeune Fille à Marier (*Maid to
        Marry*), 159, 196, 450, 452

Le Jeune Homme à Marier, 452
La Lacune, 452–3
La Leçon (*The Lesson*), 128, 145–8,
    172, 190, 195, 197, 267, 449–50,
    452
Macbett, 185, 451, 453
Le Maître (*The Leader*), 159, 196,
    450, 453
Le Nouveau Locataire (*The New
    Tenant*), 158, 164–5, 190, 195,
    450, 452
L'Œuf Dur, 452
Le Piéton de l'Air (*A Stroll in the Air*),
    174, 183–4, 451–2
Rhinocéros, 174, 180–83, 189, 195–6,
    198, 451
Le Roi se Meurt (*Exit the King*), 184,
    451–2
Le Salon de l'Automobile (*The Motor
    Show*), 159, 450, 452–3
Les Salutations, 451–2
Scène à Quatre (*Foursome*), 451–3
La Soif et la Faim (*Hunger and
    Thirst*), 184–5, 451–2
Le Tableau (*The Picture*), 165–8,
    196, 197, 450–51, 453
Tuer Sans Gages (*The Killer*),
    174–81, 193, 245, 401, 451–2
La Vase, 186
Victimes de Devoir (*Victims of Duty*),
    153–8, 160, 163, 174, 182, 195,
    450, 452
Ionesco, Rodica, *née* Burileano, 17,
    136

Jammes, Francis, 135
Janco, Marcel, 364–5
Jarry, Alfred, 165–6, 339, 356–61,
    363–4, 371, 388, 398, 467
    Ubu Enchaîné, 360
    Ubu Roi, 324, 356–61, 364–5, 367
John of the Cross, St (San Juan de la
    Cruz), 25, 426
Johnson, Samuel, 346
Johnstone, Keith, 131
Jouvet, Louis, 208, 212–13

Joyce, James, 16, 27, 30–34, 36, 44,
    50, 68–70, 264, 348, 353–4, 405,
    414, 464–5
Joyce, Lucia, 34
Jung, Carl Gustav, 94, 127, 414

Kafka, Franz, 16, 23, 158, 183, 207,
    261, 264, 310, 317, 354–6
    Der Gruftwächter, 355
    Le Procès (*The Trial* adapted by
        André Gide and J.-L. Barrault),
        355–6
Kandinsky, Vasily, 27, 176, 365
Keaton, Buster, 42, 335–6, 396
Keats, John, 346
Keystone comedies, 163, 335
Klages, Ludwig, 405
Klee, Paul, 290, 364, 421
Kleist, Heinrich von, 198
Klima, Ivan, 326
Kohout, Pavel, 326
Kokoschka, Oskar, 365–6, 391, 468
Kopit, Arthur L., 315–16, 457

Labiche, Eugène, 189, 198
Lahr, Bert, 40
Lamb, Charles, 346
Language, 25, 34, 39, 84–8, 95, 102,
    106, 129–30, 138–9, 142, 145–7
    191–4, 251, 325, 328–9, 341,
    344–5, 348, 381–2, 384, 389, 391,
    395, 405–10, 427
Lao-Tzu, 426
Lardner, Ring, 347–8, 462–3
Laurel and Hardy, 336
Lautréamont, Comte de (Isidore
    Ducasse), 201, 357
Lear, Edward, 342–6, 389, 410
Lemarchand, Jacques, 141, 145
Leno, Dan, 334–5
Lichtenberg, Georg Christoph, 347
Lorca, Federico García, 396
Losey, Joe, 261
Lugné-Poë, Aurélien-Marie, 27, 367–
    8, 385
Lynes, Carlos, Jr, 104n.

McGowran, Jack, 42
McWhinnie, Donald, 41
Madách, Imre, 352
Maeterlinck, Maurice, 135
Mallarmé, Stéphane, 266, 357, 358–9
Mann, Thomas, 183, 207
Marinetti, Filippo Tommaso, 365
Marivaux, Pierre de, 198, 334
Marx Brothers, 288, 336, 348, 384
Marxism, 22, 407
Masson, André, 133
Matisse, Henri, 364
Mauclair, Jacques, 27, 153, 158, 184
Maugham, Robin, 261
Mauriac, Claude, 38, 445
Mauthner, Fritz, 34
Melville, Herman, 38
Mendel, Deryk, 40
Mendès, Catulle, 358
Metman, Eva, 58–9, 74, 412–13, 445
Mihalovici, Marcel, 42
Miller, Arthur, 128–30
Mimus, 330–35
Modigliani, Amedeo, 365
Molière, 153, 158, 169, 334
Moreau, Gustave, 359
Moreau, Jeanne, 230
Morgenstern, Christian, 345–6, 389, 464
Mortimer, Penelope, 261
Mosley, Nicholas, 261
Mrozek, Slawomir, 318–21, 457
Music hall, 47, 61, 328, 334–5, 375, 384, 412
Musset, Alfred de, 198, 268, 380
Mystery plays, 332, 402
Mysticism, 426–8
Myth, 317, 349, 357

Nerval, Gérard de, 351
Nestroy, Johann, 338
Neveux, Georges, 25
Nietzsche, Friedrich, 329, 399
Nodier, Charles, 347
Noël, Jacques, 139
Nonsense literature, 328, 340–48

Nursery rhymes, 341

O'Casey, Sean, 129
O'Neill, Eugene, 313
Olivier, Sir Laurence, 180
Opie, Iona and Peter, 341
Osborne, John, 129–30, 431

Pantomime, 334
Paris, as centre of artistic experiment, 26–7, 30
Pataphysics, definition, 361
Pataphysique, Collège de, 137, 165–6, 180, 182, 361, 388
Pavlicek, Frantisek, 326
Pedrolo, Manuel de, 17, 281–5, 401, 458
    Cruma, 241, 282–4, 458
    Homes i No, 284–5, 458
Perelman, S. J., 348
Petresco, Camil, 135
Picasso, Pablo, 26, 176, 364–5, 386, 391–2, 418, 421, 468
Pichette, Henri, 25
Pickup, Ronald, 90
Piers Plowman (John Langland), 349
Pilgrim's Progress, The (John Bunyan), 349
Pinget, Robert, 299–302, 458
    Architruc, 301
    L'Hypothèse, 301
    Ici ou Ailleurs, 301, 458
    L'Inquisitoire, 302
    Lettre Morte, 299, 301, 458
    La Manivelle (*The Old Tune*), 300, 458
Pinter, Harold, 9, 12, 17, 21, 42, 234–64, 312–13, 332, 348, 376, 402, 432, 458
    Biographical data, 234, 237, 242–9
    Film scripts, 258
    The Basement, 258, 458
    The Betrayal, 260–61, 458
    The Birthday Party, 239–45, 253, 257, 458

Pinter, Harold,—*cont.*
  The Caretaker, 247–51, 257, 260,
    262, 458
  The Collection, 253–4, 458
  The Dumb Waiter, 237–9, 458
  The Dwarfs, 252–4, 261–2, 458
  Five Screen Plays, 458
  The Homecoming, 255–7, 458
  Landscape, 258–9, 458
  The Lover, 254–5, 257, 260, 458
  A Night Out, 246–7, 458
  Night School, 246–7, 263, 458
  No Man's Land, 260, 458
  Old Times, 458
  The Room, 235–40, 458
  Silence, 258–9, 458
  A Slight Ache, 244–6, 458
  Tea Party, 257–8, 458
Pirandello, Luigi, 40, 198
Planchon, Roger, 118
Portora Royal School, 30
Prévert, Jacques, 104, 166, 266, 361
Prouse, Derek, 149, 180
Proust, Marcel, 32, 353
Psychoanalysis, 154–8, 407–8
Puppet theatre, 134, 337, 357, 360
'Pure' theatre, 328, 360, 368, 397

Queneau, Raymond, 153, 165–6, 266,
    361, 392

Rabelais, François, 341, 357, 360
Radiguet, Raymond, 387, 468
Raimund, Ferdinand, 337–8
Regnaut, Maurice, 109–10, 171
Reich, Hermann, 330–31
Rémi, Philippe de, 340–41
Renard, Jules, 358
Renaud, Madeleine, 41, 230
Ribemont-Dessaignes, Georges, 366–
    70, 468
  Le Bourreau du Pérou, 369–70
  L'Empereur de Chine, 369–70
  Le Serin Muet, 367
  Zizi de Dada, 368
Richardson, Tony, 230
Rilke, Rainer Maria, 127

Rimbaud, Arthur, 201, 357
Ringelnatz, Joachim, 347
Ritual, 222–6, 290, 328
Rousseau, 'Douanier', 184, 391
Roussel, Raymond, 390–91, 468
Rózewicz, Tadeusz, 321–4

Sade, Donatien Alphonse François,
    Marquis de, 201, 351
Saint-Côme, Monique, 139
Salacrou, Armand, 24, 141, 387–8,
    469
San Quentin penitentiary, 19–21, 28,
    70, 414
Saroyan, William, 40
Sartre, Jean-Paul, 24, 61, 129, 156–7,
    170–71, 209–14, 392, 415
  Saint Genet, Comédien et Martyr,
    201–4, 230–31, 415, 447
Schehadé, Georges, 25, 274
Schikaneder, Emmanuel, 337
Schiller, Johann Christoph Friedrich
    von, 198
Schneider, Alan, 41–2, 44
Schopenhauer, Arthur, 89
Seneca, Lucius Annaeus, 350
Serreau, Jean-Marie, 27, 104, 164
Serusier, Paul, 364
Sewell, Elizabeth, 344–5
Shakespeare, William, 118, 198, 330,
    332–3, 338, 404, 417
  As You Like It, 338
  King Lear, 333
  Macbeth, 185
  A Midsummer Night's Dream, 333,
    350
  Measure for Measure, 332
  The Taming of the Shrew, 351
  Troilus and Cressida, 333
  The Two Gentlemen of Verona, 332
  A Winter's Tale, 350
Shaw, George Bernard, 29, 292, 404
Shepard, Sam, 434
Silent film, 335–6
Simpson, Norman Frederick, 17,
    302–10, 459

The Cresta Run, 459
The Form, 459
Gladly Otherwise, 459
The Hole, 305–7, 459
Oh, 459
One Blast and Have Done, 459
One Way Pendulum, 307–10, 459
A Resounding Tinkle, 302–4, 305–7, 401, 444
Social realism, 132–3, 163, 262, 310, 315
Sophocles, 173, 198
Soupault, Philippe, 31–2, 367–8
Stein, Gertrude, 27, 396–7, 469
Steiner, George, 407
Sterne, Laurence, 347
Stoppard, Tom, 433–4
Strindberg, August, 98, 127, 153, 198, 275, 313, 354, 404
A Dream Play, 98, 352–3
The Father, 127, 353
The Ghost Sonata, 352–3
To Damascus, 352–3
Struwwelpeter (by Dr Heinrich Hoffmann), 346
Supervielle, Jules, 153
Surrealism, 16, 317, 356, 361–2, 377–80, 395–8
Symons, Arthur, 358–9

Tardieu, Jean, 265–74, 328–9, 460
L'A.B.C. de Notre Vie, 271–2, 460
Les Amants du Métro, 270–71, 460
Candide, 460
Ce Que Parler Veut Dire, 269, 460
Cinq Divertissements, 460
Conversation-Sinfonietta, 269–70, 460
Eux Seuls Le Savent, 269, 460
Faust et Yorick, 268, 460
Le Guichet, 268–9, 460
Le Meuble, 268, 460
Monsieur Moi, 460
Oswald et Zenaïde, 269, 460
La Politesse Inutile, 267, 460
Livrets d'opéras de chambre, 460

Qui Est Là?, 266–7, 460
Rhythme à Trois Temps, 272, 460
La Serrure, 268, 460
La Société d'Apollon, 460
La Sonate, 269–70, 460
Les Temps du Verbe, 272, 460
Tonnerre Sans Orage, 273, 460
Un Geste pour un Autre, 269, 460
Une Voix Sans Personne, 272, 460
Une Soirée en Province ou le mot et le cri, 460
Tati, Jacques, 336–7
Theatre of the Absurd
  and *nouveau roman*, 302
  and politics, 125–6, 316–17
  characteristics, 402–5
  contribution to dramatic mainstream, 430–35
  critical standards for judgement of, 419–21
  delimitation of its field, 21–8
  effect on audience, 411–16
  in Eastern Europe, 316–26, 392–5
  interpretation, 44–6
  misconstruing of term, 11–12
  objectives, 305, 399–403, 424–9
  origins and antecedents, 327–98
  subject matter, 93
Torma, Julien, 388–90, 469
Touchard, Pierre-Aimé, 147
Toulouse-Lautrec, Henri de, 364
Tourneur, Cyril, 351
Trinity College, Dublin, 30–33
Trionfi, 328
Twain, Mark, 347
Tynan, Kenneth, 128–31, 133, 171, 176, 262, 316, 378, 422–3
Tzara, Tristan, 27, 364–8, 392, 469

Utrillo, Maurice, 184

Valentin, Karl, 375
Valle-Inclan, Ramón del, 395–6
Vaudeville, 334–6, 398
Vauthier, Jean, 25
Velde, Bram van, 391

Verlaine, Paul, 201, 351, 359
Verne, Jules, 139
Viala, Akakia, 144
Vian, Boris, 274–7, 361, 401, 460–61
  Les Bâtisseurs d'Empire, 274–7, 279,
    460–61
  L'Equarrissage pour Tous, 275,
    460–61
  Le Gouter des Généraux, 461
Vigny, Alfred de, 198
Vilar, Jean, 27, 103–4, 106, 274
Villon, François, 201
Vitrac, Roger, 356, 380–82, 469
Vuillard, Edouard, 364

Watson, Donald, 166
Webern, Anton, 272
Webster, John, 351
Wedekind, Frank, 339, 365, 375
Weil, Simone, 49

Weingarten, Romain, 434
Weiss, Peter
  Marat Sade, 229–30, 432–3
Welles, Orson, 131, 180
White, Ruth, 41
Wilde, Oscar, 29, 198
Wilder, Thornton, 40, 268, 292
Williams, Tennessee, 40, 129
Williamson, Nicol, 11
Wilson, Edmund, 347
Witkiewicz, Stanislaw, 392–3, 395,
  470
Wittgenstein, Ludwig, 408

Yeats, William Butler, 29, 90, 358–9,
  470

Zadek, Peter, 214–15
Zen Buddhism, 198, 427
Zola, Emile, 353

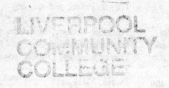